PERCEPTIONS AND ASPIRATIONS OF INDUSTRIAL WORKERS

(A Sociological Analysis of the Workers of Aligarh Lock Industry)

PERCEPTIONS AND ASPIRATIONS OF INDUSTRIAL WORKERS

(A Sociological Analysis of the Workers of Aligarh Lock Industry)

Syed Karamat Ali

Foreword

Prof. Noor Mohammad
Chairman
Department of Sociology and Social Work
Aligarh Muslim University
Aligarh (U.P.)

UPPAL PUBLISHING HOUSE
NEW DELHI – 110 002 (INDIA)

UPPAL PUBLISHING HOUSE
3, Ansari Road, Daryaganj, New Delhi-110002
Ph. : 23273756, 23286571 Fax : 91-011-23286571
E-Mail : Uppalbooks@vsnl.net

First Published 2007
ISBN 81-7658-034-1

Printed in India

Published by B.S. Uppal for Uppal Publishing House 3, Ansari Road, Daryaganj, New Delhi and Typeset by Phoenix Computer Centre, Daryaganj, New Delhi and Printed at **ARORA OFFSET PRESS, Laxmi Nagar, Delhi-**

Dedicated
to my
parents

FOREWORD

Human perceptions and aspirations are formulated and moulded by the environment under which they live. These differ from one social category to other. Since perceptions and aspirations are largely determined by the Psychological makeup and the socio-cultural environment in which the individuals live, perceive and aspire to achieve through the interactive processes with others, hence the perceptive approach and analysis differ from discipline to discipline. Psychologists and Psychiatrists give importance to Psychological traits of the individuals whereas Sociologists emphasis upon social variables like education, income, Profession etc.

Nirupama, P. and Srivastava, A.L. (1991) through their study "Perception of Scheduled Castes towards Education" highlighted these traits in the formulation and moulding of human perception and aspirations. This study concluded that the majority of the scheduled caste respondents opined that the education must be provided to children at any cost inspite of certain hurdles like caste values and traditions and their economic status. It further elaborates that the majority of the respondents of low as well as high occupational categories perceived education as a tool for acquiring prestige and status in a society and for their personality development. Members of the scheduled castes hold a very positive attitude towards the role of education in one's life. As far as the members from Scheduled Castes Social category are concerned, they showed a very positive response towards education. Similarly if we take example from other social categories like workers and the employers, a marked difference can be noticed regarding their perception and aspirations towards education and economic attainment.

Dr. S. Karamat Ali in the present study entitling **"Perceptions and Aspirations of Industrial Workers: A Sociological Analysis of the Workers of Aligarh Lock Industry"** has truly sketched out the level of aspirations and Perceptions among the industrial workers in general and the workers of Aligarh Lock Industry in particular. Since the industrial workers are generally from the low socio-economic background who are illiterate or semi-literate perceive things differently and have low level of aspirations and hence they remain within their vicious circle of poverty, illiteracy, vices and miseries. It is from this perspective Dr. S. Karamat Ali Studied these of Aligarh Lock Industry. He has also explored that the workers of Aligarh Lock Industry are having different working conditions because of the nature of Industry as it is home-based Industry and the middle-men play very dominant role and hence these workers remain on their mercy.

This is very good work on Industrial Workers of Aligarh Lock Industry and can help to the policy makers in reformulating their policies relating to the Industrial Workers as well as to the NGOs and Social Workers who can intervene and help these workers to come out of the vicious circle of poverty, ignorance vices and miseries and live like others. I do hope that this study will get the attention it deserves from everyone concerned.

Prof. Noor Mohammad
Chairman
Department of Sociology
and Social Work
Aligarh Muslim University,
Aligarh, (U.P.)

PREFACE

It gives me immense pleasure to praise the Almighty "Allah" who gave me strength, courage and helped me spiritually complete this work.

I wish to express my profound sense of gratitude to my supervisor, Dr. H.N. Singh, Reader Department of Sociology, Dharam Samaj College, Aligarh (Dr. B.R. Ambedkar University, Agra), for his valuable suggestions, encouraging guidance and stimulating discussions, which made this investigation as a rewarding experience.

I owe my gratitude to Dr. M.B. Mathur, a prominent Social Scientist of the Aligarh Muslim University, Aligarh without whose directions and timely guidance this investigation could not have been completed.

Thanks are due to Professor Nurul Hasan, Librarian, Maulana Azad Library, Aligarh Muslim University, Aligarh for providing all necessary help in getting the relevant books, journals, reports and research work accessible for the purpose of this investigation.

Help extended by Mr. Amanatullah, Computer Programmer for preparing necessary programmes on Dbase for analysis of the data in different ways has been appreciated. The untiring efforts of Mr. Amanatullah for writing the programme and furnishing the required information from district information Office, Aligarh made the analysis easy.

Thanks are due to my team members who have helped me in arranging interviews with the workers in different lock factories in the vicinity of industrial Estate and other parts of the City. I am highly indebted for the sincere efforts taken by my closest friend, who inspite of multiple preoccupations, spared time in comparing data and getting this work completed. I must not forget to think Mr. M. Asim Ali, Stenographer in AMU., Aligarh and friend, who inspite of multiple preoccupations, spared time in comparing data and getting this work completed. I must not forget to think Mr. M. Asim Ali, Stenographer in AMU., Aligarh and Mr. Tariq Ahmad Khan for doing the typing work and making their services available at any time whenever needed.

Syed Karamat Ali

CONTENTS

CHAPTER 1

INTRODUCTION

> The present investigation is an humble attempt to explore the perceptions and aspirations of workers hailing from different working groups of Aligarh Lock Industries.

Aligarh district — Located in the middle portion of Doab — Uttar Pradesh is known world over for Locks manufactured in the district. On account of superb workmanship, quality as well as attractive designs Aligarh is universally known as "City of Locks". Aligarh Lock industry has grown from a workshop established in 1860 for the services of the Postal Department of the country. Although it is stated that locks were initially manufactured in 1818 by Karim Elahi and Nabi Bakhsh[1] in Kala Mahal, Upper Kot, Aligarh, who had around 1000 workers in the workshop. Credit for development of Aligarh Lock Industry also goes to HiraLal Jha[2] way back in 1887. With the passage of time and growing demand of locks, a Training School was established in Aligarh in 1923 to provide basic or fundamental training to the aspirants interested to learn the process and technique of lock making from the point of view of employment or even starting an independent venture.

However, Aligarh lock industry was not able to meet the growing demand for locks. Therefore, the British Government started importing locks which ultimately lead to retrenchment of the workers. The retrenched lock workers having no other place to go started lock manufacturing for the local market only. They succeeded to a great

1. Kumar Sunjay: *Talon Mein Taley Aligarh Key Taley*, Asmitha Prakashan, Gandhinagar, Delhi 1993, p.7.
2. *Ibid.*

extent. However, with the gradual industrialization and application of modern tools and techniques in the production of locks, Aligarh lock industry suffered a set back as is evident from the emergence of lock industries based on latest modern techniques of production adopted by the entrepreneurs of Punjab, Haryana, Delhi, Gujrat, Maharashtra and other regions of the country. The situation is not likely to change in future as majority of capable lock workers of Aligarh are still following the traditional mode of locks production and operating from their homes. Besides, lock traders of Aligarh also directly or indirectly discourage them to venture for setting up their own independent establishments on modern lines. The traders, thus, are undoubtedly in a position to dictate terms and conditions and ask them to produce locks to promote their own (traders') trademark. Unfortunately, majority of the expert lock makers in Aligarh are poorly educated or illiterate Muslims of the city. On account of lack of education and economic constraint they are lagging far behind in competition with lock producing establishments from other states.

The individuals engaged in lock manufacturing or lock trade are of the view that State assistance and some other factors have helped in promotion and growth of lock industry in Aligarh. The Aligarh lock industry, thus, has become economically viable and competitive in the domestic market. In the initial stages of its development and growth, around 2000 workers were engaged in the lock industry. The growing demand of locks, to a great extent, sustained its growth and added to its horizontal expansion.

The first World War provided greatest filip in the phenomenal growth of lock industry in Aligarh as investors succeeded in getting highest rates of return on their investments. The lock industry of Aligarh expanded manifold and, thus, attracted additional capital for investment in the establishment of new lock manufacturing units, which ultimately resulted in the emergence of trading firms or organizations to handle the demand and supply of locks throughout the country. The economic achievements of the investors resulted in

---

3. Anand. A.L.: *SOUVENIER, Seminar on Locks*, March 21, 1982.
4. Kumar, Sunjay: *op. cit.*, Delhi 1993, p.7

the process of galvanizing the product to appear attractive in the year 1923[5].

Locational Factors

Aligarh emerged as the city of locks because of the following benefits following from locational factors:

1. Climate,
2. Availability of skilled labour,
3. Availability of raw materials,
4. Power,
5. Access to buyers, and
6. State Assistance.

Aligarh lock industry owes its growth due to good climate. Workers do not get tired early which enables them to long hours of physical work. The high labour productivity is mainly accounted for good climate of the town.

Further more, it is believed that the workers acquired Lock-making skills back in 1860 when the workshop was established to make metallic locks for the postal department. The cottage units that followed later were the training centres for workers in subsequent years. Thus, over a period of time lock-making became a traditional occupation of large section of the population of the town.

The cottage units have to mainly employ labour intensive techniques of production. Power has no significant input in these units. As compared to these, modern factories employ capital-intensive techniques of production. Power is in a way significant input there. It is fortunate that location of the town offers easy access to buyers from all over the country.

The cottage units or the small units both need the state assistance in the procurement of finance, raw-materials and subsidies, etc. The advantages in the form of special agencies which assist the lock industry here would go a long way to rejuvenate and strengthen the marginal units.

---

5. Anand, A.L, *op. cit.*, p. 2.

DEVELOPMENT OF ALIGARH LOCK INDUSTRY

Socio-politico and economic factors had a profound impact on the pattern of development of Aligarh Lock industry. The workshop for postal Department in 1860 lead to the birth of the lock industry in Aligarh. The workers who had received training in the workshop took to lock-making and became pioneer artisan entrepreneurs in lock industry and introduced from time to time improvements in design and techniques of production[5].

Aligarh lock industry received a shot in the arm during World War I, as phenomenal growth took place in the industry. Investors received high rates of return on investment in the industry during World War I. It attracted additional capital for investment in establishment of new lock manufacturing units. The industry expanded manifold and trading firms came into existence to handle distribution and sale of locks throughout the country.

Government established Metal Workshop School in Aligarh in 1935 for training of workers. Government provided foreign exchange for modernization of plants and machines. Machines were imported from Germany to make punch die locks. The industry made a successful bid to manufacture suit-case locks which were hitherto imported. Subsequently, the industry created additional capacity to expand production of punch die locks with indigenously forged devices for the domestic market. Semi automation was also introduced in the industry when manual process was substituted by the mechanized process of polishing the finished products. The innovations brought down the cost, raised labour productivity and profitability of lock industry.

The World War II period (1940) was characterized by global inflation and scarcity of industrial inputs. Aligarh lock industry was beset with scarce supply of inputs. This led to formation of Manufacturers Association and Traders Association to create healthy environment for mutual cooperation. The main objective of both these associations was to provide a forum to entrepreneurs for the pursuit

5. Anand, A.I., *op. cit.*, p. 2.

of common production and distribution policies and to avoid wasteful competition. It was not the purpose of the associations to encourage monopolies in industry and trade. On the contrary, the association lent its helping hand to new entrepreneurs and promoted expansion in the production of locks.

The immediate post independence period was marked with social and political instability which lead to disinvestment in the industry for a brief period of four years 1947-51. The industry could resume its normal functioning only after 1951 when it appeared safe to transport goods, employ workers, borrow capital and realize the credits.

KINDS OF ORGANIZATIONS IN LOCKS PRODUCTION

Firms may be classified into different types as they operate on divergent scales with different marketing systems. The industry consists of firms employing substantial capital and workers. They undertake marketing activities for direct sales to consumers. A large number of artisan entrepreneurs are also there in the industry who either make locks on their own behalf or on behalf of the middlemen and traders. The organization of firms vary from unit to unit according to the type of production and marketing systems. A brief description of such classification is presented in the following paragraphs.

1. Independent workers

The self-employed lock workers are entrepreneurs, who constitute physical resources and labour. Workers are members of their family. Such self employed workers plan production, prepare marketing strategies and coordinate activities of all the family workers engaged in different processes of lock making. The small-scale production is attributed to scanty capital invested in the business. It is difficult for them to procure raw materials in bulk or undertake bulk production. They are not financially strong to offer attractive terms and conditions to consumers in the competitive market. The standardization of production processes with division of labour cannot be introduced by these self-employed workers. In a desperate bid to affect cash sales, they resort to distress sale of their finished products at nominal profits. Their borrowing capacity is insignificant to raise additional funds for investment in the business. In fact, borrowing causes deterioration in their financial position due to inadequacy in their repaying capacity.

2. Production in factory

On the other end of the scale are firms fully organized and flush with resources. Workers are provided all basic facilities to complete a given job, in factory *viz.*, space, tools and equipment, raw materials etc. The management undertakes planning of production, schedules to complete the job and targets for individual workers. Mistries (Foremen) instruct workers about the methods of completing the job. The workers are under strict control and supervision of the management for regulating production. To fulfill the target as well as for maintaining the quality, the whole job is divided into smaller units to be completed by individual workers under the supervision of a Foreman. A worker in such factories does not carry out the whole job. Instead, he is engaged in one process to produce a part of the product. Workers are paid wages as per pieces produced by them. Thus, higher wages are received by the efficient workers producing more pieces[6].

Management-wise Categorization

The preceding discussion has brought to light the parameters within which the Aligarh Lock Industry is working, *viz.*, managerial problems, financial difficulties, inefficient production process, and labour problems. The cumulative effect of these constraints have telling effect on their credibility for investors in terms of their network, profitability, gross turnover, and labour productivity.

Total number of registered lock factories in Aligarh, which was 768 till 1992[7] has risen to 1612 as on March 1999. Classification of these units is under:

6. Anand, A.L., *op. cit.*, p. 2.
7. Kumar, Sanjay, *op. cit.* p.1.

Individual entrepreneur lock firms	724
Joint family firms	187
Partnership lock firms	685
Private Limited companies	15
Cooperative Society	01
Total:	1612

Source: Information collected personally by the investigator from the District Information Office (DIO), Aligarh.

Pattern of investment indicates that the cottage units predominate the Aligarh Lock Industry. Only 25 per cent of the firms are independent of middlemen. Those owned by artisans belong to cottage sector. These entirely depend on the middlemen's support. Such firms constitute 75 per cent of the existing units in the Aligarh Lock Industry.

Proportion of these firms may be inferred from the following table:

S. No.	*Types of the firms*	*Percentage Units in a Group*	
1.	Firms manufacturing locks on their personal account		25
2.	Firms manufacturing locks for middlemen	35	
3.	Firms manufacturing locks on behalf of both	40	

Source: Information gathered by the investigator from the DIO Aligarh.

As is apparent from the table, only one-fourth of the firms have invested enough capital to establish and organize production and marketing of their own products. Most of them (75% of the firms) are house-hold units, manufacturing locks for traders and shop-keepers in the local market. The middlemen provide working capital, which is normally adjusted against the value of products supplied by artisan entrepreneurs. Such units invest no capital in fixed assets and do not employ regular workers. In brief, Aligarh Lock Industry is largely unorganized.

An overview of Aligarh Lock Industry

Aligarh Lock Industry is one of the oldest industry in India. It occupies an important position among the small-scale economic sector of U.P. and finds favourable market in national economy, meeting 80 per cent demand of locks from Aligarh[8].

In Aligarh 38 types of locks are manufactured. Details of these are as follows:

1. Air Baggage Locks
2. Brass Pad Locks
3. Briefcase Locks
4. Batai Locks
5. Cycle Locks
6. Cupboard Locks
7. Cabinet Locks
8. Cast Iron Locks
9. Die-Punch Locks
10. Die-Pressed Locks
11. Drawer Locks
12. Double Locks
13. G.I. Pad Locks
14. Galla Locks
15. Iron Pad Locks
16. Key Holes Locks
17. Lever Pad Locks
18. Letter and Trunk Locks
19. Lorry Locks
20. Locking device for Bajaj Scooter
21. Locking device for Instrument Panel
22. Locking device for Petrol Pumps
23. Locking device for Vijay Scooter
24. Locking device for Refrigerator
25. Lock for A.C. Equipment
26. Motor Cycle Locks
27. Port Folio Locks
28. Spring Pad Locks
29. Safety Locks of Safes
30. Suit Case Locks
31. Shutter Locks
32. Servile Cared Pin-Cylinder Locks
33. Square Lever Locks
34. Showcase Locks
35. Truck Locks
36. Trunk Locks
37. Telephone Locks
38. Zinc Pin-Cylinder Locks

The products of the industry are not only popular in domestic market but also has acquired a significant position in the international market. These are constantly exported to Belgium, Behrain, Cyprus, Egypt, France, Greece, Ireland, Italy, Jordan, Kuwait, Malta,

---

8. *Anand, A.L., op. cit.*

Netherlands, United Kingdom, Canada and U.S.A. The lock industry is concentrated in urban as well as rural areas of Aligarh District. The Aligarh Lock Industry assumed its importance because it provides direct and indirect employment.

The industry has progressed considerably since the government has made numerous efforts for its development. Such endeavours include issue of licence for raw materials, loans, power and other facilities which helped in raising production to make Aligarh locks available in every corner of the country. Aligarh locks are sold not only in India and in domestic market but are also exported to foreign countries, *viz.* U.S.A., U.K., Canada, Burma, Indonesia, Malaya, Africa, Ceylon, Poland, etc. It is revealed from the trend of the foreign exchange that export of locks has shown a downward trend which may be due to competition from other countries like China, Taiwan and Hong Kong. But the main reason of decline in export is believed to be constant increasing demand of locks in national market. Thus, it may be pointed out that Aligarh Lock Industry expanded international trade with a view to securing favourable climate and balance of payments and to strengthen socio-economic relations with other countries. During three-and-half decades, this industry has grown phenomenally and today occupies a significant position in U.P. Economy. Due to pioneering skills of artisans of Aligarh and competitive labour charges, India has been able to diversify its exports throughout the world.

For development of Aligarh Lock Industries new techniques lock production will be introduced with an estimated investment of Rupees 1.25 crores. For introducing new techniques of locks, NSIC and Zakir Hussain Engineering College and Technology of AMU will join hands. It has been provided to launch Researches for developing Magnetic and Electronic Locks techniques in Aligarh from June 2000 on land to be procured in Tala Nagri. For this purpose district administration has been approached. For new techniques, machines are being imported from Taiwan, Britain, China and other countries. Besides, training will be imparted for Magnetic and Electronics Locks production. Presently, there is no institution for development and research of the Aligarh locks although its production is marketed all over the country. Central Government has arranged funds for research and training in order to develop the lock production[9].

In lock industry, major sections which constitute the industrial units are *office*, *packing* unit, *press* unit, *assembly* unit, *die making* unit, *key making* unit, *nickel polish* unit and *furnace and despatch* unit.

The larger impact on profitability can be attributed to such factors as increasing competition in the product market, especially since the establishment of lock units in other states. Besides, infrastructure provided by other state government have helped new units to become modern and more efficient, than the Aligarh lock manufacturing firms. This explains the reasons for the faster growth of lock industry outside U.P. According to Lock Manufacturers Association, establishment of *Talanagri* was demanded for development of lock industries which was considered by the then chief minister of Uttar Pradesh (Shri Kalyan Singh) and in the year 1991, a foundation stone of Talanagri was laid at Ramghat Road, leading to Atrauli, using 600 acre land of four villages, *viz.*, Devseni, Talaspur, Kithara and Harduaganj. Although electric poles and *kachcha* roads are there, yet people are not being attracted as the cost of land fixed was on higher side, *i.e.* Rs. 400/- per meter for residential plots and Rs. 120/- per meter for industrial plots, which poor workers cannot afford[10]. Resultantly, after a span of eight years, no lock industry could be shifted/established there. The state government to make the Aligarh Lock Industry economically viable and competitive, should implement the plan of Talanagri at Aligarh at least for lock units owned and run by the artisans in their homes. Talanagri would yield the advantage of large-scale economies, foster spirit of cooperation, provide opportunities to exchange expertise as well. Besides, the residential areas of the town would be free from pollution when the lock units are shifted to Talanagri.

---

9. See news item published in *Amar Ujala* — The Hindi Daily published from Agra/Aligarh dated 19.5.2000.
10. Kumar Sanjay, *op. cit.*

Problems

The industry's main problem is procurement of raw material. It is transported from distant places, *viz.*, Jamshedpur, Calcutta, Delhi, Kanpur, etc. Government has issued licences to large producers but the small artisan entrepreneurs, who own cottage units and constitute over 50 per cent of the units of the industry, do not have any licence to procure the raw materials at controlled prices. They mainly get supplies from local traders at exorbitant prices. The unsatisfactory system of distribution of the raw materials constitutes severe constraints on the growth of the Aligarh lock industry.

The town has the means of transport of goods to all the parts of the country. The private truck operators union, the sales tax, and the frequent hikes in transport rates are some of the major problems concerned with the distribution of the products of Aligarh lock industry. The taxes and the freight together push up the cost which the Industry is unable to recover due to stiff competition in the market.

The production has, at times, been severely affected by power cuts. Therefore, State Electricity Board should determine the quota of power in consultation with the representatives of the Lock Industry. The quota, once determined, should be regarded as the minimum requirements of power to be supplied on priority basis, and, if possible, the target should be exceeded to let the industry produce more.

A little investment in human capital, by way of labour welfare schemes, it is expected, would go a long way in raising the labour productivity. The labour welfare schemes, it is also expected, would impart a sense of association of the workers within the organization. At present, the lock factories at Aligarh lack even the basic amenities, viz., lavatories, catering facilities, rest places during recess for lunch, etc. There must be a change in the process of recruitment and selection, payment of wages. The factories largely employ temporary workers to circumvent the provisions of the Factory Act. The shifting labour in Aligarh lock industry breeds indiscipline and apathy. Besides recruitment of workers on permanent basis, the workers must be allowed to form associations and unions. It would serve as a forum for workers to undertake activity of common interest of mutual benefit of employees and employers.

A study on problems of the Aligarh Lock industry related to production and marketing reveals that it is well established and provides gainful employment to lots of people of Aligarh. The growth of the industry has retarded mainly due to shortage of finance, inefficient production and marketing management. Inspite of these serious hurdles, the industry holds position of unique importance in the industrial spectrum of UP State. The UP State Government has a pivotal role to play in solving the problems and take effective steps for the efficient running of the industry. Though the Aligarh lock industry provides numerous benefits, but is mismanaged by the illiterate entrepreneurs.

State should revitalize the training facilities and equip it with modern facilities. Since trained workers and modernization of the industry are indispensable to higher productivity, small entrepreneurs should have adequate funds to undertake the exercise. The state government should provide subsidized loans to entrepreneurs for modernization. Recently, the Central Government, realizing the facts of having no training programmes for the Aligarh Lock Industry workers, have arranged funds for launching research training programmes for development of lock production[11].

Perception

A study of perception by Hochberg[12] is an attempt to understand those aspects of observations of the world of things and people that depend upon the nature of the observer. Research in perception requires the most sophisticated controls of the motivational judgement and learning processes of simple and elementary experiences, or sensations, which recur in various combinations to compose the world we perceive; sensations presumably result from the excitation of

11. See news item published in *Amar Ujala* — The Hindi Daily published from Agra/ Aligarh of 19.5.2000.

12. Julian. E.Hochberg: Introduction in David L. Sill (ed.). *International Encyclopedia of the Social Science*. Vol. II, McMillan and Free Press.

individual's sensory cells, or receptor neurons, each contributing a characteristic signal, called a specific nerve energy, to the central nervous system. Whether acting alone or with a host of others, any receptor would produce the same sensation, although memories of past experiences evoked by each different context in which the sensation is embodied would usually conceal from the untrained observer (but not from the observers' trained to ignore those memories, to practice analytic introspection) the fact that the same elementary sensation has occurred.

The term perception is usually applied to the way one comes to know and observe the world or the way one experiences the world of objects or events. According to Shashi Jain (1988)[13], perception is the meaningful self-evaluation in terms of the given structural situation. The term perception has been used to know the self image and meaningful orientation of a person in a society. Ronald H. Forgus and L.E. Melamed[14] consider perception as the process by which an organism receives or extracts certain information about the environment and is an important element in the structural stability and continuity of the society.

Aspiration

Aspirations actually are the goals that, a person sets for himself in tasks which have intense personal significance. According to K. Lewin (1944)[15], "an individual while undertaking to perform a task builds up a goal structure, comprising a number of goals at varying levels. There may be a very high dream goal, an ideal goal, an action goal, and a low level goal, which the individual is sure of attaining even if luck or circumstances are against him. This type of goal where a person is determined to achieve, live and maintain it as the action

---

13. Jain, Shashi: *Status and Role Perceptions of Middle Class Women*, New Delhi, Puja Publications, 1988.
14. Forgus, Ronald H. and Melamed, L.E.: Perception — *A Cognitive Stage Approach*, New York, McGraw Hill Book Company, 1976.
15. Lewin, Kurt: Level of Aspirations in J. Mc. V. Hunt (ed.) *Personality and Behaviour Disorders*, New York, The Ronald Press Company, 1944.

goal." Lewin further holds the view that social environment plays a decisive role in determining what a person's aspirations would be. The most common factor which influence or generate aspirations are intelligence, sex, cultural traditions, competition with others, past experience, mass media and personal characteristics, etc.

A. Adler[16], emphasized that every one has a "life plan", a purpose or goal which determines his reactions. This life plan is generally developed early in life as a result of certain relationships between the person and his physical social environment. Elizabeth Hurlock[17] defines aspiration as longing for and striving after some thing higher than oneself or one's present status. This longing may be enabling or uplifting or it may be unwarranted or presumptuous.

B.C. Mutaiyyah[18], believes that aspirations of children are influenced by parents, particularly mothers. Educated mothers and working mothers hold a greater impact on children as compared to uneducated and non-working mothers.

According to E.B. Hurlock aspirations[19] are divided into three categories:

1. *Negative and Positive Aspirations*

Negative aspirations centre on the goal of avoiding failure while positive aspirations are oriented towards achieving success.

2. *Immediate and Remote Aspirations*

From early childhood, people set goals for what they want to achieve. At first, these goals are immediate but when the child grows and starts to plan for future setting goals, these goals are remote, which are generally less realistic and more fanciful than immediate goals.

---

16. Adler, A: *Individual Psychology*, New York, Harcourt Brace, 1925.
17. Hurlock, Elizabeth B.: *Personality and Development*, New York, McGraw Hill, 1974.
18. Mutayya B.C.: *Level of Aspiration and Frustation Reality* (Reserarches in Personality and Social Problems, Department of Psychology), University of Madras, 1971.
19. Hurlock, Elizabeth B.: *op. cit.*

3. *Realistic and Unrealistic Aspirations*

Realistic aspirations are those aspirations where a person is justified in expecting to achieve the goals he sets for himself, while unrealistic aspirations are those where a person lacks the potential to achieve the goals, no matter how hard he may work or sacrifice.

Behind all aspirations, there is a fundamental need for achievement. Factors like level of poverty, economic conditions and educational background etc, to a great extent play a decisive role in the socio-psychological make-up of human personality as well as in the formation and development of aspirations of the individuals.

OBJECTIVES OF THE STUDY

The major objectives of the present investigation are:

1. To throw some light on the variation in perceptions and aspirations among the workers and thereby exhibit personality differentials along with their approach towards work and social adjustments among the workers themselves as well as among the workers and the management.
2. To find out and compare perceptions and aspirations of the workers:
   - (i) Serving in the same factory but are attached to different units;
   - (ii) Representing different factories according to their units for unit-wise comparison;
   - (iii) Employed on salary and contractual workers;
   - (iv) In sex-wise categories of male and female;
   - (v) According to their literacy level, that is literate and illiterate;
   - (vi) According to their family background, that is there belonging to joint family and those to nuclear families;
   - (vii) Hailing from rural and urban areas;
   - (viii) Belonging different religions;
   - (ix) On the basis of their monthly salary (Income Groups : 0 to 3000 and 3000 & above);
   - (x) On the basis of working conditions and other benefits.

Besides 83 lock manufacturing units in Aligarh (List of these is given in Annexure II), we have 90 Lock manufacturing units scattered in Punjab, Gujarat, Maharashtra, Uttar Pradesh, Tamil Nadu and Union Territory located in different cities and towns, i.e. Chandigarh, Ropar, Kurali (Ropar), Ludhiana, Khanna, Jullundur, Suchipind (Jullundars), Amritsar, in Punjab; Gorwa (Baroda), Rajkot, Mehsana, Baroda, Ahmedabad, Jamnagar, Kela Paldi and Anand (Khera) in Gujarat; Vikhsoli (Mumbai) in Maharashtra; Kanpur, Modi Nagar and Meerut in Uttar Pradesh; Rajapalayam, Muhaveer (Ramnad District), Dindigul, Madurai, Kumbakonam, Chennail, Salem, Nolakottai Taluk and Usilampatti in Tamil Nadu.

CHAPTER 2

RESEARCH STUDIES ON PERCEPTIONS AND ASPIRATIONS

Social scientists and researchers, especially from the disciplines of sociology, psychology and psychiatry have tried to explore the avenues of knowledge related to perceptions and aspirations of human beings from their respective point of view. Since perceptions and aspirations of human beings besides other factors, are largely formulated and remoulded on the basis of psychological make up of the individual and the socio-cultural environmental conditions in which the individuals interact, hence the perceptive approach and analysis differs markedly as far as perceptions and aspirations of human beings are concerned. psychologists and psychiatrists lay major emphasis on the psychological components or traits of the individuals while sociologists on the environmental variable.

Studies on Perceptions and Aspirations

The following are some of the studies related to perceptions and aspirations as reported by different social scientists.

Gould, R *(1941)*[1] in his study *Some Sociological Determinants of Goal Settings* concluded that sociological factors like education, income and profession contribute to the differences in the levels of aspirations. The students coming from favourable socio-economic backgrounds were realistic in setting their goals for achievements and the students coming from low socio-economic status suffer from a sense of insecurity.

1. Gould, R. (1941) "Some Sociological Determinants of Goal Settings", *Journal of Social Psychology.*

Boyed, F.G. (*1952*)[1] in his study *The Level of Aspiration of White and Negro children in Non-segrated Elementary School* found out that environment affects the level of aspiration. The Negro children exhibited unrealistically higher hopes and ambitions due to their basic feeling of insecurity and had educational occuptational and professional aspirations.

Ahmad, K. (*1968*)[2] in his study *Social Background of Women Undergraduates of Delhi University* reveals that most of the undergraduates come to college without any definite aim. He further found that the girls coming from educated and economically well-off families were modern in their outlook and had higher aspiration for job.

Kamat, P. (1969)[3] in her study *A Comparative Study of Achievement of Girls with Their Intelligence and Socio-economic Status of Their Parents* finds out that female's education is more a problem of socio-religious attitudes, customs and values than any things else and that the level of school education of girls appears to be significantly related to the aspirational level of parents, their educational status, social rank, status and economic level.

Muthayya, B.C. (1971)[4], in his study *Farmers and Their Aspirations*, concludes that higher the socio-economic level the higher will be the aspirations. Furthermore, persons belonging to high socio-economic status, were more realistic than persons belonging to low socio-economic status.

Vimal, P. Shah, Tara Patel and William H. Sewell (1971)[5], in their study *Social Class and Educational Aspirations in an Indian Metropolitan* examined the relationship of socio-economic status and

---

1. Boyed, F.G. (1952), "The Level of Aspiration of White and Negro Children in a Non-segregated Elementary School", *Journal of Social Psychology*, Vol. 36.
2. Ahmad, K. (1968), "Social Background of Women Under-graduates of Delhi University", Quoted from M.B. Busch, *Survey in Research Education*, 1974.
3. Kamat, P.A. (1969), *A Comparative Study of Achievement of Girls with Their Intelligence and Socio-economic Status of the Parents*, unpublished M.Ed. Dissertation, M.S. University of Baroda.
4. Muthayya, B.C. (1971), *Farmers and Their Aspirations*, Hyderabad, NICD.
5. Shah, V.P. (1971), "Social Class and Educational Aspirations in an Indian Metropolitan", *Sociological Bulletin*.

educational aspirations of High School (SSC) students in Ahmedabad. The study reveals that the educational aspirations of female students were lower than those of males. However, little concern has been shown by sociologists to examine the influence of social background, particularly sex and social class, on the occupational aspirations of males and females.

Singh, C.P., Pandey, B.P., Dubey, G.S. and Yadav, D.R. (*1976*)[1], in their study *Educational Aspirations of Scheduled Caste Students in Eastern Uttar Pradesh* found that their was relationship between strata, time devoted to studies, economic status, level of politicisation and educational aspiration. The relationship between economic status and educational aspiration was of an inverse type. There was no relationship between sources of encouragement, father's education and age and educational levels aspired for.

Lal, Shoe Kumar (*1976*)[2], in his study *Occupational Aspiration of Scheduled Caste Students* found out the most of the Schedule Caste Students were drifting from their traditional occupations. Educated Scheduled Caste students were found following new occupations. The study also showed that a higher proprotion of Scheduled Caste students aspired for government positions followed by high-level professions. As such, to some extent, aspirations, represent their need for achievement.

Mohanty, G. (*1976*)[3], in his study *Sex Difference in Shifts and Rigidity in Level of Aspiration Experiment* took male as well as female students as sample. He concludes that female students were flexible in adjusting to the goals. The male students were rigid and non-responsive to success or failure. The non-responsiveness indicates unrealism in one level of aspiration, while the famale students were found to be realistic in finding the goals than males.

Swaleha, B. (*1979*)[4], in her study *A Study of Age and Socio-*

1. Singh, C.P. (1976), "Educational Aspirations of Schedule Caste Students in Eastern Uttar Pradesh", *Social Change*, Vol. 6.
2. Lal, Shoe Kumar (1976), "Occupational Aspirations of Schedule Caste's Students", *Social Change*, Vol. 6 (1&2).
3. Mohanty, G. (1976), "Sex Differences in Shifts and Rigidity in Level of Aspration Experiment", *Journal of Psychological Researches*, Vol. 22 (1).
4. Swaleha, B. (1979), "A Study of Age, Socio-economic Difference in Level of Aspiration", *Manavdarshan*, Vol. 14 (15-17).

Economic Differences in Level of Aspirations found that the higher the socio-economic level, the higher will be achievement. That is children from high socio-economic status, have stronger motivation to achieve, and set the aspirations.

Sharma, R.R. (*1981*)[1] investigated *Self-Concept, Level of Aspiration and Mental Health as Factors in Academic Achievement* and arrived at the following conclusions:

1. Self concept affects academic achievement.
2. Level of aspiration and mental health does not influence academic achievement.
3. High and low achievers differ significanly on certain elements of self concept of behaviour, intellectual and school status, happiness and satisfaction and physical appearance and attributes.
4. High and low achievers differ significantly in their level of aspiration. Level of aspiration is related with self concept.
5. Boys and girls differ significantly in their level of aspiration. A strong tendency in girls to set their level of aspiration below their achievement was found, whereas boys show an opposite trend.
6. No significant relationship between level of aspiration and family income, order of birth or vocational aspiration was found.

Uniyal, M.P. & Beena Shah (*1981*)[2] in their study *The Level of Aspiration of Teacher Trainees of Rural and Urban Areas in Relation to Their Achievement* found out that the high achievers were negligent in respect to their aspirations. As such, one's level of aspiration was more affected by his academic achievement rather than his social belongingness.

---

1. Sharma, R. Rani (1981), "Self Concept, Level of Aspiration and Mental Health as Factors in Academic Achievement", *Indian Educational Review*, Vol. XVI (2).
2. Uniyal, M.P. *et. al.*, (1981), "The Level of Aspiration of Teacher Trainees of Rural and Urban Areas in Relation to Their Achievement", *Indian Educational Review*, Vol. XVI (2).

Braccia, M.C. (*1981*)[1], in his study *A Comparison of the Changes in Perceptions of Ideal Leader Behaviour, Interpersonal Communication, and Work Motivation Attitudes of Students in An Educational Administration Programme Who Have and Have Not Completed Administrative Internship* found a significant increase among intern students perceptions of communication skill. Intern students also showed a significantly different change in their perceptions of ideal leader behaviour with respect to the two dimensions: initiating structure and consideration. No significant changes were found between male and female interns, less experienced and more experienced interns, elementary level or secondary level administrative interns and urban and sub-urban iterns, for initiating structure, competitiveness, desirability, willingness to seek rewards and interpersonal communications.

Decoleau, Ramona (*1981*)[2] in his study *Perceptions of Selected Groups Towards the Current and Ideal Role of Special Education Directors as Administrative Leader sin North Dakota Schools Which Have High Concentration of Ameican Indian Students* found out that there were statistically significant differences among the perceptions of all groups towards the current and the ideal role of the special Education Director/Coordinator. The special education directors/coordinators, special education teachers and school administrators viewed the ideal role as well as current role in the same way.

Kuk, Linda, S. (*1981*)[3] in his study *Perception of Work Climate and Their Relationship to the Career Aspiration of Women Student*

1. Braccia, M.C. (1981). "A comparison of the changes in perceptions of leader behaviour, interpersonal communication and work motivation attitudes of students in an educational administration programme, who have and have not completed administrative internship", *Dissertation Abstracts, International, Series 4*, Vol. 42(A).
2. Decolean R. (1981), "Perceptions of selected group toward the current and ideal role of special education directors as administrative leaders in North Dakota Schools which have high concentration of Indian Students", *Dissertation Abstracts, International, Series 4*, Vol. 42(4).
3. Kuk, Linda, S (1981). "Preceptions of work climate and their relationship to the career aspiration of women student affairs administrators", *Dissertation Abastracts, International, Series 4*, Vol. 42 (4).

Affairs Administrators indicated that women did aspire to high level positions in higher educational organizations, although they continue to perceive these positions as less attainable. In examining the existence of a relationship between women students affairs aspirations and their perceptions of the external work environment, the six job characteristics — variety, autonomy, identity, feed-back, friendship and dealings with others — were perceived to be present in the work environment. However, a difference in the perceptions of the presence of some of these factors based on aspiration was found.

Akers, Marilyn O.S., (*1981*)[1] in his study *Perceptions of Selected Eighth Grade Students Concerning Academic Achievement and Influence of Family Encouragement and Expectation* concluded that: (1) grade point average has no bearing on perceptions of students concerning family encouragement and expection. High capable achievers showed stronger family expectation than highly capable unachievers showed. Average ability over achiever males indicated stronger family encouragement than females of the group. Highly capable unachiever females indicated stronger family encouragement than males of the group. (2) Grade point average is not related to personal self-concept. With the highly capable under-achiever group, females expressed higher self concept than males (3) Average ability over achievers identified with highly capable under-achievers in personal academic achievement rather than with highly capable achievers. With the average ability over achiever group, males felt more capable academically than females of the same group.

Uploankar, Ambarao T., (*1983*)[2] in his study *Occupational Aspirations of College Students* reports that the occupational aspiration of the women students were lower than those of men. This indicated that women students in higher education did not perceive any meaningful role in terms of gainful employment. This also suggested that women students were more likely to use higher education as a

1. Akers, Marilyn, O.S. (1981), "Perceptions of Selected Eighth Grade Students Concerning Academic Achievement and Influence of Family Encouragement and Expectations", *Dissertation Abstrats International, Series 4*, Vol. 42(4).
2. Uploankar, Ambarao T (1983), "Occupational Aspirations of College Students", *Social Change*, Vol. 3(2).

status symbol, as an end in itself, than as a means of gainful employment.

Prakash Nirupma and A.L. Srivastava (*1991*)[1] in their *Perception of Scheduled Caste Towards Education* investigated that majority of the Scheduled Caste respondents held the view that education must be provided to childeren at all costs inspite of certain hurdles like caste values and traditions or economic hardships. It was further observed that majority of the respondents of low as well as high occupational categories perceived education as an instrument for acquiring prestige and status in society and for their personality development. Members of Scheduled Caste community held a verry positive attitude towards the role of education in one's life. As far as education in the upliftment of the Scheduled Caste community was concerned, the respondents showed a very positive response.

Husain, Mohd. Muzammil, (*1996*)[2] in his study *Perceptions and Aspirations of Rajputs: A Sociological Study of Rajori Distt. (J&K)* found out that the members of every community in order to retain the bonds of familial relationships should encourage among themselves for regular interactions among their families. As regard the educational backwardness, the author had proposed that more educational institutions with adequate hostel facilities for boys and girls be set up in the area and efforts be made to put pressure on the government for seeking financial help. In the political area, besides political awareness among them, philosophy of Punchayati Raj system needed to be explained through some socio-political organizations which may hold meetings to discuss political ideologies and events, educate the masses not to cast their votes on the considerations of caste or religion but on the basis of election manifestoes and that voice should be raised to impose some ban on the use of the services of religious leaders at the time of elections.

---

1. Prakash. N and Srivastava, A.L. (1991). "Perception of Schedule Castes Towards Education". *Journal of Indian Education*, Vol. XVI(5)
2. Husain. M.M. (1996). *Perceptions and Aspirations of Rajputs: A Sociological Study of Rajouri District (J & K)* — A thesis submitted for award of Ph.D at AMU, Aligarh.

In the economic area the farmers and the traders of the area needed to be educated and enlightened about the moderm technologies and system pertaining to agriculture and trade for achieving maximum return of their economic activities and that women should not be discouraged from taking part in economic activities of the families and other independent economic activities for improvement of economic situations. In the Religious Area the intellectuals and the preachers of religion should concert their efforts to enlighten the members of the community or of the area about the usefulness and importance of religious prescriptions so that people of the community may gain clear concept for offering of prayers and that the members of the society with good knowledge of religion, secular and nationalistic outlook should work and make concerted efforts and propagate against misconception among the masses so that religion is not conceived as a dividing force in the society and that for maintaining mutual trust the members of each community or of the area may feel encouraged to participate and celebrate the religious festivities of other communities collectively and for saving the humanity from religious exploitation, the person should be condemmed by the members of the society who deliberately does not extend equal respect to other religions.

Although Studies have been made on perceptions and aspirations in other areas as reported above, but no study has so far been conducted in this area of knowledge. Hence, the findings of the present analysis of the perceptions and aspirations of the Aligarh Lock Industry workers under the selected five parameters — *viz.* economic, social educational, political and religious — were expected to be of great academic value.

CHAPTER 3

METHODOLOGY OF STUDY

SAMPLE OF STUDY

The sample of the study has been drawn from the workers serving in 55 lock industries situated in the vicinity of Industrial Estate as well as in other parts of the city. Number of workers selected from the above mentioned lock industries have been shown in *Chart No. 1.* It confirms random selection of the workers from various lock industries in the vicinity of the Industrial Easte and other parts of the City. Average number of workers covered in each industry comes to seven of different units. In all 474 lock industry workers constitute the sample of the study. Respondents drawn from each of 55 industries of the sample is given in Table 1.

The data has been collected by adopting proportionate random sampling method. The sample represents respondents of various units of lock industries, like Office, Packing, Press Unit, Assembly Unit,

---

The factories covered in the vicinity of Industrial Estate are: Asia Traders: Jobex India Ltd.; Kukoo; Lakshmi Enterprise; Link Locks; Lock House: Lock Master: Maheshwari Locks: MICO Locks; Morris Bajaj: Nevy Locks; Raghav Ratan: S.Kumar Locks and U.P. Industrial Corporation. whereas other places where lock industries are situated are: Ghas ki Mandi. Nai Basti. Chowk Bundu Khan. Turkman Gate. New Idgah. Mohd. Ali Road. Usman Para. Tan Tan Para. Teela. Bani Israilan. Qureshiyan. Delhi Gate Sheikhan Street. Mamu Bhanja and the Upper Fort. The factories covered in the study are: A.D. Products: AK & Sons; AZ Lock Craft; Acron Locks: Blaze Locks: Camy Locks: Chief Lock Industries; Friend Locks; Hemco Locks; Henri Locks; Hina Locks: Hoya Locks: Huma Products; Jawaid Locks: Jay Lock Company: Laxmi Locks: Lockage: Malik Locks: Metalic Lock Manufacturing Company: Mohan Traders: Nagina Padlocks, Naaz Enterprizes; Nelco Locks; New Gold Locks: New Life Locks. Onida Locks; Prime Lock Industries; Right Locks; Rose Lock Company RoxyLocks: Talha Locks Industries; Technico India; Typson Locks; Ugrasen Locks; and United India and Wasi Locks.

Table 1: Number of Respondents in Each Lock Industry

S.No.	*Factory*	*No. of Respondents*
1.	A.D. Products	7
2.	A.K. & Sons	20
3.	Azlocks craft	7
4.	Arconlocks	7
5.	Asia Traders	8
6.	Blaze Locks	8
7.	Camy Locks	8
8.	Chief Lock Ind.	15
9.	Friend Lock	12
10.	Hemco Locks	7
11.	Henry Locks	8
12.	Hina Locks	19
13.	Hoya Locks	8
14.	Huma Products	8
15.	Jawaid Locks	8
16.	Jay Locks Co.	8
17.	Jobex India	8
18.	Kukul Locks	8
19.	Lakshmi Ent.	8
20.	Laxmi Locks	8
21.	Link Locks	8
22.	Locks House	8
23.	Lock Master	8
24.	Lockage	8
25.	M. Khurshid Lock	7
26.	Maheshwari Lock	8
27.	Malik Locks	8
28.	Manzoor Locks	5
29.	Metalic Lock Mico	8
30.	Mico Lock Mico	8
31.	Might Locks	8
32.	Mohan Trades	8
33.	Morris Bajaj	8
34.	Nagina Padlocks	8
35.	Naz Enterprizes	8
36.	Nelco Locks	8
37.	Nervy Locks	8
38.	new Gold Locks	8
39.	New Life Locks	8

S.No	Factory	No. of Respondents
40.	Onida Locks	7
41.	Prime Lock Ind.	7
42.	Raghav Ratan	8
43.	Right Locks	9
44.	Rose Lock Fact	8
45.	Roxy Locks	9
46.	S. Kumar Locks	8
47.	Security Locks	8
48.	Shiba Locks	7
49.	Talha Lock Ind.	8
50.	Technico India	8
51.	Typson Locks	7
52.	UP Industrial Co.	8
53.	Ugrasen Locks	20
54.	United India	7
55.	Wasi Locks	7

Die Making Unit, Key Making Unit, Nickle Polish Unit, Furnance and Despatch Unit. It appears from *Chart No.2* that out of the sample studied, 11 per cent belong to Assembly Unit 12 per cent to Die Making Unit; 9 per cent to Furnancing & Despatch Unit; 12 per cent to Key Making Unit; 12 per cent to Nickle Polish Unit; 13 per cent to the Office; 16 per cent to Packing Unit and 15 per cent to Press Unit. It appears from *Chart No. 3* that out of total respondents 24 per cent represent management group whereas 76 per cent represent labour group of 55 Lock Industries. *Chart No. 4* reveals that 32 percent of the respondents represent urban areas and 68 percent rural areas. *Chart No.5* reveals that 27 per cent of the workers represent joint family system and 73 percent nuclear family system. *Chart No. 6* reveals that 30 per cent of the respondents were Hindus and 70 per cent were Muslims. *Chart No. 7* reveals that 3 per cent of the respondents were females and 97 percent were male workers representing different industrial units of Lock Industries. It appears from *Chart No. 8* that 15 per cent of the respondents belong to the families adopting small family norms and 85 percent to the families which do not adopt the small family norms.

CHART 1: FACTORY-WISE DISTRIBUTION OF WORKERS

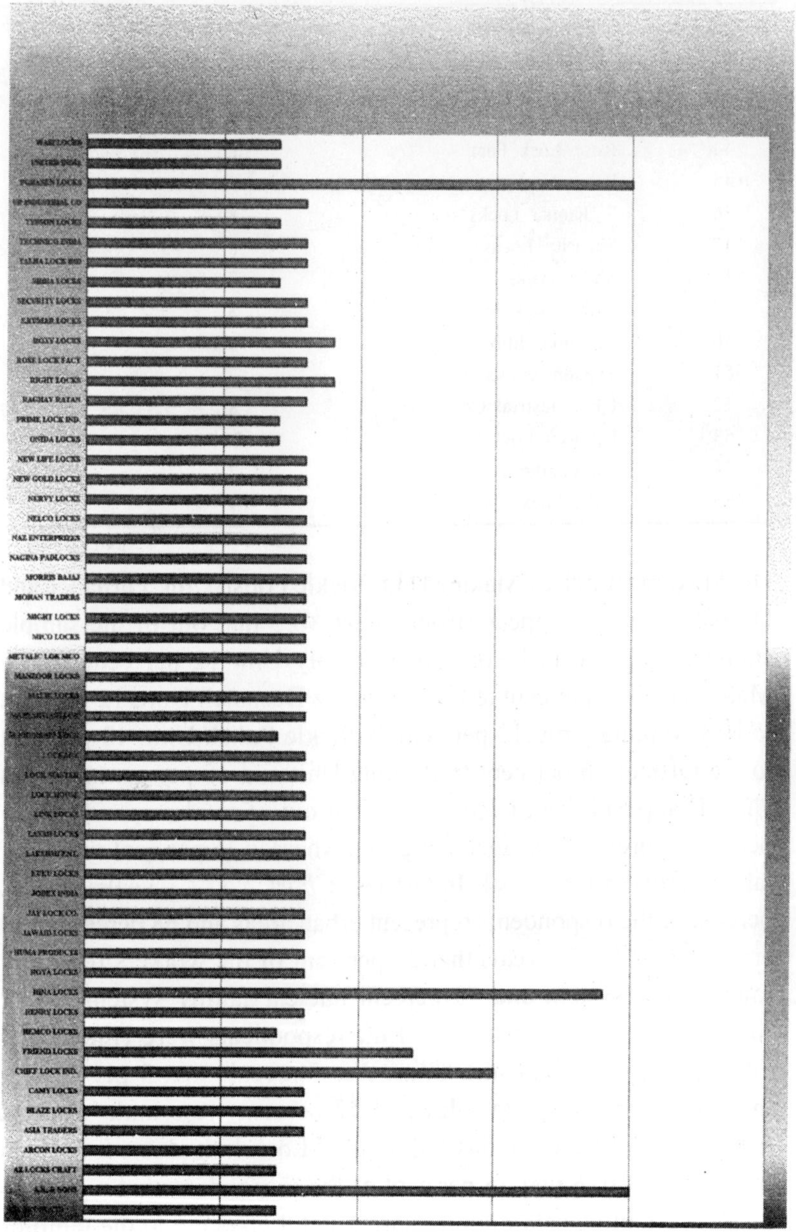

CHART 2: UNIT-WISE DISTRIBUTION OF WORKERS OF THE SAMPLE (474)

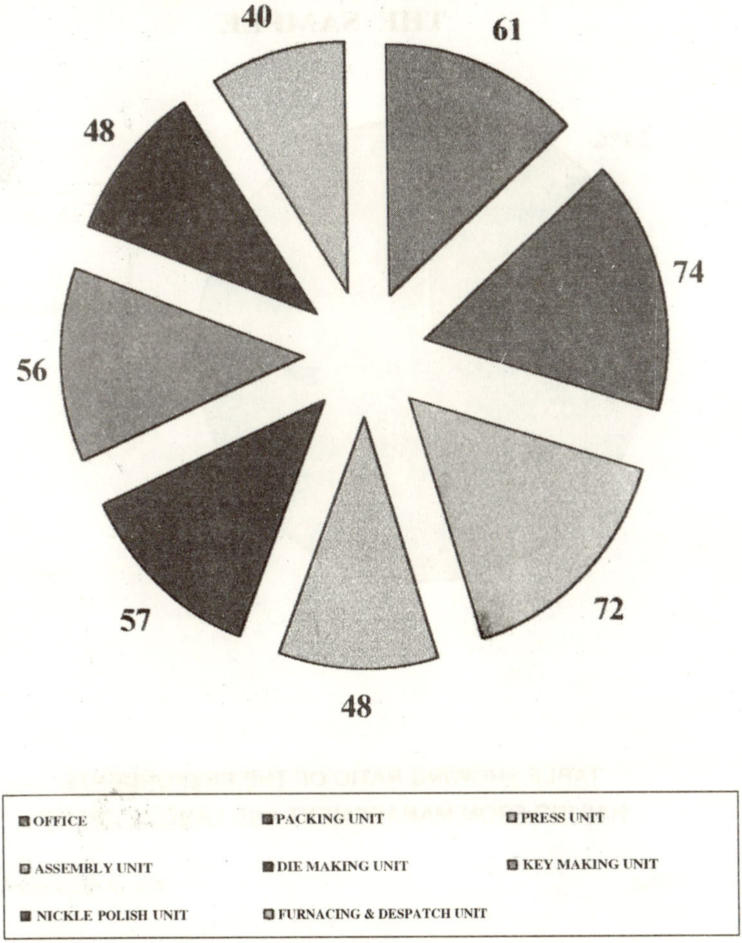

TABLE SHOWING NUMBER OF RESPONDENTS IN EACH INDUSTRIAL UNIT OF ALIGARH LOCK INDUSTRIES

INDUSTRIAL UNITS	RESPONDENTS
1. ASSEMBLY UNIT	53
2. DIE MAKING UNIT	58
3. FURNACING & DESPATCH UNIT	43
4. KEY MAKING UNIT	56
5. NICKLE POLISH UNIT	57
6. OFFICE UNIT	61
7. PACKING UNIT	74
8. PRESS UNIT	72
TOTAL	474

CHART 3: LABOUR – MANAGEMENT RATIO OF THE SAMPLE

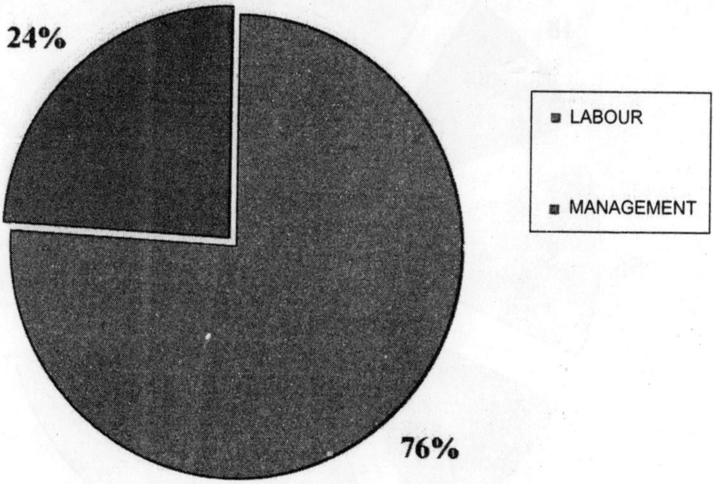

TABLE SHOWING RATIO OF THE RESPONDENTS HAILING FROM MANAGEMENT AND LABOUR GROUP

Status	No. of respondents
WORKERS REPRESENTING MANAGEMENT GROUP	358
WORKERS HAILING FROM LABOUR CLASS	116
Total	**474**

CHART 4: WORKERS HAILING FROM RURAL AREAS AND URBAN AREAS

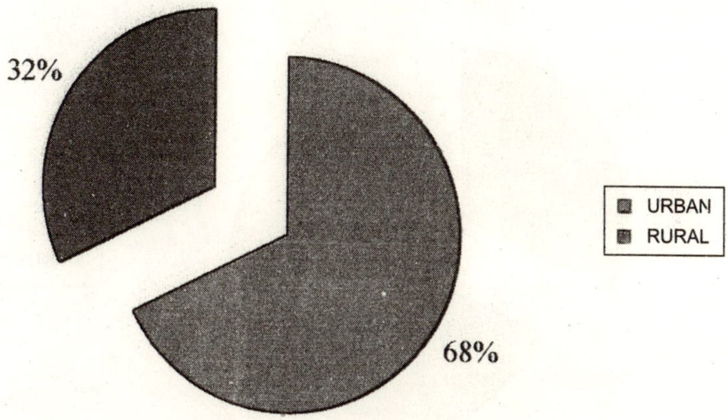

TABLE SHOWING WORKERS HAILING FROM URBAN & RURAL AREAS

Area	No. of respondents
URBAN	321
RURAL	153
Total	474

CHART 5: FAMILY STATUS OF THE RESPONDENTS

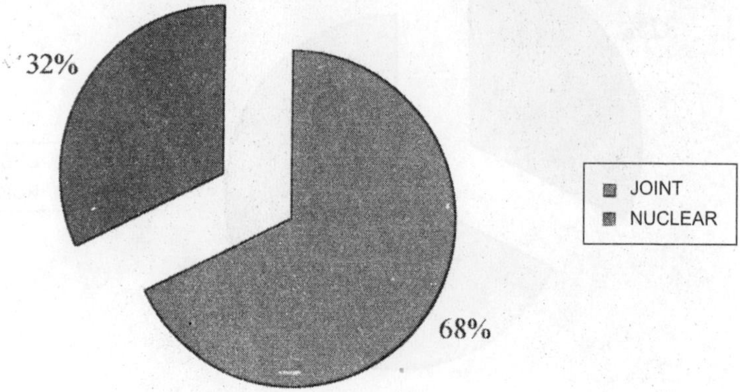

TABLE SHOWING FAMILY STATUS OF THE RESPONDENTS

Family Status	No. of respondents
WORKERS HAILING FROM JOINT FAMILIES	347
WORKERS HAILING FROM NUCLEAR FAMILIES	127
Total	**474**

CHART 6: RELIGION OF THE RESPONDENTS

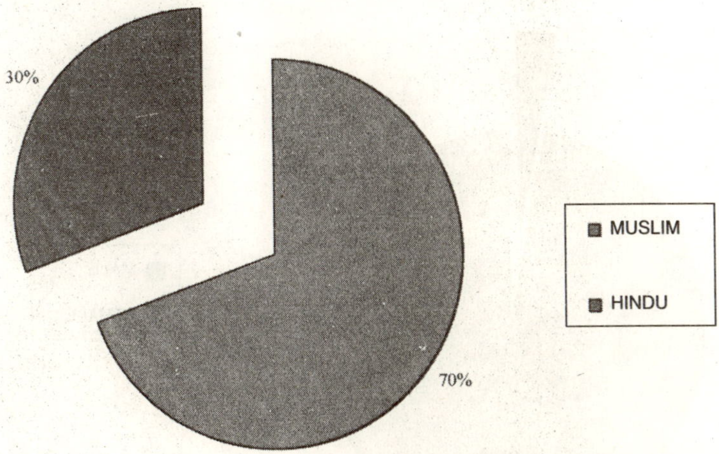

TABLE SHOWING THE RELIGION OF THE RESPONDENTS

Religion	No. of respondents
MUSLIM	326
HINDU	148
Total	474

CHART 7: RESPONDENT'S SEX

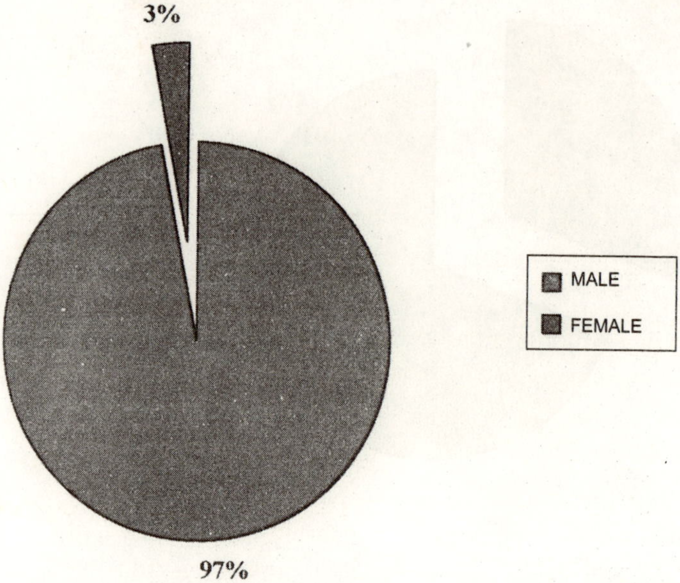

TABLE SHOWING SEX OF THE RESPONDENTS

Religion	No. of respondents
MALE	459
FEMALE	15
	Total 474

CHART 8: RATIO OF THE RESPONDENTS ADOPTING AND NOT ADOPTING THE SMALL FAMILY NORMS

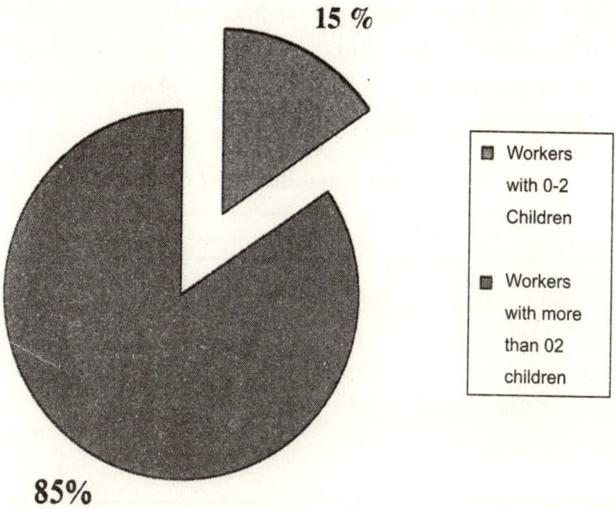

TABLE SHOWING RATIO OF THE RESPONDENTS ADOPTING AND NOT ADOPTING THE SMALL FAMILY NORMS

Category	No. of respondents
Workers with 0-2 Children	72
Workers with more than 02 children	402
Total	474

Sample Composition

The respondents constituting the sample of the study represent major sections which constitute the industrial units of each factory. The total population of workers in all the factories is 1.25 lac which constitute the universe out of which approximately 474, i.e. 0.379 per cent respondents have been interviewed personally by the investigator. The total number of workers in the registered lock industries is 7795 out of which perceptions and aspirations of 474, i.e. 6.08 per cent workers have been studied.

Table 2: Sample Composition of Lock Industries

Locks Factories	*No.*	*Sample drawn*	*Percentage*
Individual Eentrepreneur Firms	724	11	1.5
Joint family firms	187	08	4.2
Partnership firms	685	30	4.3
Private Limited Companies	15	05	33.3
Cooperative Society	01	01	100.0
Total:	1612	55	3.41

Source: Information collected personally by the investigator from the Distt. Information Office, Aligarh.

Table 3: Sample Composition of lock Industry Workers

Total Number of Registered Factories	*No. of Workers*	*Sample drawn*	*Percentage*
1612	7795	474	6.08

Source: Information collected personally by the investigator from the Distt. Information Office, Aligarh.

Representation of Respondents

Out of the total universe of 1.25 lacs workers serving in 1612 registered lock industries, 7795 workers have been identified out, of which a sample of 474 workers representing different units of the lock industries has been drawn constituting a percentage of 6.08 per cent.

Table 4: Unit-wise Sample Composition of Lock Industry Workers

S. No.	*Unit of the Factories*	*Total No. of Workers*	*Sample of Workers Drawn*	*Percentage*
1.	Assembly unit	535	53	0.990
2.	Die making unit	455	58	12.74
3.	Furnace and Despatch	430	43	10.00
4.	Key making unit	580	46	09.65
5.	Nickel polish unit	818	47	06.96
6.	Office	1612	61	03.78
7.	Packing unit	1615	74	04.58
8.	Press unit	1750	72	04.11
	Total:	7795	476	06.08

Distribution respondents coming from management and labour groups has been given in Table 5 below:

Table 5: Ratio of respondents Hailing from Management and Labour Group

Status	*No. of Respondents*
Workers Representing Management Group	358
Workers Hailing From Labour Class	116
Total:	474

Urban/rural background of respondents has been given in Table 6 below:

Table 6: Workers Hailing from Urban & Rural Areas

Status	*No. of Respondents*
Urban	321
Rural	153
Total:	474

The family status — *i.e.* distribution of respondents drawn from joint family and nucleus family — of the sample has been given in Table 7 below:

Table 7: Family Status of the Respondents

Family Status	*No. of respondents*
Workers Hailing From Joint Families	347
Workers Hailing from Nuclear Families	153
Total:	474

Religion-wise distribution of respondents has been given in Table 8 below:

Table 8: Religion of the Respondents

Religion	*No. of Respondents*
Muslim	326
Hindu	148
Total:	474

Sex-wise distribution of respondents has been given in Table 9 below:

Table 9: Sex of the Respondents

Sex	*No. of Respondents*
Male	459
Female	15
Total:	474

Distribution of adherence to small family now has been given in Table 10.

Table 10: Ratio of the Respondents Adopting and not Adopting the Small Family Norms

Category	*No. of Respondents*
Workers with 0-2 Children	72
Workers with more than 2 Children	402
Total:	474

The table indicates that from amongst the sample drawn for the survey, 53 workers were randomly selected from assembly unit; 58 from die making unit; 43 from furnace and despatch; 56 from key making unit; 57 from nickle polish unit; 61 from the office; 74 from packing unit; and 72 from press unit.

Tools and Techniques

An interview schedule was developed by the researcher for data collection and the respondents from each unit, *viz.* Office, Assembly Unit, Die Making Unit, Packing Unit, Nickle Polish Unit, Press Unit and Furnace and Despatch Unit of the lock industries were interviewed personally by the researcher and care was taken to ensure that selected sample represents the universe proportionately. The interview schedule consisted of two parts, one dealing with fact-finding information and personal data, like education, sex, income, status, and place of work; and the other contains items pertaining to perceptions and aspirations. In all, there are 100 questions in the interview schedule, fifty questions are related to perceptions and fifty questions with aspirations. The respondents were asked to express their preference towards each item in the form of "Yes", "Indifferent" and "No". The data has been collected using structural interview method with the help of interview schedule consisting open-ended and closed questions.

Since perceptions and aspirations were unlimited, the researcher has selected five parameters for investigation. These are Economic, Social, Educational, Political, and Religious. The items of the selected parameters have been numbered for convenience sake.

The economic perceptions (EP 1, EP 2, EP 3, EP 4, EP 5, EP 6, EP 7, EP 8, EP 9 and EP 10) and economic aspirations (EA 1, EA 2, EA 3, EA 4, EA 5, EA 6, EA 7, EA 8, EA 9 and EA 10) of respondents have been elicited by framing items related to economic conditions and activities.

The responses of the respondents towards social perceptions (SP 1, SP 2, SP 3, SP 4, SP 5, SP 6, SP 7, SP 8, SP9 and SP 10) and social aspirations (SA 1, SA 2, SA 3, SA 4, SA 5, SA 6, SA 7, SA

8, SA 8, SA 9 and SA 10) have been framed to collect the items related to social condition as well as social relations and interactions.

Under the educational perceptions (EDP 1, EDP 2, EDP 3, EDP 4, EDP 5, EDP 6, EDP 7, EDP 8, EDP 9 and EDP 10) and educational aspirations (EDA 1, EDA 2, EDA 3, EDA 4, EDA 5, EDA 6, EDA 7, EDA 8, EDA 9 and EDA 10) items have been framed to elicit responses from the respondents pertaining to educational system and opportunities.

Political perceptions (PP 1, PP 2, PP 3, PP 4, PP 5, PP 6 PP 7, PP 8, PP 9 and PP 10) and political aspirations (PA 1, PA 2, PA 3, PA 4, PA 5, PA 6, PA 7, PA 8, PA 9 and PA 10) of the respondents have been elicited by framing items pertaining to political activities, ideologies and political participations, etc.

Religious perceptions (RP 1, RP 2, RP 3, RP 4, RP 5, RP 6, RP 7, RP 8, RP 9 and RP 10 and religious aspirations (RA 1, RA 2, RA 3, RA 4, RA 5, RA 6, RA 7, RA 8, RA 9 and RA 10, of the respondents have been elicited by framing items related to religious practices and teachnings.

COLLECTION OF DATA

The investigator, after finalizing the interview schedule, started field investigation. The data was collected by the researcher, who visited the lock industries situated in the vicinity of industrial estate as well as other parts of the city like Ghas Ki Mandi, Chowk Bundoo Khan, Usman Para, Turkman Gate, Tan Tan Para, Azad Nagar, New Idgah, Mohammad Ali Road, Teel, Nai Basti, Johnson Compound, Pathan Mohalla, Upper Fort, Bani Israilan, ITI Road, Mohalla Qureishyan, Delhi Gate, Sheikhan Street, and Mamu Bhanja.

Input of Data

After explaining the items in the interview schedule to the respondents, the personal information was recorded on the first page of the interview schedule. There were items consisting open-ended and closed questions in the interview schedule. Perceptions and aspirations under the five parameters were read to the respondents and appropriate columns were ticked on the respective page of the interview schedule by the investigator.

Problems Faced during Data Collection

The investigator passed through some pleasant and unpleasant experiences during data collection as submitted below.

Firstly, no proper consolidated record of the lock factories and complete list of workers was available to the researcher. Hence, the investigator had to confine to the sources of the District Information Office, Aligarh, as well as the information obtained from other lock industries, Lock Manufacturers Association and the monthly journal *The Lock Times*.

Secondly, the respondents of the lock industries were mostly illiterate. They were not in a position to understand the items of the interview schedule which were put on to them. The researcher presented the items in Urdu/Hindi language, which consumed a lot of time in translation.

Thirdly, the respondents were not able to spare time for the interview in one sitting for which the investigator had to go twice and thrice to the respondents according to their convenience, which meant a lot of time and exertion.

Fourthly, some of the respondents exhibited their indifference to cooperate with the investigator because they were under some wrong impression that the collected information might not be used against them. The investigator got cooperation only when he could fully convince them about the purpose of investigation. The owners of the industries allowed the investigation to be carried on only after they were convinced that the study is a part of academic programme and may be beneficial for them in achieving their targets more efficiently and may provide better job satisfaction among the workers as well as may encourage the development of good relations between the management and labour.

Lastly, some of the respondents were residing in the interior areas of city and the investigator had to locate the places in those narrow lanes of Balai Qila (Upper Fort), Sarai Mian, Usmanpara, Tan Tan Para, Turkman Gate, etc.

DATA ANALYSIS

The entire data has been analyzed and interpreted with the help of factor analysis and *chi*-square test to find out whether any significant difference among the respondents is operative or not as far as their perceptions and aspirations were concerned. Total analysis has been done with the help of computer programming under 'Microsoft-Visual Fox Pro' and 'dBase software.'

The programme structure under Microsoft-Visual Fox prepared for initial feeding of the data of the interview schedule has been shown at the end of this thesis. Final entries of responses of the lock industries workers to the interview schedule have been made under database, the structure for which has also been shown at the end of this study. Similarly, the programming under 'dBase' used for data analysis has also been appended to the study.

While tables have been prepared under Microsoft Word, the charts have been drawn under Microsoft Excel programmes, which has helped in checking and cross checking of the data analysis from different angles.

CHAPTER

4

ANALYSIS AND INTERPRETATION OF THE DATA

In order to analyse, compare and interpret the perceptions and aspirations of the respondents, item analysis, *t*-test and *chi*-square method and techniques have been used. Furthermore, the data has been analysed and compared on the basis of perceptions and aspirations of lock industry workers of different industrial units, constituting major sections of various lock factories.

The *t*-value has been calculated to compare the perceptions and aspirations of different Lock industry workers working in various industrial units using the following formula:

$$t = \frac{P_1 - N_1}{P_c q_c \left(\frac{N_1 + N_2}{N_1 N_2} \right)}$$

Where,

P_1 = First percentage,

P_2 = Second percentage,

N_1 = Number of persons in the first group,

N_2 = Number of persons in the second group, and

N_c = Combined percentage of the two groups.

$$P_c = \frac{N_1 P_1 + N_2 P_2}{N_1 + N_2}$$

$$q_c = 1 - P_c$$

The following chi-square formula[2] has been applied to find out significance of difference, if any, among the perceptions and aspirations of Lock industry workers of different industrial units at Aligarh.

$$X^2 = \sum \frac{(f_0 - f_c)^2}{f_e}$$

Where,

f_0 = observed frequencies, and

f_e = expected frequencies

The data has been calculated with the help of computer, using MICROSOFT VISUAL FOX PRO AND DBASE Software. Details of the programmes have been shown in the preceding chapter. For calculating percentage of the data, item wise, factory wise, etc., Microsoft Excel programme has been used with the following formula:

$$= A/(A+B+C)*100$$

Similarly, charts of various tables have been prepared with the help of Microsoft Excel.

ANALYSIS AND INTERPRETATION OF DATA

As against 1612 registered lock factories in Aligarh, 55 factories were randomly selected for the study from different places, including the Industrial Estate and other parts of the city. Total number of respondents was 474, which constitutes the sample representing the eight units of the lock industries, *viz.* Packing Unit; Press Unit; Assembly Unit; Office; Die-making Unit; Key making Unit; Nickle Polish Unit; and Furnace and Despatch Unit. The sample represents respondents hailing from salaried and contractual; male and female; literate and illiterate; management and labour class; Hindu and Muslim religions; joint family system and nuclear family Urban and rural areas; with two or less children (adopting small family norms) and having more than two children (not adopting small family norms); and drawing wages below Rs. 3000 p.m. and those drawing more than Rs. 3000 per month.

Table 4.1 Parameters Included in Interview Schedule

Statement	*Yes*	*%AGE*	*INDIFF.*	*%AGE*	*NO*	*% AGE*
1. Do you perceive that your earnings are not sufficient to meet familial responsibilities and other obligations?	459	96.84	02	0.42	13	2.74
2. Do you observe that, because of economic reasons people of your community, despite mental and physical exploitation, permit their children. to seek employment?	456	96.20	08	1.69	10	2.11
3. Do you notice that, because of economic constraints, majority of the people of your community fail to fulfill their socio-cultural commitments?	455	95.99	14	2.95	05	1.05
4. Do you perceive that, on account of economic considerations, mostly people of your community give perference to their sons in place of daughters?	541	95.15	18	3.80	28	1.05
5. Do you observe that some families within your own community, where women are also working along with men, are economically much better off as compared to others?	429	90.51	17	3.59	21	5.91
6. Do you notice that constant hikes in the cost of living and limited income has compelled the economically weaker sections of your community to accept all kinds of exploitations?	434	91.56	19	4.01	359	4.43

Table 4.1 Parameters Included in Interview Schedule (Cont.)

Statement	Yes	%AGE	INDIFF.	%AGE	NO	% AGE
7. Do you notice that, on account of limited opportunities of employment, the educated youths of your community has adopted unethical and illegal means to earn money?	82	17.30	33	6.96	359	
8. Do you feel that continuous disurbed conditions like strikes and riots in the society certainly affect economic activities and per captita income of the people of the society?	441	93.04	24	5.06	09	
9. Do you notice that educated and capable youths of your community is not making adequate use of Governmental programmes or schemes meant for economic welfare of the people?	450	94.94	23	4.85	01	
10. Do you observe that, on account of financial reasons, children of your community are unable to receive adequate education, as mostly parents in general and economically weaker parents in particular, are unable to meet the prevailing high educational expenses?	453	95.57	21	4.43	00	

*Total number of respondents

The analysis is based on information furnished by 474 respondents against each of the ten parameters included in the interview schedule, irrespective of the lock industry, industrial units and working groups.

Table 4.1 reveals that predominant majority (96.84%) of the respondents 96.84% have expressed their agreement with the statement that their earnings are not sufficient to meet the familial responsibilities and other obligations, while 0.42% have exhibited indifference towards the statement and only 2.74% have expressed their disagreement with the statement. The majority of the respondents 96.20% have agreed to the statement that, because of economic reasons, people of their community, despite mental and physical exploitation, permit their children to seek employment, while 1.69% have exhibited their indifference towards the statement and only 2.11% have expressed their disagreement with the statement. Majority of the respondents 95.99% observe that because of economic constraints, majority of the people of their community fail to fulfill their socio-cultural commitments, while 2.95% have exhibited their indifference and only 1.05% have expressed their disagreement with the statement. The majority of the respondents 95.15% have agreed to the statement that on account of economic considerations most of the people of their community give preference to sons in place of daughters, while 3.80% have exhibited their indifference and only 1.05% have expressed their disagreement with the statement. It appears that majority of the respondents 90.51% have agreed to the statement that families where women are also working along with men are economically better. While 3.59% have exhibited their indifference towards the statement, only 5.91% have expressed their disagreement. Majority of the respondents 91.56% have noticed that constant hikes in the cost of living and limited income has compelled the economically weaker sections of their community to accept all kinds of exploitations, while 4.01% have exhibited their indifference towards the statement and only 4.43% have expressed their disagreement. Majority of the respondents 75.74% have not agreed to the statement that on account of limited employment opportunities the educated youths of the community have adopted unethical and illegal means to earn money, while 6.96% have exhibited their indifference towards the statement and only 17.30% have expressed their agreement. Majority of the respondents (93.04%) feel that disturbed conditions like strikes and riots in the society certainly affect economic activities and per capita income of the people while 5.06% have exhibited their indifference and only 1.90% have expressed their disagreement. As many as respondents 94.94% have noticed that educated and capable youths of the community are not making adequate use of governmental programmes or schemes meant for economic welfare of the people, while 4.85% have shown their indifference and only 0.21% have expressed their disagreement. High majority of the respondents 95.57% have observed that due to financial reasons children of their community are unable to receive adequate education as most of parents are unable to meet the prevailing high educational expenses, while 4.43% have shown their indifference, none has expressed disagreement with the statement.

It can be concluded that majority of the respondents have expressed their agreement with all the above mentioned statement except in item No. 7 where majority of respondents have expressed their disagreement.

Table 4.2 reveals that majority of the respondents 94.94% have expressed their agreement with the statement that they want to supplement their earnings by taking up some part time job or economic activities, while 2.95% have shown their indifference only 2.11% have expressed their disagreement with the statement. It is also evident from the table that 90.72% of the respondents aspire to raise their voice and fight for implementation of labour laws pertaining to children for saving them from exploitation, while 5.70% have exhibited their indifference and only 3.59% have expressed their disagreement. In all, 89.87% of the respondents have expressed their agreement with the statement for taking up some extra economic activities, yielding monetary returns for fulfillment of their socio-cultural commitments, while 3.80% have shown their indifference and only 6.33% disagree with the statement.Less then half (*i.e.*, 45.99% respondents have shown their agreement to the statement on desiring to work and educate the members of their community to treat their

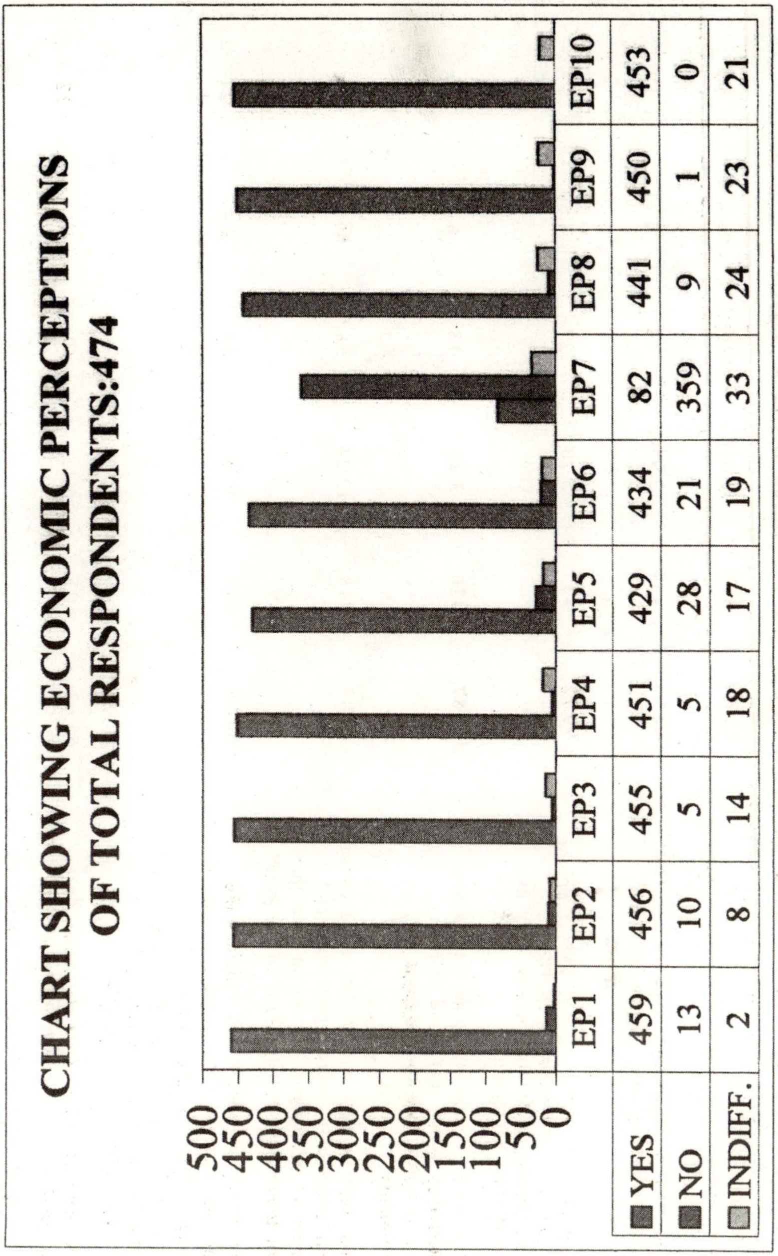

	EP1	EP2	EP3	EP4	EP5	EP6	EP7	EP8	EP9	EP10
YES	459	456	455	451	429	434	82	441	450	453
NO	13	10	5	5	28	21	359	9	1	0
INDIFF.	2	8	14	18	17	19	33	24	23	21

Table 4.2 Responses on Statements Having Bearing on Economic Aspects

STATEMENT	*%AGE*	*YES*	*%AGE*	*INDIFF.*	*%AGE*	*NO*
1. Do you want to supplement your earnings by taking up some part-time job or economic activities?	94.94	450	2.95	14	2.11	10
2. Do you earnestly aspire to raise your voice and fight for implementation of labour laws pertaining to children so that they may be saved from exploitation?	90.72	430	5.70	27	3.59	17
3. Do you aspire to take up some extra economic activities which may yield monetary returns to fulfill your socio-cultural commitments?	89.87	426	3.80	18	6.33	30
4. Do you want to work and educate the members of your community to treat their sons and daughters on equal basis, keeping in view the modern trends and changing laws of the land?	45.99	218	12.24	58	41.77	198
5. Do you aspire to educate and enlighten the ignorant members of your community and to encourage women to take part in economic activities alongwith their male counterparts to achieve greater economic stability and prosperity?	86.29	409	9.28	44	4.43	21
6. Do you aspire to educate the economically weaker sections of your community to fight against any kind of exploitation and start some extra economic activities initially on a small scale so that exploitation be controlled?	85.02	403	6.11	49	4.64	22

Table 4.2 Responses on Statements Having Bearing on Economic Aspects

	Statement	*%AGE*	*YES*	*%AGE*	*INDIFF.*	*%AGE*	*NO*
7.	Do you intend to educate the unemployed educated youth of your community that instead of adopting unethical and illegal means of earning money, they should avail facilities offered by Government to start independent economic activity?	73.63	349	6.11	29	20.25	96
8.	Do you intend to join some such judicious non-political organizations which may prove a useful instrument in settling strikes as well as in maintaining communal harmony during riot?	93.67	444	4.85	23	1.48	07
9.	Do you aspire to educate the deserving youths of your community to avail benefits of Government sponsored employment programmes and schemes so that their economic upliftment could be achieved?	89.24	423	8.02	38	2.74	13
10.	Do you intend to raise your voice through some social organization or agency to put some pressure on the Government as well as on the welfare bodies of your community to provide reading material on subsidized rates in general and scholarships in particular to the economically weaker sections of your community?	83.33	395	5.91	28	10.76	51

sons and daughters on equal basis keeping in view the modern trends and changing law of the land, while 12.24% have exhibited indifference, but a strong percentage *i.e.* 41.77% have shown their disagreement with the statement. While majority of the respondents 86.29% have expressed their agreement to the statement that they aspire to educate and enlighten the ignorant members of their community and to encourage women to take part in economic activities along with their male counterparts for achieving greater economic stability and prosperity. 9.28% have exhibited their indifference and only 4.43% have expressed their disagreement with the statement. Although a strong majority of the respondents 85.02% aspire to educate economically weaker sections of their community to fight against any kind of exploitation and start some extra economic activities initially on small scale for controlling exploitation, yet 10.34% have shown indifference and only 4.64% have expressed their disagreement with the statement. While a high majority of respondents 73.63% aspire to educate the unemployed educated youths of their community to avail loan facilities offered by Government for starting independent economic activity for earning money, 6.11% have exhibited their indifference towards the statement and only 20.25% have expressed their disagreement with the statement. Although a preponderant majority of the respondents (93.67%) intend to join non-political organizations proving a useful instrument in settling strikes as well as in maintaining communal harmony, yet 4.85% have exhibited their indifference and only 1.48% have expressed their disagreement with the statement. A strong majority of the respondents 89.24% aspire to educate the deserving youths of their community to avail the provision and benefits of government sponsored employment programmes and schemes for achieving economic upliftment, but 8.02% have shown their indifference and only 2.74% have expressed their disagreement with the statement. Happily, a strong majority of the respondents (i.e., 83.33%) intend to raise their voice through some social organization or agency for putting some pressure on the government as well as on the welfare bodies of their community to provide reading material on subsidized rates in general and on scholarships in particular to the economically weaker sections of their

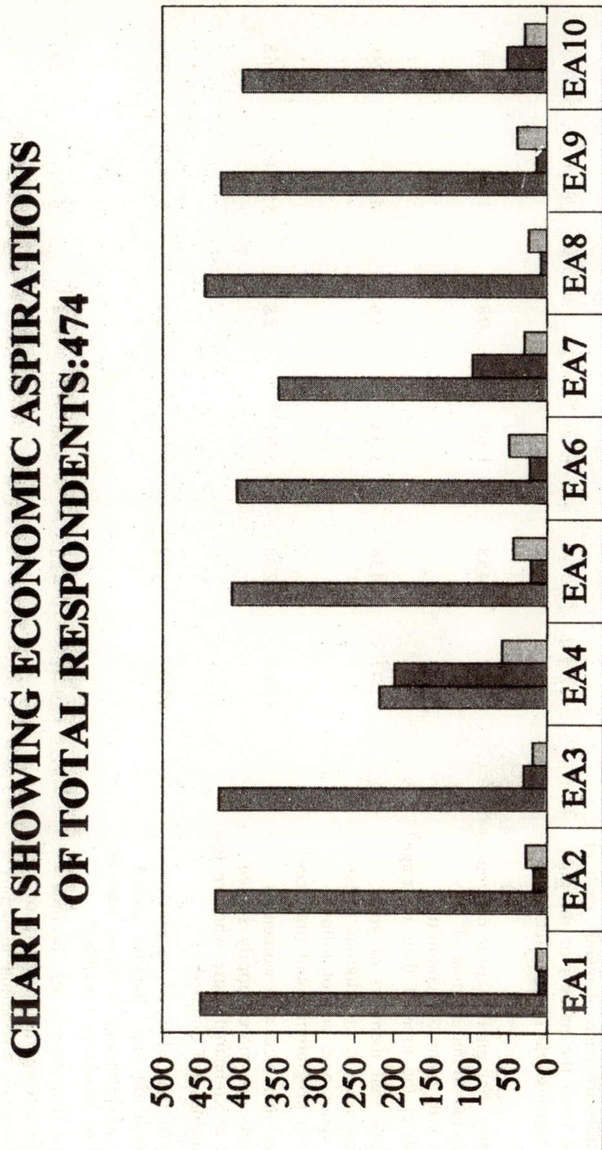

	EA1	EA2	EA3	EA4	EA5	EA6	EA7	EA8	EA9	EA10
YES	450	430	426	218	409	403	349	444	423	395
NO	10	17	30	198	21	22	96	7	13	51
INDIFF.	14	27	18	58	44	49	29	23	38	28

Table 4.3 Responses on Statements Having Bearing on Soceo-Cultural Aspets

STATEMENT	%AGE	YES	%AGE	INDIFF.	%AGE	NO
1. Do you perceive that in your community boy's parents, at the time of marriage, directly or indirectly make demand cash or kinds of gifts from the parents of the girls which is not permissible in your religion and by law?	81.43	386	1.48	07	17.09	81
2. Do you observe that girls of your community are subjected to humiliation if they fail to bring with them the committed gifts and cash at the time of their marriage?	96.62	458	1.69	08	1.69	08
3. Do you observe that members of your community, on account of religious consideration and ignorance, do not follow family planning programmes and practices?	92.41	438	3.38	16	4.22	20
4. Do you notice that men and women in your community are more happily settled in their lives as compared those who are less educated or uneducated couples?	57.66	278	5.91	28	35.44	168
5. Do you observe that educated couples of your community are more happily settled in their lives as compared to those who are less educated or uneducated couples?	89.87	422	5.06	24	5.91	28
6. Do you notice that divorce has become fairly common among the members of our society which is amounting to family disorganization?	89.03	422	5.06	24	5.91	28

Table 4.3 Responses on Statements Having Bearing on Soceo-Cultural Aspets

	STATEMENT	*%AGE*	*YES*	*%AGE*	*INDIFF.*	*%AGE*	*NO*
7.	Do you observe that women window remarriage though legally permissible, yet is being discouraged by certain sections of the community.	38.19	181	8.65	41	53.16	252
8.	Do you notice that in your community it is somewhat difficult to find suitable matches for educated boys and girls?	93.88	445	4.64	22	1.48	07
9.	Do you perceive that on account of growing nuclear family patterns, the traditional familial bonds of feeling among the members of the community have weakened?	95.36	422	2.95	14	1.69	08

community, while 5.91% have exhibited their indifference and only 10.76% have expressed their disagreement with the statement.

It can be concluded that majority of the respondents have expressed their strong agreement with all the above statements.

Table 4.3 reveals that majority of respondents 81.43% expressed agreement with the statement that in their community parents of the boys, at the time of their marriage, demand gifts in cash and kind from parents of girls which is not permissible in the religion and law, while 1.48% exhibited their indifference only 17.09% expressed their disagreement with the statement. Overwhelming majority of the respondents 96.62% expressed agreement with the statement that girls of their community are subjected to humiliation if they fail to bring with them the committed gifts and cash at the time of their marriage; 1.69% exhibited their indifference and only 1.69% expressed their disagreement with the statement. While majority of respondents 92.41% expressed their agreement with the statement that the members of their community due to religious consideration and ignorance do not follow family planning programmes and practices, 3.38% exhibited indifference and only 4.22% expressed their disagreement with the statement. Most of the respondents 58.66% agreed that men and women in their community enjoy equal authority in family matters, but while 5.91% exhibited their indifference a significant 35.44% expressed their disagreement with the statement.A respondent majority (89.87%) expressed their agreement that educated couples of the community are more happily settled in their lives as compared to less or uneducated couples, while 6.96% exhibited indifference and only 3.16% expressed their disagreement with the statement. Majority of the respondents 89.03% agreed that members of their community go for early marriage of their daughters even to elderly settled persons because of economic reasons, while 5.06% exhibited indifference and only 5.91% expressed their disagreement with the statement. Majority of the respondents (89.03%) have expressed their agreement to the statement that divorce has become fairly common among the members of their society which is amounting to family disorganization, while 5.06% exhibited their indifference and 5.91% expressed their disagreement with the statement. Most of the respondents 53.16% have expressed their disagreement with the statement that women widow remarriage, through legally permissible, yet it is being discouraged by certain sections of the community; while 8.65% exhibited their indifference towards the statement, only 38.19% have agreed to the statement. While a huge majority (93.88%) agreed that in their community it is somewhat difficult to find suitable matches for educated boys and girls, 4.64% have expressed indifference and only 1.48% expressed disagreement with the statement. Majority of the respondents 95.36% agreed that on account of growing nuclear family patterns, the traditional familial bonds of the feelings among the members of their community have weakened, 2.95% exhibited indifference and only 1.69% expressed disagreement with the statement.

It can be concluded that majority of the respondents have expressed their agreement with all the above statements except in item No.8, where the majority of respondents (53.16%) exhibited their disagreement while 38.19% have exhibited their agreement and 8.65% showed their indifference to the statements.

Table 4.4 reveals that majority of the respondents 94.09% have aspired to work against the system of demanding cash or kind at the time of marriage. While 4.22% exhibited indifference, only 1.69% expressed their disagreement with it. Majority of the respondents 91.98% aspired to organize or join such organization working for rehabilitation of such girls of their community who become victims of humiliation after their marriage, while 6.75% exhibited their indifference only 1.27% expressed their disagreement with the statement. Majority of the respondents 67.93% aspired to appeal the enlightened, educated and expert members of their community to come forward and educate the masses about socio-economic and physiological advantages of family planning. While 6.96% exhibited indifference only 25.11% expressed disagreement with it. Clear majority of respondents 52.11% wished to voice in support of women's right of equality in family matters of their community. While 4.85% exhibited indifference only 43.04% have expressed their disagreement with it. Vast majority of the respondents 85.65% aspired to educate

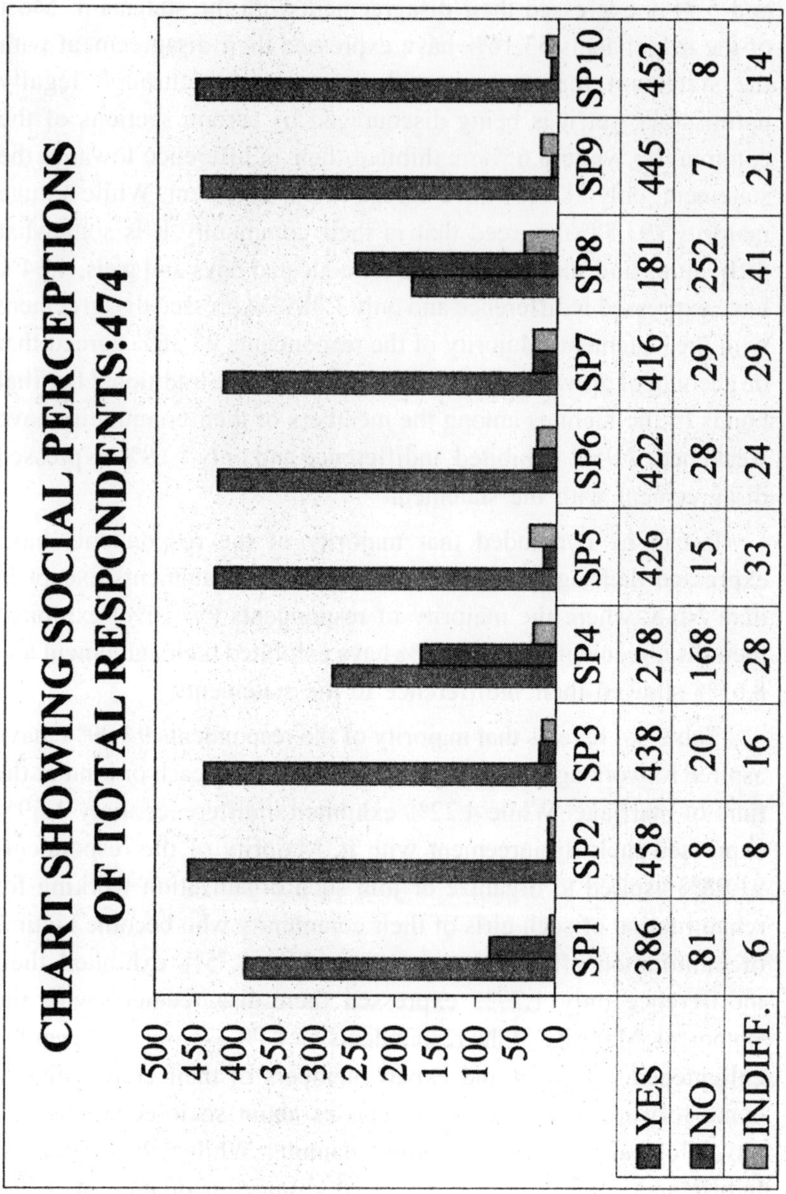

	SP1	SP2	SP3	SP4	SP5	SP6	SP7	SP8	SP9	SP10
YES	386	458	438	278	426	422	416	181	445	452
NO	81	8	20	168	15	28	29	252	7	8
INDIFF.	6	8	16	28	33	24	29	41	21	14

Table 4.4 Responses on Aspects Having Bearing on Family

STATEMENT	*%AGE*	*YES*	*%AGE*	*INDIFF.*	*%AGE*	*NO*
1. Do you aspire to work against the system of demand in cash and kind by the boys parents of your community at the time of their marriage as is not permissible in your religion and by law?	94.09	446	4.22	20	1.69	08
2. Do you aspire to organize or join such organization which work for the rehabilitation of such girls of your community who became victims of humiliation after their marriage?	91.98	436	6.75	32	1.27	06
3. Do you aspire to appeal the enlightened, educated and expert members of your community to come forward and educate the masses about the socio-economic and physiological advantages of family planning?	67.93	322	6.96	33	25.11	119
4. Do you wish to raise your voice in support of women's rights of equality in family matters of your community?	52.11	247	4.85	23	43.04	204
5. Do you aspire to educate the members of your community not to marry their children till they receive porper education?	85.65	406	11.60	55	2.74	11
6. Do you aspire to educate the members of your community not to marry their daughters to elderly settled persons on account of economic reasons?	90.72	434	5.91	28	2.53	12

Table 4.4 Responses on Aspects Having Bearing on Family (Contd)

STATEMENT	*%AGE*	*YES*	*%AGE*	*INDIFF.*	*%AGE*	*NO*
7. Do you aspire to propagate against the evils of divorce among the members of your society so that families could be saved from being disorganized?	91.56	434	5.91	28	2.53	12
8. Do you aspire to propagate among the masses of your community to encourage women widow remarriage in order to rehabilitate and rescue them from expected future exploitations?	91.35	433	6.96	33	1.69	08
9. Do you aspire to be associated with some such voluntary social organizations which may help in selecting matches for educated boys and girls of your community?	94.30	447	4.43	21	1.27	06
10. Do you aspire to enlighten the members of your community to interact among themselves quite frequently so that the traditional bonds of family proximity are maintained?	92.19	437	4.22	20	3.59	17

* Total number of respondents

the members of their community not to marry their children till they receive proper education. While 11.60% exhibited their indifference, only 2.74% expressed their disagreement with the statement. Majority of the respondents 90.72% aspired to educate the members of their community not to marry their daughters to elderly settled persons on account of economic reasons and instead start some extra economic activity to improve their financial condition. While 5.91% exhibited their indifference towards the statement, only 2.53% expressed their disagreement. Majority of the respondents (91.56%) aspired to propagate against the evils of divorce among the members of their society for saving the families from disorganization. While 5.91% exhibited their indifference, only 2.53% expressed their disagreement with the statement. Majority of the respondents 91.35% aspired to propagate among the masses of their community to encourage widow remarriage in order to rehabilitate and rescue them from expected future exploitations. While 6.96% exhibited their indifference only 1.69% have expressed their disagreement with the statement. Vast majority of the respondents (94.30%) aspired to associate themselves with some such voluntary social organization which may help in selecting matches for educated boys and girls of their community. While 4.43% exhibited their indifference only 1.27% expressed their disagreement with the statement. Huge majority of 92.19% aspired to enlighten the members of their community to interact among themselves quite frequently so that the traditional bonds of family proximity are maintained. While 4.22% exhibited their indifference only 3.59% have expressed their disagreement with the statement.

It can be concluded that majority of the respondents have expressed their agreement with all the above statement except that with regard to item No. 4 where 43.04% of the respondents expressed their disagreement towards the statement.

Table 4.5 reveals that huge majority of the respondents 83.97% expressed their disagreement with the statement that the members of their community take keen interest in the political affairs and also adopt unethical practices to achieve their goals. While 1.48% exhibited indifference only 14.56% expressed their agreement with the statement. Vast majority of 94.09% expressed their agreement with the statement that members of their society do not support political parties on the basis of their election manifesto. While 4.01% exhibited their indifference, only 1.90% expressed their disagreement with the statement. Majority of the respondents 71.31% expressed their disagreement with the statement that fair elections are held in the society. While 3.38% exhibited indifference, only 25.32% expressed their agreement with the statement A preponderant majority of 93.04% expressed their agreement with the statement that political bosses misuse their position and power for selfish ends by exploiting the authorities. While 5.91% exhibited their indifference, only 1.05% expressed their disagreement with the statement. A massive majority of 93.30% expressed their agreement with the statement. that candidates and political parties freely use money and muscle power during elections. While 5.91% exhibited their indifference, only 1.05% expressed their disagreement with the statement. A massive majority of 94.30% expressed their agreement with the statement that economically well off people of their community extend financial support to all important parties and candidates because they take advantage of them after their victories. While 4.43% exhibited their indifference, only 1.27% expressed their disagreement with the statement. The huge majority of 94.05% expressed their agreement with the statement that in elections political parties issue tickets and extend full support to persons having established criminal background. While 5.70% exhibited their indifference, only 0.21% disagreed with the statement. Overwhelming majority of the respondents 94.94% expressed their agreement with the statement that the political parties or even independent candidates, in order to win elections, do not hesitate in giving communal or caste turn to any event during election period, if it suits them. While 4.64% expressed indifference only 0.42% expressed their disagreement with the statement. A convincing majority of 94.09% expressed their agreement with the statement that the members of their community lack the required political awareness in selecting right type of person or party and hence do not cast their votes. While 4.64% exhibited their indifference only 0.42% expressed

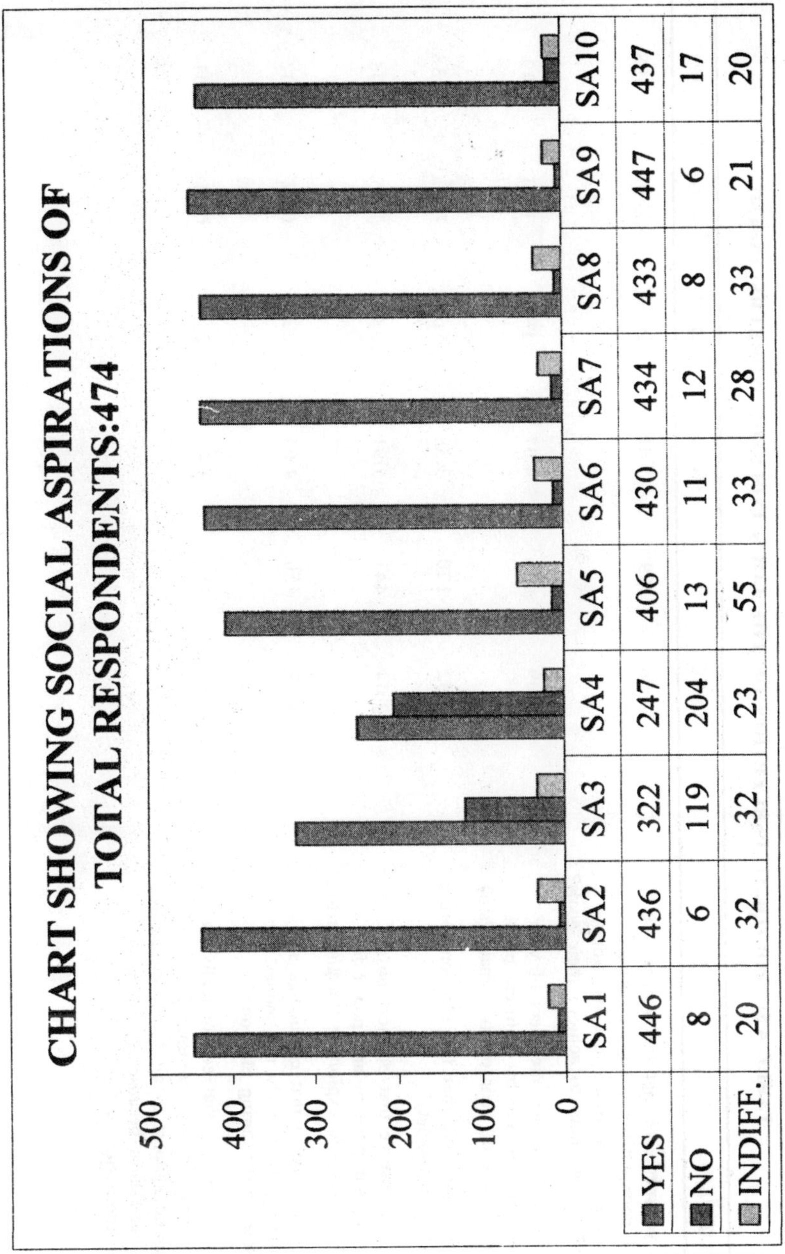

	SA1	SA2	SA3	SA4	SA5	SA6	SA7	SA8	SA9	SA10
YES	446	436	322	247	406	430	434	433	447	437
NO	8	6	119	204	13	11	12	8	6	17
INDIFF.	20	32	32	23	55	33	28	33	21	20

TABLE 4.5: POLITICAL PERCEPTION OF THE LOCK INDUSTRY WORKERS: (N=474)

STATEMENT	*%AGE*	*YES*	*%AGE*	*INDIFF.*	*%AGE*	*NO*
1. Do you perceive that the members of your community take keen interest in the political affairs and also adopt unethical practices to achieve their goals?	14.56	69	1.48	07	83.97	398
2. Do you notice that members of your society do not support political parties on the basis of their election manifesto?	94.09	446	4.01	19	1.90	09
3. Do you perceive that fair elections are held in our society?	25.32	120	3.38	16	7131	338
4. Do you observe that political bosses misuse their position and power for selfish ends and exploiting the authorities?	93.04	441	5.91	28	1.05	05
5. Do you perceive that candidates and political parties freely use money and muscle power during elections?	94.94	450	4.64	22	0.42	02
6. Do you observe that economically well off people of your community extend financial support to all important parties and candidates because they encash it after their victories?	95.36	452	4.43	21	0.21	01

TABLE 4.5: POLITICAL PERCEPTION OF THE LOCK INDUSTRY WORKERS: (N=474) (Cond.)

STATEMENT	*%AGE*	*YES*	*%AGE*	*INDIFF.*	*%AGE*	*NO*
7. Do you observe that in elections, political parties issue tickets and extend full support to persons having established criminal background?	94.30	446	5.70	27	0.21	01
8. Do you notice that political parties or even independent candidates, in order to win the election, do not hesitate in giving communal or caste turn to any event during election period, if it suits to them?	94.94	450	4.64	22	0.42	02
9. Do you perceive that the members of your community lack the required political awareness in selecting right type of person or party and hence do not cast their votes?	94.94	450	4.64	22	0.42	02
10. Do you observe that political parties and independent candidates mostly make false promises at the time of elections but never attend to them?	95.36	452	4.43	21	0.21	01

* Total number of respondents

disagreement with the statement. A vast majority of the respondents (95.36%) expressed their agreement with the statement that political parties and independent candidates mostly make false promises at the time of elections but never attend to them. While 4.43% exhibited their indifference, only 0.21% have expressed their disagreement with the statement.

It can be concluded that majority of the respondents expressed agreement with all the above statements except in case of items No.1 and 3 where the majority of respondents exhibited their disagreement with the statements.

Table 4.6 reveals that a huge majority of the respondents 95.36% expressed their desire to generate judicious and ethical political awareness among the masses of their community for not adopting unethical practices in the political affairs of the society, if they get a chance. While 2.53% exhibited indifference, only 2.11% expressed agreement with it. A big chunk of 93.04% aspired to propagate among the members of their society the idea to support political parties on the basis of their election manifesto and not on any other considerations. While 4.64% exhibited their indifference only 2.32% expressed disagreement with the statement. A huge majority of the respondents 90.51% aspired to become member of such organization which may fight against the malpractices operative during elections. While 6.54% exhibited their indifference, only 2.95% expressed their disagreement with the statement. An impressive majority of the respondents 82.49% aspired to expose such political persons who misuse their positions and power for their selfish ends. While 15.61% exhibited their indifference only 1.90% expressed their disagreement with the statement. A clear majority of the respondents (78.27%) aspired to work and raise their voice against such parties and persons who use money and muscle power during elections. While 19.41% exhibited their indifference, only 2.32% expressed their disagreement with the statement. Majority of the respondents 81.22% aspired to raise their voice that government should impose some financial limits in election expenditure which should be subject to accountability. While 13.08% exhibited their indifference, only 5.70% expressed

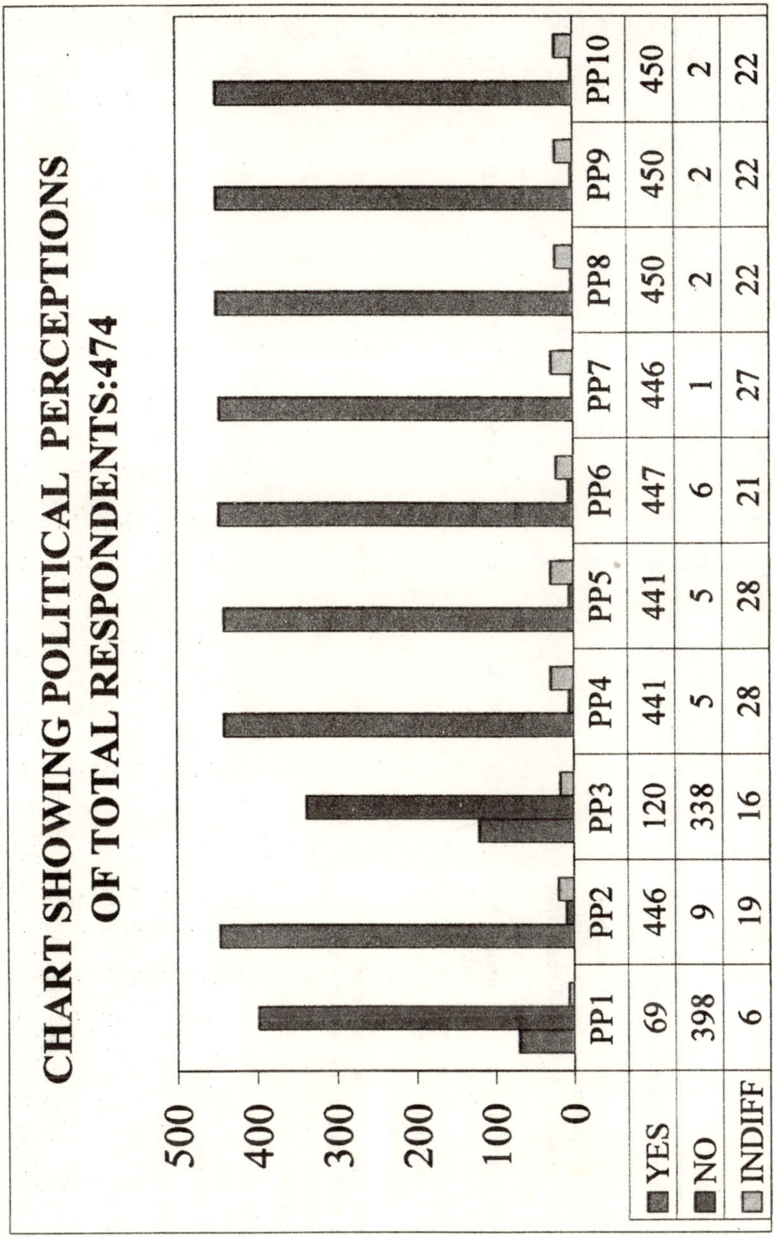

	PP1	PP2	PP3	PP4	PP5	PP6	PP7	PP8	PP9	PP10
YES	69	446	120	441	441	447	446	450	450	450
NO	398	9	338	5	5	6	1	2	2	2
INDIFF	6	19	16	28	28	21	27	22	22	22

TABLE 4.6: POLITICAL PERCEPTION OF LOCK INDUSTRY WORKERS (N=474)

STATEMENT	%AGE	YES	%AGE	INDIFF.	%AGE	NO
1. Do you aspire to generate judicious and ethical political awareness among the masses of your community, if and when you get an opportunity not to adopt unethical practices in the political affairs of the society?	9536	452	2.53	12	2.11	10
2. Do you aspire to propagate among the members of your society to support political parties on the basis of their election manifesto and not on any other considerations?	93.04	441	4.46	22	2.32	11
3. Do you aspire to become member of some such organization which may fight against malpartices which are operative during elections?	90.51	429	6.54	31	2.95	14
4. Do you aspire to expose such political persons who misuse their positions and power for their selfish ends?	82.49	391	15.61	74	1.90	09
5. Do you aspire to work and raise voice against such parties and persons who use money and muscle power during elections?	78.27	371	19.41	92	2.32	11
6. Do you aspire to raise your voice that government should impose some financial limits in election expenditure which should be subject to accountability?	81.22	385	13.08	62	5.70	27

TABLE 4.6: POLITICAL PERCEPTION OF LOCK INDUSTRY WORKERS (N=474)

7. Do you aspire to propose or request the elightened and judicious members of your community to come forward and put pressure on the Government to impose a ban on permitting any contestant, having criminal background, to seek election?	91.77	435	7.81	37	0.42	02
8. Do you earnestly wish to protest vigorously through some organization or independently against such political parties and independent candidates who, in order to win elections, exploit the election scence on the basis of religion or caste?	94.09	446	5.06	24	0.84	04
9. Do you wish to educate independently or through your community organizations to press the members of the community to caste this votes and support right type of person or party, based on their election manifesto?	94.03	431	8.23	39	0.84	04
10. Do you aspire to join some such non-political organization through which you may raise your protest effectively in highlighting non-fulfillment of promises to communities made by the political parties and independent candidates after winning the elections?	94.09	446	5.49	26	042	02

* Total number of respondents

disagreement with the statement. A big majority of 91.77% aspired to pursue the enlightened and judicious members of their community to come forward and put pressure on the government to impose ban on permitting any contestant having criminal background to seek election. While 7.81% exhibited their indifference, only 0.42% expressed disagreement with the statement. Majority of the respondents (94.09%) earnestly wished to protest vigorously through some organization or independently against such political parties or independent candidates who, in order to win elections, exploit the election scene on the basis of religion or caste. While 5.06% exhibited indifference towards the statement only 0.84% expressed disagreement with the statement. Huge majority of respondents 94.03% wished to educate independently or through their community organizations to press the members of the community to cast their votes and support right type of person or party based on their election manifestoes. While 8.23% exhibited indifference, only 0.84% expressed disagreement with the statement. A great majority of the respondents 94.09% aspired to join some such non-political organization through which they may raise their voice effectively in highlighting non-fulfillment of promises made to communities by the political parties and independent candidates but failed to fulfil them after winning the elections. While 5.49% exhibited their indifference only 0.42% expressed their disagreement with the statement.

Thus, it can be concluded that majority of the respondents have expressed their agreement with all the above statements.

Table 4.7 reveals that majority of respondents 84.18% are not satisfied with the prevailing educational system during the present era of advancement. While 1.69% exhibited indifference, only 14.14% expressed their disagreement with the statement. Huge majority of the respondents 93.67% noticed that on account of higher cost of education, majority of the parents hailing from economically weaker sections of their community do not encourage their children to receive full education. While 5.06% exhibited indifference, only 1.27% have expressed their disagreement with the statement. An impressive majority of respondents 91.14% perceived that education was mainly responsible for the socio-economic development of the members of

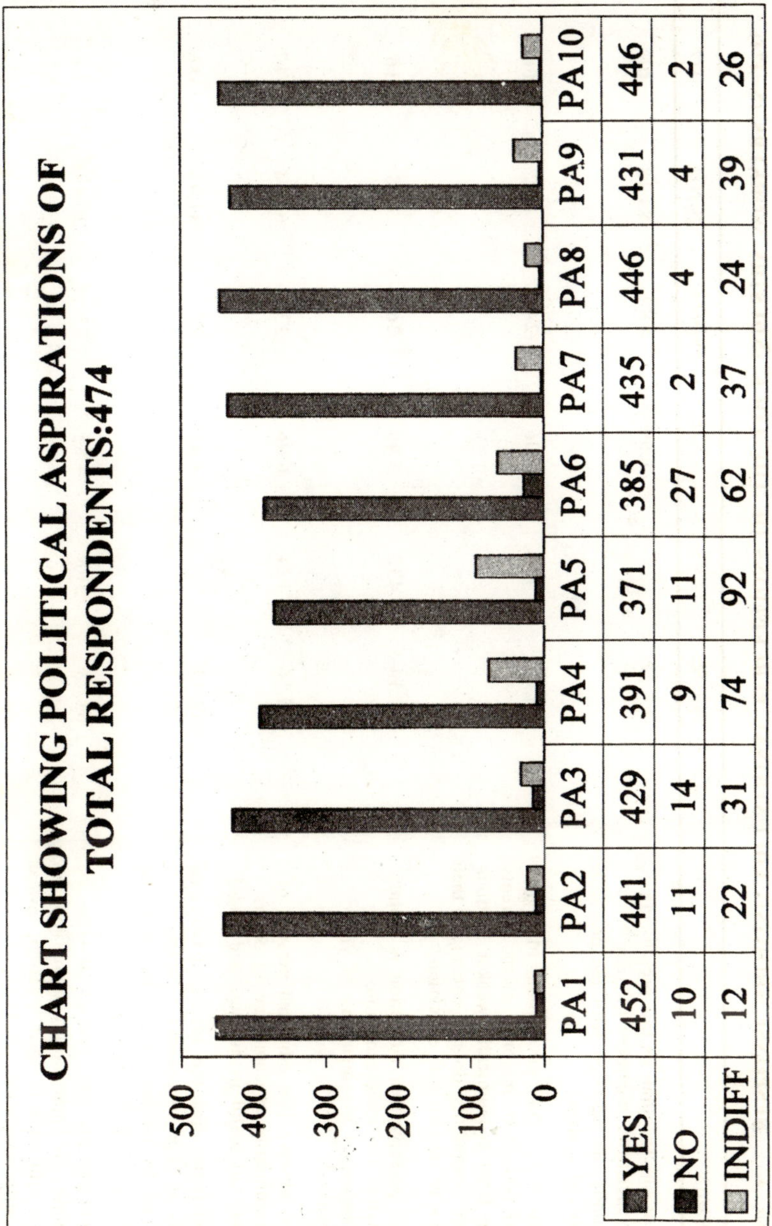

	PA1	PA2	PA3	PA4	PA5	PA6	PA7	PA8	PA9	PA10
YES	452	441	429	391	371	385	435	446	431	446
NO	10	11	14	9	11	27	2	4	4	2
INDIFF	12	22	31	74	92	62	37	24	39	26

TABLE 4.7: RESPONSE SHOWING EDUCATIONAL PERCEPTIONS OF THE LOCK INDUSTRY WORKERS (N=474)

STATEMENT	%AGE	YES	%AGE	INDIFF.	%AGE	NO
1. Do you observe that in the present era of advancement, members of your community are satisfied with the prevailing educational system?	14.14	67	1.69	08	84.18	06
2. Do you notice that, on account of higher cost of education, majority of the parents hailing from economically weaker sections of your community do not encourage their children to receive full education?	93.67	444	5.06	24	1.27	06
3. Do you perceive that education is mainly responsible for socio-economic development of the members of your community?	91.14	432	5.49	26	3.38	16
4. Do you observe that educated persons of your community as compared to others, are more successful in business and trade?	26.16	124	6.96	33	66.88	317
5. Do you notice that the advice of educated persons of your community is always sought by the uneducated and less educated ones to settle their disputes?	14.14	67	4.43	21	81.43	386
6. Do your perceive that parents of your community are more in favour of imparting religious education to their children, instead of scientific education?	64.98	308	4.85	23	30.17	14

TABLE 4.7: RESPONSE SHOWING EDUCATIONAL PERCEPTIONS OF THE LOCK INDUSTRY WORKERS (N=474) (Cont.)

STATEMENT	*%AGE*	*YES*	*%AGE*	*INDIFF.*	*%AGE*	*NO*
7. Do you observe that majority of parents of your community are ignorant about importance of their children's education?	92.62	439	6.12	29	1.27	05
8. Do you notice that women of your community are more educationally backward, as compared to the women of other communities?	94.51	448	5.49	26	0.00	00
9. Do you observe that the leaders of your community are indifferent towards the educational upliftment of the community and do not seek help from the Government?	94.51	448	5.49	26	0.00	00
10. Do you observe that in the present era, education has become highly commerciali-zed because teachers do not judiciously perform their teaching duties in shools and colleges as either they have opened their coaching centres or teaching in other coaching centres on the basis of payment?	94.30	447	5.49	26	0.21	01

* Total number of respondents

their community. While 5.49% exhibited indifference, only 3.38% have expressed their disagreement with the statement. A clear majority of respondents 66.88% expressed disagreement with the statement that the educated persons of their community as compared to others, were more successful in business and trade, although 26.16% of the respondents expressed their agreement, and 6.96% showed their indifference towards the statement. Huge majority of respondents 81.43% showed their disagreement with the statement that advice of educated persons of their community was always sought by the uneducated and less educated ones to settle disputes. While 4.43% exhibited indifference only 14.14% expressed agreement with the statement. A class majority of the respondents 64.98% perceived that parents of their community are more in favour of imparting religious education to their children instead of scientific education. While 485% exhibited indifference, only 30.17% expressed disagreement with the statement. A vast majority of the respondents 92.62% observed that majority of parents of their community were ignorant about the importance of their children's education. While 6.12% exhibited indifference, only 1.27% expressed disagreement with the statement. A great majority of the respondents 94.51% have noticed that women of their community were more educationally backward as compared to the women of other communities. While 5.49% exhibited indifference, none expressed their disagreement with the statement. As many as 94.51% observed that the leaders of their community are indifferent towards the educational upliftment of the community and do not seek help from the government, while 5.49% exhibited their indifference towards the statement. An overwheleing majority of the respondents (94.30%) observed that in the present era education has become highly commercialized because teachers do not judiciously perform their teaching duties in schools and colleges as either they have opened their own coaching centres or teach at other coaching centres on payment. While 5.49% exhibited indifference, only 0.21% expressed disagreement with the statement.

It can, therefore be concluded that majority of the respondents expressed their agreement with all the above statements, except in case of items No. 1, 4 and 5, where the majority of respondents exhibited disagreement with the statements.

Table 4.8 reveals that majority of the respondents 58.23% expressed their agreement with the statement wishing to establish some contact with members of their community, connected with the system of education to suggest ways and means to the government for evolving better system of education. While 1.27% exhibited indifference, only 40.51% expressed disagreement with the statement. Huge majority of respondents 92.83% aspired to work and fight independently or through some social organization to press the government for free and full education to the children hailing from the economically backward strata of the community. While 6.12% exhibited indifference, only 1.05% expressed their disagreement with the statement. A clear majority of respondents 54.64% aspired to work with some social organization of their community, who claim to look after the interest of the poor children hailing from the lower economic strata. While 5.72% exhibited their indifference only 39.66% expressed their disagreement with the statement. A huge majority of respondents 77.85% aspired to propagate that children should not be engaged in any economic activity till they receive proper education so that they may be more successful in business and trade. While 7.17% exhibited their indifference only 14.98% expressed their disagreement with the statement. A vast majority of the respondents 85.44% aspired to educate the uneducated and less educated masses of their community to settle their disputes amicably with the help of educated persons and not to use physical force or adopt unethical practices or to go to court of law as it is very expensive and time-consuming. While 6.33% exhibited their indifference, only 8.23% expressed their disagreement with the statement. Only 45.57% aspired to propagate among the members of their community the usefulness of scientific education based on analytical and rational principles instead of religious education alone. Whereas 46.84% of the respondents expressed their disagreement and 7.51% exhibited indifference to the statement. A huge majority of the respondents 91.77% aspired to seek help from the educated members of their community to enlighten the ignorant parents about the importance of children's education. While 4.85% exhibited their indifference towards the statement only 3.38% expressed their disagreement with the

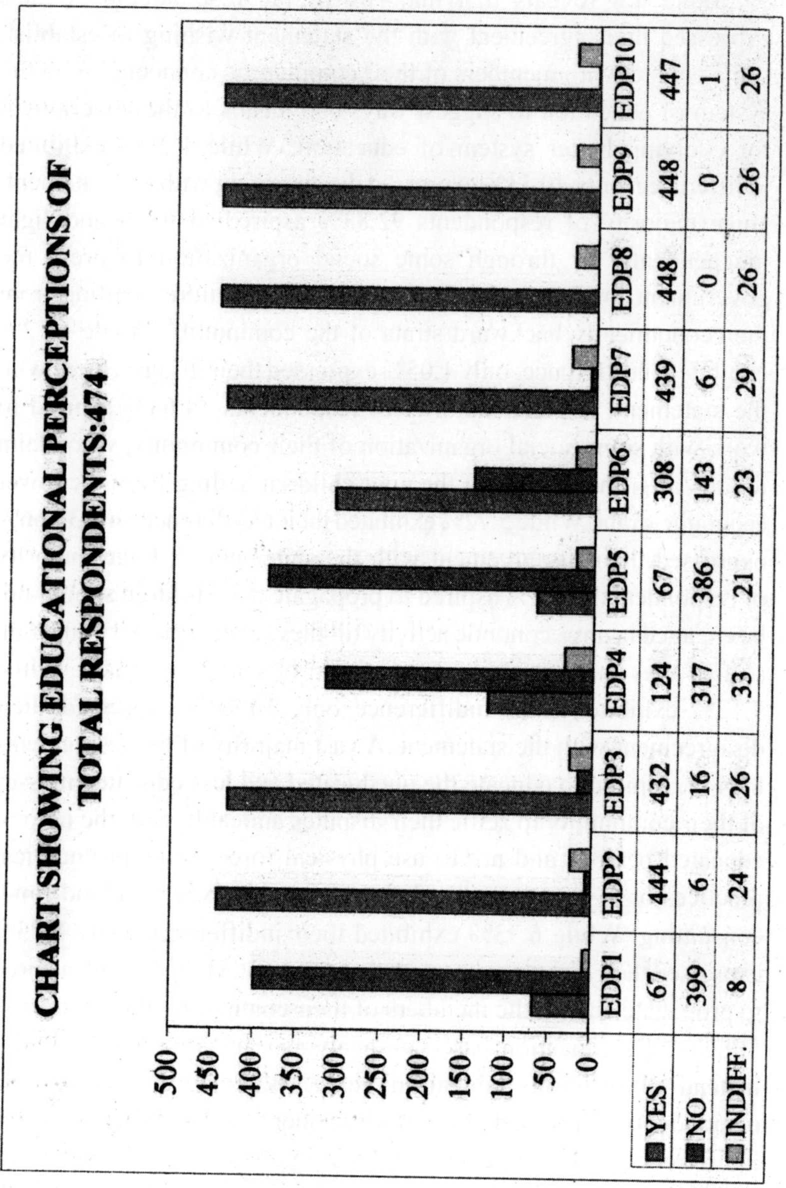
CHART SHOWING EDUCATIONAL PERCEPTIONS OF
TOTAL RESPONDENTS:474
500
450
400
350
300
250
200
150
100
50
0
EDP1 EDP2 EDP3 EDP4 EDP5 EDP6 EDP7 EDP8 EDP9 EDP10
YES 67 444 432 124 67 308 439 448 448 447
NO 399 6 16 317 386 143 6 0 0 1
INDIFF. 8 24 26 33 21 23 29 26 26 26

TABLE 4.8: RESPONSES SHOWING EDUCATIONAL ASPIRATIONS OF THE LOCK INDUSTRY WORKERS (N=474)

	EDUCATIONAL ASPIRATIONS	*%AGE*	*YES*	*%AGE*	*INDIFF.*	*%AGE*	*NO*
1.	Do you wish, in case members of your community are not satisfied with the present education system, to establish some contact with members of your community who are connected with the system of education to suggest ways and means to the government so that some better system of education may be evolved?	58.23	276	1.27	06	40.51	192
2.	Do you aspire to work and fight independently or though some social organization to press the Government for free and full education to the children hailing from economically backward strata of the community?	92.83	440	6.12	29	1.05	05
3.	Do you aspire to work with some social organizations of your community who claim to look after the interests of the poor children hailing from lower economic strata?	54.64	259	5.72	27	39.66	188
4.	Do you aspire to propagate that children should not be engaged in any economic activity till they receive proper education so that they may be more successful in business and trade?	77.85	369	7.17	34	14.98	71

TABLE 4.8: RESPONSES SHOWING EDUCATIONAL ASPIRATIONS OF THE LOCK INDUSTRY WORKERS (N=474)

5. Do you aspire to educate uneducated and less educated masses of your community to settle their disputes amicably with the help of educated persons and not to use physical force or adopt unethical practices or to go to court of law as it is very expansive and time was consuming?	85.44	405	6.33	30	8.23	39
6. Do you aspire to propagate among the members of your community about the usefulness of scientific education based analytical and rational principles instead of religious education alone?	45.57	216	7.51	36	46.84	222
7. Do you aspire to seek help from educated members of your community to enlighten the ignorant parents about importance of child's education?	91.77	435	4.85	23	3.38	16
8. Do you aspire to establish some women social organization in your community which should keep regular contact with the leader sof the community and press them to work and seek Government help in getting adequate educational facilities for the sake of the community?	92.41	438	5.27	25	2.32	11
9. Do you wish that the educated and respectable members of your community should keep regular contract with the leaders of community and press them to work and seek Government help in getting adequate educational facilities for the sake of the community.	94.51	448	5.27	25	0.21	01

TABLE 4.8: RESPONSES SHOWING EDUCATIONAL ASPIRATIONS OF THE LOCK INDUSTRY WORKERS (N=474)

10. Do you support the view that services of teachers who are not performing their educational duties in their institutions and are engaged in coaching centres, be terminated and the coaching centres banned by the Government?	94.51	448	506	24	0.42	02

statement. A great majority of the respondents 92.41% aspired to establish some women social organization in their community for enlightening and encouraging women of the community to receive education who may, thus, not remain educationally backward. While 5.27% exhibited their indifference, only 2.32% expressed their disagreement with the statement. A overwheling majority of 94.51% wished that the educated and respectable members of their community should keep regular contact with the leaders of the community and press them to work and seek government help in getting adequate educational facilities for the sake of the community. While 5.27% exhibited their indifference only 0.21% expressed their disagreement with the statement. A great majority of the respondents 94.51% supported the view that teachers, who are not performing their educational duties in their institutions and are instead engaged in coaching centres, the services of such teachers should be terminated and the coaching centres be banned by the government. While 5.06% exhibited their indifference only 0.42% expressed their disagreement with the statement.

It can, thus be concluded that majority of the respondents have expressed their agreement with all the above mentioned statements except in items No. 1, 3, and 6 where 40.51%, 39.66% and 46.84% of the respondents exhibited their disagreement with the statements.

Table 4.9 reveals that most of the respondents 80.59% disagreed with the statement that majority of the members of their community offer the perscribed prayers regularly. While a minimum of 0.63% exhibited their indifference, only 18.78% expressed their agreement with the statement. A vast majority of 81.43% held the view that members of their community strictly follow and practice the laws as prescribed in Holy Scriptures. While 5.49% exhibited indifference, only 13.08% expressed their agreement with the statement. Most of the respondents (67.30%) exhibited their disagreement with the statement that members of their community extend equal respect to other religions. Although 128(27%) agreed with the statement yet 5.70% have shown their indifference to the statement. A huge majority of respondents (93.25%) have noticed that certain number of the members of their community, on account of vested interests,

CHART SHOWING EDUCATIONAL ASPIRATIONS OF TOTAL RESPONDENTS:474

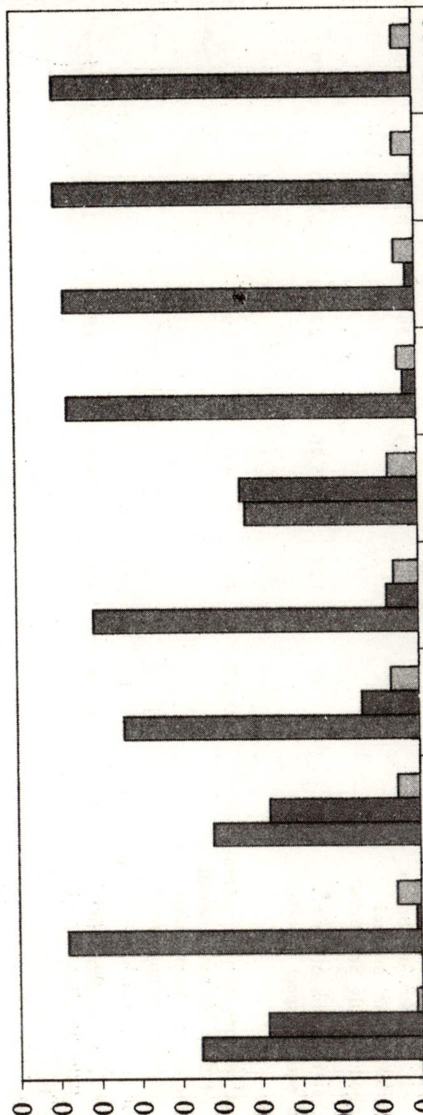

	EDA1	EDA2	EDA3	EDA4	EDA5	EDA6	EDA7	EDA8	EDA9	EDA10
YES	276	440	259	369	405	216	435	438	448	448
NO	192	5	188	71	39	222	16	11	1	2
INDIFF.	6	29	27	34	30	36	23	25	25	24

TABLE 4.9: RESPONSES SHOWING RELIGIOUS PERCEPTIONS OF THE LOCK INDUSTRY WORKERS (N=474)

RELIGIOUS PERCEPTIONS	*%AGE*	*YES*	*%AGE*	*INDIFF.*	*%AGE*	*NO*
1. Do you notice that majority of members of your community offer prayers regularly as prescribed?	18.78	89	0.63	03	80.59	382
2. Do you perceive that members of your community strictly follow and practice the laws as prescribed in Holy Scriptures?	13.08	62	5.49	26	81.43	386
3. Do you observe that members of your community extend equal respect to other religions?	27.00	128	5.70	27	67.30	319
4. Do you notice that sections of your community, on account of their ignorance about the teaching of religion, maintain social distance with the members hailing from other religions?	93.25	442	4.01	19	2.74	13
5. Do you notice that certain number of members of your community, on account of their ignorance about the teaching of religion maintain social distance with the members hailing from other religions?	94.94	450	4.01	19	1.05	05
6. Do you observe that the preachers of religion of your community have not adequately succeeded in transmitting proper understanding and knowledge about religion to the masses?	85.44	405	5.70	27	8.86	42

TABLE 4.9: RESPONSES SHOWING RELIGIOUS PERCEPTIONS OF THE LOCK INDUSTRY WORKERS (N=474)

7. Do you perceive that religious heads of your community have imposed certain restrictions which are not prescribed in the Holy Scriptures?	91.77	435	4.64	22	3.59	17
8. Do you notice that members in our society are distinctly discriminated on the basis of religion and caste in all matters of life?	94.51	448	5.27	25	0.21	01
9. Do you notice that the members in our society are distinctly discriminated on the basis of religion and caste in all the matters of life?	94.51	448	5.49	26	0.00	00
10. Do you perceive that funds collected in the name of religion by the religious leaders of your community are not utilized religiously by them?	94.51	448	5.27	25	0.21	01

deviated from the prescribed religious codes of conduct. While 4.01% exhibited their indifference only 2.74% expressed their disagreement with the statement. Most of the respondents 94.94% have noticed that sections of their community on account of their ignorance about teaching of religion maintain social distance with the members hailing from other religions. While 4.01% exhibited their indifference, only 1.05% expressed their disagreement with the statement. Vast majority of the respondents 85.44% observed that preachers of religion of their community have not adequately succeeded in transmitting proper understanding and knowledge about religion to the masses. While 5.70% exhibited indifference, only 8.86% expressed their disagreement with the statement. Most of the respondents 91.77% perceived that religious heads of their community have imposed certain restrictions which are not prescribed in the Holy Scriptures. While 4.64% exhibited their indifference, only 3.59% expressed their disagreement with the statement. Majority of the respondents 94.51% observed that religious heads of their community, on account of their vested material gains and popularity, offer their services to political parties during elections, which is against their religious ethics. While 5.27% exhibited their indifference only 0.21% expressed their disagreement with the statement. A huge majority of respondents 94.51% noticed that the members in their society were distinctly discriminated on the basis of religion and caste in all the matters of life; only 5.49% exhibited their indifference towards the statement. A overwheling majority of the respondents (94.51%) perceived that funds were collected in the name of religion by the religious leaders of their community which are not utilized religiously by them. While 5.27% exhibited their indifference, an insignificant 0.21% expressed their disagreement with the statement.

It can, thus be concluded that majority of the respondents have expressed their agreement with all the above stated statements except in the case of items No 1, 2, & 3, where majority of the respondents have exhibited their disagreement with the statements.

Table 4.10 reveals that most of the respondents 95.57% aspire, if possible, to educate the importance of offering prayers to such members of their community who do not offer prescribed prayers regularly. While 3.59% exhibited their indifference, only 0.84% expressed their disagreement with the statement. Majority of the respondents 94.51% intend to follow themselves and educate other members of their community to follow and practice the laws as laid down in their Holy Scripture. While 4.64% exhibited their indifference only 0.84% expressed their disagreement with the statement. Most of the respondents 90.30% aspired to educate such members of their community who, out of their ignorance, failed to offer equl respect to other religions. While 8.65% exhibited indifference, only 1.05% expressed disagreement with the statement. A vast majority of the respondents 89.03% wished to enlighten members of their community not to violate the prescribed religious prescriptions for the sake of their personal gains. While 8.44% exhibited indifference, only 2.53% expressed their disagreement with the statement. Most of the respondents 72.57% aspired to enlighten people about certain prevailing misconceptions about teachings of religion so that the members of their community, on the basis of religion, do not maintain social distance with members representing other religions. While 18.99% exhibited their indifference, only 8.44% expressed disagreement with the statement. A vast majority of the respondents 86.71% aspired to gain full and real knowledge about their religion from religious scholars so that in their spare time they may transmit it judiciously to the masses of their community. While 10.34% exhibited their indifference, only 2.95% expressed disagreement with the statement.

Most of the respondents (90.70%) aspired to take guidance from religious scholars and fight against such restrictions as are not prescribed in their religious scriptures, but have been imposed by the preachers of religion of their community. While 8.02% exhibited their indifference, only 1.27% expressed disagreement with the statement. Vast majority of respondents 89.03% aspired to raise their voice and condemn such religious heads of their community who, on account of their vested interests, offered services to political parties. While 6.12% exhibited their indifference, only 4.85% expressed disagreement with the statement. A huge majority of 83.33% aspired to work and fight against the operative practices of discrimination in their society

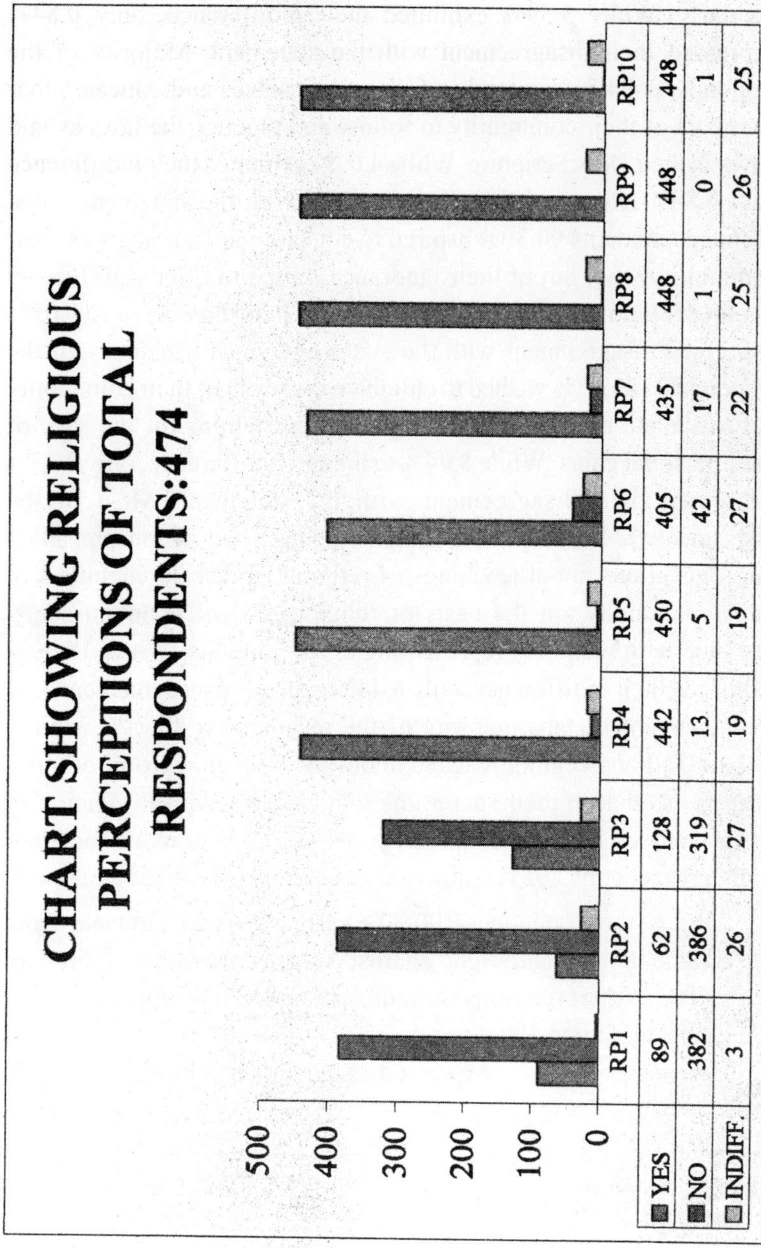
CHART SHOWING RELIGIOUS PERCEPTIONS OF TOTAL RESPONDENTS:474
500
400
300
200
100
0
RP1 RP2 RP3 RP4 RP5 RP6 RP7 RP8 RP9 RP10
YES 89 62 128 442 450 405 435 448 448 448
NO 382 386 319 13 5 42 17 1 0 1
INDIFF. 3 26 27 19 19 27 22 25 26 25

TABLE 4.10: RESPONSES SHOWING RELIGIOUS ASPIRATIONS OF LOCK INDUSTRY WORKERS (N=474)

RELIGIOUS ASPIRATIONS	*%AGE*	*YES*	*%AGE*	*INDIFF.*	*%AGE*	*NO*
1. Do you aspire, if possible, to educate the importance of offering prayers to such members of your community who do not offer prayers regularly as prescribed?	95.57	453	3.59	17	0.84	04
2. Do you intend to follow yourself and educate other members of your community to follow and practice the laws as laid down in your Holy Scriptures?	94.51	448	4.64	22	0.84	04
3. Do you aspire to educate such members of your community to extend equal respect to other religions who, out of their ignorance, are failing to offer equal respect to other religions?	90.30	422	8.65	41	1.05	05
4. Do you wish to enlighten members of your community not to violate the prescribed religious prescriptions for the sake of their personal gains?	89.03	422	8.44	40	2.53	12
5. Do you aspire to enlighten people about certain prevailing misconceptions about the teachings of religion so that the members of your community,	72.57	344	18.99	90	8.44	40

TABLE 4.10: (Cont.)

on the basis of religion, do not maintain social distance with members representing other religions?						
6. Do you aspire to gain full and real knowledge about your religion from religious scholars so that in your spare time you may transmit it judiciously to the masses of your community?	86.71	411	10.34	49	2.95	14
7. Do you aspire to take guidance from religious scholars and fight against such restrictions as are not prescribed in your religious scriptures but have been imposed by the preachers of religion of your community?	90.72	430	8.02	38	1.27	06
8. Do you aspire to raise your voice and condemn such religious heads of your community who, on account of their vested interests, offer services to political parties?	89.03	422	6.12	29	4.85	23
9. Do you aspire to work and fight against the operative practices of discrimination in our society by seeking support from the enlightened members hailing from other communities?	83.33	395	13.92	66	2.74	13

TABLE 4.10: (Cont.)

10. Do you aspire to propagate in your community that religious fund collectors must submit the programmes and regular accounts before the General Body of the community so that misuse of the funds be checked?	94.94	450	5.06	24	0.00	00

by seeking support from the enlightened members hailing from other communities. While 13.92% exhibited their indifference only 2.74% expressed disagreement with the statement.

A thumping majority of respondents 94.94% aspired to propagate in their community that the religious fund collectors must submit the programmes and regular accounts before the general body of the community so that misuse of the funds be checked. While 5.06% exhibited indifference, none opposed the validity of the statement.

It can, thus, be concluded that majority of the respondents have expressed their agreement with all the above mentioned statements.

COMPARATIVE ANALYSIS OF PERCEPTIONS AND ASPIRATIONS OF LOCK INDUSTRY WORKERS HAILING FROM FAMILIES WHICH ADOPTED SMALL FAMILTY NORMS AND THOSE WHICH DID NOT ADOPT THESE NORMS

As against 474 respondents representing 55 factories from various working groups, 72 workers have been identified from the families who adopted small family norms- i.e., having only one or two children (first group), whereas, 402 workers are from the families having more than 02 children, thus not adopting small family norms (second group). An attempt has been made to analyse and compare the perceptions and aspirations of these two groups hailing from different working units of the lock industries.

CHART SHOWING RESPONSES OF RESPONDENTS WHO ADOPTED & DID NOT ADOPT SMALL FAMILY NORMS

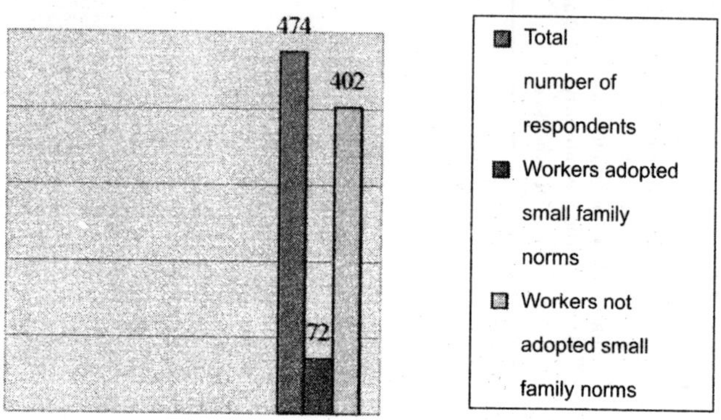

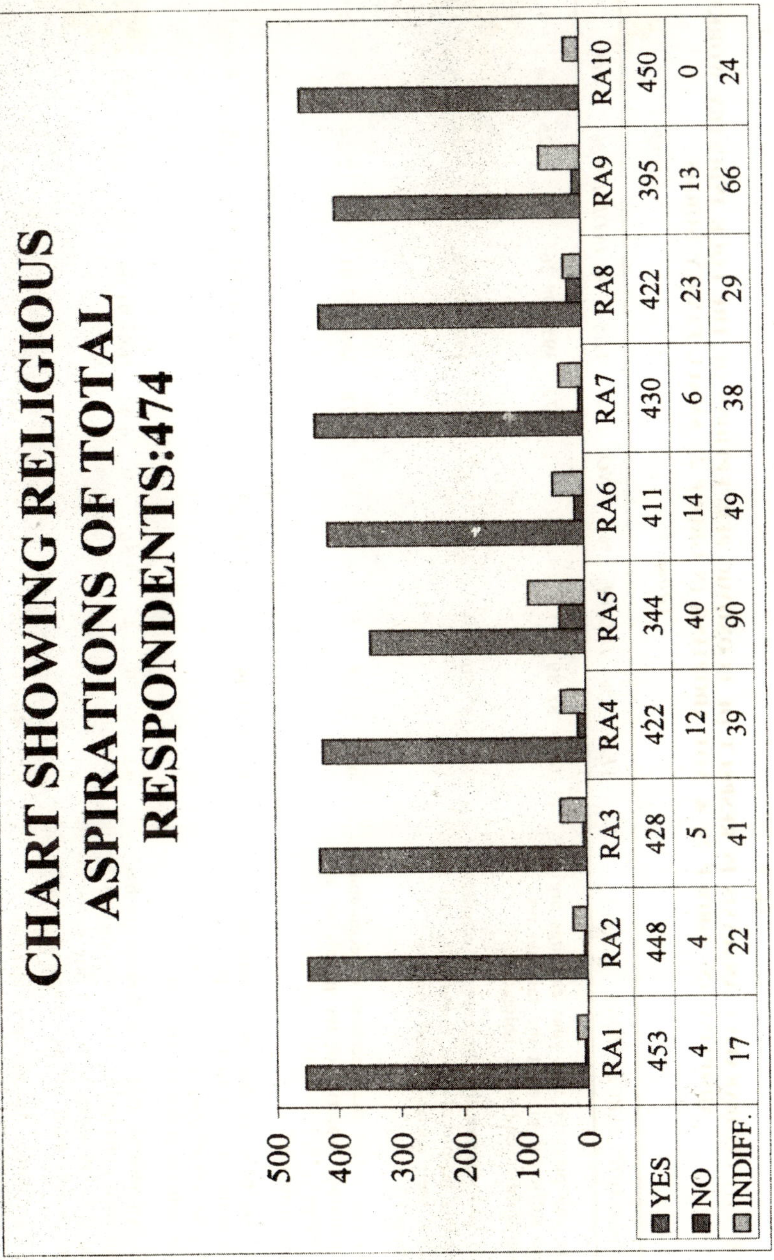

	RA1	RA2	RA3	RA4	RA5	RA6	RA7	RA8	RA9	RA10
YES	453	448	428	422	344	411	430	422	395	450
NO	4	4	5	12	40	14	6	23	13	0
INDIFF.	17	22	41	39	90	49	38	29	66	24

TABLE 4.11: COMPARATIVE ANALYSIS IN RESPECT OF ECONOMIC PERCEPTIONS OF THE LOCK INDUSTRY WORKERS ADOPTING (N= GROUP 2); & NOT ADOPTING (N GROUP 2); SMALL FAMILY NORMS

	Group 1						Group 2					
ECONOMIC PERCEPTIONS	YES	%	INDIFF.	%	NO	%	YES	%	INDIFF.	%	NO	%
1. Do you perceive that your earnings are not sufficient to meet the familial responsibilities and other obligations?	64	88.89	1	1.39	7	9.72	395	98.26	1	0.25	6	1.49
2. Do you observe that because of economic reasons people of your community fail to fulfill their social-cultural commitments?	63	87.50	3	4.17	6	8.33	393	97.76	5	1.24	4	1.00
3. Do you notice that, because of economic constraints, majority of the people of your community fail to fulfill their socio-cultural commitments?	65	90.28	5	6.94	2	2.78	390	97.01	9	2.24	3	0.75
4. Do you perceive that on account of economic considerations, mostly people of your community give perference to their sons in place of daughters?	67	93.06	4	5.56	1	1.39	384	95.52	14	3.48	4	1.00
5. Do you observe that some families within your own community, where women are also working along with men, are economically much better off as compared to others?	63	87.50	4	5.56	5	6.94	366	91.04	13	3.23	23	5.72
6. Do you notice that constant hikes in the cost of living and limited income has	62	86.11	6	8.33	4	5.56	372	92.54	13	3.23	17	4.23

(TABLE 4.11 Contd.)

compelled the economically weaker sections of your community to accept all kinds of exploitations?												
7. Do you notice that on account of limited opportunities of employment, educated youths of your community have adopted unethical and illegal means to earn money?	16	22.22	11	15.28	45	62.50	66	16.42	22	5.47	314	78.11
8. Do you feel that continuous disturbed conditions, like strikes and riots, in our society certainly affect economic activities and per captita income of the people of the society?	67	93.06	4	5.56	1	1.39	374	93.03	20	4.98	8	1.99
9. Do you notice that educated and capable youths of your community are not making adequate use of Governmental programmes or schemes meant for economic welfare of the people?	65	90.28	7	9.72	0	0.00	385	95.77	16	3.98	1	0.25
10. Do you observe that, on account of financial reasons, children of your community are unable to receive adequate education as mostly parents, in general and economically weaker sections in particular, are unable to meet the prevailing high educational expenses?	65	90.28	7	9.72	0	0.00	388	96.52	14	3.48	0	0.00

Analysis of Economic Perception of Both the groups

Table 4.11 reveals that 88.89% of the workers hailing from families with two or less children (Group 1) agreed that earnings are not sufficient for meeting financial responsibilities and other obligations, whereas 98.26% of the workers hailing from families with more than two children (Group 2) agreed with the statement.

Majority of the respondents of Group 1 87.50% expressed their agreement with the statement that because of economic reasons people of their community, despite mental and physical exploitation, permit their children to seek employment, whereas a much larger group 97.76% of the workers hailing from Group 2 agreed with the statement.

A still bigger majority of respondents (90.28%) of Group 1 expressed their agreement with the statement that because of economic constraints majority of the people of their community fail to fulfill their socio-cultural commitments, whereas a monolith of 97.01% from Group 2 agreed with the statement.

As many as 93.06 of majority of the respondents from Group 1 expressed their agreement with the statement that on account of economic considerations most of the people of their community give preference to sons in place of daughters, whereas 95.52% of the workers from Group 1 endorsed the statement.

While a vast majority of respondents 87.50% from group 1 agreed that families where women along with men are also working are economically better, 91.04% of the workers hailing from the families with more than two children (second group) have agreed with that statement.

A strong majority of the respondents 86.11% hailing from Group 1 manifested that constant hike in the cost of living and limited income has compelled economically weaker sections of their community to accept all kinds of exploitations. However, with a much bigger majority (92.54%) of workers hailing from group 2 exhibited their agreement with the statement.

A clear majority of respondents 62.50% hailing from Group 1 did not perceive that the educated unemployed youths of their community adopt unethical and illegal means to earn money, whereas a still bigger majority 78.11% of workers hailing from Group 2 exhibited their disagreement with the statement.

A clear majority of respondents 93.06% hailing from Group I felt that disturbed conditions like strikes and riots in the society certainly affect economic activities and per capita income of the people of the society, whereas an almost equal percentage (93.03) of the workers hailing from Group 2 agreed with the statement.

Although a vast majority of respondents 90.28% hailing from Group 1 noticed that educated and capable youths of their community are not making adequate use of governmental programmes or schemes meant for economic welfare of the people, whereas a still bigger percentage 95.77% of workers hailing from Group 2 agreed with the statement.

Although a huge majority of respondents 90.28% hailing from Group 1 observed that due to financial reasons children of their community are unable to receive adequate education as mostly parents are unable to meet the prevailing high educational expenses, yet a much bigger percentage 96.54% of workers hailing from Group 2 agreed with the statement.

It can, therefore, be concluded that both the groups have expressed their agreement with the statements.

ANALYSIS OF ECONOMIC ASPIRATION OF BOTH THE GROUPS

Table 4.12 reveals that a vast majority of the respondents 95.83% hailing from Group 1 intend to supplement their earnings by taking up some part-time job or economic activities, whereas 94.78% of the workers hailing from Group 2 expressed their agreement with the statement.

While a strong majority of respondents 79.17% hailing from Group 1 aspired to raise their voice and fight for implementation of labour laws pertaining to children for saving them from exploitation, a much bigger majority (92.79%) of workers from Group 2 agreed with the statement.

TABLE 4.12 COMPARATIVE ANALYSIS IN RESPECT OF ECONOMIC ASPIRATIONS OF LOCK INDUSTRY WORKERS ADOPTING & NOT ADOPTING SMALL FAMILY NORMS

		GROUP I						GROUP 2					
	ECONOMIC ASPIRATIONS	*YES*	%	*INDIFF.*	%	*NO*	%	*YES*	%	*INDIFF.*	%	*NO*	%
1.	Do you want to supplement your earnings by taking up some part-time job or economic activities?	69	95.83	2	2.78	1	1.39	381	94.78	12	2.99	9	2.24
2.	Do you earnestly aspire to raise your voice and fight for implementation of labour laws pertaining to children so that they may be saved from exploitation?	57	79.17	10	13.89	5	6.94	373	92.79	17	4.23	12	2.99
3.	Do you aspire to take up some extra economic activities, which may yield monetary returns in order to fulfill your committed socio-cultural commitments?	60	83.33	5	6.94	7	9.72	366	91.04	13	3.23	23	5.72
4.	Do you want to work and educate the members of your community to treat their sons and daughters on equal basis, keeping in view modern trends and changing laws of the land?	41	56.94	9	12.50	22	30.56	171	44.03	49	12.1	176	43.78
5.	Do you aspire to educate and enlighten the ignorant members of your community to encourage women also to take part in economic activities along with their male counterparts in order to achieve greater economic stability and prosperity?	60	83.33	7	9.72	5	6.94	349	86.82	37	9.20	16	3.98
6.	Do you aspire to educate the economically weaker sections of your community to fight	58	80.56	11	15.28	3	4.17	345	8582	38	9.45	19	4.73

TABLE 4.12 (CONT.)

	against any king of exploitation and start some extra economic activities initially on a small scale so that exploitation be controlled?											
7.	Do you intend to educate the unemployed educated youth of your community that instead of adopting unethical and illegal means of earning, they should avail loan facilities as offered by the Government to start independent economic activity?	51	70.83	4	5.56	17	23.61	298	74.13	25	6.22	79	19.65
8.	Do you intend to join some such judicious and non-political organization which may prove to be a useful instrument in settling strikes as well as in maintaining communal harmony at the time of riot?	63	87.50	5	6.94	4	5.56	381	94.78	18	4.48	3	0.75
9.	Do you aspire to educate the deserving youths of your community to avail the provisions and benefits of Government sponsored employment programmes and schemes so that economic upliftment could be achieved?	54	75.00	11	15.28	7	9.72	369	91.79	27	6.72	6	1.49
10.	Do you intend to raise your voice through some social organization or agency to put some pressure on the Government as well as on the welfare bodies of your community to provide reading material on subsidized rates in general and scholarship in particular to economically weaker sections of your community?	51	70.83	8	11.11	13	18.06	344	85.57	20	4.98	38	9.45

While 83.33% respondents hailing from families of Group 1 expressed their aspiration to take up some extra economic activities yielding monetary returns for fulfillment of their socio-cultural commitments, (91.04%) of the workers from Group 2 families also agreed with the statement.

While a dim majority of respondents (56.94%) hailing from Group 1 expressed their desire to work and educate the members of their community to treat their sons and daughters on equal basis keeping in view the modern trends and changing laws of the land, only 44.03% of respondents from Group 2 agreed with the statement. While 83.33% of workers hailing from Group 1 families desired to educate and enlighten the ignorant members of the community to encourage women also for taking part in economic activities along with their male counterparts for achieving greater economic stability and prosperity, a bigger number (86.82%) of the respondents from Group 2 agreed to the statement.

While a majority of 80.56% hailing from Group 1 families aspired to educate economically weaker sections of their community to fight against any kind of exploitation and start some extra economic activities initially on small scale for controlling exploitation, a still bigger number (85.82%) of workers from Group 2 agreed with the statement.

Similarly while a majority of respondents 70.83% from Group 1 families aspired to educate the unemployed educated youths of their community to avail loan facilities as offered by the government for starting independent economic activity for earning money, a bigger number 74.13% of workers from Group 2 families agreed with the statement.

While 87.50% families from Group 1 exhibited their disagreement with the statement that joining non-political organizations may prove to be a useful instrument in settling strikes and maintaining communal harmony, a much bigger number (94.78%) of workers hailing from Group 2 exhibited their disagreement with the statement.

While a majority (75.00%) of the respondents from Group 1 families aspired to educate the deserving youths of their community to avail the provisions and benefits of government-sponsored employment programmes and schemes for achieving economic upliftment, a much bigger percentage (91.79%) of workers from Group 2 families agreed with the statement.

While 70.83% families from Group 1 intended to raise their voice through some social organization or agency for putting some pressure on the government as well as on welfare bodies of their community to provide reading material on subsidized rates in general and scholarships in particular to the economically weaker sections of their community, a relatively bigger number (87.57%) of workers hailing from Group 2 families agreed with the statement.

It can, thus, be concluded that both the groups have expressed their agreement with the statements in this area.

ANALYSIS OF SOCIAL PERCEPTION OF BOTH THE GROUPS

Table 4.13 reveals that 69.44% respondents hailing from Group 1 families perceived that in their community parents of the boys, at the time of their marriage, demand gifts in cash and kind from parents of the girls, which is not permissible in the religion and law, whereas (83.79%) of workers hailing from Group 2 families agreed with the statement.

Similarly 93.06% hailing from families of Group 1 observed that girls of their community are subjected to humiliation if they fail to bring with them the committed gifts and cash at the time of their marriage, whereas 97.26% of workers hailing from Group 2 families agreed with the statement.

Majority of the respondents 88.89% hailing from Group 1 families observed that the members of their community, due to religious consideration and ignorance, do not follow family planning programmes and practices, whereas a larger number (93.03%) of the workers from Group 2 families agreed with the statement.

Only 44.44% respondents hailing from Group 1 families noticed that men and women in their community enjoy equal authority in family matters, whereas a healthy majority of 61.19% of the workers from Group 2 families agreed with the statement.

TABLE 4.13 COMPARATIVE ANALYSIS IN RESPECT OF SOCIAL PERCEPTIONS OF LOCK INDUSTRY WORKERS ADOPTING GROUP 1 & NOT ADOPTING GROUP 2 SMALL FAMILY NORMS

		GROUP 1						GROUP 2					
	ECONOMIC ASPIRATIONS	*YES*	*%*	*INDIFF.*	*%*	*NO*	*%*	*YES*	*%*	*INDIFF.*	*%*	*NO*	*%*
1.	Do you perceive that in your community parents of boys at the time of marriage directly or indirectly demand gifts in cash or kind from the parents of the girls which is not permissible in your religion and by law?	50	6944	3	4.17	19	26.39	333	83.79	3	0.75	62	15.46
2.	Do you observe that girls of your community are subjected to humiliation if they fail to bring with them the committed gifts and cash at the time of their marriage?	67	93.06	3	4.17	2	2.78	391	97.26	5	1.24	6	1.49
3.	Do you observe that the members of your community on account of religious consideration and ignorance do not follow family planning programmes and practices?	64	88.89	3	4.17	5	6.94	374	93.03	13	3.23	15	3.73
4.	Do you notice that men and women in your community are enjoying equal authority in family matters?	34	44.44	9	12.50	31	43.06	246	61.19	19	4.73	137	34.08
5.	Do you observe that educated couples of your community are more happily settled in their lieves as compared to less or uneducated couples?	59	81.94	8	11.11	5	6.94	367	91.29	25	6.22	10	2.49
6	Do you perceive that members of your community go for early marriage of their daughters even to elderly settle persons because of economic reasons?	60	83.33	6	6.94	7	9.72	362	90.05	19	4.73	21	5.22

TABLE 4.13 COMPARATIVE ANALYSIS IN RESPECT OF SOCIAL PERCEPTIONS OF LOCK INDUSTRY WORKERS ADOPTING GROUP 1 & NOT ADOPTING GROUP 2 SMALL FAMILY NORMS

		GROUP 1						GROUP 2					
7.	Do you notice that divorce had become fairly common among members of our society which is amounting to family disorganization?	58	80.56	5	6.94	9	12.50	358	89.05	24	5.97	20	4.98
8.	Do you observe that remarriage of widow though legally permissible yet is being discouraged by certain sections of the communities.	27	37.50	9	12.50	36	50.00	154	38.31	32	7.96	216	53.73
9.	Do you notice that in your community it is somewhat difficult to find suitable matches for educated boys and girls?	67	93.06	3	4.17	2	2.78	379	94.28	18	4.48	5	1.24
10.	Do you perceive that on account of growing nuclear family patterns, the traditional familial bonds among the members of the community have weakened?	67	93.06	3	4.17	2	2.78	385	95.77	11	2.74	6	1.49

While a majority of 81.94% hailing from Group 1 families observed that educated couples of the community were more happily settled in their lives as compared to less or uneducated couples, whereas a bigger number 91.29% of the workers hailing from Group 2 families agreed with the statement.

While 83.33% respondents from Group 1 families agreed to the statement that members of their community go for early marriage of their daughters even to elderly settled persons because of economic reasons, whereas a bigger numbers 90.05% of the workers hailing from Group 2 families agreed with the statement.

While a majority of 80.56% hailing from Group 1 families noticed that divorce had become fairly common among the members of their society which is amounting to family disorganization, whereas a bigger number 89.05% of workers from families agreed with the statement.

While 50.00% respondents from Group 1 families did not perceive discouragement of widow remarriage, whereas a majority of 53.73% of workers from Group 2 families did not agreed with the statement.

While an overwhelming majority of the respondents (93.06%) hailing from Group 1 families noticed that in their community it is somewhat difficult to find suitable matches for educated boys and girls, a greater number 94.28% of the workers hailing from Group 2 families agreed with the statement.

While a majority of the respondents 93.06% hailing from Group 1 families perceived that on account of growing nuclear family patterns, the traditional familial bonds of the feelings among the members of their community have weakened, whereas a much bigger number (95.77%) of workers hailing from Group 2 families agreed with the statement.

It can, thus, be concluded that respondents hailing from the Group 2 families appear to be more enlightened as compared to the respondents hailing from Group 1 families.

ANALYSIS OF SOCIAL ASPIRATION OF BOTH THE GROUPS

Table 4.14 reveals that 88.89% respondents hailing from Group 1 families aspired to work against the system of demand in cash or kind by boy's parents at the time of marriage, whereas 95.02% of workers hailing from Group 2 families agreed with the statement.

Majority of the respondents 88.89% hailing from Group 1 families aspired to organize or join such organization which are working for rehabilitation of such girls of their community who become victims of humiliation after their marriage, whereas a bigger number (92.54%) of the workers hailing from Group 2 families agreed with the statement.

While a solid majority of respondents 68.06% hailing from Group 1 families aspired to appeal to the enlightened, educated and expert members of their community to come forward and educate the masses about the socio-economic and physiological advantages of family planning, a bigger number 74.45% of workers hailing from Group 2 families agreed with the statement.

While only 45.83% respondents hailing from Group 1 families wished to raise voice in support of women's rights of equality in family matters of their community, a clear majority 53.23% of the workers hailing from the Group 2 families agreed with the statement.

A majority of respondents 84.72% hailing from Group 1 families aspired to educate members of their community not to marry their children till they receive proper education, and a matching figure 85.82% of workers hailing from Group 2 families agreed with the statement.

While a heavy majority of the respondents 84.72% hailing from Group 1 families aspired to educate the members of their community not to marry their daughters to elderly settled persons on account of economic reasons and instead start some extra economic activity to improve their financial conditions, a greater number 91.79% of workers hailing from Group 2 families agreed with the statement.

A thumping majority of the respondents 90.28% hailing from Group 1 families aspired to propagate against the evils of divorce among the members of their society for saving the families from disorganization, which was also endorsed by a matching figure (91.79%) of workers hailing from Group 2 families.

TABLE 4.14 COMPARATIVE ANALYSIS IN RESPECT OF SOCIAL ASPIRATIONS OF LOCK INDUSTRY WORKERS ADOPTING (GROUP 1) & NOT ADOPTING (GROUP 2) SMALL FAMILY NORMS

		GROUP 1						GROUP 2					
	ECONOMIC ASPIRATIONS	*YES*	*%*	*INDIFF.*	*%*	*NO*	*%*	*YES*	*%*	*INDIFF.*	*%*	*NO*	*%*
1.	Do you aspire to work against the system of demand in cash and kind by the boy's parents of your community at the time of their marriage as is not permissible in your religion and by law?	64	88.89	7	9.72	1	1.39	382	95.02	13	3.23	7	1.74
2.	Do you aspire to organize or join such organization which work for the rehabilitation of such girls of your community who becomes victims of humiliation after their marriage?	64	88.89	6	8.33	2	2.78	372	92.54	26	6.47	4	1.00
3.	Do you aspire to appeal the enlightened, educated and expert members of your community to come forward and educate the masses about the socio-economic and physiological advantages of family planning?	49	68.06	13	18.06	10	13.89	373	74.45	19	3.79	109	21.76
4.	Do you wish to raise your voice in support of womens's rights of equality in family matters of your community?	33	45.83	5	6.94	34	47.22	214	53.23	18	4.48	170	42.29
5.	Do you aspire to educate the members of your community not to marry their children till they receive proper education?	61	84.72	10	13.89	1	1.39	345	85.82	45	11.19	12	2.99

TABLE 4.14 (CONT.)

6.	Do you aspire to educate the members of your community not to marry their daughters to elderly settled persons on account of economic reasons and instead start some extra economic activity to improve their financial conditions?	61	84.72	7	9.72	4	5.56	369	91.79	26	6.47	7	1.74
7.	Do you aspire to propagate against the evils of divorcee among the members of your society so that families could be saved from being disorganized?	65	90.28	7	9172	0	0.00	369	91.79	21	5.22	12	2.99
8.	Do you aspire to propagate among the masses of your community to encourage women window remarriage in order to rehabilitate and rescue them from expected future exploitations?	61	84.72	11	15.28	0	0.00	372	92.54	22	5.47	8	1.99
9.	Do you aspire to be associated with some such voluntary social organizations which may help in selecting matches for educated boys and girls of your community?	67	93.06	5	6.94	0	0.00	380	94.53	16	3.98	6	1.49
10.	Do you aspire to enlighten the members of your community to interact among themselves quite frequently so that the traditional bonds of family proximity are maintained?	63	87.50	6	8.33	3	4.17	374	93.03	14	3.48	14	3.48

While a majority of respondents 84.72% hailing from Group 1 families aspired to propagate among the masses of their community to encourage widow remarriage in order to rehabilitate and rescue them from expected future exploitations, a bigger number 92.54% of workers hailing from Group 2 families agreed with the statement.

A huge majority of respondents 93.06% hailing from Group 1 families aspired to associate themselves with some such voluntary social organization which may help in selecting matches from educated boys and girls of their community, and a similar figure 94.53% of workers hailing from Group 1 families agreed with the statement.

While a huge majority of 87.50% hailing from Group 1 families aspired to enlighten members of their community to interact among themselves quite frequently so that the traditional bonds of family proximity are maintained, a much bigger number 93.03% of workers hailing from Group 2 families agreed with the statement.

It can, thus, be concluded that both the groups expressed their agreement with the statements.

ANALYSIS OF POLITICAL PERCEPTION OF BOTH THE GROUPS

Table 4.15 reveals that only 22.54% respondents hailing from Group 1 families perceived that members of their community take keen interest in political affairs and also adopt unethical practices to achieve their goals, while a much lesser number 13.18% of workers hailing from the families agreed with the statement.

While solid majority of respondents 86.11% hailing from Group 1 families noticed that members of their society do not support political parties on the basis of their election manifesto, a much bigger figure 95.52% of workers hailing from Group 2 families agreed with the statement.

While a clear majority of respondents 66.67% hailing from Group 1 families did not perceive that fair elections are held in the society, a much bigger number 72.14% of workers hailing from Group 2 families did not agree with the statement.

TABLE 4.15 COMPARATIVE ANALYSIS IN RESPECT OF POLITICAL PERCEPTION OF THE LOCK INDUSTRY WORKERS ADOPTING (GROUP 1) & NOT ADOPTING (GROUP 2) SMALL FAMILY NORMS WORKERS

		GROUP 1						GROUP 2					
	POLITICAL PERCEPTIONS	*YES*	%	*INDIFF.*	%	*NO*	%	*YES*	%	*INDIFF.*	%	*NO*	%
1.	Do you perceive that members of your community take keen interest in political affairs and also adopt unethical practices to achieve their goals?	16	22.54	3	4.23	52	73.24	53	13.18	3	0.75	346	86.07
2.	Do you notice that members of your society do not support political parties on the basis of their election manifesto?	62	86.11	8	11.11	2	2.78	384	95.52	11	2.74	7	1.74
3.	Do you perceive that fair elections are held in our society?	20	27.78	4	‘5.56	48	66.67	100	24.88	12	2.99	290	72.14
4.	Do you observe that political bosses misuse their position and power for selfish ends by exploiting the authorities?	62	86.11	8	11.11	2	2.78	376	94.28	20	4.98	3	0.75
5.	Do you perceive that candidates and political parties freely use money and muscles power during elections?	65	90.28	7	9.72	0	0.00	376	93.53	21	5.22	5	1.24
6.	Do you observe that economically weil off people of your community extend financial support to all important parties and candidates because they encash them after their victories?	65	90.28	5	6.94	2	2.78	382	95.02	16	3.98	4	1.00

TABLE 4.15 (CONTD.)

POLITICAL PERCEPTIONS	YES	%	INDIFF.	%	NO	%	YES	%	INDIFF.	%	NO	%
7. Do you observe that in elections, political parties issue tickets and extend full support to persons having established criminal background?	64	88.89	8	11.11	0	0.00	382	95.02	19	4.73	1	0.25
8. Do you notice that political parties or even independent candidates, in order to win the election, do not hesitate in giving communal or caste turn to any event during election period, if it suits them?	63	87.50	8	11.11	1	1.39	387	96.27	14	3.48	1	0.25
9. Do you perceive that the members of your community lack the required political awareness in selecting right type of persons or party hence they do not cast their votes?	64	88.89	8	11.11	0	0.00	386	96.02	14	3.48	2	0.50
10. Do you observe that political parties and independent candidates mostly make false promises at the time of elections but never attend to them?	64	88.89	8	11.11	0	0.00	388	96.52	13	3.23	1	0.25

Although a majority of the respondents 86.11% hailing from Group 1 families observed that political bosses misuse their position and power for selfish ends by exploiting the authorities, a larger number 94.28% of workers hailing from Group 2 families agreed with the statement.

While a solid majority of respondents 90.28% hailing from Group 1 families perceived that candidates and political parties freely use money and muscle power during elections, a bigger number 93.53% of workers hailing from Group 2 families agreed with the statement.

While a thumping majority of respondents 90.28% hailing from Group 1 families observe that economically well off people of their community extend financial support to all important parties and candidates because they take advantage after their victories, a still bigger figure of 95.02% of workers hailing from Group 2 families agreed with the statement.

On similar pattern, a thumping majority of respondents 88.89% hailing from Group 1 families observed that in elections political parties issue tickets and extend full support to persons having established criminal background, whereas 95.02% of workers hailing from Group 2 families agreed with the statement.

While a vast majority of the respondents 87.50% hailing from Group 1 families noticed that political parties or even independent candidates, in order to win elections, do not hesitate in giving communal or caste turn to any event during election period if it suits them, whereas a much bigger figure 96.27% of workers hailing from Group 2 families endorsed the statement.

On similar pattern, a thumping majority of the respondents 88.89% hailing from Group 1 families perceived that members of their community lack the required political awareness in selecting right type of person or party, hence, they do not cast their votes, whereas a much bigger percentage 96.02 of the workers hailing from Group 2 families agreed with the statement.

Again, on similar pattern, while a vast majority of respondents (88.89%) hailing from Group 1 families observed that political parties and independent candidates mostly make false promises at the time of elections but never attend to them, whereas a much bigger figure 96.52% of the workers from Group 2 families agreed with the statement.

It can, thus, be concluded that both the groups expressed their agreement with the statements.

ANALYSIS OF POLITICAL ASPIRATION OF BOTH THE GROUPS

Table 4.16 reveals that a heavy majority of respondents 91.67% hailing from Group 1 families aspired to generate judicious and ethical political awareness among the masses of their community for not adopting unethical practices in the political affairs of the society, if they get a chance, whereas a bigger majority of 96.02% of workers hailing from Group 2 families agreed with the statement.

While 86.11% respondents hailing from Group 1 families aspired to propagate among the members of their society to support political parties on the basis of their election manifesto and not on any other consideration, whereas a much bigger number 94.28% of the workers hailing from Group 2 families agreed with the statement.

While a majority of the respondents 88.89% hailing from Group 1 families aspired to become members of such organization which may fight against the malpractices operative during elections, whereas a slightly bigger percentage 90.80% of the workers hailing from Group 2 families endorsed the statement.

While majority of the respondents 86.11% hailing from Group 1 families aspired to expose such political persons who misuse their positions and power for their selfish ends, whereas a lesser number 81.84% of the workers hailing from Group 2 families agreed with the statement.

A majority of the respondents 84.72% hailing from Group 1 families aspired to work and raise voice against such parties and persons who use money and muscle power during elections, whereas a lesser number 77.11% of the workers hailing from Group 2 families agreed with the statement.

TABLE 4.16 COMPARATIVE ANALYSIS IN RESPECT OF POLITICAL ASPIRATIONS OF LOCK INDUSTRY WORKERS ADOPTING (GROUP 1) & NOT ADOPTING (GROUP 2) SMALL FAMILY NORMS

		Group 1						Group 2					
	POLITICAL ASPIRATIONS	*YES*	*%*	*INDIFF.*	*%*	*NO*	*%*	*YES*	*%*	*INDIFF.*	*%*	*NO*	*%*
1.	Do you aspire to generate judicious and ethical political awareness among the masses of your community, if and when you get an opportunity, and not to adopt unethical parties in the political affairs of the society?	66	91.67	4	5.56	2	2.78	386	96.02	8	1.99	8	1.99
2.	Do you aspire to propagate among the members of your society to support political parties on the basis of their election manifesto and not on any other considerations?	62	86.11	9	12.5	1	1.39	379	94.28	13	3.23	10	2.49
3.	Do you aspire to become member of some such organization which may fight against the malpractices which are operative during elections?	64	88.89	6	8.33	2	2.78	365	90.80	25	6.22	12	2.99
4.	Do you aspire to expose such political persons who misuse their positions and power for their selfish ends?	62	86.11	10	13.89	0	0.00	329	8184	64	15.92	9	2.24
5.	Do you aspire to work and raise your voice against such parties and persons who use money and muscle power during elections?	61	84.72	8	11.11	3	4.17	310	77.10	84	20.90	8	1.99

Table 4.16 (cont.)

6.	Do you aspire to raise your voice that government should impose some financial limits in election expenditure which should be subject to accountability?	51	70.83	12	16.67	9	12.50	334	83.08	50	12.44	18	4.48
7.	Do you aspire to pursue or request the enlightened and judicious members of your community to come forward and put pressure on the Government to impose a ban and not permit any contestant having criminal background to seek election?	61	84.72	10	13.89	1	1.39	374	93.03	27	6.72	1	0.25
8.	Do you earnestly wish to protest vigorously through some organization or independently against such political parties and independent candidates who, in order to win election, exploit the election scene on the basis of religion or caste?	65	90.28	6	8.33	1	1.39	381	94.78	18	4.48	3	0.75
9.	Do you wish to educate independently or through your community organizations to press the members of the community to caste this votes and support right type of person or party based on their election manifestoes?	58	80.56	12	16.67	2	2.78	373	92.79	27	6.72	2	0.50
10.	Do you aspire to join some such non-political organization through which you may raise your protest effectively highlighting the non-fulfillment of the promises to communities made by the political parties and independent candidates who failed to fulfill them after winning the elections?	65	90.28	6	8.33	1	1.39	381	94.78	20	4.98	1	0.25

While a relatively lesser majority of the respondents (70.93%) hailing from Group 1 families aspired to raise their voice that government should impose some financial limits in election expenditure which should be subject to accountability, whereas a bigger number 83.08% of the workers hailing from Group 2 families agreed with the statement.

While a majority of the respondents 84.72% from Group 1 families aspired to pursue the enlightened and judicious members of their community to come forward and put pressure on the government to impose ban and not permit any contestant having criminal background to seek election, whereas a much bigger number, i.e. 93.03% of the workers hailing from Group 2 families agreed with the statement.

While majority of respondents 90.28% hailing from Group 1 families earnestly wished to protest vigorously through some organization or independently against such political parties or independent candidates who, in order to win elections exploit the election, scene on the basis of religion or caste, whereas a slightly bigger percentage (94.78%) of the workers hailing from the families with more than two children (second group) have agreed with the statement.

While majority of the respondents 80.56% hailing from Group 1 families wished to educate independently or through their community organizations to press the members of the community to cast their votes and support the right type of persons or party based on their election manifestos, whereas a bigger figure 92.79% of the workers from Group 2 families agreed with the statement.

While a huge majority of the respondents 90.28% from Group 1 families aspired to join some such non-political organization through which they may raise their voice effectively to highlight non-fulfillment of the promises to communities made by the political parties and independent candidates who failed to fulfil them after winning the eléctions, whereas a still bigger number 94.78% of workers hailing from Group 2 families agreed with the statement.

It can, thus, be concluded that both the groups expressed their agreement with the statements.

ANALYSIS OF EDUCATIONAL PERCEPTION OF BOTH THE GROUPS

Table 4.17 reveals that majority of the respondents 75.00% from Group 1 families were not satisfied with the prevailing educational system during the present era of advancement, whereas a larger number (85.82%) of the workers hailing from Group 2 families disagreed with the statement.

While majority of the respondents 84.72% hailing from Group 1 families noticed that on account of higher cost of education, majority of the parents hailing from economically weaker sections of their community did not encourage their children to receive full education, whereas 95.27% of the workers hailing from Group 2 families agreed with the statement.

Majority of the respondents (77.78%) hailing from Group 1 families perceived that education is mainly responsible for the socio-economic development of the members of their community, whereas 93.53% of the workers hailing from Group 2 families agreed with the statement.

While majority of respondents 55.56% hailing from Group 1 families have not observed that the educated persons of their community as compared to others are more successful in business and trade, whereas 68.91% of the workers hailing from Group 2 families did not agree with the statement.

While majority of respondents 62.90% hailing from Group 1 families expressed their disagreement with the statement that the advice of educated persons of their community is always sought by the uneducated and less educated ones to settle their disputes, whereas 83.83% of the workers hailing from Group 2 families did not agree with the statement.

A majority of the respondents 62.50% hailing from Group 1 families perceived that parents of their community are more in favour of imparting religious education to their children instead of scientific education, whereas 65.59% of the workers hailing from Group 2 families agreed with the statement.

TABLE 4.17 COMPARATIVE ANALYSIS IN RESPECT OF EDUCATIONAL PERCEPTION OF LOCK INDUSTRY WORKERS ADOPTING (GROUP 1) & NOT ADOPTING (GROUP 2) SMALL FAMILY NORMS

		GROUP 1						GROUP 2					
	EDUCATION PERCEPTIONS	*YES*	*%*	*INDIFF.*	*%*	*NO*	*%*	*YES*	*%*	*INDIFF.*	*%*	*NO*	*%*
1.	Do you observe that in the present era of advancement members of your community are satisfied with the prevailing educational system?	13	18.06	5	6.94	54	75.00	54	13.43	3	0.75	345	85.82
2.	Do you notice that on account of higher cost of education, majority of parents hailing from economically weaker sections of your community do not encourage their children to receive full education?	61	84.72	11	15.28	0	0.00	383	95.27	13	3.23	6	1.49
3.	Do you perceive that education is mainly responsible for socio-economic development of the members of your community?	56	77.78	12	16.67	4	5.56	376	93.53	14	3.48	12	2.99
4.	Do you observe that educated persons of your community, as compared to others, are more successful in business and trade?	24	33.33	8	11.11	40	55.56	100	24.88	25	6.22	277	68.91
5.	Do you notice that the advice of educated persons of your community is always sought by the uneducated and less educated ones to settle their disputes?	17	27.42	6	9.68	39	62.90	50	12.44	15	3.73	337	83.83
6.	Do you perceive that parents of your community are more in favour of imparting religious education to their children instead of scientific education?	45	62.50	6	8.33	21	29.17	263	65.59	16	3.99	122	30.42

TABLE 4.17 (CONT.)

7.	Do you observe that majority of the parents of your community are ignorant about importance of their children's education?	64	88.89	8	11.11	0	0.00	375	93.28	21	5.22	6	1.49
8.	Do you notice that women of your community are more educationally backward as compared to the women of other communities?	64	88.89	8	11.11	0	0.00	384	95.52	18	4.48	0	0.00
9.	Do you observe that the leaders of your community are indifferent towards the educational upliftment of the community and do not seek help from the Government?	64	88.89	8	11.11	0	0.00	384	95.52	18	4.48	0	0.00
10.	Do you observe that in the present era, education has become highly commercialized, because teachers do not judiciously perform their teaching duties in schools and colleges as either they have opened their Coaching Centers or teaching in other coaching centers on the basis of payment?	64	88.89	8	11.11	0	0.00	383	95.27	18	4.48	1	0.25

While majority of respondents 88.89% hailing from Group 1 families observed that majority of parents of their community were ignorant about the importance of their children's education, whereas a bigger majority (93.28%) of the workers hailing from Group 2 families have agreed with the statement.

While majority of the respondents 88.89% hailing from Group 1 families noticed that women of their community were more educationally backward as compared to the women of other communities, whereas **95.52%** of the workers hailing from Group 2 families agreed with the statement.

A solid majority of respondents (88.89%) hailing from Group 1 families observed that leaders of the community were in different towards the educational upliftment of the community and did not seek help from the government, whereas 95.52% of the workers hailing from the Group 2 families agreed with the statement.

A solid majority of the respondents 88.89% hailing from Group 1 families observed that in the present era education has become highly commercialized because teachers do not judiciously perform their teaching duties in schools and colleges as either they have opened their coaching centers or teaching in other coaching centers on payment, whereas 95.27% of the workers hailing from Group 2 families endorsed the statement.

It can, thus, be concluded that both the groups have expressed their agreement with the statements.

ANALYSIS OF EDUCATIONAL ASPIRATION OF BOTH THE GROUPS

Table 4.18 reveals that half of respondents 50.00% hailing from Group 1 families wished to establish some contact with members of their community connected with the system of education to suggest ways and means to government for evolving better system of education, whereas a clear majority 59.70% of the workers from Group 2 families agreed with the statement.

While a relatively smaller majority of the respondents 79.17% from Group 1 families aspired to work and fight independently or through some social organization to press the government for free and full education to the children hailing from the economically backward strata of the community, a huge majority 95.27% of workers from Group 2 families agreed with the statement.

While only 43.06% respondents from Group 1 families aspired to work with some social organization of their community who claim to look after the interest of the poor and the children hailing from the lower economic strata, whereas a clear majority 56.72% of workers from Group 2 families endorsed the statement.

While a majority of the respondents 77.78% hailing from Group 1 families aspired to propagate that children should not be engaged in any economic activity till they receive proper education so that they may be more successful in business and trade, almost an equal number 77.86% of workers hailing from Group 2 families endorsed the statement.

While a majority of respondents 87.50% hailing from Group 1 families aspired to educate the uneducated and less educated masses of their community to settle their disputes amicably with the help of educated persons and not to use physical force or adopt unethical practices or go to court of law as it was very expensive and time consuming, whereas almost a similar number 85.07% of the workers hailing from Group 2 families agreed with the statement.

While only one-third majority of the respondents 33.33% hailing from Group 1 families aspired to propagate among members of their community about the usefulness of scientific education based on analytical and rational principles instead of religious education alone, whereas a bigger number 47.76% of the workers from Group 2 families agreed with the statement.

While a huge majority of respondents 86.11% hailing from Group 1 families aspired to seek help from the educated members of their community to enlighten the ignorant parents about the importance of children's education, a bigger number 92.79% of workers from Group 2 families agreed with the statement.

TABLE 4.18 COMPARATIVE ANALYSIS IN RESPECT OF EDUCATIONAL ASPIRATIONS OF LOCK INDUSTRY WORKERS ADOPTING (GROUP 1) & NOT ADOPTING (GRUOP 2) SMALL FAMILY NORMS

	GROUP 1						GROUP 2					
EDUCATION ASPIRATIONS	*YES*	%	*INDIFF.*	%	*NO*	%	*YES*	%	*INDIFF.*	%	*NO*	%
1. Do you wish, in case members of your community are not satisfied with the present education system, to establish some contact with members of your community, who are connected with the system of education, to suggest ways and means to the government so that some better system of education may be evolved?	36	50.00	3	4.17	33	45.83	240	59.70	3	0.75	159	39.55
2. Do you aspire to work and fight independently or though some social organization to press the government for free and full education to the children hailing from economically backward strata of the community?	57	79.17	15	20.83	0	0.00	383	95.27	14	3.48	5	1.24
3. Do you aspire to work with some social organizations of your community, who claim to look after the interest of the poor children hailing from the lower economic strata?	31	43.06	9	12.50	32	44.44	228	56.72	18	4.48	156	38.81
4. Do you aspire to propagate that children should not be engaged in any economic activity till they receive proper education so that they may be more successful in business and trade?	56	77.78	8	11.11	8	11.11	313	77.86	26	6.47	63	15.67

TABLE 4.18 (CONTD.)

5.	Do you aspire to educate the uneducated and less educated masses of your community to settle their disputes amicably with the help of educated persons and not to use physical force or adopt unethical practices or go to court of law as it was very expensive and time consuming?	63	87.50	5	6.94	4	5.56	342	85.07	25	6.22	35	8.71
6.	Do you aspire to propagate among members of your community about the usefulness of scientific education based on analytical and rational principles, instead of religious education alone?	24	33.33	10	13.89	38	52.78	192	47.76	26	6.47	184	45.77
7.	Do you aspire to seek help from the educated members of your community to enlighten the ignorant parents about the importance of child's education?	62	86.11	7	9.72	3	4.17	373	92.79	16	3.98	13	3.23
8.	Do you aspire to establish some women social organization in your community to enlighten and encourage women of the community to receive education so that they may not remain educationally backward?	58	80.56	9	12.50	5	6.94	380	94.53	16	3.98	6	1.49
9.	Do you wish that the educated and respectable members of your community should keep regular contract with leaders of the community and press them to work and seek Government help in getting adequate educational facilities for the sake of	64	88.89	8	11.11	0	0.00	384	95.52	17	423	1	0.25

TABLE 4.18 (CONTD.)

10.	Do you support the view that teachers, who are not performing their educational duties in their institutions and are instead engaged in coaching centers, the services of such persons should be terminated and the coaching centers be banned by the Government.	63	87.50	8	11.11	1	1.39	385	95.77	16	3.98	1	0.25

As many as 80.56% respondents from Group 1 families aspired to establish some women social orgnisation in their community for enlightening and encouraging women of the community to receive education so that they may not remain educationally backward, whereas a much bigger number 94.53% of workers hailing from Group 2 families agreed with the statement.

While a large majority of the respondents 88.89% hailing from Group 1 families wished that the educated and respectable members of their community should keep regular contact with the leaders of the community and press them to work and seek government help in getting adequate educational facilities for the sake of the community, whereas a much bigger number 95.52% of workers hailing from Group 2 families agreed with the statement.

While a large majority of the respondents 87.50% hailing from Group 1 families supported the view that teachers who are not performing their educational duties in their institutions and are instead engaged in coaching centers, the services of such persons should be terminated and the coaching centers be banned by the government, whereas a much bigger number (95.77%) of workers hailing from Group 2 families agreed with the statement.

It can, thus, be concluded that both the groups expressed their agreement with the statements.

ANALYSIS OF RELIGIOUS PERCEPTION OF BOTH THE GROUPS

Table 4.19 reveals that most of the respondents (62.50%) hailing from Group 1 families did not agree that majority of members of their community offer prescribed prayers regularly, whereas a much bigger number 84.04% of workers hailing from Group 2 families did not agree with the statement.

While a majority of the respondents (73.61%) hailing from Group 1 families disagreed with the view that members of their community strictly follow and practice laws as prescribed in Holy Scriptures, whereas a bigger number (82.84%) of the workers hailing from Group 2 families did not agree with the statement.

TABLE 4.19 COMPARATIVE ANALYSIS IN RESPECT OF RELIGIOUS PERCEPTION OF THE LOCK INDUSTRY WORKERS ADOPTING (GROUP 1) & NOT ADOPTING (GROUP 2) SMALL FAMILY NORMS

		GROUP 1						GROUP 2					
	RELIGIOUS PERCEPTIONS	*YES*	*%*	*INDIFF.*	*%*	*NO*	*%*	*YES*	*%*	*INDIFF.*	*%*	*NO*	*%*
1.	Do you notice that majority of members of your community offer prayers regularly as prescribed?	27	37.50	0	0.00	45	62.50	62	15.46	2	0.50	337	8404
2.	Do you perceive that members of your community strictly follow and practice the laws as prescribed in Holy Scriptures?	11	15.28	8	11.11	53	73.61	51	12.69	18	4.489	333	82.84
3.	Do you observe that members of your community extend equal respect to other religions?	24	33.33	10	13.89	38	52.78	104	25.87	17	4.23	281	69.90
4.	Do you notice that certain number of the members of your community on account of their vested interests, deviate from the prescribed religious codes of conduct?	62	86.11	6	8.33	4	5.56	380	94.53	13	3.23	9	2.24
5.	Do you notice that sections of your community on account of their ignorance about the teaching of religion, maintain social distance with members hailing from other religions?	68	94.44	4	5.56	0	0.00	382	95.02	15	3.73	5	1.24
6.	Do you observe that the preachers of religion of your community have not adequately succeeded in transmitting proper understanding and knowledge about religion to the masses?	56	77.78	7	9.72	9	12.50	349	86.82	20	4.98	33	8.21

TABLE 4.19 (CONTD.)

7.	Do you perceive that religious heads of your community have imposed certain restrictions which are not prescribed in the Holy Scriptures?	61	8472	5	6.94	6	8.33	374	93.03	17	4.23	11	2.74
8.	Do you observe that the religious heads of your community on account of their vested material gains and popularity, offer their services to political parties during elections which is against their religious ethics?	65	90.28	7	9.72	9	12.50	349	36.82	20	4.98	33	8.21
9.	Do you notice that same members in our society are distinctly discriminated on the basis of the religion and caste in all the matters of life?	65	90.28	7	9.72	0	0.00	383	95.27	19	4.73	0	0.00
10.	Do you perceive that funds collected in the name of religion by the religious leaders of your community are not utilized religiously by them?	65	90.28	7	9.72	0	0.00	383	95.27	18	4.48	1	0.25

While simple majority of respondents 52.78% hailing from Group 1 families disagreed that members of their community extend equal respect to other religions, whereas a larger majority 69.90% of workers hailing from Group 2 families did not agree with the statement.

While a strong majority of respondents (86.11%) hailing from Group 1 families noticed that certain number of members of their community, on account of their vested interests deviated from the prescribed religious codes of conduct, whereas a much bigger number 94.53% of the workers hailing from Group 2 families agreed with the statement.

While a thumping majority of respondents 94.44% hailing from Group 1 families noticed that sections of their community, on account of their ignorance about the teaching of religion, maintain social distance with the members hailing from other religions, whereas a still larger number (95.02%) of workers hailing from Gruop 2 families agreed with the statement.

While a strong majority of respondents 77.78% hailing from Group 1 families observed that preachers of religion of their community have not adequately succeeded in transmitting proper understanding and knowledge about religion to the masses, whereas much bigger number 86.82% of workers hailing from Group 2 families agreed with the statement.

Although a strong majority of respondents 84.72% hailing from Group 1 families perceived that religious heads of their community have imposed certain restrictions which are not prescribed in the Holy Scriptures, whereas a much larger number 93.03% of the workers hailing from Group 2 families agreed with the statement.

While a thumping majority of respondents 90.28% hailing from Group 1 families observed that religious heads of their community, on account of their vested material gains and popularity, offer their services to political parties during elections which is against their religious ethics, whereas a stronger majority 95.27% of the workers hailing from Group 2 families agreed with the statement.

While a huge majority of respondents 90.28% hailing from Group 1 families noticed that members in their society are distinctly discriminated on the basis of religion and caste in all the matters of life, a stronger majority 95.27% of the workers hailing from Group 2 families agreed with the statement.

While a strong majority of respondents 90.28% hailing from Group 1 families perceived that funds collected in the name of religion by the religious leaders of their community are not utilized religiously by them, a much stronger number 95.27% of workers hailing from Group 2 families agreed with the statement.

It can, thus, be concluded that both the groups expressed agreement with the statements.

ANALYSIS OF RELIGIOUS ASPIRATION OF BOTH THE GROUPS

Table 4.20 reveals that most of the respondents 99.22% hailing from Group 1 families aspired, if possible, to educate the importance of offering prayers to such members of their community who do not offer prescribed prayers regularly, whereas a lesser number (95.27%) of the workers hailing from Group 2 families agreed with the statement.

While a strong majority of respondents 93.06% hailing from Group 1 families intended to follow themselves and educate other members of their community to follow and practice the laws as laid down in their Holy Scriptures, a stronger number 95.02% of the workers hailing from Group 2 families agreed with the statement.

While a strong majority of respondents 84.72% hailing from Group 1 families aspired to educate such members of their community to extend equal support to other religions who out of their ignorance, are failing to offer equal respect to other religions, whereas a stronger majority 91.29% of workers hailing from Group 2 families agreed with the statement.

While a huge majority of respondents (87.50%) hailing from Group 1 families wished to enlighten members of their community not to violate the prescribed religious prescriptions for the sake of their personal gains, a stronger number 89.78% of workers hailing from Group 2 families agreed with the statement.

TABLE 420 COMPARATIVE ANALYSIS IN RESPECT OF RELIGIOUS ASPIRATIONS OF LOCK INDUSTRY WORKERS ADOPTING (GROUP 1) & NOT ADOPTING (GROUP 2) SMALL FAMILY NORMS

	RELIGIOUS PERCEPTIONS	*YES*	*%*	*INDIFF.*	*%*	*NO*	*%*	*YES*	*%*	*INDIFF.*	*%*	*NO*	*%*
1	Do you aspire, if possible, to educate the importance of offering prayers to such members of your community who do not offer prayers regularly as prescribed?	70	97.22	2	2.78	0	0.00	383	95.27	15	3.73	4	1.00
2	Do you intend to follow yourself and educate other members of your community to follow and practice the laws as laid down in your Holy Scriptures?	67	93.06	4	5.56	1	1.39	382	95.02	17	4.23	3	0.75
3	Do you aspire to educate such members of your community to extend equal respect to other religions who out of their ignorance are failing to offer equal respect to other religions?	61	8472	10	13.989	1	1.39	367	91.29	31	7.71	4	1.00
4	Do you wish to enlighten the members of your community not to violate the prescribed religious prescriptions for the sake their personal gains?	63	87.50	6	8.33	3	4.17	360	89.78	33	8.23	8	2.00
5	Do you aspire to enlighten about certain prevailing misconceptions about teachings of religion so that the members of your community, on the basis of religion, do not maintain social distance with the members representing other religions?	55	76.39	12	16.67	5	6.94	289	71.89	78	19.40	35	8.71

TABLE 4.20 (CONTD.)

6	Do you aspire to gain full and real knowledge about your religion from religious scholars so that in your spare time you may transmit it judiciously to the masses of your community?	59	81.94	12	16.67	1	1.39	353	87.81	36	8.96	13	3.23
7	Do you aspire to take guidance from religious scholars and fight against such restrictions which are not prescribed in your religious scriptures but have been imposed by the preachers of religion of your community?	65	90.28	6	8.33	1	1.39	364	90.55	33	8.21	5	1.24
8	Do you aspire to raise your voice and condemn such religious heads of your community who, on account of their vested interests, offer services to political parties?	61	84.72	7	9.72	4	5.56	362	90.02	21	5.22	19	4.73
9	Do you aspire to work and fight against the operative practices by discrimination in your society by seeking support from the enlightened members hailing from other communities?	50	49.44	19	26.39	3	4.17	346	86.07	46	11.44	10	2.49
10	Do you aspire to propagate in your community that the religious fund collectors must submit the programmes and regular accounts before the general body of the community so that misuse of the funds be checked?	66	91.67	6	8.33	0	0.00	385	95.77	17	4.23	0	0.00

While a strong majority of the respondents 76.39% hailing from Group 1 families aspired to enlighten about certain prevailing misconceptions about the teachings of religion so that the members of their community on the basis of religion, do not maintain social distance with the members representing other religions, a lesser majority 7189% of workers hailing from Group 2 families agreed with the statement.

While a big majority of respondents 81.94% hailing from Group 1 families aspired to gain full and real knowledge about their religion from religious scholars so that in their spare time they may transmit it judiciously to masses of their community, a stronger numbers 87.81% of workers hailing from Group 2 families agreed with the statement.

While a strong majority of the respondents 90.28% hailing from Group 1 families aspired to take guidance from religious scholars and fight against such restrictions which are not prescribed in their religious scriptures but have been imposed by the preachers of religion of their community, an almost equal number 90.55% of the workers hailing from Group 2 families agreed with the statement.

While a thumping majority of respondents 84.72% hailing from Group 1 families aspired to raise their voice and condemn such religious heads of their community who, on account of their vested interests offer services to political parties, a stronger number 90.05% of the workers hailing from Group 2 families agreed with the statement.

While a majority of respondents 69.44% hailing from Group 1 families aspired to work and fight against the operative practices of discrimination in their society by seeking support from enlightened members hailing from the other communities, a much larger number 86.07% of the workers hailing from Group 2 families agreed with the statement.

While a strong majority of respondents 91.67% hailing from Group 1 families aspired to propagate in their community that the religious fund collectors must submit the programmes and regular accounts before the general body of the community so that misuse of the funds be checked, a much larger number 95.77% of workers hailing from Group 2 families agreed with the statement.

It can, thus, be concluded that both the groups expressed their agreement with the statements.

ITEMWISE ANALYSIS

For the purpose of itemwise analysis, the respondents have been categorized in 25 broad groups as specified below:

1. Workers of different industrial units belonging to the same factory —one group
2. Workers of different factories belong to the same industrial unit —eight group
3. Salaried & contractual workers —two groups
4. Male & female workers —two groups
5. Literate & illiterate workers —two groups
6. Workers belonging to joint families & nuclear families —two groups
7. Workers from the rural areas and urban areas —two groups
8. Workers representing different religions —two groups
9. Workers hailing from the different income groups —two groups
10. Workers belonging to management & labour class —two groups

The investigator framed one hundred (100) items in order to elicit responses from the workers for the purpose of the present investigation. Ten items have been framed from each parameter, reflecting towards perceptions and aspirations of the respondents, *viz.* economic perceptions, economic aspirations, social perceptions, social aspirations, political perceptions, political aspirations, educational perceptions, educational aspirations, religious perceptions and religious aspirations.

Table 4.21 reveals that majority of the workers 96.84% representing different units of 55 factories have agreed with the statement that earnings are not sufficient to meet their familial responsibilities and other obligations. While 0.42% have exhibited their indifference towards the statement only 2.74% have expressed their disagreement with the statement. Unit wise analysis reveals that 96.23% workers hailing from assembly units; 98.28% hailing from diemaking units; 97.67% representing furnace and despatch units; 98.21% hailing from key making units; 96.49% hailing from nickle polish units; 96.72% hailing from office; 95.95% hailing from packing units and 95.83% from press units have expressed their agreement with the statement. Similarly 97.89% salaried workers and 95.40% contractual workers have also expressed their agreement with the statement. Similarly, 96.95% male workers and 92.86% female workers; 97.30% literate and 96.43% illiterate workers; 97.41% workers hailing from joint family system and 95.28% representing nuclear family system; 96.73% rural and 96.88% urban workers; 96.88% Hindu workers and 97.2% Muslim workers; 96.65% workers; receiving salary up to Rs. 3000/-and 97.41% workers receiving salary more than 3000/-per month; have also exhibited their agreement with the statement. 96.65% workers hailing from Labour class and 97.59% workers hailing from management group have all expressed their agreement with the statement.

It can, thus, be concluded that the respondents representing different units of the factory as well as majority of the total subjects (96.84) has expressed their agreement with the statement that "earnings are not sufficient to meet their familial responsibilities and other obligations".

Table 4.22 reveals that majority of the workers (96.20%) representing different units of 55 factories have agreed with the statement that because of economic reasons people of their community, despite mental and physical exploitation, permit their children to seek employment, while 1.6% have exhibited their indifference towards the statement and only 2.1% have expressed their disagreement with the statement. Units wise analysis reveals that 98.1% workers hailing from assembly units; 98.2% from die-making units; 97.6% from

TABLE 4.21 ECONOMIC PERCEPTION: (1) EARNINGS ARE NOT SUFFICIENT TO MEET THE FAMILAL RESPONSIBILITIES AND OTHER OBLIGATIONS

	RESPONDENTS CATEGORY	*YES*	*%*	*INDIFF.*	*%*	*NO*	*%*
1.	Workers of different industrial units belonging to same factory.	459	96.84	2	0.42	13	2.74
2.	Workers of different factories belonging to assembly units.	51	96.23	1	1.89	1	1.89
3.	Workers of different factories belonging to die-making units.	57	98.28	0	0.00	1	1.72
4.	Workers of different factories belonging to furnace & despatch units.	42	97.67	0	0.00	1	2.33
5.	Workers of different factories belonging to key-making units.	55	98.21	0	0.00	1	1.79
6.	Workers of different factories belonging to nickle polish units.	55	96.49	0	0.00	2	3.51
7.	Workers of different factories belonging to office.	59	96.72	0	0.00	2	3.28
8.	Workers of different factories belonging to packing units.	71	95.95	1	1.35	2	2.70
9.	Workers of different factories belonging to press units.	69	95.83	0	0.00	3	4.17
10.	Salaried workers.	232	97.89	2	0.84	3	1.27

11. Contractual workers	228	95.40	1	0.42	10	4.18
12. Male workers	445	96.95	2	0.44	12	2.61
13. Female workers	13	92.86	0	0.00	1	7.14
14. Literate workers	217	97.30	0	0.00	6	2.70
15. Illiterate workers	243	96.43	2	0.79	7	2.78
16. Joint family workers	339	97.41	1	0.29	8	2.31
17. Nuclear family workers	121	95.28	1	0.79	5	3.94
18. Rural workers	149	96.73	2	1.31	3	1.96
19. Urban workers	311	96.88	0	0.00	10	3.12
20. Hindu workers	142	97.26	1	0.68	3	2.05
21. Muslim workers	317	96.65	1	0.30	10	3.05
22. Workers' in income group below 3000	346	96.65	2	0.00	10	2.79
23. Workers in income group of 3000 plus	113	97.41	0	0.00	3	2.59
24. Workers belonging to Labour Class	375	96.65	2	0.52	11	2.84
25. Workers belonging to Management Class	81	97.59	0	00	2	241

furnace and dispatch units 96.4% from key-making units; 96.4% from nickle polish units; 96.7 from office; 91.8% from packing units; 95.8% from press units; 97.4% salaried workers and 94.9% contractual workers; 96.2% male workers and 92.8% female workers; 96.8% literate and 95.6% illiterate workers; 96.8 % workers representing joint family system and 94.4% hailing from nuclear family system; 97.3% rural and 95.6% urban workers; also 92.2% Hindu workers and 95.7% Muslim workers; 95.81% workers receiving salary up to Rs. 3000/- and 97.41% workers receiving salary more than 3000/- per month; and 97.59% workers hailing from management group expressed their agreement with the statement.

It can, thus, be concluded that the respondents representing different units of the factory as well as majority of the total subjects (96.2%) have expressed their agreement with the statement that "because of economic reasons people of the community, despite mental and physical exploitation, permit their children to seek employment.

Table 4.23 reveals that majority of workers (95.99%) representing different units of 55 factories have agreed with the statement that because of economic constraints majority of the people of community fail to fulfil their socio-cultural commitments, while 12.17% exhibited their indifference towards the statement, only 4.42% have expressed their disagreement with the statement. Unit-wise analysis reveals that 92.45% workers hailing from assembly units; 98.28% from die-making units; 100% from furnace and dispatch units 96.43% from key-making units; 96.49% from nickle polish units; 95.08% from office; 9730% from packing units; and 93.06% from press units 97.05% salaried workers and 94.98% contractual workers; 95.86% male workers and 100% female workers; 96.85% literate and 95.24% illiterate workers; 96.83% workers from joint family system and 9370% representing nuclear family system; 96.73% rural and 95.64% urban workers; 96.58% Hindu workers 95.73% Muslim workers; 95.53% workers receiving salary up to Rs. 3000/- and 97.41% workers receiving salary of more than 3000/-per month; 96.13%

TABLE 4.22 ECONOMIC PERCEPTION: (2) BECAUSE OF ECONOMIC REASONS PEOPLE OF THEIR COMMUNITY DESPITE MENTAL & PHYSICAL EXPLOITATION, PERMIT THEIR CHILDREN TO SEEK EMPLOYMENT

	RESPONDENTS CATEGORY	*YES*	*%*	*INDIFF.*	*%*	*NO*	*%*
1.	Workers of different industrial units belonging to same factory.	456	96.2	8	1.6	10	2.1
2.	Workers of different factoreis belonging to Assembly units.	52	98.1	0	0	1	1.8
3.	Workers of different factories belonging to Die-Making units.	57	98.2	0	00	1	1.8
4.	Workers of different factories belonging to furnace & despatch units.	42	97.6	00	00	1	2.3
5.	Workers of different factories belonging to key-making units.	54	96.4	1	1.7	1	1.7
6.	Workers of different factories belonging to Nickle Polish units.	55	96.4	1	1.7	1	1.7
7.	Workers of different factories belonging to office.	59	96.7	0	00	2	3.2
8.	Workers of different factories belonging to packing units.	68	91.8	5	6.7	1	1.3
9.	Workers of different factories belonging to press units.	69	95.8	1	1.3	2	2.7
10.	Salaried workers.	231	97.4	4	1.6	2	0.8

(Cont.)

11. Contractual workers	227	94.9'	4	1.6	8	3.3
12. Male workers	442	96.2	7	1.5	10	2.1
13. Female workers	13	92.8	1	7.1	0	0
14. Literate workers	215	96.8	2	0.9	5	2.2
15. Illiterate workers	241	95.6	6	2.3	5	1.9
16. Joint family workers	336	96.8	6	1.7	5	1.4
17. Nuclear family workers	120	94.4	2	1.5	5	3.9
18. Rural workers	149	97.3	3	1.9	1	0.6
19. Urban workers	307	95.6	5	1.5	9	2.8
20. Hindu workers	142	92.2	4	2.5	8	5.1
21. Muslim workers	314	95.7	4	1.2	10	3.0
22. Workers in income group 0 – 3000	343	95.81	7	1.96	8	2.23
23. Workers in income group of over 3000	113	97.41	1	0.86	2	1.72
24. Workers belonging to Labour Class	372	95.88	8	2.06	8	2.06
25. Workers belonging to Management Class	81	97.59	0	00	2	2.41

TABLE 4.23 ECONOMIC PERCEPTION: (3) NON FULFILLMENT OF THEIR SOCIO-CULTURAL COMMITMENTS DUE TO ECONOMIC CONSTRAINTS

	RESPONDENTS CATEGORY	*YES*	*%*	*INDIFF.*	*%*	*NO*	*%*
1.	Workers of different industrial units belonging to same factory.	455	95.99	14	12.17	5	4.42
2.	Workers of different factoreis belonging to Assembly units.	49	92.45	4	4.15	0	0.00
3.	Workers of different factories belonging to Die-making units.	57	98.28	1	1.01	0	0.00
4.	Workers of different factories belonging to furnace & despatch units.	43	100.00	0	0.00	0	0.00
5.	Workers of different factories belonging to key-making units.	54	96.43	2	2.03	0	0.00
6.	Workers of different factories belonging to nickle polish units.	55	96.49	1	1.02	1	1.02
7.	Workers of different factories be[illegible]ging to office.	58	95.08	2	2.04	1	1.02
8.	Workers of different factories belonging to packing units.	72	97.30	1	1.01	1	1.01
9.	Workers of different factories belonging to press units.	67	93.06	3	3.06	2	2.04
10.	Salaried workers.	230	97.05	4	3.84	3	2.89

(Contd.)

11. Contractual workers	227	94.98	10	9.35	2	1.88
12. Male workers	440	95.86	14	12.19	5	4.42
13. Female workers	14	100.00	0	0.00	0	0.00
14. Literate workers	215	96.85	6	5.78	1	0.97
15. Illiterate workers	240	95.24	8	7.45	4	3.75
16. Joint family workers	336	96.83	7	6.49	4	3.73
17. Nuclear family workers	119	93.70	7	6.88	1	0.98
18. Rural workers	148	96.73	4	3.93	1	0.98
19. Urban workers	307	95.64	10	9.12	4	3.68
20. Hindu workers	141	96.58	3	2.95	2	1.97
21. Muslim workers	314	95.73	11	10.02	3	2.76
22. Workers in income group 0 – 3000	342	95.53	11	9.86	5	4.53
23. Workers in income group of over 3000.	113	97.41	3	2.99	0	0.00
24. Workers belonging to Labour Class	373	96.13	11	2.84	4	1.03
25. Workers belonging to Management Class	79	95.18	3	3.61	1	1.20

workers hailing from Labour class and 95.18% workers hailing from management group have all expressed their agreement with the statement.

It can, thus, be concluded that the respondents representing different units of the factory as well as majority of the total subjects (95.99%) have expressed their agreement with the statement that "because of economic constraints majority of the people of the community fail to fulfil their socio-cultural commitments".

Table 4.24 reveals that majority of workers (95.14%) representing different units of 55 factories have agreed with the statement that on account of economic considerations, people of their community give preference to their sons in place of daughters, while 1.05% exhibited their indifference, only 3.79% expressed their disagreement with the statement. Units wise analysis reveals that 98.11% workers hailing from assembly units; 96.55% from die-making units; 100% from furnace and dispatch units, 98.21% from key-making units; 94.74% from nickle polish units; 95.08% from Office; 89.19% from packing units; 93.06% from press units 95.78% salaried workers and 94.56% contractual workers; 95.21% male workers and 92.86% female workers; 96.85% literate and 93.65% illiterate workers; 96.25% workers from joint family system and 92.13% representing nuclear family system; 91.50% rural and 96.88% urban workers; 93.15% Hindu workers and 96.04% Muslim workers; 94.41% workers receiving salary up to Rs. 3000/- and 97.41% workers receiving salary of more than 3000/-per month 94.85% workers hailing from Labour class have also exhibited their agreement with the statement. 96.39% workers hailing from management group all expressed their agreement with the statement.

It can, thus, be concluded that respondents representing different units of the factory as well as majority of the total subjects (95.14%) expressed their agreement with the statement that "on account of economic considerations, people of their community give preference to their sons in place of daughters".

TABLE 4.24 ECONOMIC PERCEPTION: (4) ON ACCOUNT OF ECONOMIC CONSIDERATIONS PEOPLE OF THEIR COMMUNITY GIVE PREFERENCE TO THEIR SONS IN PLACE OF DAUGHTERS

	RESPONDENTS CATEGORY	*YES*	*%*	*INDIFF.*	*%*	*NO*	*%*
1.	Workers of different industrial units belonging to same factory.	451	95.14	5	1.05	18	3.79
2.	Workers of different factoreis belonging to assembly units.	52	98.11	1	1.01	0	0.00
3.	Workers of different factories belonging to Die-making units.	56	96.55	2	2.03	0	0.00
4.	Workers of different factories belonging to furnace & despatch units.	43	100.00	0	0.00	0	0.00
5.	Workers of different factories belonging to key-making units.	55	98.21	1	1.01	0	0.00
6.	Workers of different factories belonging to nickle polish units.	54	94.74	2	2.05	1	1.02
7.	Workers of different factories belonging to office.	58	95.08	2	2.04	1	1.02
8.	Workers of different factories belonging to packing units.	66	89.19	6	6.17	2	2.05
9.	Workers of different factories belonging to press units.	67	93.06	4	4.08	1	1.02
10.	Salaried workers.	227	95.78	7	6.62	3	2.85

(Contd.)

11. Contractual workers	226	94.56	11	10.23	2	1.87
12. Male workers	437	95.21	17	14.50	5	4.36
13. Female workers	13	92.86	1	1.07	0	0.00
14. Literate workers	215	96.85	5	4.81	2	1.93
15. Illiterate workers	236	93.65	13	11.86	3	2.76
16. Joint family workers	334	96.25	9	8.24	4	3.69
17. Nuclear family workers	117	92.13	9	8.81	1	0.98
18. Rural workers	140	91.50	11	10.53	2	1.92
19. Urban workers	311	96.88	7	6.55	3	2.82
20. Hindu workers	136	93.15	10	9.69	0	0.00
21. Muslim workers	315	85.94	7	6,34	5	4.51
22. Workers in income group 0 – 3000	338	94.41	15	13.11	5	4.44
23. Workers in income group of over 3000	133	97.41	3	2.99	0	0.00
24. Workers belonging to Labour Class	368	94.85	16	4.12	4	1.03
25. Workers belonging to Management Class	80	96.39	2	2.41	1	1.20

Table 4.25 reveals that majority of the workers (90.51%) representing different units of 55 factories have agreed with the statement that some families within the community, where women are also working along with men are economically much better off as compared to others, while 3.59% have exhibited their indifference only 5.91% have expressed their disagreement with the statement. Unit-wise analysis reveals that 94.34% workers hailing from assembly units; 94.83% from die-making units; 90.70% from furnace and dispatch units 83.93% from key-making units; 85.96% from nickle polish units; 91.80% from Office; 90.54% from packing units; 91.67% from press units; 88.61% salaried workers and 91.63% contractual workers; 90.85% male workers and 78.57% female workers; 90.09% literate and 90.87% illiterate workers; 89.63% workers from joint family system and 92.91% representing nuclear family system; 87.58% rural and 91.90% urban workers; 86.30% Hind workers and 92.38% Muslim workers; 92.46% workers receiving salary up to Rs. 3000/ - and 84.48% workers receiving salary more than 3000/-per month; 90.21% workers hailing from Labour class 91.57% workers hailing from management group expressed their agreement with the statement.

It can, thus, be concluded that the respondents representing different units of the factory as well as majority of the total subjects (90.51%) expressed their agreement with the statement that "some families within the community, where women are also working along with men, are economically much better off as compared to others".

Table 4.26 reveals that majority of the workers (91.56%) representing different units of 55 factories agreed with the statement that constant hikes in the cost of living and limited income has compelled the economically weaker sections of the community to accept all kinds of exploitations, while 4.01% exhibited their indifference, only 4.43% have expressed their disagreement with the statement. Unit-wise analysis reveals that 94.34% workers hailing from assembly units; 93.10% from die-making units; 97.67% from

TABLE 4.25 ECONOMIC PERCEPTION: (5) FAMILIES WHERE WOMEN ARE ALSO WORKING ARE ECONOMICALLY MUCH BETTER OFF AS COMPARED TO OTHERS

	RESPONDENTS CATEGORY	*YES*	*%*	*INDIFF.*	*%*	*NO*	*%*
1.	Workers of different industrial units belonging to same factory.	429	90.51	17	3.59	28	5.91
2.	Workers of different factories belonging to assembly units	50	94.34	0	0.00	3	5.66
3.	Workers of different factories belonging to Die-making units.	55	94.83	1	1.72	2	3.45
4.	Workers of different factories belonging to furnace & despatch units.	39	90.70	1	2.33	03	6.98
5.	Workers of different factories belonging to key-making units.	47	83.93	5	8.93	4	7.14
6.	Workers of different factories belonging to nickle polish units.	49	85.96	4	7.02	4	7.02
7.	Workers of different factories belonging to office.	56	91.80	2	3.28	3	4.92
8.	Workers of different factories belonging to packing units.	67	90.54	1	1.35	6	8.11
9.	Workers of different factories belonging to press units.	66	91.67	3	4.17	3	4.17
10.	Salaried workers.	210	88.61	11	4.64	16	6.75

(Contd.)

11. Contractual workers	219	91.63	6	2.51	14	5.86
12. Male workers	417	90.85	17	3.70	25	5.45
13. Female workers	11	78.57	0	0.00	3	21.43
14. Literate workers	200	90.09	5	2.25	17	7.66
15. Illiterate workers	229	90.87	12	4.76	11	4.37
16. Joint family workers	311	89.63	11	3.17	25	7.20
17. Nuclear family workers	118	92.91	6	4.72	3	2.36
18. Rural workers	134	87.58	10	6.54	9	5.88
19. Urban workers	295	91.90	19	5.92	7	2.18
20. Hindu workers	126	86.30	9	6.16	11	7.53
21. Muslim workers	303	92.38	8	2.44	17	5.18
22. Workers in income group 0 – 3000	331	92.46	13	3.63	14	3.91
23. Workers in income group of over 3000	98	84.48	4	2.34	14	12.07
24. Workers belonging to Labour Class	350	90.21	15	3.87	23	5.93
25. Workers belonging to Management Class	76	91.57	2	2.41	5	6.02

TABLE 4.26 ECONOMIC PERCEPTION: (6) CONSTANT HIKES IN THE COST OF LIVING AND LIMITED INCOME HAS COMPELLED THE ECONOMICALLY WEAKER SECTIONS OF THE COMMUNITY TO ACCEPT ALL KINDS OF EXPLOITATIONS

	RESPONDENTS CATEGORY	*YES*	*%*	*INDIFF.*	*%*	*NO*	*%*
1.	Workers of different industrial units belonging to same factory.	434	91.56	19	4.01	21	4.43
2.	Workers of different factories belonging to assembly units.	50	94.34	1	1.89	2	3.77
3.	Workers of different factories belonging to Die-making units.	54	93.10	2	3.45	2	3.45
4.	Workers of different factories belonging to furnace & despatch units.	42	97.67	1	2.33	0	0.00
5.	Workers of different factories belonging to key-making units.	50	89.29	2	3.57	4	7.14
6.	Workers of different factories belonging to nickle polish units.	50	87.72	4	7.02	3	5.26
7.	Workers of different factories belonging to office.	58	95.08	1	1.64	2	3.28
8.	Workers of different factories belonging to packing units.	67	90.54	3	4.05	4	5.41
9.	Workers of different factories belonging to press units.	63	87.50	5	6.94	4	5.56
10.	Salaried workers.	218	91.98	11	4.64	8	3.38

(Contd.)

11. Contractual workers	218	91.21	8	3.35	13	5.44
12. Male workers	419	91.29	19	4.14	21	4.58
13. Female workers	14	100.00	0	0.00	0	0.00
14. Literate workers	209	94.14	4	1.80	9	4.05
15. Illiterate workers	225	89.29	15	5.95	12	4.76
16. Joint family workers	322	95.55	6	1.78	9	2.67
17. Nuclear family workers	112	88.19	10	7.87	5	3.94
18. Rural workers	137	89.54	8	5.23	8	5.23
19. Urban workers	297	92.52	11	3.43	13	4.05
20. Hindu workers	132	90.41	10	6.85	4	2.74
21. Muslim workers	302	92.07	9	2.74	17	5.18
22. Workers in income group 0 – 3000	327	91.34	14	3.91	17	4.75
23. Workers in income group of over 3000	107	97.24	5	4.31	4	3.45
24. Workers belonging to Labour Class	350	90.21	19	4.90	19	4.90
25. Workers belonging to Management Class	81	97.59	0	00	2	2.41

furnace and dispatch units; 89.29% from key-making units; 987.72% from nickle polish units; 95.08% from Office; 90.54% from packing units and 87.50% from press units; 91.98% salaried workers and 91.21% contractual workers; 91.29% male workers and 100% female workers; 94.14% literate and 89.29% illiterate workers; 95.55% workers from joint family system and 88.19% representing nuclear family system; 89.54% rural and 92.52% urban workers; 90.41% Hindu workers and 92.07% Muslim workers; 91.34% workers receiving salary up to Rs. 3000/- and 92.24% workers receiving salary of more than 3000/- per month; 90.21% workers hailing from labour class and 97.59% workers hailing from management group all expressed their agreement with the statement.

It can, thus, be concluded that the respondents representing different units of the factory as well as majority of the total subjects (91.56%) have expressed their agreement with the statement that "constant hikes in the cost of the living and limited income has compelled the economically weaker sections of the community to accept all kinds of exploitations".

Table 4.27 reveals that majority of workers (75.74%) representing different units of 55 factories have disagreed with the statement that on account of limited opportunities of employment, the educated youths of the community have adopted unethical and illegal means to earn money, while 6.96% respondents exhibited their indifference, only 17.30% expressed their agreement with the statement. Unit-wise analysis reveals that 81.13% workers hailing from assembly units; 77.59% from die-making units; 88.37% from furnace and dispatch units; 78.57% from key-making units; 75.44% from nickle polish units; 78.69% from Office, 67.57% from packing units; 66.67% from press units; 73% salaried workers and 77.82% contractual workers; 75.38% male workers and 85.71% female workers; 81.53% literate and 70.63% illiterate workers; 78.10% workers from joint family system and 69.29% representing nuclear family system 67.32% rural workers and 79.75% urban workers; 68.49% Hindu workers and 78.96% Muslim workers; 73.46% workers receiving salary up to Rs. 3000/- and 82.76% workers receiving salary. More than

TABLE 4.27 ECONOMIC PERCEPTION: (7) ON ACCOUNT OF LIMITED OPPORTUNITIES OF EMPLOYMENT, THE EDUCATED YOUTH OF THE COMMUNITYHERE ADOPTED UNETHICAL AND ILLEGAL MEANS TO EARN MONEY

	RESPONDENTS CATEGORY	*YES*	*%*	*INDIFF.*	*%*	*NO*	*%*
1.	Workers of different industrial units belonging to same factory.	82	17.30	33	6.96	359	75.74
2.	Workers of different factories belonging to assembly units.	6	11.32	4	7.55	43	81.13
3.	Workers of different factories belonging to Die-making units.	7	12.07	6	10.34	45	77.59
4.	Workers of different factories belonging to furnace & despatch units.	5	11.63	0	0.00	38	88.37
5.	Workers of different factories belonging to key-making units.	9	16.07	3	5.36	44	78.57
6.	Workers of different factories belonging to nickle polish units.	8	14.04	6	10.53	43	75.44
7.	Workers of different factories belonging to office.	9	14.75	4	6.56	48	78.69
8.	Workers of different factories belonging to packing units.	20	27.03	4	5.41	50	67.57
9.	Workers of different factories belonging to press units.	18	25.00	6	8.33	48	66.67
10.	Salaried workers.	43	18.14	21	8.86	173	73.00

11. Contractual workers	41	17.15	12	5.02	186	77.82
12. Male workers	80	17.43	33	7.19	346	75.38
13. Female workers	2	14.29	0	0.00	12	85.71
14. Literate workers	28	12.61	13	5.56	181	81.53
15. Illiterate workers	54	21.43	20	7.94	178	70.63
16. Joint family workers	56	16.14	20	5.76	271	78.10
17. Nuclear family workers	26	20.47	13	10.24	88	69.29
18. Rural workers	41	26.80	9	5.88	103	67.32
19. Urban workers	41	12.77	24	7.48	256	79.75
20. Hindu workers	35	23.97	11	7.53	100	68.49
21. Muslim workers	47	14.35	22	6.71	259	78.96
22. Workers in income group 0–3000	73	20.39	22	6.15	263	73.46
23. Workers in income group of over 3000	9	7.76	11	9.48	96	82.76
24. Workers belonging to Labour Class	74	19.07	29	7.47	285	73.45
25. Workers belonging to Management Class	8	9.64	4	4.82	71	85.54

3000/-per month and 73.45% workers hailing from labour class and 85.54% belong to managers class, all expressed have exhibited their disagreement with the statement. Against this, only 19.07% and 9.64% workers hailing from management group expressed their agreement with the statement.

It can, thus, be concluded that the respondents representing different units of the factory as well as majority of the total subjects (75.74%) expressed their disagreement with the statement that "on account of limited opportunities of employment, the educated youths of the community have adopted unethical and illegal means to earn money". The trend indicates that the respondents do not agree that the educated youths of their community have adopted unethical and illegal means to earn money. On the other hand, 6.96% of the respondents exhibited their indifference towards the statement white only 17.30% of the respondents exhibited their agreement with the statement. Similar trend is also notice-able among the respondents representing different units of the factory.

Table 4.28 reveals that majority of the workers (93.04%) representing different units of 55 factories have agreed with the statement that continuous disturbed conditions, like strikes and riots, in the society certainly affect economic activities and per capita income of the people of the society, while 5.06% have exhibited their indifference, only 1.90% expressed their disagreement with the statement. Unit-wise analysis reveals that 94.34% workers hailing from assembly units; 94.83% from die-making units; 95.35% from furnace and dispatch units; 91.07% from key-making units; 91.23% from nickle polish units; 100% from Office; 89.19% from packing units; 90.28% from press units; 92.41% salaried workers and 94.14% contractual workers; 93.03% male workers and 92.86% female workers; 95.95% literate and 90.48% illiterate workers; 93.37% workers from joint family system and 92.13% representing nuclear family system; 83.66% rural workers and 97.51% urban workers; 88.36% Hindu workers and 95.12% Muslim workers; 91.90% workers receiving salary up to Rs. 3000/- and 96.55% workers receiving

TABLE 4.28 (8) CONTINUOUS DISTURBED CONDITIONS LIKE STRIKES & RIOTS IN THE SOCIETY CERTAINLY AFFECT ECONOMIC ACTIVITIES AND PER CAPITA INCOME OF THE PEOPLE OF THE SOCIETY

	RESPONDENTS CATEGORY	*YES*	*%*	*INDIFF.*	*%*	*NO*	*%*
1.	Workers of different industrial units belonging to same factory.	441	93.04	24	5.06	09	1.90
2.	Workers of different factories belonging to assembly units.	50	94.34	1	1.89	2	3.77
3.	Workers of different factories belonging to Die-making units.	55	94.83	3	5.17	0	0.00
4.	Workers of different factories belonging to furnace & despatch units.	41	95.35	0	0.00	2	4.65
5.	Workers of different factories belonging to key-making units.	51	91.07	5	8.93	0	0.00
6.	Workers of different factories belonging to nickle polish units.	52	91.23	3	5.26	2	3.51
7.	Workers of different factories belonging to office.	61	100.00	0	0.00	0	0.00
8.	Workers of different factories belonging to packing units.	66	89.19	8	10.81	0	0.00
9.	Workers of different factories belonging to press units.	65	90.28	4	5.56	3	4.17
10.	Salaried workers.	219	92.41	14	5.91	4	1.69

(Contd.)

11. Contractual workers	225	94.14	9	3.77	5	2.09
12. Male workers	427	93.03	23	5.01	9	1.96
13. Female workers	13	92.86	1	7.14	0	0.00
14. Literate workers	213	95.95	5	2.25	4	1.80
15. Illiterate workers	228	90.48	19	7.54	5	1.98
16. Joint family workers	324	93.37	15	4.32	8	2.31
17. Nuclear family workers	117	92.13	9	7.09	1	0.79
18. Rural workers	128	83.66	19	12.42	6	3.92
19. Urban workers	313	97.51	5	1.56	3	0.93
20. Hindu workers	129	88.36	12	8.22	5	3.42
21. Muslim workers	312	95.12	12	3.66	4	1.22
22. Workers in income group 0-3000	329	91.90	20	5.59	9	2.51
23. Workers in income group of over 3000	112	96.55	0	3.45	4	0.00
24. Workers belonging to Labour Class	355	91.49	24	6.19	9	2.32
25. Workers belonging to Management Class	83	100	0	00	0	00

salary of more than 3000/-per month; 91.49% workers hailing from Labour class 100.00% workers hailing from management group expressed their agreement with the statement.

It can, thus, be concluded that the respondents representing different units of the factory as well as majority of the total subjects (93.04%) expressed their agreement with the statement that "continuous disturbed conditions, like strikes and riots, in the society certainly affect economic activities and per capita income of the people of the society".

Table 4.29 reveals that majority of the workers 94.94% representing different units of 55 factories agreed with the statement that educated and capable youths of the community are not making adequate use of Governmental Programmes or schemes meant for economic welfare of the people, while 4.85% have exhibited their indifference only an insignificant 0.21% expressed their disagreement with the statement.

Unit-wise analysis reveals that 96.23% workers hailing from assembly units; 94.83% from die-making units; 95.35% from furnace and dispatch units; 94.64% from key-making units; 89.47% from nickle polish units; 100% from Office; 9189% from packing units; 97.22% from press unit 92.41% salaried workers and 97.49% contractual workers; 94.77% male workers and 100% female workers; 97.75% literate and 92.46% illiterate workers; 96.25% workers from joint family system and 91.34% representing nuclear family system; 90.85% rural workers and 96.88% urban workers; 93.15% Hindu workers and 89.06% Muslim workers; 94.69% workers receiving salary up to Rs. 3000 and 95.69% workers receiving salary of more than 3000 per moth 93.81% workers hailing from Labour class and 100.00% workers hailing from management group expressed their agreement with the statement.

It can, thus, be concluded that the respondents representing different units of the factory as well as majority of the total subjects (94.94%) have expressed their agreement with the statement that "educated and capable youths of the community are not making

TABLE 4.29 (9) ECONOMIC PERCEPTION: (9) EDUCATED AND CAPABLE YOUTHS OF THE COMMUNITY ARE NOT MAKING ADEQUATE USE OF GOVERNMENT PROGRAMMES OF SCHEMES MEANT FOR ECONOMIC WELFARE OF THE PEOPLE

	RESPONDENTS CATEGORY	*YES*	*%*	*INDIFF.*	*%*	*NO*	*%*
1.	Workers of different industrial units belonging to same factory.	450	94.94	23	4.85	1	0.21
2.	Workers of different factories belonging to assembly units.	51	96.23	2	3.77	0	0.00
3.	Workers of different factories belonging to Die-making units.	55	94.83	3	5.17	0	0.00
4.	Workers of different factories belonging to furnace & despatch units.	41	95.35	1	2.33	1	2.33
5.	Workers of different factories belonging to key-making units.	53	94.64	3	5.36	0	0.00
6.	Workers of different factories belonging to nickle polish units.	51	89.47	6	10.53	0	0.00
7.	Workers of different factories belonging to office.	61	100.00	0	0.00	0	0.00
8.	Workers of different factories belonging to packing units.	68	91.89	6	8.11	0	0.00
9.	Workers of different factories belonging to press units.	70	97.22	2	2.78	0	0.00
10.	Salaried workers.	219	92.41	17	7.17	1	0.42

(*Contd.*)

11. Contractual workers	233	97.49	6	251	0	0.00
12. Male workers	435	94.77	23	5.01	1	0.22
13. Female workers	14	1000.00	0	0.00	0	0.00
14. Literate workers	217	97.75	4	1.80	1	0.45
15. Illiterate workers	233	92.46	19	7.54	0	0.00
16. Joint family workers	334	96.25	12	3.46	1	0.29
17. Nuclear family workers	116	91.34	11	3.66	0	0.00
18. Rural workers	139	90.85	14	9.15	0	0.00
19. Urban workers	311	96.88	9	2.80	1	0.31
20. Hindu workers	136	93.15	10	6.85	0	0.00
21. Muslim workers	114	89.06	13	10.16	1	0.78
22. Workers in income group 0–3000	339	94.69	18	5.03	1	0.28
23. Workers in income group of 3000 and above	111	95.69	5	4.31	0	0.00
24. Workers belonging to Labour Class	364	93.81	23	5.93	1	0.26
25. Workers belonging to Management Class	83	100	0	00	0	00

adequate use of Governmental Programmes or schemes meant for economic welfare of people".

Table 4.30 reveals that majority of the workers 95.57% representing different units of 55 factories agreed with the statement that on account of financial reasons children of the community are unable to receive adequate education as mostly parents in general and economically weaker in particular are unable to meet the prevailing high educational expenses, while 4.43% have exhibited their indifference, none expressed disagreement with the statement.

Unit-wise analysis reveals that 96.23% workers hailing from assembly units; 94.83% from die-making unit 97.67% from furnace and dispatch units 94.64% from key-making units; 91.23% from nickle polish units; 100% from Office; 93.24% from packing units 97.22% from press units; 93.67% salaried workers and 97.91% contractual workers; 95.42% male workers and 100% female workers; 98.20% literate and 93.25% illiterate workers; 95.39% workers from joint family system and 93.70% representing nuclear family system; 92.16% rural workers and 97.20% urban workers; 93.84% Hindu workers and 96.34% Muslim workers; 95.53% workers receiving salary up to Rs. 3000/- and 95.69% workers receiving salary of more than 3000/- per month; 94.59% workers hailing from Labour class and 100.00% workers hailing from management group expressed their agreement with the statement.

It can, thus, be concluded that the respondents representing different units of the factory as well as majority of the total subjects (95.57%) have expressed their agreement with the statement that "on account of financial reasons, children of the community are unable receive adequate education as mostly parents in general and economically weaker in particular were unable to meet the prevailing high educational expenses."

Table 4.31 reveals that majority of the workers 94.94% representing different units of 55 factories have agreed with the statement to desire to supplement their earning by taking up some part time jobs or economic activities, while 2.95% have exhibited their indifference towards the statement and only 2.11% have expressed their disagreement with the statement.

TABLE 4.30 ECONOMIC PERCEPTION: (10) CHILDREN OF THE COMMUNITY ARE UNABLE TO RECEIVE ADEQUATE EDUCATION AS MOSTLY PARENTS IN GENERAL AND ECONOMICALLY WEAKERS IN PARTICULARS ARE UNABLE TO MEET THE PREVAILING HIGH EDUCATIONAL EXPENSES

	RESPONDENTS CATEGORY	*YES*	*%*	*INDIFF.*	*%*	*NO*	*%*
1.	Workers of different industrial units belonging to same factory.	453	95.57	21	4.43	0	0.00
2.	Workers of different factories belonging to assembly units.	51	96.23	2	3.77	0	0.00
3.	Workers of different factories belonging to Die-making units.	55	94.83	3	5.17	0	0.00
4.	Workers of different factories belonging to furnace & despatch units.	42	97.67	1	2.33	0	0.00
5.	Workers of different factories belonging to key-making units.	53	94.64	3	5.36	0	0.00
6.	Workers of different factories belonging to nickle polish units.	52	91.23	5	8.77	0	0.00
7.	Workers of different factories belonging to office.	61	100.00	0	0.00	0	0.00
8.	Workers of different factories belonging to packing units.	69	93.24	5	6.76	0	0.00
9.	Workers of different factories belonging to press units.	70	97.22	2	2.78	0	0.00
10.	Salaried workers.	222	93.67	15	6.33	0	0.00

(*Contd.*)

11. Contractual workers	234	97.91	5	2.09	0	0.00
12. Male workers	438	95.42	21	4.58	0	0.00
13. Female workers	14	100.00	0	0.00	0	0.00
14. Literate workers	218	98.20	4	1.80	0	0.00
15. Illiterate workers	235	93.25	17	6.75	0	0.00
16. Joint family workers	331	95.39	7	2.02	9	2.59
17. Nuclear family workers	119	93.70	7	5.51	1	0.79
18. Rural workers	141	92.16	12	7.84	0	0.00
19. Urban workers	312	97.20	9	2.80	0	0.00
20. Hindu workers	137	93.84	9	6.16	0	0.00
21. Muslim workers	316	96.34	12	3.66	0	0.00
22. Workers in income group 0–3000	342	95.53	16	4.47	0	0.00
23. Workers income group 3000 and above	111	95.69	5	4.31	0	0.00
24. Workers belonging to Labour Class	367	94.59	21	5.41	0	0.00
25. Workers belonging to Management Class	83	100	0	00	0	00

TABLE 4.31 ECONOMIC ASPIRATION: (1) TO SUPPLEMENT EARNINGS BY TAKING UP SOME PART-TIME JOB OR ECONOMIC ACTIVITIES

	RESPONDENTS CATEGORY	*YES*	*%*	*INDIFF.*	*%*	*NO*	*%*
1.	Workers of different industrial units belonging to same factory.	450	94.94	14	2.95	10	2.11
2.	Workers of different factories belonging to assembly units.	50	94.34	1	1.89	2	3.77
3.	Workers of different factories belonging to Die-making units.	56	96.55	1	1.72	1	1.72
4.	Workers of different factories belonging to furnace & despatch units.	43	100.00	0	0.00	0	0.00
5.	Workers of different factories belonging to key-making units.	53	94.64	3	5.36	0	0.00
6.	Workers of different factories belonging to nickle polish units.	54	94.74	2	3.51	1	1.75
7.	Workers of different factories belonging to office.	57	93.44	2	3.28	2	3.28
8.	Workers of different factories belonging to packing units.	69	93.24	1	1.35	4	5.41
9.	Workers of different factories belonging to press units.	68	94.44	4	5.56	0	0.00
10.	Salaried workers.	226	95.36	7	2.95	4	1.69

(Contd.)

11. Contractual workers	234	97.91	225	94.14	7	2.93
12. Male workers	435	94.77	14	3.05	10	2.18
13. Female workers	14	100.00	0	0.00	0	0.00
14. Literate workers	211	95.05	7	3.15	4	1.80
15. Illiterate workers	239	94.84	7	2.78	6	2.38
16. Joint family workers	319	91.93	15	4.32	13	3.75
17. Nuclear family workers	111	87.40	12	9.45	4	3.15
18. Rural workers	143	93.46	6	3.92	4	2.61
19. Urban workers	307	95.64	8	2.49	6	1.87
20. Hindu workers	136	93.15	6	4.11	4	2.74
21. Muslim workers	314	95.73	8	2.44	6	1.83
22. Workers in income group 0–3000	338	94.41	10	2.79	10	2.79
23. Workers in income group 3000 and above	112	96.55	4	3.45	0	0.00
24. Workers belonging to Labour Class	369	95.10	12	3.09	7	1.80
25. Workers belonging to Management Class	78	93.98	2	2.41	3	3.61

Unit-wise analysis reveals that 93.34% workers hailing from assembly units; 96.55% from die-making units; 100% from furnace and dispatch units; 94.65% from key making unit; 94.74% from nickle polish units; 93.44% from Office; 93.24% from packing units; 94.44% from press units; 95.36% salaried workers and 94.14% contractual workers; 94.77% male workers and 100% female workers; 95.05% literate workers and 94.84% illiterate workers; 91.93% workers from joint family system and 87.40% representing nuclear family system; 93.46% rural workers and 95.64% urban workers; 93.15% Hindu workers and 95.73% Muslim workers; 94.41% workers receiving salary up to Rs. 3000/- and 96.55% workers receiving salary of more than 3000/- per month; 95.10% workers hailing from Labour class and 93.98% workers hailing from management group all expressed their agreement with the statement.

It can, thus, be concluded that the respondents representing different units of the factory as well as majority of the total subjects (94.94%) expressed their agreement with the statement that "they are keenly interested to supplement their earnings by taking up some part time jobs or economic activities."

Table 4.32 reveals that majority of workers (90.72%) representing different units of 55 factories agreed to raise their voice and fight for implementation of labour laws pertaining to children so that they may be saved from exploitations; while 5.70% have exhibited indifference, only 3.59% have expressed their disagreement with the statement.

Unit-wise analysis reveals that 92.45% workers hailing from assembly units; 89.66% from die making units; 100% from furnace and dispatch units; 92.86% from key-making units; 89.47% from nickle polish units; 90.16% from Office; 85.14% from packing units; 91.67% from press units; 89.03% salaried workers and 92.05% contractual workers; 90.63% male workers and 92.86% female workers; 91.89% literate and 89.68% illiterate workers; 89.91% workers from joint family system and 89.76% representing nuclear

TABLE 4.32 ECONOMIC ASPIRATION (2): TO RAISE VOICE AND FIGHT FOR THE IMPLEMENTATION OF LABOUR LAWS PERTAINING TO CHILDREN FOR SAVING THEM FROM EXPLOITATION

	RESPONDENTS CATEGORY	*YES*	*%*	*INDIFF.*	*%*	*NO*	*%*
1.	Workers of different industrial units belonging to same factory.	430	90.72	27	5.70	17	3.59
2.	Workers of different factories belonging to assembly units.	49	92.45	3	5.66	1	1.89
3.	Workers of different factories belonging to Die-making units.	52	89.66	4	6.90	2	3.45
4.	Workers of different factories belonging to furnace & dispatch units.	42	100.00	0	0.00	0	0.00
5.	Workers of different factories belong to Key-making units.	52	92.86	3	3.36	1	1.79
6.	Workers of different factories belonging to nickle polish units.	51	89.47	3	5.26	3	5.26
7.	Workers of different factors belonging to Office.	55	90.16	5	6.56	2	3.28
8.	Workers of different factories belonging to packing units.	63	85.14	5	6.76	6	8.11
9.	Workers of different factories belonging to press units.	66	9167	5	6.94	1	1.39
10.	Salaried workers.	211	89.03	17	7.17	9	3.80

(Contd.)

11. Contractual workers	220	92.05	10	4.18	9	3.77
12. Male workers	416	90.63	27	5.88	16	3.49
13. Female workers	13	92.86	0	0.00	1	7.14
14. Literate workers	204	91.89	11	4.95	7	3.15
15. Illiterate workers	226	89.68	16	6.35	10	3.97
16. Joint family workers	312	89.91	11	3.17	24	6.92
17. Nuclear family workers	114	89.76	7	5.51	6	4.72
18. Rural workers	138	90.20	6	3.92	9	5.88
19. Urban workers	292	90.97	21	6.54	8	2.49
20. Hindu workers	129	88.36	10	6.85	7	4.79
21. Muslim workers	301	91.77	17	5.18	10	3.05
22. Workers in income group 0–3000	324	90.50	18	5.03	16	4.47
23. Workers in income group 3000 and above	106	91.38	9	7.76	1	0.86
24. Workers belonging to Labour Class	349	989.95	24	6.19	15	3.87
25. Workers belonging to Management Class	78	93.98	3	3.61	2	2.41

family system; 90.20% rural 90.97% urban workers; 88.36% Hindu workers and 91.77% Muslim workers 90.50% workers receiving salary up to Rs. 3000/- and 91.38% workers receiving salary of more than 3000/; 89.95% workers hailing from Labour class and 93.98% workers hailing from management group all expressed their agreement with the statement.

It can, thus, be concluded that the respondents representing different units of the factory as well as majority of the total subjects (90.72%) expressed their agreement "to raise their voice and fight for the implementation of labour laws pertaining to children so that they may be saved from exploitations".

Table 4.33 reveals that majority of the workers (89.87%) representing different units of 55 factories agreed to take up some extra economic activities which may yield monetary returns in order to fulfill their socio-cultural commitments, while 3.80% exhibited indifference, only 6.33% have expressed their disagreement with it.

Unit-wise analysis reveal that 90.57% workers hailing from assembly units; 93.10% from die-making units; 100% from furnace and dispatch units; 91.07% from key-making units; 85.96% from Nickle polish units; 95.08% from Office; 90.54% from packing units; 79.17% from press units;

92.83% salaried workers and 87.03% contractual workers; 89.76% male workers and 92.86% female workers; 95.05% literate workers and 85.32% illiterate workers; 89.91workers from joint family system and 89.76% representing nuclear family system; 83.01% rural workers and 93.15% urban workers; 89.04% Hindu workers and 90.24% Muslim workers 88.27% workers receiving salary up to Rs. 3000/ and 94.83% workers receiving salary of more than 3000/-per month 88.66% workers hailing from Labour class and 95.18% workers hailing from management group all expressed their agreement with the statement.

It can, thus, be concluded that respondents representing different units of the factory as well as majority of the total subjects (89.87%)

TABLE 4.33 ECONOMIC ASPIRATION: (3) TO TAKE UP SOME EXTRA ECONOMIC ACTIVITIES YIELDING MONETARY RETURNS FOR FULFILLMENTS OF SOCIO-CULTURAL COMMITMENTS

	RESPONDENTS CATEGORY	*YES*	*%*	*INDIFF.*	*%*	*NO*	*%*
1.	Workers of different industrial units belonging to same factory.	426	89.87	18	3.80	30	6.33
2.	Workers of different factories belonging to assembly units.	48	90.57	2	3.77	3	5.66
3.	Workers of different factories belonging to Die-making units.	54	93.10	1	1.72	3	5.17
4.	Workers of different factories belonging to furnace & dispatch units.	42	100.00	0	0.00	1	0.00
5.	Workers of different factories belonging to key-making units.	51	91.07	2	3.57	3	5.36
6.	Workers of different factories belonging to nickle polish units.	49	85.96	3	5.26	5	8.77
7.	Workers of different factories belonging to Office.	58	95.08	0	0.00	3	4.92
8.	Workers of different factories belonging to packing units.	67	90.54	1	1.35	6	8.11
9.	Workers of different factories belonging to press units.	57	79.17	9	12.50	6	8.33
10.	Salaried workers.	220	92.83	7	2.95	10	4.22

11. Contractual workers	208	87.03	11	4.60	20	8.37
12. Male workers	412	89.76	18	3.92	29	6.32
13. Female workers	13	92.86	0	0.00	1	7.14
14. Literate workers	211	95.05	2	0.90	9	4.05
15. Illiterate workers	215	85.32	16	6.35	21	8.33
16. Joint family workers	312	89.91	11	3.17	24	6.92
17. Nuclear family workers	114	88.76	7	5.51	6	4.72
18. Rural workers	127	83.01	11	7.19	15	9.80
19. Urban workers	299	93.15	7	2.18	15	4.67
20. Hindu workers	130	89.04	9	6.16	7	4.79
21. Muslim workers	296	90.24	9	2.74	23	7.01
22. Workers in income group 0–3000	316	88.27	16	7.26	26	4.47
23. Workers in income group of 3000 and above	110	94.83	5	1.72	4	3.45
24. Workers belonging to Labour Class	344	88.66	18	4.64	26	6.70
25. Workers belonging to Management Class	799	95.18	0	0	4	4.82

expressed their agreement "to take up some extra economic activities which may yield monetary returns in order to fulfill their committed socio-cultural commitments."

Table 4.34 reveals that only 44.90% workers representing different units of 55 factories have agreed with the statement to work and educate members of the community to treat their sons and daughters on equal basis, keeping in view the modern trends and changing laws of the land, while 12.24% have exhibited indifference, 41.77% expressed their disagreement with it.

Unit-wise analysis reveals that 45.28% workers hailing from assembly units; 4138% from die-making units; 39.53% from furnace and dispatch units; 48.21% from key-making units; 52.63% from nickle polish unit; 44.66% from Office, 47.30% from packing units; 47.22% from press units expressed their agreement with the statement; while 41.51% workers from assembly units; 44.83% from die-making units; 53.49% from furnace and dispatch units; 37.50% from key-making units; 40.35% from Nickle polish units; 47.54% from Office; 36.49% from packing units and 37.50% from press units have expressed their disagreement with the statement. Again, 42.62% salaried workers and 40.21% contractual workers also expressed their agreement with the same while 43.04% salaried workers and 40.17% contractual workers expressed their disagreement with the statement. While 41.44% literate and 50% illiterate workers are also in support of the statement whereas 48.20% literate workers and 36.11% illiterate workers have expressed their disagreement with the statement. 44.38% workers from joint family system and 50.39% representing nuclear family system with the statement, 42.94% workers from joint family system and 38.58% from nuclear family system expressed their disagreement with the statement. While 48.37% rural workers and 44.86% urban workers exhibited their support or the statement, 33.99% rural workers and 45.48% urban workers expressed their disagreement with the statement. While 45.21% Hindu workers and 46.34% Muslim workers expressed their agreement with the statement, 38.36% Hindu and 43.29% Muslim workers expressed their disagreement with the statement. While 46.65% workers receiving salary up to Rs. 3000/- and 43.97% workers receiving salary of more than 3000/- per month exhibited their agreement with the statement

TABLE 4.34 ECONOMIC ASPIRATION (4) TO WORK AND EDUCATE THE COMMUNITY MEMBERS FOR TREATING THEIR SONS AND DAUGHTERS EQUAL, KEEPING IN VIEW THE MODERN TRENDS AND CHANGING LAWS OF THE LAND

	RESPONDENTS CATEGORY	*YES*	*%*	*INDIFF.*	*%*	*NO*	*%*
1.	Workers of different industrial units belonging to same factory.	218	45.99	48	12.24	198	41.77
2.	Workers of different factories belonging to assembly units.	24	4528	7	13.21	22	41.51
3.	Workers of different factories belonging to Die-making units.	24	41.38	8	13.79	26	44.83
4.	Workers of different factories belonging to furnace & dispatch units.	17	39.53	3	6.98	23	53.49
5.	Workers of different factories belonging to Key-making units.	27	48.21	8	14.29	21	37.50
6.	Workers of different factories belonging to nickle polish units.	30	52.63	4	7.02	23	40.35
7.	Workers of different factories belonging to Office.	27	44.26	5	8.20	29	47.54
8.	Workers of different factories belonging to packing units.	35	478.30	12	16.22	27	36.49
9.	Workers of different factories belonging to press units.	34	47.22	11	15.28	27	37.50
10.	Salaried workers.	101	42.62	34	14.35	102	43.04

(Contd.)

11. Contractual workers	120	50.21	23	9.62	96	40.17
12. Male workers	211	45.97	57	12.42	191	41.61
13. Female workers	7	50.00	1	7.14	6	42.86
14. Literate workers	92	41.44	23	10.36	107	48.20
15. Illiterate workers	126	50.00	35	13.89	91	36.11
16. Joint family workers	154	44.38	44	12.68	149	42.94
17. Nuclear family workers	64	50.39	14	11.02	49	38.58
18. Rural workers	74	48.37	27	17.65	52	3.99
19. Urban workers	144	44.86	31	9.66	146	45.48
20. Hindu workers	66	45.21	24	16.44	56	38.36
21. Muslim workers	152	46.34	34	10.37	142	43.29
22. Workers in income group 0–3000	167	46.65	49	13.69	142	39.66
23. Workers in income groups 3000 and above	51	43.97	9	7.76	56	48.28
24. Workers belonging to Labour Class	176	45.36	52	13.40	160	41.24
25. Workers belonging to Management Class	42	50.60	6	7.23	35	42.17

39.66% workers receiving salary up to Rs. 3000/-and 48.28% workers receiving salary of more than 3000/-per month expressed their agreement with the statement. While just 45.36% workers hailing from Labour class exhibited their agreement a bigger numbers of 50.50% workers from management class expressed their agreement with the statement.

It can, thus, be concluded that less than half of the respondents (45.99%) representing different units of the factories expressed their agreement with the statement. The trend indicates that the respondents want to work and educate the community members for treating their sons and daughters on equal terms, keeping in view the trends and changing laws of the land. While only 12.24% of the respondents exhibited their indifference, 41.77% of the respondents disagreed with the statement. Similar trend was also noticeable among the respondents representing different units of the factory. It can, thus, be inferred that majority of the respondents were in favour of the statement.

Table 4.35 reveal that majority of workers (86.29%) representing different units of 55 factories agreed to educate and enlighten the ignorant members of the community to encourage women also to take part in economic activities along with their male counterparts in order to achieve greater economic stability and prosperity, while 9.28% exhibited their indifference only 4.43% have expressed their disagreement with the statement.

Unit-wise analysis reveals that 92.45% workers hailing from assembly units; 84.48% from die-making units; 93.02% from furnace and dispatch units; 89.29% from key-making unit 91.23% from Nickle polish unit 85.25% from office; 78.38% from packing units; 81.94% from press units; 82.70% salaried workers and 89.96% contractual workers; 86.06% male workers and 92.86% female workers; 90.54% literate workers and 82.54% illiterate workers; 87.61% workers from joint family system and 82.68% representing nuclear family system; 80.39% rural workers and 89.10% urban workers; 83.56% Hindu workers and 87.54% Muslim workers; 85.47% workers receiving salary up to Rs. 3000/- and 88.79% workers receiving salary more

TABLE 4.35 ECONOMIC ASPIRATION: (5) TO EDUCATE AND ENLIGHTEN THE IGNORANT MEMBERS OF THE COMMUNITY TO ENCOURAGE WOMEN ALSO FOR TAKING PART IN ECONOMIC ACTIVITIES ALONGWITH THEIR MALE COUNTERPARTS FOR ACHIEVING GREATER ECONOMIC STABILITY AND PROSPERITY

	RESPONDENTS CATEGORY	*YES*	*%*	*INDIFF.*	*%*	*NO*	*%*
1.	Workers of different industrial units belonging to same factory.	409	86.29	44	9.28	21	4.49
2.	Workers of different factories belonging to assembly units.	49	92.45	3	5.66	1	1.89
3.	Workers of different factories belonging to Die-making units.	49	84.48	7	12.07	2	3.45
4.	Workers of different factories belonging to furnace & dispatch units.	40	93.02	2	4.65	1	2.33
5.	Workers of different factories belonging to key-making units.	50	89.29	3	5.36	3	5.36
6.	Workers of different factories belonging to nickle polish units.	52	91.23	4	7.02	1	1.75
7.	Workers of different factories belonging to Office	52	85.25	8	13.11	1	1.64
8.	Workers of different factories belonging to packing units.	58	78.38	10	13.51	6	8.11
9.	Workers of different factories belonging to press units.	59	81.94	7	9.72	6	8.33
10.	Salaried workers.	196	82.70	28	11.81	13	5.49

(Contd.)

11. Contractual workers	215	89.96	15	6.28	9	3.77
12. Male workers	395	86.06	44	9.59	20	4.36
13. Female workers	13	92.86	0	0.00	1	7.14
14. Literate workers	201	90.54	14	6.31	7	3.15
15. Illiterate workers	208	82.54	30	11.90	14	5.56
16. Joint family workers	304	87.61	29	8.36	14	4.03
17. Nuclear family workers	105	82.68	15	11.81	7	5.51
18. Rural workers	123	80.39	23	15.03	7	4.58
19. Urban workers	286	89.10	21	6.54	14	4.36
20. Hindu workers	122	83.56	13	8.90	11	7.53
21. Muslim workers	287	87.50	31	9.45	10	3.05
22. Workers in income group 0–3000	306	85.47	35	9.78	17	4.75
23. Workers in income group of 3000 and above	103	88.79	9	7.76	4	3.45
24. Workers belonging to Labour Class	332	85.57	37	9.54	19	4.90
25. Workers belonging to Management Class	74	89.16	7	8.43	2	2.41

than 3000/-per month; and 85.57% workers hailing from Labour class exhibited their agreement with the statement.

It can, thus, be concluded that respondents representing different units of the factory as well as majority of the total subjects (86.29%) have expressed their agreement with the statement that "to educate and enlighten the ignorant members of the community to encourage women also to take part in economic activities along with their male counterparts in order to achieve greater economic stability and prosperity".

Table 4.36 reveal that majority of the workers (85.02%) representing different units of 55 factories agreed to educate the economically weaker sections of the community to fight against any kind of exploitation and start some extra economic activities initially on a small scale, for controlling exploitation. While 10.34% respondents exhibited their indifference, only 4.64% subjects expressed their disagreement with the statement.

Unit-wise analysis reveals that 93.65% workers hailing from assembly units; 87.93% hailing from die-making units; 88.37% representing from furnace and dispatch units; 85.71% from key-making units; 85.96% from nickle polish units; 88.52% hailing from Office; 78.38% from packing units; 77.78% from press units; 77.78% salaried workers; 74.14% contractual workers; 85.19% male workers; 78.57% female workers; have also expressed their agreement with the same. 84.68% literate and 85.32% illiterate workers; 85.30% workers hailing from joint family system and 84.25% representing nuclear family system; 79.74% rural and 86.20% urban workers; 79.45% Hindu workers and 87.50% Muslim workers; 85.47% workers receiving salary up to Rs. 3000 and 83.62% workers receiving salary of more than 3000/-per month 84.02% workers hailing from Labour class and 89.16% workers hailing from management group expressed their agreement with the statement.

It can, thus, be concluded that the respondents representing different units of the factories as well as majority of the total subjects (88.02%) expressed their agreement with the statement that "to

TABLE 4.36 ECONOMIC ASPIRATION: (6) TO EDUCATE ECONOMICALLY WEAKER SECTIONS OF THE COMMUNITY TO FIGHT AGAINST ANY KIND OF EXPLOITATION AND START SOME EXTRA ECONOMIC ACTIVITIES INITIALLY ON A SMALL SCALE FOR CONTROLLING THE EXPLOITATION

	RESPONDENTS CATEGORY	*YES*	*%*	*INDIFF.*	*%*	*NO*	*%*
1.	Workers of different industrial units belonging to same factory.	403	85.02	49	10.34	22	4.64
2.	Workers of different factories belonging to assembly units.	59	93.65	4	6.35	0	0.00
3.	Workers of different factories belonging to die-making units.	51	87.93	4	6.90	3	5.17
4.	Workers of different factories belonging to furnace & dispatch units.	38	88.37	4	9.30	1	2.33
5.	Workers of different factories belonging to key-making units.	48	85.71	5	8.93	3	5.36
6.	Workers of different factories belonging to Nickle polish units.	49	85.96	5	8.77	3	5.26
7.	Workers of different factories belonging to Office.	54	88.52	3	4.92	4	6.56
8.	Workers of different factories belonging to packing units.	58	78.38	11	14.86	5	6.76
9.	Workers of different factories belonging to press units.	56	77.78	13	18.06	3	4.17
10.	Salaried workers.	195	74.14	28	10.65	40	15.21

(Contd.)

11. Contractual workers	210	87.87	21	8.79	8	3.35
12. Male workers	391	85.19	47	10.24	21	4.58
13. Female workers	11	78.57	2	14.29	1	7.14
14. Literate workers	188	84.68	24	10.81	10	4.50
15. Illiterate workers	215	85.32	25	9.92	12	4.76
16. Joint family workers	296	85.30	35	10.09	16	4.61
17. Nuclear family workers	107	84.25	14	11.02	6	4.72
18. Rural workers	122	79.74	22	14.38	9	5.88
19. Urban workers	281	86.20	27	8.28	18	5.52
20. Hindu workers	116	79.45	21	14.38	9	6.16
21. Muslim workers	287	87.50	28	8.54	13	3.96
22. Workers in income group 0–3000	306	85.47	36	10.06	16	4.47
23. Workers in income group of 3000 and above	97	83.62	13	11.21	6	5.17
24. Workers belonging to Labour Class	326	84.02	45	11.60	17	4.38
25. Workers belonging to Management Class	74	89.16	4	4.82	5	6.02

educate the economically weaker section of the community to fight against any kind of exploitation and start some extra economic activities, initially on a small scale, for controlling the exploitation."

Table 4.37 reveals that majority of the workers 73.63% representing different units of 55 factories agreed to educate the unemployed educated youths that instead of using unethical and illegal means of earning money, they should avail loan facilities as offered by the government to start independent economic activity. While 6.12% exhibited their indifference, only 20.25% expressed their disagreement with the statement.

Unit-wise analysis reveals that 73.58% workers hailing from assembly units; 76.47% from the die-making units; 83.72% from furnace and dispatch units; 69.64% from key-making units; 70.18% from nickle polish units; 78.69% from Office; 74.32% from packing units; 69.44% from press units; 78.06% salaried workers and 69.46% contractual workers; 73.86% male workers and 64.29% female workers; 78.38% literate workers and 69.44% illiterate workers; 74.64% workers from joint family system and 70.87% representing nuclear family system; 74.51% rural workers and 73.21% urban workers; 73.97% Hindu workers and 73.48% Muslim workers; 72.91% workers receiving salary up to Rs. 3000/-and 75.86% workers receiving salary of more than 3000/- per month; 73.45% workers hailing from Labour class and 73.40% workers hailing from management group all expressed their agreement with the statement.

It can, thus, be concluded that the respondents representing different units of the factory as well as majority of the total subjects (73.63%) expressed their"to educate the unemployed educated youths instead of using unethical & illegal means of earning money, they should avail loan facilities as offered by the government to start independent economic activity".

Table 4.38 reveals that majority of workers (93.67%) representing different units of 55 factories agreed to join some judicious and non-political organizations which may prove a useful instrument in setling strikes and in maintaining communal harmony at the time of riot.

TABLE 4.37 ECONOMIC ASPIRATION: (7) TO EDUCATE UNEMPLOYED EDUCATED YOUTHS THAT INSTEAD OF USING UNETHICAL & ILLEGAL MEANS OF EARNING MONEY, THEY SHOULD AVAIL LOAN FACILITIES AS OFFERED BY THE GOVERNMENT TO START INDEPENDENT ECONOMIC ACTIVITY

	RESPONDENTS CATEGORY	*YES*	*%*	*INDIFF.*	*%*	*NO*	*%*
1.	Workers of different industrial units belonging to same factory.	349	73.63	29	6.12	96	20.25
2.	Workers of different factories belonging to assembly units.	39	73.58	1	1.89	13	24.53
3.	Workers of different factories belonging to die-making units.	52	76.47	4	5.88	12	17.65
4.	Workers of different factories belonging to furnace & dispatch units.	36	83.72	0	0.00	7	16.28
5.	Workers of different factories belonging to key-making unit.	39	69.64	5	8.93	12	21.43
6.	Workers of different factories belonging to nickle polish units.	40	70.18	4	7.02	13	22.81
7.	Workers of different factories belonging to Office	48	78.69	2	3.28	11	18.03
8.	Workers of different factories belonging to packing units.	55	74.32	7	9.46	12	16.22
9.	Workers of different factories belonging to press units.	50	69.44	6	8.33	16	22.22
10.	Salaried workers.	185	78.06	11	4.64	41	17.30

11. Contractual workers	166	69.46	17	7.11	56	23.43
12. Male workers	339	73.86	28	6.10	92	20.04
13. Female workers	9	64.29	1	7.14	4	28.57
14. Literate workers	174	78.38	6	2.70	42	18.92
15. Illiterate workers	175	69.44	23	9.13	54	21.43
16. Joint family workers	259	74.64	18	5.19	70	20.17
17. Nuclear family workers	90	70.87	11	8.66	26	20.47
18. Rural workers	114	74.51	13	8.50	26	16.99
19. Urban workers	235	73.21	16	4.98	70	21.81
20. Hindu workers	108	73.97	10	6.85	28	19.18
21. Muslim workers	241	73.48	19	5.79	68	20.73
22. Workers in income group 0–3000	261	72.91	21	5.87	76	21.23
23. Workers in income group of 3000 and above	88	75.86	8	6.90	20	17.24
24. Workers belonging to Labour Class	285	73.45	27	6.96	76	19.59
25. Workers belonging to Management Class	61	73.40	2	2.41	20	24.10

While 4.85% exhibited their indifference, only 1.48% expressed their disagreement with the statement.

Unit-wise analysis reveals that 98.11% workers from assembly units; 93.10% from die-making units; 100% from furnace and dispatch units; 94.64% from key-making units; 91.23% from nickle polish units; 95.08% from Office; 89.19% from packing units; 91.67% from press units; 91.98% salaried workers and 95.40% contractual workers; 93.68% male workers and 92.86% female workers; 95.95% literate and 91.67% illiterate workers; 94.24% workers from joint family system and 92.13% representing nuclear family system; 90.85% rural and 95.02% urban workers; 92.47% Hindu workers and 94.21% Muslim workers; 93.30% workers receiving salary up to Rs.3000/- and 94.83% workers receiving salary of more than 3000/- per month; 93.04% workers hailing from Labour class have also exhibited their agreement with the statement. 96.39% workers hailing from management group all expressed their agreement with the statement.

It can, thus, be concluded that the respondents representing different units of the factory as well as majority of the total subjects (93.67%) expressed their agreed "to join some judicious and nonpolitical organizations, which may prove useful instrument in setling strikes and in maintaining communal harmony at the time of riot".

Table 4.39 reveals that majority of the workers (89.24%) representing different units of 55 factories agreed to educate the deserving youths of the community to avail the provisions and benefits of governments sponsored employment programmes and schemes for economic upliftment. While 8.02% exhibited their indifference and only 2.74% disagreed with the statement.

Unit wise analysis reveals that 94.34% workers hailing from assembly units; 87.93% from die-making units; 93.02% from furnace and dispatch units; 89.29% from key-making units; 85.96% from nickle polish units; 91.80% from Office; 83.78% from packing unit and 90.28% from press units; 86.50% salaried workers and 92.47% contractual workers; 89.11% male workers and 92.86% female

TABLE 4.38 ECONOMIC ASPIRATION (8) TO JOIN SOME JUDICIOUS AND NON-POLITICAL ORGANIZATIONS WHICH MAY PROVE USEFUL INSTRUMENT IN SETTLING STRIKES AND IN MAINTAINING COMMUNAL HARMONY AT THE TIME OF RIOT

	RESPONDENTS CATEGORY	*YES*	*%*	*INDIFF.*	*%*	*NO*	*%*
1.	Workers of different industrial units belonging to same factory.	444	93.67	23	4.85	7	1.48
2.	Workers of different factories belonging to assembly units.	52	98.11	0	0.00	1	1.89
3.	Workers of different factories belonging to die-making units.	54	93.10	4	6.90	0	0.00
4.	Workers of different factories belonging to furnace & dispatch units.	43	100.00	0	0.00	0	0.00
5.	Workers of different factories belonging to key-making units.	53	94.64	2	3.57	1	1.79
6.	Workers of different factories belonging to nickle polish units.	52	91.23	4	7.02	1	1.75
7.	Workers of different factories belonging to Office.	58	95.08	2	3.28	1	1.64
8.	Workers of different factories belonging to packing units.	64	89.19	7	9.46	1	1.35
9.	Workers of different factories belonging to press units.	66	91.67	4	5.56	2	2.78
10.	Salaried workers.	218	91.98	16	6.75	3	1.27

(*Contd.*)

11.	Contractual workers	228	95.40	7	2.93	4	1.67
12.	Male workers	430	93.68	22	4.79	7	1.53
13.	Female workers	13	92.86	1	7.14	0	0.00
14.	Literate workers	213	95.95	7	3.15	2	0.90
15.	Illiterate workers	231	91.67	16	6.35	5	1.98
16.	Joint family workers	327	94.24	13	3.75	7	2.02
17.	Nuclear family workers	117	92.13	10	7.87	0	0.00
18.	Rural workers	139	90.85	11	7.19	3	1.96
19.	Urban workers	305	95.02	12	3.74	4	1.25
20.	Hindu workers	135	92.47	8	5.48	3	2.05
21.	Muslim workers	309	94.21	15	4.57	4	1.22
22.	Workers in income group 0–3000	334	93.30	18	5.03	6	1.68
23.	Workers in income group of 3000 and above	110	94.83	5	4.31	1	0.86
24.	Workers belonging to Labour Class	361	93.04	21	5.41	6	1.55
25.	Workers belonging to Management Class	80	96.39	2	2.41	1	1.20

TABLE 4.39 ECONOMIC ASPIRATION: (9) TO EDUCATE THE DESERVING YOUTHS OF THE COMMUNITY TO AVAIL PROVISIONS AND BENEFITS OF SCHEMES FOR ECONOMIC UPLIFTMENT

	RESPONDENTS CATEGORY	*YES*	*%*	*INDIFF.*	*%*	*NO*	*%*
1.	Workers of different industrial units belonging to same factory.	423	89.24	38	8.02	13	2.74
2.	Workers of different factories belonging to assembly units.	50	94.34	2	3.77	1	1.89
3.	Workers of different factories belonging to die-making units.	51	87.93	6	10.34	1	1.72
4.	Workers of different factories belonging to furnace & dispatch units.	40	93.02	1	2.33	2	4.65
5.	Workers of different factories belonging to key-making units.	50	89.29	6	10.71	0	0.00
6.	Workers of different factories belonging to nickle polish units.	49	85.96	7	12.28	1	[illegible]
7.	Workers of different factories belonging to Office.	56	91.80	2	3.28	[illegible]	[illegible]
8.	Workers of different factories belonging to packing units.	62	83.78	10	13.51	2	[illegible]
9.	Workers of different factories belonging to press units.	65	90.28	4	5.56	3	4.17
10.	Salaried workers.	205	86.50	25	10.55	7	2.95

(Contd.)

11. Contractual workers	221	92.47	12	5.02	6	2.51
12. Male workers	409	89.11	37	8.06	13	2.83
13. Female workers	13	92.86	1	7.14	0	0.00
14. Literate workers	205	92.34	10	5.50	7	3.15
15. Illiterate workers	218	86.51	28	11.11	6	2.38
16. Joint family workers	319	91.93	21	6.05	7	2.02
17. Nuclear family workers	104	81.89	17	13.39	6	4.72
18. Rural workers	132	86.27	19	12.42	2	1.31
19. Urban workers	291	90.65	19	5.92	11	3.43
20. Hindu workers	129	88.36	15	10.27	2	1.37
21. Muslim workers	294	89.63	23	7.01	11	3.35
22. Workers in income group 0– 000	320	89.39	29	8.10	9	2.51
23. Workers in income group of 3000 and above	103	88.79	9	7.76	4	3.45
24. Workers belonging to Labour Class	342	88.14	36	9.28	10	2.58
25. Workers belonging to Management Class	78	93.96	2	2.41	3	3.61

workers; 92.34% literate and 86.51% illiterate workers; 91.93% workers from joint family system and 81.89% representing nuclear family system; rural workers and 90.65% urban workers; 88.36% Hindu workers and 89.63% Muslim workers; 89.39% workers receiving salary up to Rs. 3000/- and 88.79% workers receiving salary of more than 3000/-per month; 88.14% workers hailing from Labour class and 93.96% workers from Muslim class agreed with the statement.

It can, thus, be concluded that the respondents representing different units of the factory as well as majority of the total subjects (89.24%) agreed "to educate the deserving youths of the community to avail the provisions and benefits of government-sponsored employment programmes and schemes for economic upliftment".

Table 4.40 reveals that majority of the workers (83.33%) representing different units of 55 factories agreed to raise voice through some social organization or agency for pressurizing the government and welfare bodies of the community for providing reading material on subsidized rates in general and scholarships in particular for the economically weaker sections. While 5.91% exhibited their indifference, only 10.76% expressed disagreement with the statement.

Unit-wise analysis reveals that 86.79% workers hailing from assembly units; 82.76% from the making units; 90.70% from furnace and dispatch units 82.14% from key-making units; 78.95% from nickle polish units; 83.33% from Office; 77.03% from packing units; 86.11% from press units; 78.48% salaried workers and 88.70% contractual workers; 83.22% male workers and 85.71% female workers; 87.39% literate workers and 79.76% illiterate workers; 86.17% workers from joint family system and 75.59% representing nuclear family system; 78.43% rural and 85.67% urban workers; 83.56% Hindu workers and 83.23% Muslim workers; 83.80% workers receiving salary up to Rs. 3000/-and 81.90% workers receiving salary of more than 3000/-per month; 82.99% workers hailing from Labour

TABLE 4.40 ECONOMIC ASPIRATION: (10) TO RAISE VOICE THROUGH SOME GOVERNMENT AND WELFARE BODIES OF THE COMMUNITY FOR PROVIDING READING MATERIAL ON SUBSIDIZED RATES IN GENERAL AND SCHOLARSHIPS IN PARTICULAR FOR THE ECONOMICALLY WREAKERS SECTIONS

	RESPONDENTS CATEGORY	*YES*	*%*	*INDIFF.*	*%*	*NO*	*%*
1.	Workers of different industrial units belonging to same factory.	395	83.33	28	5.91	51	10.76
2.	Workers of different factories belonging to assembly units.	46	86.79	1	1.89	6	11.32
3.	Workers of different factories belonging to die-making units.	48	82.76	4	6.90	6	10.34
4.	Workers of different factories belonging to furnace & dispatch units.	39	90.70	1	2.33	3	6.98
5.	Workers of different factories belonging to key-making units.	46	82.14	4	7.14	6	10.71
6.	Workers of different factories belonging to nickle polish units.	45	78.95	6	10.53	6	10.53
7.	Workers of different factories belonging to Office	57	86.36	2	3.03	7	10.61
8.	Workers of different factories belonging to packing units.	57	77.03	7	9.46	10	13.51
9.	Workers of different factories belonging to press units.	62	86.11	3	4.17	7	9.72
10.	Salaried workers.	186	78.48	19	8.02	32	13.50

(Contd.)

11. Contractual workers	212	88.70	8	3.35	19	7.95
12. Male workers	382	83.22	27	5.88	50	10.89
13. Female workers	12	85.71	1	7.14	1	7.14
14. Literate workers	194	87.39	7	3.15	21	9.46
15. Illiterate workers	201	79.76	21	8.33	30	11.90
16. Joint family workers	299	86.17	17	4.90	31	8.93
17. Nuclear family workers	96	75.59	11	8.66	20	15.75
18. Rural workers	120	78.43	16	10.46	17	11.11
19. Urban workers	275	85.67	12	3.74	34	10.59
20. Hindu workers	122	83.56	13	8.90	11	7.53
21. Muslim workers	273	83.23	40	12.20	15	4.47
22. Workers in income group 0–3000	300	83.80	22	6.15	36	10.06
23. Workers in income group of 3000 and above	95	81.90	6	5.17	15	12.93
24. Workers belonging to Labour Class	322	82.99	26	6.70	40	10.31
25. Workers belonging to Management Class	70	84.34	2	2.41	11	13.25

class and 84.34% workers from management flass all expressed their agreement with the statement.

It can, thus, be concluded that respondents representing different units of the factory as well as majority of the total subjects (83.33) agreed "to raise voice through some social organization or agency for pressurizing the government and welfare bodies of the community for providing reading material on subsidized rates in general and scholarships in particular for the economically weaker sections".

Table 4.41 reveals that majority of the workers (81.43%) representing different units of 55 factories agreed that boy's parents at the time of marriage directly or indirectly demand gifts in cash and kind from parents of girls which is not permissible in religion and law. While 1.48% exhibited their indifference, only 17.09% have expressed their disagreement with the statement.

Unit-wise analysis reveals that 83.02% workers hailing from assembly units; 79.31% from die-making units; 76.74% from furnace and dispatch units; 83.93% from key-making units; 97.87% from nickle polish units; 78.69% from Office; 83.56% from packing units; 84.72% from press units; 81.43% salaried workers and 81.93% contractual workers; 81.56% male workers and 85.71% female workers; 81.45% literate workers and 81.75% illiterate workers; 80.64% workers from joint family system and 84.25% representing nuclear family system; 85.62% rural workers and 79.69% urban workers; 89.04% Hindu workers and 78.29% Muslim workers; 80.39% workers receiving salary up to Rs. 300/- and 85.34% workers receiving salary of more than 3000/-per month;82.69% workers hailing from Labour class and 79.52% workers from management class agreed with the statement.

It can, thus, be concluded that the respondents representing different units of the factory as well as majority of the total subjects (81.43%) expressed their agreement with the statement that, "boy's parents at the time of marriage directly or indirectly demand gifts in cash and kind from parents of girls, which is not permissible in the religion and law."

TABLE 4.41 SOCIAL PERCEPTION: BOY'S PARENTS AT THE TIME OF MARRIAGE DIRECTLY OR INDIRECTLY DEMAND GIFT IN CASH AND KIND FROM PARENTS OF GIRLS WHICH IS NOT PERMISSIBLE IN RELIGION AND LAW

	RESPONDENTS CATEGORY	*YES*	*%*	*INDIFF.*	*%*	*NO*	*%*
1.	Workers of different industrial units belonging to same factory.	386	81.43	7	1.48	81	17.09
2.	Workers of different factories belonging to assembly units.	44	83.02	1	1.89	8	15.09
3.	Workers of different factories belonging to die-making units.	46	79.31	1	1.72	11	18.97
4.	Workers of different factories belonging to furnace & dispatch units.	33	76.74	0	0.00	10	23.26
5.	Workers of different factories belonging to key-making units.	47	83.93	0	0.00	9	16.07
6.	Workers of different factories belonging to nickle polish units.	46	97.87	1	2.13	0	0.00
7.	Workers of different factories belonging to Office.	48	78.69	0	0.00	13	21.31
8.	Workers of different factories belonging to packing units.	61	83.56	2	2.74	10	13.70
9.	Workers of different factories belonging to press units.	61	84.72	1	1.39	10	13.89
10.	Salaried workers.	193	81.43	4	1.69	40	16.88

(Contd.)

11.	Contractual workers	195	81.93	2	0.84	41	17.23
12.	Male workers	376	81.56	6	1.30	79	17.14
13.	Female workers	12	85.71	0	0.00	2	14.29
14.	Literate workers	180	81.45	2	0.90	39	17.65
15.	Illiterate workers	206	81.75	4	1.59	42	16.67
16.	Joint family workers	279	80.64	3	0.87	64	18.50
17.	Nuclear family workers	107	84.25	3	2.36	17	13.39
18.	Rural workers	131	85.62	2	1.31	20	13.07
19.	Urban workers	255	79.69	4	1.25	61	19.06
20.	Hindu workers	130	89.04	2	1.37	14	9.59
21.	Muslim workers	256	78.29	4	1.22	67	20.49
22.	Workers in income group 0–3000	287	80.39	6	1.68	64	17.93
23.	Workers in income group of 3000 and above	99	85.34	0	0.00	17	14.66
24.	Workers belonging to Labour Class	320	82.69	6	1.55	61	15.76
25.	Workers belonging to Management Class	66	79.52	0	0	17	20.48

Table 4.42 reveals that majority of workers (96.62%) representing different units of 55 factories agreed that girls are subjected to humiliation if they fail to bring with them the committed gifts and cash at the time of their marriage. While only 1.69% each either exhibited their indifference expressed disagreement with the statement.

Unit-wise analysis reveals that 98.11% workers hailing from assembly units; 98.28% from die-making units; 95.35% from furnace and dispatch units; 98.21% from key-making units; 92.98% from nickle polish units; 96.72% from Office; 95.95% from package units; 9722% from press units; 95.36% salaried workers and 97.49% contractual workers; 96.73% male workers and 92.86% female workers; 97.75% literate workers and 95.63% illiterate workers; 96.25% workers from joint family system and 97.64% representing nuclear family system; 95.42% rural workers and 97.20% urban workers; 95.81% workers receiving salary up to Rs. 3000/- and 99.14% workers receiving salary of more than 3000/-per month; 96.39% workers hailing from Labour class and 97.59% workers hailing from management class all expressed their agreement with the statement.

It can, thus, be concluded that the respondents representing different units of the factory as well as majority of the total subjects (96.62%) expressed their agreement with the statement that, "girls are subjected to humiliation if they fail to bring with them the committed gifts and cash at the time of their marriage".

Table 4.43 reveals that majority of workers (92.41%) representing different units of 55 factories agreed that earnings were not sufficient to meet familial responsibilities and other obligations. While 3.38% exhibited their indifference only 4.22% have expressed their disagreement with the statement.

Unit-wise analysis revealed that 94.34% workers hailing from assembly units; 89.66% from die-making units; 97.67% from furnace and dispatch units; 91.07% from key-making units; 89.47% from nickle polish units; 93.44% from Office; 91.89% from packing units;

TABLE 4.42 SOCIAL PERCEPTION: (2) GIRLS ARE SUBJECTED TO HUMILIATION IF THEY FAIL TO BRING WITH THEM THE COMMITTED GIFTS AND CASH AT THE TIME OF THEIR MARRIAGE

	RESPONDENTS CATEGORY	*YES*	*%*	*INDIFF.*	*%*	*NO*	*%*
1.	Workers of different industrial units belonging to same factory.	458	96.62	8	1.69	8	1.69
2.	Workers of different factories belonging to assembly units.	52	98.11	1	1.89	0	0.00
3.	Workers of different factories belonging to die-making units.	57	98.28	1	1.72	0	0.00
4.	Workers of different factories belonging to furnace & dispatch units.	41	95.35	0	0.00	2	4.65
5.	Workers of different factories belonging to key-making units.	55	98.21	0	0.00	1	1.79
6.	Workers of different factories belonging to nickle polish units.	53	92.98	3	5.26	1	1.75
7.	Workers of different factories belonging to Office.	59	96.72	1	1.64	1	1.64
8.	Workers of different factories belonging to packing units.	71	95.95	2	2.70	1	1.35
9.	Workers of different factories belonging to press units.	70	97.22	0	0.00	2	2.78
10.	Salaried workers.	226	95.36	7	2.95	4	1.69

(Contd.)

11. Contractual workers	233	97.49	1	0.42	5	2.09
12. Male workers	444	96.73	7	1.53	8	1.74
13. Female workers	13	92.86	1	7.14	0	0.00
14. Literate workers	217	97.75	1	0.45	4	1.80
15. Illiterate workers	241	95.63	7	2.78	4	1.59
16. Joint family workers	334	96.25	6	1.73	7	2.02
17. Nuclear family workers	124	97.64	2	1.57	1	0.79
18. Rural workers	146	95.42	6	3.92	1	0.65
19. Urban workers	312	97.20	2	0.62	7	2.18
20. Hindu workers	140	95.89	4	2.74	2	1.37
21. Muslim workers	318	96.95	4	1.22	6	1.83
22. Workers in income group 0–3000	343	95.81	7	1.96	8	2.23
23. Workers in income group 3000 and above	115	99.14	1	0.86	0	0.00
24. Workers belonging to Labour Class	374	96.39	7	1.80	7	1.80
25. Workers belonging to Management Class	81	97.59	1	1.20	1	1.20

TABLE 4.43 SOCIAL PERCEPTION: (3) EARNINGS ARE NOT SUFFICIENT TO MEET THE FAMILIAL RESPONSIBILITIES AND OTHER OBLIGATIONS

	RESPONDENTS CATEGORY	*YES*	*%*	*INDIFF.*	*%*	*NO*	*%*
1.	Workers of different industrial units belonging to same factory.	438	92.41	16	2.38	20	4.22
2.	Workers of different factories belonging to assembly units.	50	94.34	0	0.00	3	5.66
3.	Workers of different factories belonging to die-making units.	52	89.66	3	5.17	3	5.17
4.	Workers of different factories belonging to furnace & dispatch units.	42	97.67	0	0.00	1	2.33
5.	Workers of different factories belonging to key-making units.	51	91.07	3	5.36	2	3.57
6.	Workers of different factories belonging to nickle polish units.	51	89.47	2	3.51	4	7.02
7.	Workers of different factories belonging to Office.	47	93.44	2	3.28	2	3.28
8.	Workers of different factories belonging to packing units.	68	91.89	4	5.41	2	2.70
9.	Workers of different factories belonging to Press unit.	67	93.06	2	2.78	3	4.17
10.	Salaried workers.	215	90.72	12	5.06	10	4.22

(Contd.)

11. Contractual workers	225	94.14	4	1.67	10	4.18
12. Male workers	425	92.59	14	3.05	20	4.36
13. Female workers	12	85.71	2	14.29	0	0.00
14. Literate workers	210	59.59	4	1.80	8	3.60
15. Illiterate workers	228	90.48	12	4.76	12	4.76
16. Joint family workers	332	93.26	15	4.21	9	2.53
17. Nuclear family workers	115	90.55	1	0.79	11	8.66
18. Rural workers	132	86.27	11	7.19	10	6.54
19. Urban workers	306	95.33	5	1.56	10	3.12
20. Hindu workers	131	89.73	5	3.42	10	3.85
21. Muslim workers	307	93.60	11	3.35	10	3.05
22. Workers in income group 0–3000	328	94.25	5	1.44	15	4.31
23. Workers in income group of 3000 and above	110	94.83	1	0.86	5	4.31
24. Workers belonging to Labour Class	356	91.75	14	3.61	18	4.64
25. Workers belonging to Management Class	79	95.18	2	2.41	2	2.41

93.06% from press units; 90.72% salaried workers and 94.14% contractual workers; 94.59% literate workers and 90.48% illiterate workers; 93.26% workers from joint family system and 90.55% representing nuclear family system; 86.27% rural workers and 95.33% urban workers; 89.73% Hindu workers and 93.60% Muslim workers; 94.25% workers receiving salary up to Rs. 3000/-and 94.83% workers receiving salary of more than 3000/-per month; 91.75% workers hailing from labour class and 95.18% workers hailing from management class exhibited their agreement with the statement.

It can, thus, be concluded that respondents representing different units of the factory as well as majority of the total subjects (92.41%) expressed their agreement with the statement that, "earnings were not sufficient to meet familial responsibilities and other obligations".

Table 4.44 revealed that majority of workers (58.65%) representing different units of 55 factories agreed that men and women are enjoying equal authority in family matters. While 5.91% exhibited indifference only 35.44% expressed their disagreement with the statement.

Unit wise analysis revealed that 56.60% workers hailing from assembly unit; 53.45% from die-making units; 65.12% from furnace and dispatch units; 51.79% from key-making units; 54.39% from nickle polish units; 55.74% from Office; 64.86% from packing units; and 65.28% from press units; 56.54% salaried workers and 80.45% contractual workers; 58.61% male workers and 57.14% female workers; 57.21% literate workers and 59.92% illiterate workers; 61.38% workers from joint family system and 51.18% representing nuclear family system; 62.75% rural and 53.37% urban workers; 64.38% Hindu workers and 56.10% Muslim workers; 61.17% workers receiving salary up to Rs. 3000/ and 50.86% workers receiving salary more than 3000/- per month; 60.05% workers hailing from Labour class and 50.60% workers hailing from management group expressed their agreement with the statement.

It can, thus, be concluded that majority of the respondents (58.65%) representing different units of the factory expressed their agreement

TABLE 4.44 SOCIAL PERCEPTION: (4) MEN AND WOMEN ENJOYING EQUAL AUTHORITY IN FAMILY MATTERS

RESPONDENTS CATEGORY	YES	%	INDIFF.	%	NO	%
1. Workers of different industrial units belonging to same factory.	278	58.65	28	5.91	168	35.44
2. Workers of different factories belonging to assembly units.	30	56.60	2	3.77	21	39.62
3. Workers of different factories belonging to die-making units.	31	53.45	5	8.62	22	37.93
4. Workers of different factories belonging to furnace & dispatch units.	28	65.12	0	0.00	15	34.88
5. Workers of different factories belonging to key-making units.	29	51.79	4	7.14	23	41.07
6. Workers of different factories belonging to nickle polish units.	31	54.39	3	5.26	23	40.35
7. Workers of different factories belonging to Office	34	55.74	3	4.92	24	39.34
8. Workers of different factories belonging to packing units.	48	64.86	6	8.11	20	27.03
9. Workers of different factories belonging to press units.	47	65.28	5	6.94	20	27.78
10. Salaried workers.	134	56.54	21	8.86	82	34.60

(*Contd.*)

11. Contractual workers	144	80.45	7	3.91	28	15.64
12. Male workers	269	58.61	26	5.66	164	35.73
13. Female workers	8	57.14	2	14.29	4	28.57
14. Literate workers	127	57.21	84	37.84	11	4.95
15. Illiterate workers	151	59.92	17	6.75	84	33.33
16. Joint family workers	213	61.38	18	5.19	116	33.43
17. Nuclear family workers	65	51.18	10	787	52	40.94
18. Rural workers	96	62.75	13	8.50	44	28.76
19. Urban workers	182	53.37	15	4.40	144	42.23
20. Hindu workers	94	64.38	14	9.59	38	26.03
21. Muslim workers	184	56.10	14	4.27	130	39.63
22. Workers in income group 0–3000	219	61.17	24	6.70	115	32.12
23. Workers in income group of 3000 and above	59	50.86	4	3.45	53	45.69
24. Workers belonging to Labour Class	233	60.05	26	6.70	129	33.25
25. Workers belonging to Management Class	42	50.80	2	2.41	39	46.99

with the statement. The trend indicates that the respondents perceived that men and women are enjoying equal authority in family matters. On the other hand, 5.91% of the respondents have exhibited their indifference towards the statement and, on the other hand 35.44% of the respondents exhibited their disagreement towards the statement. Similar trend is also noticeable among the respondents representing different units of the factory. It can thus be inferred that majority of the respondents were in favour of the statement.

Table 4.45 reveals that majority of the workers (89.87%) representing different units of 55 factories agreed that educated couples are more happily settled in their lives as compared to less or uneducated couples. While 6.96% exhibited their indifference, only 3.16% expressed their disagreement with the statement.

Unit-wise analysis reveals that 94.34% workers hailing from assembly units; 93.10% from die-making units; 100.00% from furnace and dispatch units; 87.50% from key making units; 85.96% from nickle polish units; 91.80% from Office, 85.14% from packing units; 86.11% from press units; 88.19% salaried workers and 91.63% contractual workers; 89.54% male workers and 100.00% female workers; 91.89% literate and 88.10% illiterate workers; 92.51% workers from joint family system and 82.68% representing nuclear family system; 86.93% rural and 91.28% urban workers; 83.56% Hindu workers and 92.68% Muslim workers; 88.83% workers receiving salary up to Rs. 3000/- and 93.10% workers receiving salary of more than 3000/-per month; 88.92% workers hailing from Labour class and 93.98% workers hailing from management group expressed their agreement with the statement.

It can, thus, be concluded that respondents representing different units of the factory as well as majority of the total subjects (89.87%) expressed their agreement with the statement that, "educated couples are more happily settled in their lives as compared to less or uneducated couples".

TABLE 4.45 SOCIAL PERCEPTION: (5) EDUCATED COUPLES ARE MORE HAPPILY SETTLED IN THEIR LIVES AS COMPARED TO LESS OR UNEDUCATED COUPLES

	RESPONDENTS CATEGORY	*YES*	*%*	*INDIFF.*	*%*	*NO*	*%*
1.	Workers of different industrial units belonging to same factory.	426	89.87	33	6.96	15	3.16
2.	Workers of different factories belonging to assembly units.	50	94.34	2	3.77	1	1.89
3.	Workers of different factories belonging to die-making units.	54	93.10	2	3.45	2	3.45
4.	Workers of different factories belonging to furnace & dispatch units.	43	100.00	0	0.00	0	0.00
5.	Workers of different factories belonging to key-making units.	49	87.50	5	8.93	2	3.57
6.	Workers of different factories belonging to nickle polish units.	49	85.96	7	12.28	1	1.75
7.	Workers of different factories belonging to Office	56	91.80	2	9.28	3	4.92
8.	Workers of different factories belonging to packing units.	63	85.14	9	12.1	2	2.70
9.	Workers of different factories belonging to press units.	62	86.11	4	5.56	6	8.33
10.	Salaried workers.	209	88.19	20	8.44	8	3.38

(*Contd.*)

11.	Contractual workers	219	91.63	13	5.44	7	2.93
12.	Male workers	411	89.54	33	7.19	15	3.27
13.	Female workers	14	100.00	0	0.00	0	0.00
14.	Literate workers	204	91.89	9	4.05	9	4.05
15.	Illiterate workers	222	88.10	24	9.52	6	2.38
16.	Joint family workers	321	92.51	16	4.61	10	2.88
17.	Nuclear family workers	105	82.68	17	13.3	5	3.94
18.	Rural workers	133	86.93	14	9.15	6	3.92
19.	Urban workers	293	91.28	19	5.92	9	2.80
20.	Hindu workers	122	83.56	16	10.9	8	5.48
21.	Muslim workers	304	92.68	12	5.18	7	2.13
22.	Workersin income group 0–3000	318	88.83	26	7.26	14	3.91
23.	Workers in income group of 3000 and above	108	93.10	7	6.03	1	0.86
24.	Workers belonging to Labour Class	345	88.92	31	7.99	12	3.09
25.	Workers belonging to Management Class	78	93.98	2	2.41	3	3.61

Table 4.46 reveals that majority of workers (89.03%) representing different units of 55 factories agreed that people going for early marriage of their daughters even to elderly settled persons, because of economic reasons, while 5.06% exhibited their indifference, and only 5.91% expressed their disagreement with the statement.

Unit-wise analysis reveals that 88.68% workers hailing from assembly units; 89.66% from die-making units; 100.00% from furnace and dispatch units; 85.71% from key-making units; 85.96% from nickle polish units; 93.44% from Office; 89.19% from packing units; 83.33% from press units; 89.45% salaried workers and 88.28% contractual workers; 88.67% male workers and 100.00% female workers; 92.34% literate and 86.11% illiterate workers; 90.78% workers from joint family system and 84.25% representing nuclear family system; 84.31% rural and 91.28% urban workers; 85.62% Hindu workers and 90.55% Muslim workers; 87.71% workers receiving salary up to Rs. 3000/- and 93.10% workers receiving salary of more than 3000/-per month; 87.63% workers hailing from Labour class; 95.18% workers hailing from management group expressed agreement with the statement.

It can, thus, be concluded that the respondents representing different units of the factory as well as majority of the total subjects (89.03%) expressed their agreement with the statement that, "people going for early marriage of their daughters even to elderly settled persons because of economic reasons."

Table 4.47 reveals that majority of the workers (87.76%) representing different units of 55 factories agreed that divorce has become fairly common among members of the society amounting to family disorganisation. While 61.12% exhibited their indifference, only 6.12% have expressed their disagreement with the statement.

Unit-wise analysis reveals that 90.57% workers hailing from assembly units; 94.83% from die-making units; 88.73% from furnace and dispatch units; 91.07% from key-making units; 84.21% from nickle polish units; 88.52% from Office; 84.38% from packing unit and 80.56% from press units; 85.23% salaried workers and 90.38% contractual workers; 88.48% male workers and 85.71% female

TABLE 4.46 SOCIAL PERCEPTION: (6) PEOPLE GOING FOR EARLY MARRIAGE OF THEIR DAUGHTERS EVEN TO ELDERLY SETTLED PERSONS BECAUSE OF ECONOMIC REASONS

	RESPONDENTS CATEGORY	*YES*	*%*	*INDIFF.*	*%*	*NO*	*%*
1.	Workers of different industrial units belonging to same factory.	422	89.03	24	5.06	28	5.91
2.	Workers of different factories belonging to assembly units.	47	88.68	1	1.89	5	9.43
3.	Workers of different factories belonging to die-making units.	52	89.66	3	5.17	3	5.17
4.	Workers of different factories belonging to furnace & dispatch units.	43	100.00	0	0.00	0	0.00
5.	Workers of different factories belonging to key-making units.	48	85.71	5	8.93	3	5.36
6.	Workers of different factories belonging to nickle polish unit.	49	85.96	4	7.02	4	7.02
7.	Workers of different factories belonging to Office.	57	93.44	0	0.00	4	6.56
8.	Workers of different factories belonging to packing unit.	60	89.19	5	6.76	3	4.05
9.	Workers of different factories belonging to press unit.	60	83.33	6	8.33	6	8.33
10.	Salaried workers.	212	89.45	15	6.33	10	4.22

11.	Contractual workers	211	88.28	9	3.77	19	7.95
12.	Male workers	407	88.67	24	5.23	28	6.10
13.	Female workers	14	100.00	0	0.00	0	0.00
14.	Literate workers	205	92.34	7	3.15	10	4.50
15.	Illiterate workers	217	86.11	17	6.75	18	7.14
16.	Joint family workers	315	90.78	15	4.32	17	4.90
17.	Nuclear family workers	107	84.25	9	7.09	11	8.66
18.	Rural workers	129	84.31	13	8.50	11	7.19
19.	Urban workers	293	91.28	11	3.43	17	5.30
20.	Hindu workers	125	85.62	11	7.53	10	6.85
21.	Muslim workers	297	90.55	13	3.96	18	5.49
22.	Workers in income group 0–3000	314	57.71	19	5.31	25	6.98
23.	Workers in income group of 3000 and above	108	93.10	5	4.31	3	2.59
24.	Workers belonging to Labour Class	340	87.63	24	6.19	24	6.19
25.	Workers belonging to Management Class	79	95.18	0	0	4	4.82

TABLE 4.47 SOCIAL PERCEPTION: (7) DIVORCE HAS BECOME FAIRLY COMMON AMONG MEMBERS OF THE SOCIETY AMOUNTING TO FAMILY DISORGANISATION

	RESPONDENTS CATEGORY	*YES*	*%*	*INDIFF.*	*%*	*NO*	*%*
1.	Workers of different industrial units belonging to same factory.	416	87.76	29	6.12	29	6.12
2.	Workers of different factories belonging to assembly unit.	48	90.57	2	3.77	3	5.66
3.	Workers of different factories belonging to die making unit.	55	94.83	3	5.17	0	0.00
4.	Workers of different factories belonging to furnace & dispatch unit.	38	88.37	2	4.65	3	5.36
5.	Workers of different factories belonging to Key making unit.	51	91.07	2	3.57	3	5.36
6.	Workers of different factories belonging to nickle polish unit.	48	84.21	5	8.77	4	7.02
7.	Workers of different factories belonging to Office	54	88.52	2	3.28	5	8.20
8.	Workers of different factories belonging to packing unit	54	84.38	7	10.94	3	4.69
9.	Workers of different factories belonging to press unit	58	80.56	6	8.33	8	11.11
10.	Salaried workers.	202	85.23	21	8.86	14	5.91

(Contd)

11. Contractual workers	216	90.38	7	2.93	16	6.69
12. Male workers	430	88.48	28	5.76	28	5.76
13. Female workers	12	85.71	1	7.14	1	7.14
14. Literate workers	202	90.99	8	3.60	12	5.41
15. Illiterate workers	214	84.92	21	8.33	17	6.75
16. Joint family workers	315	90.78	12	3.46	20	5.76
17. Nuclear family workers	101	79.53	17	13.39	9	7.09
18. Rural workers	128	83.66	14	9.15	11	7.19
19. Urban workers	288	89.72	15	4.67	18	5.61
20. Hindu workers	122	83.56	14	9.59	10	6.85
21. Muslim workers	294	89.63	15	4.57	19	5.79
22. Workers in income group 0–3000	313	87.43	22	6.15	23	6.42
23. Workers in income group of 3000 and above	103	88.79	7	6.03	6	5.17
24. Workers belonging to Labour Class	339	87.37	27	6.96	22	5.67
25. Workers belonging to Management Class	74	89.16	2	2.41	7	8.43

workers; 90.99% literate and 84.92% illiterate workers; 90.78% workers from joint family system and 79.53% representing nuclear family system; 83.66% rural workers and 89.72% urban workers; 83.56% Hindu workers and 89.63% Muslims workers; 87.43% workers receiving salary up to Rs. 3000/- and 88.79% workers receiving salary of more than 3000/- per month; 87.37% workers hailing from Labour class and 89.16% workers hailing from management group expressed their agreement with the statement.

It can, thus, be concluded that the respondents representing differents units of the factory as well as majority of the total subjects (87.76%) expressed their agreement with the statement. that, "divorce has become fairly common among the members of the society amounting to family disorganisation."

Table 4.48 reveals that majority of the workers 38.19% representing different units of 55 factories agreed that windows' remarriage, though legally permissible, yet is being discouraged by certain sections of the community. While 8.65% exhibited their indifference, only 53.16% expressed their disagreement with the statement.

Unit-wise analysis reveals that 35.85% workers hailing from assembly units; 36.21% from die-making units; 34.88% from furnace and dispatch units; 37.50% from key-making units; 35.09% from nickle polish units; 39.34% from Office; 37.84% from packing units; 45.83% from press units; 35.02% salaried workers and 41.84% contractual workers; 37.91% male workers and 50.00% female workers; 34.23% literate and 41.67% illiterate workers; 38.04% workers from joint family system and 38.58% representing nuclear family system; 45.10% rural workers and 34.89% urban workers; 40.41% Hindu workers and 37.20% Muslim workers; 41.34% workers receiving salary up to Rs. 3000/-and 28.45% workers receiving salary more than 3000/- per month; 36.60% workers hailing from Labour class and; exhibited their agreement with the statement. However; 53.61% workers from Labour class while 53.61%. However, 46.99%

TABLE 4.48 SOCIAL PERCEPTION: (8) WINDOWS' REMARRIAGE THOUGH LEGALLY PERMISSIBLE YET IS BEING DISCOURAGED BY CERTAIN SECTIONS OF THE COMMUNITY

	RESPONDENTS CATEGORY	*YES*	*%*	*INDIFF.*	*%*	*NO*	*%*
1.	Workers of different industrial units belonging to same factory.	181	38.19	41	8.65	252	53.16
2.	Workers of different factories belonging to assembly unit	19	35.85	3	5.66	31	85.49
3.	Workers of different factories belonging to die-making unit.	21	36.21	4	6.90	33	56.90
4.	Workers of different factories belonging to furnace & dispatch unit.	15	34.88	0	0.00	28	65.12
5.	Workers of different factories belonging to key-making unit.	21	37.50	4	7.14	31	55.36
6.	Workers of different factories belonging to nickle polish unit.	20	35.09	6	10.53	31	54.39
7.	Workers of different factories belonging to Office.	24	39.34	5	8.20	32	52.46
8.	Workers of different factories belonging to packing unit.	28	37.84	11	14.86	35	47.30
9.	Workers of different factories belonging to press unit.	33	45.83	8	11.11	31	43.06
10.	Salaried workers.	83	35.02	24	10.13	130	54.85

(Contd.)

11. Contractual workers	100	41.84	16	6.69	123	41.46
12. Male workers	174	37.91	39	8.50	246	53.59
13. Female workers	7	50.00	2	14.29	5	35.71
14. Literate workers	76	34.23	10	4.50	136	61.26
15. Illiterate workers	105	41.67	31	12.30	116	46.03
16. Joint family workers	132	38.04	26	7.49	189	54.47
17. Nuclear family workers	49	38.58	15	11.81	63	49.61
18. Rural workers	69	45.10	15	9.80	69	45.10
19. Urban workers	112	34.89	26	8.10	183	57.01
20. Hindu workers	59	40.41	19	13.01	68	46.58
21. Muslim workers	122	37.20	22	6.17	184	56.10
22. Workers in income group 0–3000	148	41.34	32	8.94	178	49.72
23. Workers in income group of 3000 and above	33	28.45	9	7.76	74	63.79
24. Workers belonging to Labour Class	142	36.60	38	9.79	208	53.61
25. Workers belonging to Management Class	39	46.99	3	3.00	41	49.40

workers; and while 49.40% workers from management class expressed their disagreement with the statement.

Table 4.49 reveals that majority of the workers (93.88%) representing different units of 55 factories agreed that it was difficult to find suitable matches for educated boys and girls. While 4.64% exhibited their indifference towards the statement and only 1.48% have expressed their disagreement with the statement.

Unit-wise analysis reveals that 96.23% workers hailing from assembly units; 94.83% from die-making units; 77.36% from furnace and dispatch units; 94.64% from key-making units; 87.72% from nickle polish units; 98.36% from Office; 94.59% from packing unit and 90.28% from press units; 94.49% salaried workers and 94.14% contractual workers; 93.89% male workers and 100.00% female workers; 97.30% literate workers and 91.27% illiterate workers; 95.68% workers from joint family system and 9.76% representing nuclear family system; 90.20% rural and 95.95% urban workers; 90.41% Hindu workers and 95.73% Muslim workers; 93.30% workers receiving salary up to Rs. 3000/- and 96.55% workers receiving salary of more than 3000/-per month; 92.78% workers hailing from Labour class; and 100.00% workers hailing from management group all agreed with the statement.

It can, thus, be concluded that the respondents representing different units of the factory as well as majority of the total subjects (93.88%) expressed their agreement with the statement that, "it is difficult to find suitable matches for educated boys and girls".

Table 4.50 reveals that majority of the workers (95.36%) representing different units of 55 factories agreed that on account of growing nuclear family patterns the traditional familial bonds of feelings among the members of the community have weakened. While 2.95% exhibited their indifference only 1.69% expressed their disagreement with the statement.

TABLE 4.49 SOCIAL PERCEPTION: (9) IT IS DIFFICULT TO FIND SUITABLE MATCHES FOR EDUCATED BOYS AND GIRLS

	RESPONDENTS CATEGORY	*YES*	*%*	*INDIFF.*	*%*	*NO*	*%*
1.	Workers of different industrial units belonging to same factory.	445	93.88	22	4.64	07	1.48
2.	Workers of different factories belonging to assembly unit.	51	96.23	3.77	5.66	0	0.00
3.	Workers of different factories belonging to die-making unit.	55	94.83	5.17	6.90	0	0.00
4.	Workers of different factories belonging to furnace & dispatch unit.	41	77.36	0.00	0.00	12	22.64
5.	Workers of different factories belonging to key-making unit.	53	94.64	3.57	7.14	1	1.79
6.	Workers of different factories belonging to nickle polish unit.	50	87.72	8.77	10.53	2	3.51
7.	Workers of different factories belonging to Office.	60	98.36	1.64	8.20	0	0.00
8.	Workers of different factories belonging to packing unit.	70	94.59	4.05	14.86	1	1.35
9.	Workers of different factories belonging to press unit.	65	90.28	6.94	11.11	2	2.78
10.	Salaried workers.	223	94.49	4.24	10.13	3	1.27

(*Contd.*)

11.	Contractual workers	225	94.14	4.18	6.69	4	1.67
12.	Male workers	430	93.89	4.59	8.50	7	1.53
13.	Female workers	14	100.00	0.00	14.29	0	0.00
14.	Literate workers	216	97.30	1.80	4.50	2	0.90
15.	Illiterate workers	230	91.27	6.75	12.30	5	1.98
16.	Joint family workers	332	95.68	3.17	7.49	4	1.15
17.	Nuclear family workers	114	89.76	7.87	11.81	3	2.36
18.	Rural workers	138	90.20	7.19	9.80	4	2.61
19.	Urban workers	308	95.95	3.12	8.10	3	0.93
20.	Hindu workers	132	90.41	8.22	13.01	2	1.37
21.	Muslim workers	314	95.73	2.74	6.71	5	1.52
22.	Workers in income group 0–3000	334	93.30	5.31	8.94	5	1.40
23.	Workers in income group of 3000 and above	112	96.55	1.72	7.76	2	1.72
24.	Workers belonging to Labour Class	360	92.78	21	5.41	7	1.80
25.	Workers belonging to Management Class	83	100.00	0	0	0	0

TABLE 4.50 ON SOCIAL ASPIRATION: (10) ACCOUNT OF GROWING NUCLEAR FAMILY PATTERNS, THE TRADITIONAL FAMILIAL BONDS OF FEELINGS AMONG MEMBERS OF THE COMMUNITY HAVE WEAKENED

	RESPONDENTS CATEGORY	*YES*	*%*	*INDIFF.*	*%*	*NO*	*%*
1.	Workers of different industrial units belonging to same factory.	452	95.36	14	2.95	08	1.69
2.	Workers of different factories belonging to assembly unit	51	96.23	2	3.77	0	0.00
3.	Workers of different factories belonging to die-making unit.	54	93.10	2	3.45	2	3.45
4.	Workers of different factories be onging to furnace & dispatch unit.	43	100.00	0	0.00	0	0.00
5.	Workers of different factories belonging to key-making unit.	55	98.21	1	1.79	0	0.00
6.	Workers of different factories belonging to nickle polish unit.	56	98.25	1	1.75	0	0.00
7.	Workers of different factors belcnging to office.	58	95.08	2	3.28	1	1.64
8.	Workers of different factories belonging to packing unit.	67	90.54	4	5.41	3	4.05
9.	Workers of different factories belonging to press unit.	68	94.44	2	2.78	3	4.05
10.	Salaried workers.	225	94.94	6	2.53	6	2.53

(Contd.)

11. Contractual workers	230	96.23	7	2.93	2	0.84
12. Male workers	439	95.64	13	2.83	7	1.53
13. Female workers	12	85.71	1	7.14	1	7.14
14. Literate workers	214	94.69	6	2.65	6	2.65
15. Illiterate workers	238	94.44	8	3.17	6	2.38
16. Joint family workers	330	95.10	10	2.88	7	2.02
17. Nuclear family workers	122	96.06	4	3.15	1	0.79
18. Rural workers	143	93.46	7	4.58	3	1.96
19. Urban workers	309	96.26	7	2.18	5	1.56
20. Hindu workers	134	91.78	8	5.48	4	2.74
21. Muslim workers	318	96.95	6	1.83	4	1.22
22. Workers in income group 0–3000	337	94.13	14	3.91	7	1.96
23. Workers in income group of 3000 and above	115	99.14	0	0.00	1	0.86
24. Workers belonging to Labour Class	369	95.10	12	3.09	7	1.80
25. Workers belonging to Management Class	80	96.39	2	2.41	1	1.20

Unit-wise analysis reveals that 96.23% workers hailing from assembly units; 93.10% from die-making units; 100.00% from furnace and dispatch units; 98.21% from key-making units; 98.25% from nickle polish units; 95.08% from Office; 90.54% from packing units; 94.44% from press units; 94.94% salaried workers and 96.23% contractual workers; 95.64% male workers and 85.71% female workers; 94.69% literate workers and 94.44% illiterate workers; 95.10% workers from joint family system and 96.06% representing nuclear family system; 93.46% rural and 96.26% urban workers; 91.78% Hindu workers and 96.95% Muslim workers; 94.13% workers receiving salary up to Rs. 3000/- and 99.14% workers receiving salary of more than 3000/- per month 95.10% workers hailing from Labour class; and 96.39% workers hailing from management group expressed their agreement with the statement.

It can, thus, be concluded that the respondents representing different units of the factory as well as majority of the total subject (95.36) expressed their agreement with the statement that, "on account of growing nuclear family patterns the traditional familial bonds of the feelings among the members of the community have weakened."

Table 4.51 reveals that majority of workers (94.09%) representing different units of 55 factories agreed to work against the system of demanding gifts in cash or kind by the boys' parents at the time of marriage, as is not permissible in the religion and law. While 4.22% have exhibited their indifference, only 1.69% expressed their disagreement with the statement.

Unit-wise analysis reveals that 96.23% workers hailing from assembly units; 92.86% from die-making units; 97.67% from furnace and dispatch units; 98.21% from key-making.units; 92.98% from nickle polish units; 93.44% from Office; 93.24% from packing units; 90.28% from press units; 93.67% salaried workers and 94.98% contractual workers have 100.00% female workers; 95.95% literate workers and 92.46% illiterate workers; 94.81% workers from joint

TABLE 4.51 SOCIAL ASPIRATIONS: (1) WORKING AGAINST THE SYSTEM OF DEMANDING GIFTS IN CASH OR KIND BY THE BOYS, PARENTS AT THE TIME OF MARRIAGE AS IS NOT PERMISSIBLE IN RELIGION AND LAW

	RESPONDENTS CATEGORY	*YES*	*%*	*INDIFF.*	*%*	*NO*	*%*
1.	Workers of different industrial units belonging to same factory.	446	94.09	20	4.22	8	1.69
2.	Workers of different factories belonging to assembly unit.	51	96.23	1	1.89	1	1.89
3.	Workers of different factories belonging to die-making unit.	52	92.86	3	5.36	1	1.79
4.	Workers of different factories belonging to furnace & dispatch unit.	42	97.67	1	2.33	0	0.00
5.	Workers of different factories belonging to key-making unit.	55	98.21	1	1.79	0	0.00
6.	Workers of different factories belonging to nickle polish unit	53	92.98	3	5.26	1	1.75
7.	Workers of different factories belonging to Office.	57	93.44	3	4.92	1	1.64
8.	Workers of different factories belonging to packing unit.	69	93.24	2	2.70	3	4.05
9.	Workers of different factories belonging to press unit.	65	90.28	6	8.33	1	1.39
10.	Salaried workers.	222	93.67	12	5.06	3	1.27

(Contd.)

11. Contractual workers	227	94.98	7	2.93	5	2.09
12. Male workers	431	93.90	20	4.36	8	1.74
13. Female workers	14	100.00	0	0.00	0	0.04
14. Literate workers	213	95.95	7	3.15	2	0.90
15. Illiterate workers	233	92.46	13	5.16	6	2.38
16. Joint family workers	329	94.81	12	3.46	6	1.73
17. Nuclear family workers	117	85.40	18	13.14	2	1.46
18. Rural workers	142	92.81	7	5.58	4	2.61
19. Urban workers	304	94.70	13	4.05	4	1.25
20. Hindu workers	136	87.18	16	10.26	4	2.56
21. Muslim workers	310	94.51	14	4.27	4	1.22
22. Workers in income group 0-3000	337	94.13	13	3.63	8	2.23
23. Workers in income group 3000 and above	109	93.97	7	6.03	0	0.00
24. Workers belonging to Labour Class	363	93.56	17	4.38	8	2.06
25. Workers belonging to Management Class	80	9639	3	3.61	0	0

family system and 85.40% representing nuclear family system; 92.81% rural workers and 94.70% urban workers; 87.18% Hindu workers and 94.51% Muslim workers; 94.13% workers receiving salary up to Rs. 3000/- and 93.97% workers receiving salary more than 3000/ -per month; 93.56% workers hailing from Labour class; and 96.39% workers hailing from management group all expressed their agreement with the statement.

It can, thus, be concluded that the respondents representing different units of the factory as well as majority of the total subjects (94.09%) expressed their agreement "working against the system of demanding cash or kind by the boys' parents at the time of marriage, as is not permissible in the religion and law."

Table 4.52 reveals that majority of the workers (91.98%) representing different units of 55 factories agreed that organizing or joining such organization which is working for rehabilitation of girls becoming victims of humiliation after marriage. While 6.75% exhibited their indifference only 1.27% have expressed their disagreement with the statement.

Unit-wise analysis reveals that 94.34% workers hailing from assembly units; 94.83% from die-making units; 100.00% from furnace and dispatch units; 92.86% from key-making units; 89.47% from nickle polish units; 95.085% from Office; 89.19 from packing units; 84.72% from press units; 91.98% salaried workers and 92.05% contractual workers; 92.05% contractual workers; 91.72% male workers and 100.00% female workers; 95.95% literate workers and 88.49% illiterate workers; 92.80% workers from joint family system and 89.76% representing nuclear family system; 86.93% rural workers and 94.39% urban workers; 86.93% rural and 94.39% urban workers; 90.41% Hindu workers and 92.68% Muslim workers; 90.50% workers receiving salary up to Rs. 3000/- and 96.55% workers receiving salary of more than 3000/- per month; 90.72% workers hailing from Labour class; and 97.59% workers hailing from management group all expressed their agreement with the statement.

TABLE 4.52 SOCIAL ASPIRATION: (2) ORGANISING OR JOINING SUCH ORGANIZATION WHICH IS WORKING FOR REHABILITATION OF GIRLS BECOMING VICTIMS OF HUMILIATION AFTER MARRIAGE

	RESPONDENTS CATEGORY	*YES*	*%*	*INDIFF.*	*%*	*NO*	*%*
1.	Workers of different industrial units belonging to same factory.	436	91.98	32	6.75	6	1.27
2.	Workers of different factories belonging to assembly unit.	50	94.34	3	5.66	0	0.00
3.	Workers of different factories belonging to die making unit	55	94.83	2	3.45	1	1.72
4.	Workers of different factories belonging to furnace & dispatch unit.	43	100.00	0	0.00	0	0.00
5.	Workers of different factories belonging to key making unit.	52	92.86	4	7.14	0	0.00
6.	Workers of different factories belonging to nickle polish unit.	51	89.47	5	8.77	1	1.75
7.	Workers of different factories belonging to Office.	58	95.08	2	3.28	1	1.64
8.	Workers of different factories belonging to packing unit.	66	89.19	6	8.11	2	2.70
9.	Workers of different factories belonging to press unit.	61	84.72	10	13.89	1	1.39
10.	Salaried workers.	218	91.98	18	7.59	1	0.42

(Contd.)

11. Contractual workers	220	92.05	14	5.86	5	2.09
12. Male workers	421	91.72	32	6.97	6	1.31
13. Female workers	14	100.00	0	0.00	0	0.00
14. Literate workers	213	95.95	7	3.15	2	0.90
15. Illiterate workers	223	88.49	25	9.92	4	1.59
16. Joint family workers	322	92.80	19	5.48	6	1.73
17. Nuclear family workers	114	89.76	13	10.24	0	0.00
18. Rural workers	133	86.93	16	10.46	4	1.61
19. Urban workers	303	94.39	16	4.98	2	1.62
20. Hindu workers	132	90.41	12	8.22	2	1.37
21. Muslim workers	304	92.68	20	6.10	4	1.22
22. Workers in income group 0–3000	324	90.50	28	7.82	6	1.68
23. Workers in income group of 3000 and above	112	96.55	4	3.45	0	0.00
24. Workers belonging to Labour Class	352	90.72	30	7.73	6	1.55
25. Workers belonging to Management Class	81	97.59	2	2.41	0	0

It can, thus, be concluded that the respondents representing different units of the factory as well as majority of the total subjects (91.98%) expressed their agreement with the statement that, "organising or joining such organisation working for the rehabilitation of girls becoming victims of humiliation after marriage".

Table 4.53 reveals that majority of the workers (67.93%) representing different units of 55 factories agreed to appeal the enlightened, educated and expert members of the community for coming forward and educating the masses about the socio-economic and physiological advantages of family planning. While 6.96% have exhibited their indifference, only 25.11% expressed their disagreement with the statement.

Unit-wise analysis reveals that 66.04% workers hailing from assembly units; 70.69% from die-making units; 57.14% from furnace and dispatch units; 69.64% from key-making units; 7193% from nickle polish units; 67.21% from Office; 674.86% from packing units; 73.61% from press units; 62.29% salaried workers and 74.48% contractual workers; 67.25% male workers and 92.86% female workers; 62.44% literate and 72.16% illiterate workers; 67.92% workers from joint family system and 68.50% representing nuclear family system; 69.08% rural workers and 67.60% urban workers; 64.14% Hindu workers and 69.82% Muslim workers; 69.47% workers receiving salary up to Rs. 3000/-and 63.79% workers receiving salary of more than 3000/-per month; 67.27% workers hailing from Labour class; and 71.08% workers hailing from management group expressed their agreement with the statement.

It can, thus, be concluded that the respondents representing different units of the factories as well as majority of the total subjects (67.93%) expressed their agreement "to appeal to the enlightened, educated and expert members of the community for coming forward and educating the masses about the socio-economic and physiological advantages of family planning."

Table 4.54 reveals that majority of the workers (52.11%) representing different units of 55 factories agreed raising of voice

TABLE 4.53 SOCIAL ASPIRATION: (3) TO APPEAL TO THE ENLIGHTENED EDUCATED AND EXPERT MEMBERS OF THE COMMUNITY FOR COMMING FORWARD AND EDUCATING THE MASSES ABOUT THE SOCIO-ECONOMIC LAND PHYSIOLOGICAL ADVANTAGES OF FAMILY PLANNING

	RESPONDENTS CATEGORY	*YES*	*%*	*INDIFF.*	*%*	*NO*	*%*
1.	Workers of different industrial units belonging to same factory.	322	67.93	33	6.96	119	25.11
2.	Workers of different factories belonging to assembly unit.	35	66.04	4	7.55	14	26.42
3.	Workers of different factories belonging to die making unit	41	70.69	2	3.45	15	25.86
4.	Workers of different factories belonging to furnace & dispatch unit.	24	57.14	3	7.14	15	35.71
5.	Workers of different factories belong to key making unit.	39	69.64	3	5.36	14	25.00
6.	Workers of different factories belonging to nickle polish unit	41	71.93	2	3.51	14	24.56
7.	Workers of different factories belonging to Office.	41	67.21	5	8.20	15	24.59
8.	Workers of different factories belonging to packing unit.	48	64.86	8	10.81	18	24.32
9.	Workers of different factories belonging to press unit.	53	73.61	5	6.94	14	19.44
10.	Salaried workers.	147	62.29	20	8.47	69	29.24

11. Contractual workers	178	74.48	11	4.60	50	20.92
12. Male workers	308	67.25	31	6.77	119	25.98
13. Female workers	13	92.86	1	7.14	0	0.00
14. Literate workers	138	62.44	11	4.98	72	32.58
15. Illiterate workers	184	72.16	24	9.41	47	18.43
16. Joint family workers	235	67.92	17	4.91	94	27.17
17. Nuclear family workers	87	68.50	15	11.81	25	19.69
18. Rural workers	105	69.08	14	9.21	33	21.71
19. Urban workers	217	67.60	18	5.61	86	2679
20. Hindu workers	93	64.14	9	6.21	43	29.66
21. Muslim workers	229	69.82	23	7.01	76	23.17
22. Workers in income group 0–3000	248	69.47	22	6.16	87	24.37
23. Workers in income group of 3000 and above	74	63.79	10	8.62	32	27.59
24. Workers belonging to Labour Class	261	67.27	27	6.96	100	25.77
25. Workers belonging to Management Class	59	71.08	5	6.02	19	22.89

TABLE 4.54 SOCIAL ASPIRATION (4) RAISING OF VOICE IN SUPPORT OF WOMEN'S RIGHTS OF EQUALITY IN FAMILY MATTERS OF THE COMMUNITY

	RESPONDENTS CATEGORY	*YES*	*%*	*INDIFF.*	*%*	*NO*	*%*
1.	Workers of different industrial units belonging to same factory.	247	52.11	23	4.85	204	43.04
2.	Workers of different factories belonging to assembly unit.	28	52.83	0	0.00	25	47.17
3.	Workers of different factories belonging to die-making unit.	30	51.72	3	5.17	25	43.10
4.	Workers of different factories belonging to furnace & dispatch unit.	23	53.49	2	4.65	18	41.86
5.	Workers of different factories belonging to key making unit.	26	46.43	5	8.93	25	44.64
6.	Workers of different factories belonging to nickle polish unit.	31	54.39	2	3.51	24	42.11
7.	Workers of different factories belonging to Office.	30	49.18	3	9.92	28	45.90
8.	Workers of different factories belonging to packing unit.	38	51.35	7	9.46	29	39.19
9.	Workers of different factories belonging to press unit.	41	56.94	1	1.39	30	41.67
10.	Salaried workers.	138	58.23	16	6.75	83	35.02

(Contd.)

11. Contractual workers	109	45.61	7	2.93	123	51.46
12. Male workers	245	53.38	21	4.58	193	42.05
13. Female workers	2	14.29	2	14.29	10	71.43
14. Literate workers	113	50.90	10	4.50	99	44.59
15 Illiterate workers	134	53.17	13	5.16	105	41.67
16. Joint family workers	181	52.16	16	4.61	150	43.23
17. Nuclear family workers	66	51.97	7	5.51	54	42.52
18. Rural workers	90	58.82	13	8.50	50	32.68
19. Urban workers	157	71.04	10	4.52	54	24.43
20. Hindu workers	93	63.70	7	4.79	46	31.51
21. Muslim workers	154	46.95	16	4.80	158	48.17
22. Workers in income group 0–3000	190	53.07	17	4.75	151	42.18
23. Workers in income group of 3000 and above	57	49.14	6	5.17	53	45.69
24. Workers belonging to Labour Class	204	52.58	20	5.15	164	42.27
25. Workers belonging to Management Class	42	50.60	3	3.61	38	45.78

in support of women's rights of equality in family matters of the community. While 4.85% exhibited their indifference, only 43.04% expressed their disagreement with the statement.

Unit-wise analysis reveals that 52.83% workers hailing from assembly units; 51.72% from die-making units; 53.49% from furnace and dispatch units; 64.43% from key-making units; 54.39% from nickle polish units; 49.18% from Office; 51.35% from packing units; 56.94% from press units; 58.23% salaried workers and 45.61% contractual workers; 53.38% male workers and 14.29% female workers; 50.90% literate workers and 53.17% illiterate workers; 52.16% workers from joint family system and 51.79% representing nuclear family system; 58.82% rural and 71.04% urban workers; 63.70% Hindu workers and 46.95% Muslim workers; 53.07% workers receiving salary up to Rs. 3000/-and 49.14% workers receiving salary of more than 3000/-per month; 52.58% workers hailing from Labour class; and 50.60% workers hailing from management group all expressed their agreement with the statement.

It can, thus, be concluded that majority of the respondents (52.11%) representing different units of the factory have expressed their agreement with the statement. The trend indicates that the respondents want to raise voice in support of women's rights of equality in family matters of the community. On the other hand, 4.85% of the respondents exhibited their indifference, 43.04% exhibited their disagreement towards the statement. Similar trend is also noticeable among the respondents representing different units of the factory. It can, thus, be inferred that majority of the respondents were in favour of the statement.

Table 4.55 reveals that majority of the workers (85.65%) representing different units of 55 factories agreed that educating members of community for not marrying their children till they receive proper education. While 11.60% have exhibited their indifference, only 2.74% expressed their disagreement with the statement.

Unit-wise analysis reveals that 88.68% workers hailing from assembly units; 79.31% from die-making units; 93.02% from furnace and dispatch units; 85.71% from key-making units; 85.96% from nickle polish units; 86.89% from Office; 81.08% packing unit and

TABLE 4.55 SOCIAL ASPIRATION: (5) EDUCATING MEMBERS OF COMMUNITY FOR NCT MARRYING THEIR CHILDREN TILL THEY RECEIVE PROPER EDUCATION

	RESPONDENTS CATEGORY	*YES*	*%*	*INDIFF.*	*%*	*NO*	*%*
1.	Workers of different industrial units belonging to same factory.	406	85.65	55	11.60	13	2.74
2.	Workers of different factories belonging to assembly unit.	47	88.68	5	9.43	1	1.89
3.	Workers of different factories belonging to die-making unit.	46	7931	8	13.79	4	6.90
4.	Workers of different factories belonging to furnace & dispatch unit.	40	93.02	2	4.65	1	2.33
5.	Workers of different factories belonging to key-making unit.	48	85.71	5	8.93	3	5.36
6.	Workers of different factories belonging to nickle polish unit.	49	85.96	8	14.04	0	0.00
7.	Workers of different factories belonging to Office.	53	86.89	7	11.48	1	1.64
8.	Workers of different factories belonging to packing unit.	60	81.08	12	16.22	2	2.70
9.	Workers of different factories belonging to press unit.	63	87.50	8	11.11	1	1.39
10.	Salaried workers.	194	81.86	33	13.92	10	4.22

(Contd.)

11.	Contractual workers	215	89.96	21	8.79	3	1.26
12.	Male workers	392	85.40	54	11.76	13	2.83
13.	Female workers	13	92.86	1	7.14	0	0.00
14.	Literate workers	201	90.54	17	7.66	4	1.80
15.	Illiterate workers	205	81.35	38	15.08	9	3.57
16.	Joint family workers	295	92.19	14	4.38	11	3.44
17.	Nuclear family workers	111	87.40	14	11.02	2	1.57
18.	Rural workers	128	83.66	20	13.07	5	3.27
19.	Urban workers	278	86.60	35	10.90	8	2.49
20.	Hindu workers	120	82.19	23	15.75	3	2.05
21.	Muslim workers	286	87.20	32	9.76	10	3.05
22.	Workers in income group 0–3000	305	85.20	43	12.01	10	2.79
23.	Workers in income group of 3000 and above	101	87.07	12	10.34	3	2.59
24.	Workers belonging to Labour Class	332	85.57	46	11.86	10	2.58
25.	Workers belonging to Management Class	72	86.75	9	10.84	2	2.41

87.50% from press units; 81.86% salaried workers and 89.96% contractual workers; 85.40% male workers and 92.86% female workers; 90.54% literate and 81.35% literate workers; 92.19% workers from joint family system and 87.40% representing nuclear family system; 83.66% rural and 86.60% urban workers; 82.19% Hindu workers and 87.20% Muslim workers; 85.20% workers receiving salary up to Rs. 3000/- and 87.07% workers receiving salary of more than 3000/- per month; 85.57% workers hailing from Labour class; and 86.75% workers hailing from management group all expressed their agreement with the statement.

It can, thus, be concluded that the respondents representing different units of the factory as well as majority of the total subjects (85.65%) agreed "educating members of community for not marrying their children till they receive proper education".

Table 4.56 reveal that majority of the workers (90.72%) representing different units of 55 factories agreed on educating members of the community for not marrying their daughters to elderly settled persons due to economic reasons but instead start some extra economic activity to improve their financial conditions. While 6.96% exhibited their indifference, only 2.34% expressed their disagreement with the statement.

Unit-wise analysis reveals that 96.23% workers hailing from assembly units; 89.66% from die-making units; 100.00% from furnace and dispatch units; 94.64% from key-making units 91.23% from press units; 89.45% salaried workers and 92.05% contractual workers; 90.41% male workers and 100.00% female workers; 94.59% literate workers and 87.30% illiterate workers; 93.66% workers from joint family system and 82.68% representing nuclear family system; 89.54% rural workers and 91.28% urban workers; 85.62% Hindu workers and 92.99% Muslim workers; 90.50% workers receiving salary up to Rs. 3000/- and 91.38% workers receiving salary more than 3000/ per month; 90.21% workers hailing from Labour class; and 92.77% workers hailing from management group all expressed their agreement with the statement.

TABLE 4.56 SOCIAL ASPIRATION: (6) EDUCATING MEMBERS OF COMMUNITY FOR NOT MARRYING THEIR DAUGHTERS TO ELDERLY SETTLED PERSONS DUE TO ECONOMIC REASONS BUT INSTEAD START SOME EXTRA ECONOMIC ACTIVITY TO IMPROVE THEIR FINANCIAL CONDITIONS

	RESPONDENTS CATEGORY	YES	%	INDIFF.	%	NO	%
1.	Workers of different industrial units belonging to same factory.	430	90.72	33	6.96	11	2.34
2.	Workers of different factories belonging to assembly unit.	51	96.23	1	1.89	1	1.89
3.	Workers of different factories belonging to die-making unit.	52	89.66	5	8.62	1	1.72
4.	Workers of different factories belonging to furnace & dispatch unit.	43	100.00	0	0.00	0	0.00
5.	Workers of different factories belonging to key making unit.	53	94.64	2	3.57	1	1.79
6.	Workers of different factories belonging to nickle polish unit.	52	91.23	4	7.02	1	1.75
7.	Workers of different factories belonging to Office	53	89.83	3	5.08	3	5.08
8.	Workers of different factories belonging to packing unit.	66	89.19	6	8.11	2	2.70
9.	Workers of different factories belonging to press unit.	58	80.56	12	16.67	2	2.78
10.	Salaried workers.	212	89.45	16	6.75	9	3.80

(Contd.)

11. Contractual workers	220	92.05	17	7.11	2	0.84
12. Male workers	415	90.41	33	7.19	11	2.40
13. Female workers	14	100.00	0	0.00	0	0.00
14. Literate workers	210	94.59	9	4.05	3	1.35
15. Illiterate workers	220	87.30	24	92.52	8	3.17
16. Joint family workers	325	93.66	15	4.32	7	2.02
17. Nuclear family workers	105	82.68	18	14.17	4	3.15
18. Rural workers	137	89.54	12	7.84	4	2.61
19. Urban workers	293	91.28	21	6.54	7	2.18
20. Hindu workers	125	85.62	18	12.33	3	2.05
21. Muslim workers	305	92.99	15	4.57	8	2.44
22. Workers in income group 0–3000	324	90.50	27	7.54	7	1.96
23. Workers' income group of 3000 and above	106	91.38	6	5.17	4	3.45
24. Workers belonging to Labour Class	350	90.21	30	7.73	8	2.06
25. Workers belonging to Management Class	77	92.77	3	361	3	3.61

It can, thus, be concluded that respondents representing different units of the factory as well as majority of the total subjects (90.27%) expressed their agreement "educating members of community for not marrying their daughters to elderly settled persons due to economic reasons but instead start some extra economic activity to improve their financial conditions".

Table 4.57 reveals that majority of the workers (91.56%) representing different units of 55 factories agreed to propagating against the evils of divorce for saving the families from disorganization. While 5.91% exhibited their indifference, only 2.53% expressed their disagreement with the statement.

Unit-wise analysis reveals that 96.23% workers hailing from assembly units; 93.10% from die-making units; 97.67% from furnace and dispatch units; 94.64% from key-making units; 91.23% from nickle polish units; 98.36% from Office; 83.78% from packing units; 83.33% from press units; 91.56% salaried workers and 92.05% contractual workers; 91.50% male workers and 92.86% female workers; 95.95% literate workers and 87.70% illiterate workers; 93.37% workers from joint family system and 86.61% representing nuclear family system; 86.27% Hindu 94.08% urban workers; 86.30% Hindu workers and 93.90% Muslim workers; 90.78% workers receiving salary up to Rs. 3000/- and 93.97% workers receiving salary more than 3000/- per month; 89.95% workers hailing from Labour class; and 98.80% workers hailing from management group all expressed their agreement with the statement.

It can, thus, be concluded that respondents representing different units of factory as well as majority of the total subjects (91.56%) agreed to "propagating against the evils of divorce for saving the families from disorganisation".

TABLE 4.57 SOCIAL ASPIRATION: (7) PROPAGATING AGAINST THE EVILS OF DIVORCE FOR SAVING THE FAMILIES FROM DISORGANISATION

	RESPONDENTS CATEGORY	*YES*	*%*	*INDIFF.*	*%*	*NO*	*%*
1.	Workers of different industrial units belonging to same factory.	434	91.56	28	5.91	12	2.53
2.	Workers of different factories belonging to assembly unit	51	96.23	2	3.77	0	0.00
3.	Workers of different factories belonging to die-making unit	54	93.10	3	5.17	1	1.72
4.	Workers of different factories belonging to furnace & dispatch unit.	42	97.67	1	2.33	0	0.00
5.	Workers of different factories belonging to Key making unit.	53	94.64	1	1.79	2	3.57
6.	Workers of different factories belonging to nickle polish unit.	52	91.23	3	5.26	2	3.51
7.	Workers of different factories belonging to Office.	60	98.36	1	1.64	0	0.00
8.	Workers of different factories belonging to packing unit.	62	83.78	7	9.46	5	6.76
9.	Workers of different factories belonging to press unit.	60	83.33	10	13.89	2	2.78
10.	Salaried workers.	217	91.56	12	5.06	8	3.38

(Contd.)

11.	Contractual workers	220	92.05	15	6.28	4	1.67
12.	Male workers	420	91.50	27	5.88	12	2.61
13.	Female workers	13	92.86	1	7.14	0	0.00
14.	Literate workers	213	95.95	6	2.70	3	1.35
15.	Illiterate workers	221	87.70	22	8.73	9	3.57
16.	Joint family workers	324	93.37	16	4.61	7	2.02
17.	Nuclear family workers	110	86.61	12	9.45	5	3.94
18.	Rural workers	132	86.27	15	9.80	6	3.92
19.	Urban workers	302	94.08	13	4.05	6	1.87
20.	Hindu workers	126	86.30	15	10.27	5	3.42
21.	Muslim workers	308	93.90	13	3.96	7	2.13
22.	Workers in income group 0–3000	325	90.78	23	6.42	10	2.79
23.	Workers in income group of 3000 and above	109	93.97	5	4.31	2	1.72
24.	Workers belonging to Labour Class	349	89.95	27	6.96	12	3.09
25.	Workers belonging to Management Class	82	98.80	1	1.20	0	0

Table 4.58 reveals that majority of the workers (91.35%) representing different units of 55 factories agreed to propagating to encourage women widow remarriage in order to rehabilitate and rescue them from expected future exploitation. While 6.96% exhibited their indifference, only 1.69% expressed their disagreement with the statement.

Unit-wise analysis reveals that 94.34% workers hailing from assembly units; 98.28% from die-making units; 97.67% from furnace and dispatch units; 92.98% from key-making units; 91.23% from nickle polish units; 96.72% from Office; 78.38% from packing units; 87.50% from press units; 90.30% salaried workers and 92.47% contractual workers; 92.16% male workers and 64.29% female workers; 95.05% literate workers and 88.10% illiterate workers; 93.66% workers from joint family system and 85.04% representing nuclear family system; 88.24% rural workers and 92.83% urban workers; 84.93% Hindu workers and 94.26% Muslim workers; 89.66% workers receiving salary up to Rs. 3000/- and 96.55% workers receiving salary more than 3000/- per month; 89.95% workers hailing from Labour class; and 97.59% workers hailing from management group all expressed their agreement with the statement.

It can, thus, be concluded that respondents representing different units of the factory as well as majority of the total subjects (91.35%) agreed to "propagating to encourage women widow remarriage in order to rehabilitate and rescue them from expected future exploitation."

Table 4.59 reveals that majority of the workers (94.30%) representing different units of 55 factories have agreed that the associate with some such voluntary social organizations which may help in selecting matches for educated boys and girls. While 4.43% their indifference, only 1.27 % expressed their disagreement with the statement.

Unit-wise analysis reveals that 96.23% workers hailing from assembly units; 94.83% from die-making units; 97.67% from furnace

TABLE 4.58 SOCIAL ASPIRATION: (8) PROPAGATING TO ENCOURAGE WOMEN WIDOW REMARRIAGE IN ORDER TO REHABILITATE AND RESCUE THEM FROM EXPECTED FUTURE EXPLOITATION

	RESPONDENTS CATEGORY	*YES*	*%*	*INDIFF.*	*%*	*NO*	*%*
1.	Workers of different industrial units belonging to same factory.	433	91.35	33	6.96	8	1.69
2.	Workers of different factories belonging to assembly unit	50	94.34	1	1.89	2	3.77
3.	Workers of different factories belonging to die-making unit	57	98.28	0	0.00	1	1.72
4.	Workers of different factories belonging to furnace & dispatch unit.	42	97.67	1	2.33	0	0.00
5.	Workers of different factories belonging to key-making unit.	53	92.98	1	1.75	3	5.26
6.	Workers of different factories belonging to nickle polish unit.	52	91.23	5	8.77	0	0.00
7.	Workers of different factories belonging to Office.	59	96.72	2	3.28	0	0.00
8.	Workers of different factories belonging to packing unit.	58	78.38	13	17.57	3	4.05
9.	Workers of different factories belonging to press unit.	63	87.50	9	12.50	0	0.00
10.	Salaried workers.	214	90.30	17	7.17	6	2.53

(*Contd.*)

11.	Contractual workers	221	92.47	16	6.69	2	0.84
12.	Male workers	423	92.16	29	6.32	7	1.53
13.	Female workers	9	64.29	4	28.57	1	7.14
14.	Literate workers	211	95.05	9	4.05	2	0.90
15.	Illiterate workers	222	88.10	24	9.52	6	2.38
16.	Joint family workers	325	93.66	16	4.61	6	1.73
17.	Nuclear family workers	108	85.04	17	13.39	2	1.57
18.	Rural workers	135	88.24	13	8.50	5	3.27
19.	Urban workers	298	92.83	20	6.23	3	0.93
20.	Hindu workers	124	84.93	18	12.33	4	2.74
21.	Muslim workers	309	94.21	15	4.57	4	1.22
22.	Workers in income group 0–3000	321	89.66	30	8.38	7	1.96
23.	Workers in income group of 3000 and above	112	96.55	3	2.59	1	0.86
24.	Workers belonging to Labour Class	349	89.95	31	7.99	8	2.06
25.	Workers belonging to Management Class	81	97.59	2	2.41	0	0

and dispatch units; 94.64% from key-making units; 94.74% from nickle polish units; 96.72% from Office; 89.19% from packing units; 93.06% from press units; 92.83% salaried workers and 96.23% contractual workers; 94.12% male workers and 100.00% female workers; 97.75% literate workers and 91.27% illiterate workers; 95.39% workers from joint family system and 91.34% representing nuclear family system; 90.85% rural workers and 95.95% urban workers; 91.10% Hindu workers and 95.73% Muslim workers; 93.58% workers receiving salary up to Rs. 3000/- and 96.55% workers receiving salary more than 3000/- per month; 93.30% workers hailing from Labour class; and 98.80% workers hailing from management group all expressed their agreement with the statement.

It can, thus, be concluded that the respondents representing different units of the factory as well as majority of the total subjects (94.30%) expressed their agreed "to associate with some such voluntary social organizations, which may help in selecting matches for educated boys and girls".

Table 4.60 reveals that majority of the workers (92.19%) representing different units of 55 factories agreed to enlighten community members to interact among themselves quite frequently so that the traditional bonds of family proximity are maintained. While 4.22% have exhibited their indifference, only 3.59% have expressed their disagreement with the statement.

Unit-wise analysis reveals that 88.68% workers hailing from assembly units; 93.10% from die-making units; 100.00% from furnace and dispatch units; 92.86% from key-making units; 92.98% from nickle polish units; 91.80% from Office; 90.54% from packing unit and 90.28% from press units; 91.14% salaried workers and 93.31% contractual workers; 91.94% male workers and 100.00% female workers;95.05% literate workers and 89.68% illiterate workers; 93.37% workers from joint family system and 88.89% representing nuclear family system; 88.89% rural workers and 93.77% urban workers; 91.10% Hindu workers and 92.68% Muslim workers; 90.78%

TABLE 4.59 SOCIAL ASPIRATION: (9) TO ASSOCIATE WITH SOME SUCH VOLUNTARY SOCIAL ORGANISATIONS WHICH MAY HELP IN SELECTING MATCHES FOR EDUCATED BOYS AND GIRLS

	RESPONDENTS CATEGORY	*YES*	*%*	*INDIFF.*	*%*	*NO*	*%*
1.	Workers of different industrial units belonging to same factory.	447	94.30	21	4.43	6	1.27
2.	Workers of different factories belonging to assembly unit.	51	96.23	2	3.77	0	0.00
3.	Workers of different factories belonging to die-making unit.	55	94.83	3	5.17	0	0.00
4.	Workers of different factories belonging to furnace & dispatch unit	42	97.67	1	2.33	0	0.00
5.	Workers of different factories belonging to key-making unit.	53	94.64	2	3.57	1	1.79
6.	Workers of different factories belonging to nickle polish unit	54	94.74	3	5.26	0	0.00
7.	Workers of different factories belonging to Office.	59	96.72	1	1.64	1	1.64
8.	Workers of different factories belonging to packing unit.	66	89.19	4	5.41	4	5.41
9.	Workers of different factories belonging to press unit.	67	93.06	5	6.94	0	0.00
10.	Salaried workers.	220	92.83	11	4.64	6	2.53

(Contd.)

11. Contractual workers	230	96.23	9	3.77	0	0.00
12. Male workers	432	94.12	21	4.58	6	1.31
13. Female workers	14	100.00	0	0.00	0	0.00
14. Literate workers	217	97.75	3	1.35	2	0.90
15. Illiterate workers	230	91.27	18	7.14	4	1.59
16. Joint family workers	331	95.39	12	3.46	4	1.15
17. Nuclear family workers	116	91.34	9	7.09	2	1.57
18. Rural workers	139	90.85	10	6.54	4	2.61
19. Urban workers	308	95.95	11	3.43	2	0.62
20. Hindu workers	133	91.10	10	6.85	3	2.05
21. Muslim workers	314	95.73	11	3.35	3	0.91
22. Workers in income group 0–3000	335	93.58	17	4.75	6	1.68
23. Workers in income group of 3000 and above	112	96.55	4	3.45	0	0.00
24. Workers belonging to Labour Class	362	93.30	21	5.41	5	1.29
25 Workers belonging to Management Class	82	98.80	0	0	1	1.20

TABLE 4.60 SOCIAL ASPIRATION: (10) TO ENLIGHTEN COMMUNITY MEMBERS TO INTERACT AMONG THEMSELVES QUITE FREQUENTLY SO THAT THE TRADITIONAL BONDS OF FAMILY PROXIMITY ARE MAINTAINED

RESPONDENTS CATEGORY	*YES*	%	*INDIFF.*	%	*NO*	%
1. Workers of different industrial units belonging to same factory.	437	92.19	20	4.22	17	3.59
2. Workers of different factories belonging to assembly unit.	47	88.68	4	7.55	2	3.77
3. Workers of different factories belonging to die-making unit.	54	93.10	3	5.17	1	1.72
4. Workers of different factories belonging to furnace & dispatch unit.	43	100.00	0	0.00	0	0.00
5. Workers of different factories belonging to key-making unit.	52	92.86	2	3.57	2	3.57
6. Workers of different factories belonging to nickle polish unit	53	92.98	3	5.26	1	1.75
7. Workers of different factories belonging to Office.	56	91.80	2	3.28	3	4.92
8. Workers of different factories belonging to packing unit.	67	90.54	3	4.05	4	5.41
9. Workers of different factories belonging to press unit.	65	90.28	3	4.17	4	5.56
10. Salaried workers.	216	91.14	12	5.06	9	3.80

(Contd.)

11. Contractual workers	223	93.31	7	2.93	9	3.77
12. Male workers	422	91.94	20	4.36	17	3.70
13. Female workers	14	100.00	0	0.00	0	0.00
14. Literate workers	211	905.05	5	2.25	6	2.70
15. Illiterate workers	226	89.68	15	5.95	11	4.37
16. Joint family workers	324	93.37	12	3.46	11	3.17
17. Nuclear family workers	113	88.98	8	6.30	6	4.72
18. Rural workers	136	88.89	10	6.54	7	4.58
19. Urban workers	301	93.77	10	3.12	10	3.12
20. Hindu workers	133	91.10	10	6.85	3	2.05
21. Muslim workers	304	92.68	10	3.05	14	4.27
22. Workers in income group 0–3000	325	90.78	19	5.31	14	3.91
23. Workers in income group of 3000 and above	112	96.55	1	0.86	3	2.59
24. Workers belonging to Labour Class	356	91.75	19	4.90	13	3.35
25. Workers belonging to Management Class	78	93.98	1	1.20	4	4.82

workers receiving salary up to Rs. 3000/- and 96.55% workers receiving salary of more than 3000/- per month; 91.75% workers hailing from Labour class; and 93.98% workers hailing from management group all expressed their agreement with the statement.

It can, thus, be concluded that respondents representing different units of the factory as well as majority of the total subjects (92.19%) expressed their agreed "to enlighten the community members to interact among themselves quite frequently so that the traditional bonds of family proximity are maintained".

Table 4.61 reveals that only 14.56% workers representing different units of 55 factories agreed that community members should take keen interest in political affairs and also adopt unethical practices to achieve their goals. While 1.48% have exhibited their indifference, only 83.97% expressed their disagreement with the statement.

Unit-wise analysis reveals that 9.43% workers hailing from assembly units; 12.07% from die-making units; 2.33% from furnace and dispatch units; 12.50% from key-making units; 10.53% from nickle polish units; 13.11% from Office; 28.38% from packing unit and 19.72% from press units; 17.30% salaried workers and 11.76% contractual workers; 14.19% male workers and 28.57% female workers; 9.91% literate workers and 18.73% illiterate workers; 13.26% workers from joint family system and 18.25% representing nuclear family system; 22.88% rural workers and 10.63% urban workers; 24.66% Hindu workers and 10.09% Muslim workers; 17.37% workers receiving salary up to Rs. 3000/- and 6.03% workers receiving salary more than 3000/- per month; 82.17% workers hailing from Labour class; and while only 16.28% workers hailing from Labour class and only 7.23% workers from management class expressed their agreement with the statement. However, 82.75 of workers from Labour class and 92.77% workers hailing from management group all expressed their disagreement with the statement.

It can, thus, be concluded that the respondents representing different units of the factory as well as majority of the total subjects (83.97%) expressed their disagreement with the statement that, community members taking keen interest in the political affairs and also adopt unethical practices to achieve their goals. On the other

TABLE 4.61 POLITICAL PERCEPTION: (1) COMMUNITY MEMBERS TAKING KEEN INTEREST IN POLITICAL AFFAIRS AND ALSO ADOPT UNETHNICAL PRACTICES TO ACHIEVE THEIR GOALS

	RESPONDENTS CATEGORY	*YES*	*%*	*INDIFF.*	*%*	*NO*	*%*
1.	Workers of different industrial units belonging to same factory.	69	14.56	7	1.48	398	83.97
2.	Workers of different factories belonging to assembly unit.	5	9.43	1	1.89	47	88.68
3.	Workers of different factories belonging to die-making unit.	7	12.07	0	0.00	51	87.93
4.	Workers of different factories belonging to furnace & dispatch unit.	1	2.33	0	0.00	42	97.67
5.	Workers of different factories belonging to key-making unit.	7	12.50	0	0.00	49	87.50
6.	Workers of different factories belonging to nickle polish unit	6	10.53	4	7.02	47	82.46
7.	Workers of different factories belonging to Office.	8	13.11	0	0.00	53	86.89
8.	Workers of different factories belonging to packing unit.	21	28.38	0	0.00	53	71.67
9.	Workers of different factories belonging to press unit.	14	19.72	1	1.41	56	78.87
10.	Salaried workers.	41	17.30	1	0.42	195	82.28

(*Contd.*)

11. Contractual workers	28	11.76	5	2.10	205	86.13
12. Male workers	65	14.19	6	1.31	387	84.50
13. Female workers	4	28.57	0	0.00	10	71.43
14. Literate workers	22	9.91	0	0.00	200	90.09
15. Illiterate workers	47	18.73	6	2.39	198	78.88
16. Joint family workers	46	13.26	5	1.44	296	85.30
17. Nuclear family workers	23	18.25	1	0.79	102	80.95
18. Rural workers	35	22.88	2	1.31	116	75.82
19. Urban workers	34	10.63	4	1.25	2892	88.13
20. Hindu workers	36	24.66	2	1.37	108	73.97
21. Muslim workers	33	10.09	4	1.22	290	88.69
22. Workers in income group 0–3000	62	17.37	5	1.40	290	81.23
23. Workers in income group of 3000 and above	7	6.03	1	0.86	108	93.10
24. Workers belonging to Labour Class	63	16.28	6	1.55	318	82.17
25. Workers belonging to Management Class	6	7.23	0	0	77	92.77

hand 1.48% of the respondents have exhibited their indifference towards the statement and 14.56% of the respondents have exhibited their agreement towards the statement. Similar trend is also noticeable among the respondents representing different unit of the factory.

Table 4.62 reveals that majority of workers (94.09%) representing different units of 55 factories agreed that members of the society do not support political parties on the basis of their election manifesto. While 4.01% exhibited their indifference, only 1.90% expressed their disagreement with the statement.

Unit-wise analysis reveals that 96.23% workers hailing from assembly units; 93.10% from die-making units; 95.35% from furnace and dispatch units; 100.00% from key-making units; 91.23% from nickle polish units; 96.72% from Office; 90.54% from packing units; 91.67% from press units; 93.25% salaried workers and 95.40% contractual workers; 94.12% male workers and 92.86% female workers; 96.40% literate workers and 92.06% illiterate workers; 94.81% workers from joint family system and 92.13% representing nuclear family system; 93.46% rural and 94.39% urban workers; 93.84% Hindu workers and 94.21% Muslim workers; 93.85% workers receiving salary up to Rs. 3000/- and 94.83% workers receiving salary more than 3000/- per month; 93.56% workers hailing from Labour class; and 97.59% workers hailing from management group expressed their agreement with the statement.

It can, thus, be concluded that the respondents representing different units of the factory as well as majority of the total subjects (94.09%) expressed their agreement with the statement that, "members of the society do not support political parties on the basis of their election manifesto".

Table 4.63 reveals that only majority of the workers 25.32% representing different units of 55 factories agreed that fair elections are held in our society, while 3.38% exhibited their indifference, only 71.31% expressed their disagreement with the statement.

TABLE 4.62 POLITICAL PERCEPTION: (2) MEMBERS OF THE SOCIETY DO NOT SUPPORT POLITICAL PARTIES ON THE BASIS OF THEIR ELECTION MANIFESTO

	RESPONDENTS CATEGORY	*YES*	*%*	*INDIFF.*	*%*	*NO*	*%*
1.	Workers of different industrial units belonging to same factory.	446	94.09	19	4.01	9	1.90
2.	Workers of different factories belonging to assembly unit.	51	96.23	2	3.77	0	0.00
3.	Workers of different factories belonging to die-making unit.	54	93.10	2	3.45	2	3.45
4.	Workers of different factories belonging to furnace & dispatch unit.	41	95.35	0	0.00	2	4.65
5.	Workers of different factories belonging to key-making unit.	56	100.00	0	0.00	0	0.00
6.	Workers of different factories belonging to nickle polish unit	52	91.23	5	8.77	0	0.00
7.	Workers of different factories belonging to Office.	59	96.72	1	1.64	1	1.64
8.	Workers of different factories belonging to packing unit.	67	90.54	5	6.76	2	2.70
9.	Workers of different factories belonging to press unit.	66	91.67	4	5.56	2	2.78
10.	Salaried workers	221	93.25	10	4.22	6	2.53

(Contd.)

11. Contractual workers	228	95.40	9	3.77	2	0.84
12. Male workers	432	94.12	18	3.92	9	1.96
13. Female workers	13	92.86	1	7.14	0	0.00
14. Literate workers	214	96.40	5	2.25	3	1.35
15. Illiterate workers	232	92.06	14	5.56	6	2.38
16. Joint family workers	329	94.81	13	3.75	5	1.44
17. Nuclear family workers	117	92.13	6	4.72	4	3.15
18. Rural workers	143	93.46	4	2.61	6	3.92
19. Urban workers	303	94.39	15	4.67	3	0.93
20. Hindu workers	137	93.84	4	2.74	5	3.42
21. Muslim workers	309	94.21	15	4.57	4	1.22
22. Workers in income group 0–3000	336	93.85	16	4.47	6	1.68
23. Workers in income group of 3000 and above	110	94.83	3	2.59	3	2.59
24. Workers belonging to Labour Class	363	93.56	18	4.64	7	1.80
25. Workers belonging to Management Class	81	97.59	1	1.20	1	1.20

TABLE 4.63 POLITICAL PERCEPTION: (3) FAIR ELECTIONS ARE HELD IN OUR SOCIETY

RESPONDENTS CATEGORY	*YES*	*%*	*INDIFF.*	*%*	*NO*	*%*
1. Workers of different industrial units belonging to same factory.	120	25.32	16	3.38	338	71.31
2. Workers of different factories belonging to assembly unit.	12	22.64	2	3.77	39	73.58
3. Workers of different factories belonging to die-making unit.	13	22.41	3	5.17	42	72.41
4. Workers of different factories belonging to furnace & dispatch unit.	8	18.60	1	2.33	34	79.07
5. Workers of different factories belonging to key-making unit.	11	19.64	4	7.14	41	73.21
6. Workers of different factories belonging to nickle polish unit.	14	24.56	2	3.51	41	71.93
7. Workers of different factories belonging to Office.	14	22.95	0	0.00	47	77.05
8. Workers of different factories belonging to packing unit.	27	36.49	3	4.05	44	59.46
9. Workers of different factories belonging to press unit.	21	29.17	1	1.39	50	69.44
10. Salaried workers.	56	23.63	11	4.64	170	71.73

(Contd.)

11.	Contractual workers	64	26.78	4	1.67	171	71.55
12.	Male workers	112	24.40	16	3.49	331	72.11
13.	Female workers	8	57.14	0	0.00	6	42.86
14.	Literate workers	49	22.07	3	1.35	170	76.58
15.	Illiterate workers	71	28.17	13	5.16	168	66.67
16.	Joint family workers	85	24.50	10	2.88	252	72.62
17.	Nuclear family workers	35	27.56	6	4.72	86	67.72
18.	Rural workers	44	28.76	9	5.88	100	65.36
19.	Urban workers	76	23.68	7	2.18	238	74.14
20.	Hindu workers	46	31.51	3	2.05	97	66.44
21.	Muslim workers	74	22.56	13	3.96	241	73.48
22.	Workers in income group 0–3000	100	27.93	13	3.63	245	68.44
23.	Workers in income group of 3000 and above	20	17.24	3	2.59	93	80.17
24.	Workers belonging to Labour Class	100	25.77	16	4.12	272	70.10
25.	Workers belonging to Management Class	20	24.10	0	0	63	75.90

Unit-wise analysis reveals that 22.64% workers hailing from assembly units; 22.41% from die-making units; 18.60% from furnace and dispatch units; 19.64% from key-making units; 24.56% from nickle polish units; 22.95% from Office; 36.49% from packing units; and 29.17% from press units; 23.63% salaried workers and 26.78% contractual workers; 24.40% male workers and 57.14% female workers; 22.07% literate workers and 28.17% illiterate workers; 24.50% workers from joint family system and 27.56 representing nuclear family system; 28.76% rural workers and 23.68% urban workers; 31.51% Hindu workers and 22.56% Muslim workers; 27.93% workers receiving salary up to Rs. 3000/- and 17.24% workers receiving salary more than 3000/- per month exhibited their agreement with the statement. However, 70.10% workers hailing from Labour class; and while only 25.77% expressed their agreement with the statement. Besides 75.90% workers hailing from management group have also expressed their disagreement with the statement, while only 24.10% expressed their agreement with the statement.

It can, thus, be concluded that the respondents representing different units of the factory as well as majority of the total subjects (71.31%) expressed their disagreement with the statement that, fair elections are held in our society. On the other hand, 3.38% of the respondents have exhibited their indifference towards the statement and on the other hand 25.32% of the respondents have exhibited their agreement towards the statement. Similar trend is also noticeable among the respondents representing different units of the factory.

Table 4.64 reveals that majority of the workers (93.04%) representing different units of 55 factories agreed that political bosses misuse their position and power for selfish ends by exploiting the authorities. While 5.91% exhibited their indifference, only 1.05% expressed their disagreement with the statement.

Unit-wise analysis reveals that 92.45% workers hailing from assembly units; 94.83% from die-making units; 95.35% from furnace and dispatch units; 94.64% from key-making units; 94.74% from nickle polish units; 95.08% from Office; 83.78% from packing units; 95.83% from press units; 91.98% salaried workers and 94.56%

TABLE 4.64 POLITICAL PERCEPTION: (4) POLITICAL BOSSES MISUSE THEIR POSITION AND POWER FOR SELFISH ENDS BY EXPLOITING THE AUTHORITIES

RESPONDENTS CATEGORY	*YES*	*%*	*INDIFF.*	*%*	*NO*	*%*
1. Workers of different industrial units belonging to same factory.	441	93.04	28	5.91	5	1.05
2. Workers of different factories belonging to assembly unit	49	92.45	3	5.66	1	1.89
3. Workers of different factories belonging to die-making unit	55	94.83	3	5.17	0	0.00
4. Workers of different factories belonging to furnace & dispatch unit.	41	95.35	1	2.33	1	2.33
5. Workers of different factories belonging to key-making unit.	53	94.64	2	3.57	1	1.79
6. Workers of different factories belonging to Nickle polish unit	54	94.74	2	3.51	1	1.75
7. Workers of different factories belonging to Office	58	95.08	3	4.92	0	0.00
8. Workers of different factories belonging to packing unit.	62	83.78	11	14.86	1	1.35
9. Workers of different factories belonging to press unit.	69	95.83	3	4.17	0	0.00
10. Salaried workers.	218	91.98	18	7.59	1	0.42

(Contd.)

11. Contractual workers	226	94.56	9	3.77	4	1.67
12. Male workers	429	93.46	25	5.45	5	1.09
13. Female workers	11	78.57	3	21.43	0	0.00
14. Literate workers	214	96.40	6	2.70	2	0.90
15. Illiterate workers	227	90.08	22	8.73	3	1.19
16. Joint family workers	325	93.66	20	5.76	2	0.58
17. Nuclear family workers	116	91.34	8	6.30	3	2.36
18. Rural workers	135	88.24	17	11.11	1	0.65
19. Urban workers	306	95.33	11	3.43	4	1.25
20. Hindu workers	132	90.41	12	8.22	2	1.36
21. Muslim workers	309	94.21	16	4.88	3	1.12
22. Workers in income group 0-3000	329	91.90	25	6.98	4	0.86
23. Workers in income group of 3000 and above	112	96.55	3	2.59	1	0.29
24. Workers belonging to Labour Class	357	92.01	26	6.70	5	1.29
25. Workers belonging to Management Class	81	57.59	2	2.41	0	0

contractual workers; 93.46% male workers and 78.57% female workers; 96.40% literate worker and 90.08% illiterate workers; 93.66% workers from joint family system and 91.34% representing nuclear family system; 88.24% rural workers and 95.33% urban workers; 90.41% Hindu workers and 94.21% Muslim workers; 91.90% workers receiving salary up to Rs. 3000/- and 96.55% workers receiving salary of more than 3000/- per month; 92.01% workers from Labour class and 97.59% workers from management group expressed their agreement with the statement.

It can, thus, be concluded that the respondents representing different units of the factory as well as majority of the total subjects (93.04%) expressed their agreement with the statement that "political bosses misuse their position and power for selfish ends by exploiting the authorities."

Table 4.65 reveals that majority of the workers (93.04%) representing different units of 55 factories agreed that candidates and political parties freely use money and muscle power during elections. While 5.91% exhibited their indifference only 1.05% expressed their disagreement with the statement.

Unit-wise analysis reveals that 92.45% workers hailing from assembly units; 94.83% from die-making units; 95.35% from furnace and dispatch units; 94.64% from key-making units; 94.74% from nickle polish units; 95.08% from Office; 83.78% from packing units; 95.83% from press units; 91.98% salaried workers and 94.56% contractual workers; 93.46% male workers and 78.57% female workers; 96.40% literate workers and 90.08% illiterate workers; 93.66% workers from joint family system and 91.34% representing nuclear family system; 88.24% rural workers and 95.33% urban workers; 90.41% Hindu workers and 94.21% Muslim workers; 91.90% workers receiving salary up to Rs. 3000/- and 96.55% workers receiving salary of more than 3000/- per month; 92.27% workers from Labour class; and 96.39% workers hailing from management group expressed their agreement with the statement.

TABLE 4.65 POLITICAL PERCEPTION: (5) CANDIDATES AND POLITICAL PARTIES FREELY USE MONEY AND MUSCLE POWER DURING ELECTIONS

	RESPONDENTS CATEGORY	*YES*	*%*	*INDIFF.*	*%*	*NO*	*%*
1.	Workers of different industrial units belonging to the same factory	441	93.04	28	5.91	5	1.05
2.	Workers of different factories belonging to assembly unit.	47	92.45	5	5.66	2	1.89
3.	Workers of different factories belonging to die-making units.	53	94.83	3	5.17	2	0.00
4.	Workers of different factories belonging to furnace & dispatch unit.	42	95.35	1	2.33	0	2.33
5.	Workers of different factories belonging to key-making units.	53	94.64	2	3.57	1	1.79
6.	Workers of different factories belonging to nickle polish unit.	54.	94.74	3	3.51	0	1.75
7.	Workers of different factories belonging to Office.	58	95.08	3	4.92	9	0.00
8.	Workers of different factories belonging to packing unit.	65	83.78	8	14.86	1	1.35
9.	Workers of different factories belonging to press unit.	69	95.83	3	4.17	0	0.00
10.	Salaried workers.	216	91.98	18	7.59	3	0.42

(Contd.)

11.	Contractual workers	228	94.56	10	3.77	1	1.67
12.	Male workers	429	93.46	26	5.45	4	1.09
13.	Female workers	11	78.57	2	21.43	1	0.00
14.	Literate workers	213	96.40	7	2.70	2	0.90
15.	Illiterate workers	228	90.08	21	8.73	3	1.19
16.	Joint family workers	323	93.66	20	5.76	4	0.58
17.	Nuclear family workers	118	91.34	8	6.30	1	2.36
18.	Rural workers	132	88.24	18	11.11	3	0.65
19.	Urban workers	309	95.33	10	3.43	2	1.25
20.	Hindu workers	132	90.41	13	8.22	1	1.37
21.	Muslim workers	309	94.21	15	4.88	4	0.91
22.	Workers in income group 0–3000	328	91.90	26	6.98	4	1.12
23.	Workers in income groups 3000 and above	113	96.55	2	2.59	1	0.86
24.	Workers belonging to Labour Class	358	93.81	25	5.15	5	1.03
25.	Workers belonging to Management Class	80	96.39	3	1.20	0	2.41

It can, thus, be concluded that the respondents representing different units of the factory as well as majority of the total subjects (93.04%) expressed their agreement with the statement that "candidates and political parties freely use money and muscle power during elections".

Table 4.66 reveals the majority of that workers (94.30%) representing different units of 55 factories agreed that economically well off people extend financial support to important parties and candidates because they cash them after their victories. While 4.43% exhibited their indifference, only 1.27% have expressed their disagreement with the statement.

Unit-wise analysis reveals that 96.23% workers hailing from assembly units; 96.55% from die-making units; 97.67% from furnace and dispatch units; 98.21% from key-making units; 94.74% from nickle polish units; 96.72% from Office; 86.49% from packing units; 91.67% from press units; 92.41% salaried workers and 96.23% contractual workers; 94.34% male workers and 92.86% female workers; 95.50% literate workers and 93.33% illiterate workers; 94.81% workers from joint family system and 92.91% representing nuclear family system; 91.50% rural workers and 95.64% urban workers; 91.10% Hindu workers and 95.73% Muslim workers; 93.02% workers receiving salary up to Rs. 3000/- and 98.28% workers receiving salary of more than 3000/- per month; 93.81% workers hailing from Labour class and 96.39% workers hailing from management group expressed their agreement with the statement.

It can, thus, be concluded that the respondents representing different units of the factory as well as majority of the total subjects (94.03%) expressed their agreement with the statement that "economically well off people extend financial support to the important parties and candidates because they cash them after their victories."

TABLE 4.66 POLITICAL PERCEPTION: (6) ECONOMICALLY WELL OFF PEOPLE EXTEND FINANCIAL SUPPORT TO THE IMPORTANT PARTIES AND CANDIDATES BECAUSE THEY CASH THEM AFTER THEIR VICTORIES

	RESPONDENTS CATEGORY	YES	%	INDIFF.	%	NO	%
1.	Workers of different industrial units belonging to same factory.	447	94.30	21	4.43	6	1.27
2.	Workers of different factories belonging to assembly unit.	51	96.23	2	3.77	0	0.00
3.	Workers of different factories belonging to diemaking unit.	56	96.55	1	2.33	0	0.00
4.	Workers of different factories belonging to furnace & dispatch unit.	42	97.67	1	2.33	0	0.00
5.	Workers of different factories belonging to key-making unit.	55	98.21	0	0.00	1	1.79
6.	Workers of different factories belonging to nickle polish unit.	54	94.74	2	3.51	1	1.75
7.	Workers of different factories belonging to Office.	59	96.72	0	0.00	2	3.28
8.	Workers of different factories belonging to packing unit.	64	86.49	9	12.16	1	1.35
9.	Workers of different factories belonging to press unit.	66	91.67	5	6.94	1	1.39
10.	Salaried workers.	219	92.41	13	5.49	5	2.11

(Contd.)

11. Contractual workers	230	96.23	8	3.35	1	0.42
12. Male workers	433	94.34	20	4.36	6	1.31
13. Female workers	212	95.50	8	3.60	2	0190
14. Literate workers	238	93.33	13	5.10	4	1.57
15. Illiterate workers	329	94.81	14	4.03	4	1.15
16. Joint family workers	118	92.91	7	5.51	2	1.57
17. Nuclear family workers	140	91.50	9	5.88	4	2.61
18. Rural workers	307	95.64	12	3.74	2	0.62
19. Urban workers	133	91.10	10	6.85	3	2.95
20. Hindu workers	314	95.73	11	3.35	3	0.91
21. Muslim workers	133	93.02	20	5.59	5	1.40
22. Workers in income group 0–3000	328	91.90	26	6.98	4	1.12
23. Workers in income group of 3000 and above	113	96.55	2	2.59	1	0.86
24. Workers belonging to Labour Class	358	93.81	25	5.15	5	1.03
25. Workers belonging to Management Class	80	96.39	3	1.20	0	2.41

Table 4.67 reveals that majority of the workers (94.09%) representing different units of 55 factories agreed that in elections, political parties issue tickets and extend full support to persons having established criminal background. While 5.70% exhibited their indifference, only 0.21% expressed their disagreement with the statement.

Unit-wise analysis reveals that 94.34% workers from assembly units; 96.55% from die-making units; 97.67% from furnace and dispatch units; 94.64% from key-making units; 87.72% from nickle polish units; 98.36% from Office; 90.54% from packing units; 94.44% from press units; 96.04% salaried workers and 96.23% contractual workers; 94.12% male workers and 92.86% female workers; 97.75% literate workers and 90.87% illiterate workers; 95.10% workers from joint family system and 91.34% representing nuclear family system; 88.89% rural workers and 96.57% urban workers; 91.10% Hindu workers and 95.43% Muslim workers; 93.30% workers receiving salary up to Rs. 3000/- and 96.55% workers receiving salary more than 3000/- per month; 93.04% workers hailing from Labour class and 98.80% workers hailing from management group expressed their agreement with the statement.

It can, thus, be concluded that the respondents representing different units of the factory as well as majority of the total subjects (94.09%) expressed their agreement with the statement that "in elections political parties issue tickets and extend full support to persons having established criminal background".

Table 4.68 reveals that majority of workers (94.94%) representing different units of 55 factories agreed that political parties and even independent candidates, for winning the election, do not hesitate in giving communal or caste turn to any event during election period if it suits them. While 4.64% exhibited their indifference, only 0.42 have expressed their disagreement with the statement.

Unit-wise analysis reveals that 96.23% workers hailing from assembly units; 96.55% from die-making units; 97.67% from furnace

TABLE 4.67 POLITICAL PERCEPTION: (7) IN THE ELECTIONS POLITICAL PARTIES ISSUE TICKETS AND EXTEND FULL SUPPORT TO PERSONS HAVING ESTABLISHED CRIMINAL BACKGROUND

	RESPONDENTS CATEGORY	*YES*	*%*	*INDIFF.*	*%*	*NO*	*%*
1.	Workers of different industrial units belonging to same factory.	446	94.09	27	5.70	1	0.21
2.	Workers of different factories belonging to assembly unit.	50	94.34	3	5.66	0	0.00
3.	Workers of different factories belonging to die-making units	56	96.55	2	3.45	0	0.00
4.	Workers of different factories belonging to furnace & dispatch unit.	42	97.67	1	2.33	0	0.00
5.	Workers of different factories belonging to key making unit.	53	94.64	3	5.36	0	0.00
6.	Workers of different factories belonging to nickle polish unit.	50	87.72	6	10.53	1	1.75
7.	Workers of different factories belonging to Office.	60	98.36	1	1.64	0.	0.00
8.	Workers of different factories belonging to packing unit.	67	90.54	7	9.46	0	0.00
9.	Workers of different factories belonging to press unit.	68	94.44	4	5.56	0	0.00
10.	Salaried workers.	218	96.04	9	3.96	0	0.00

(Contd.)

11.	Contractual workers	230	96.23	8	3.35	1	0.42
12.	Male workers	432	94.12	26	5.66	1	0.22
13.	Female workers	13	92.86	1	7.14	0	0.00
14.	Literate workers	217	97.75	5	2.25	0	0.00
15.	Illiterate workers	229	90.87	22	8.73	1	0.40
16.	Joint family workers	330	95.10	16	4.61	1	0.29
17.	Nuclear family workers	116	91.34	11	8.66	0	0.00
18.	Rural workers	136	88.89	16	10.46	1	0.65
19.	Urban workers	310	96.57	11	3.43	0	0.00
20.	Hindu workers	133	91.10	12	8.22	1	0.68
21.	Muslim workers	313	95.43	15	4.57	0	0.00
22.	Workers in income group 0–3000	334	93.30	23	6.42	1	0.28
23.	Workers in income group of 3000 and above	112	96.55	4	3.45	0	0.00
24.	Workers belonging to Labour Class	361	93.04	26	6.70	1	0.26
25.	Workers belonging to Management Class	82	98.80	1	1.20	0	0

TABLE 4.68 POLITICAL PERCEPTION: (8) POLITICAL PARTIES AND EVEN INDEPENDENT CANDIDATES FOR WINNING THE ELECTION DO NOT HESITATE IN GIVING COMMUNAL OR CASTE TURN TO ANY EVENT DURING ELECTION PERIOD IF IT SUITS THEM

	RESPONDENTS CATEGORY	*YES*	*%*	*INDIFF.*	*%*	*NO*	*%*
1.	Workers of different industrial units belonging to same factory.	450	94.94	22	4.64	2	0.42
2.	Workers of different factories belonging to assembly unit.	51	96.23	2	3.77	0	0.00
3.	Workers of different factories belonging to die-making unit.	56	96.55	2	3.45	0	0.00
4.	Workers of different factories belonging to furnace & dispatch unit.	42	97.67	1	2.33	0	0.00
5.	Workers of different factories belonging to key making unit.	53	94.64	3	5.36	0	0.00
6.	Workers of different factories belonging to nickle polish unit.	52	91.23	5	8.77	0	0.00
7.	Workers of different factories belonging to Office.	61	100.00	0	0.00	0	0.00
8.	Workers of different factories belonging to packing unit.	66	89.19	7	9.46	1	1.35
9.	Workers of different factories belonging to press unit.	69	95.83	2	2.78	1	1.39
10.	Salaried workers.	219	92.41	17	7.17	1	0.42

(Contd.)

11. Contractual workers	233	97.49	5	2.09	1	0.42
12. Male workers	437	95.21	21	4.58	1	0.22
13. Female workers	12	85.71	1	7.14	1	7.14
14. Literate workers	218	98.20	4	1.80	0	0.00
15. Illiterate workers	232	92.06	18	7.14	2	0.79
16. Joint family workers	333	95.97	12	3.46	2	0.58
17. Nuclear family workers	117	92.13	10	7.87	0	0.00
18. Rural workers	139	90.85	12	7.84	2	1.31
19. Urban workers	311	96.88	10	3.12	0	0.00
20. Hindu workers	133	91.10	11	7.53	2	1.37
21. Muslim workers	317	96.65	11	3.35	0	0.00
22. Workers in income group 0-3000	338	94.41	18	5.03	2	0.56
23. Workers in income group of 3000 and above	112	96.55	4	3.45	0	0.00
24. Workers belonging to Labour Class	364	93.81	22	5.67	2	0.52
25. Workers belonging to Management Class	83	100.0	0	0	0	0

and dispatch units; 94.64% from key-making units; 91.23% from nickle polish units; 100.00% from Office; 89.19% from packing units; 95.83% from press units; 92.41% salaried workers and 97.49% contractual workers; 95.21% male workers and 85.71% female workers; 98.20% literate workers and 92.06% illiterate workers; 95.97% workers from joint family system and 92.13% representing nuclear family system; 90.85% rural workers and 96.88% urban workers; 91.10% Hindu workers and 96.65% Muslim workers; 94.41% workers receiving salary up to Rs. 3000/- and 96.55% workers receiving salary more than 3000/- per month; 93.81% workers hailing from Labour class and 100.00% workers hailing from management group also expressed their agreement.

It can, thus, be concluded that the respondents representing different units of the factory as well as majority of the total subjects (94.94%) have expressed their agreement with the statement that "political parties and even independent candidates for winning the election do not hesitate in giving communal or caste turn to any event during election period if it suits them."

Table 4.69 reveals that majority of the workers (94.94%) representing different units of 55 factories agreed that community members lacking required political awareness in selecting right type of person or party do not caste their votes. While 4.64% exhibited their indifference, only 0.42% expressed their disagreement with the statement.

Unit-wise analysis reveals that 96.23% workers hailing from assembly units; 93.10% from die-making units; 97.67% from furnace and dispatch units; 94.64% from key-making units; 91.23% from nickle polish units; 100.00% from Office; 90.54% from packing unit and 97.22% from press units; 92.41% salaried workers and 97.91% contractual workers; 94.99% male workers and 92.86% female workers; 98.20% literate workers and 92.06% illiterate workers; 96.25% workers from joint family system and 91.34% representing nuclear family system; 89.76% rural workers and 96.57% urban workers; 9247% Hindu workers and 96.04% Muslim workers; 94.69%

TABLE 4.69 POLITICAL PERCEPTION: (9) COMMUNITY MEMBERS LACKING THE REQUIRED POLITICAL AWARENESS IN SELECTING RIGHT TYPE OF PERSON OR PARTY DO NOT CASTE THEIR VOTES

	RESPONDENTS CATEGORY	*YES*	*%*	*INDIFF.*	*%*	*NO*	*%*
1.	Workers of different industrial units belonging to same factory.	450	94.94	22	4.64	2	0.42
2.	Workers of different factories belonging to assembly unit.	51	96.23	2	3.77	0	0.00
3.	Workers of different factories belonging to die making unit.	54	93.10	3	5:17	1	1.72
4.	Workers of different factories belonging to furnace & dispatch unit	42	97.67	1	2.33	0	0.00
5.	Workers of different factories belonging to key making unit.	53	94.64	3	5.36	0	0.00
6.	Workers of different factories belonging to nickle polish unit	52	91.23	5	8.77	0	0.00
7.	Workers of different factories belonging to Office.	61	100.00	0	0.00	0	0.00
8.	Workers of different factories belonging to packing unit.	67	90.54	6	8.11	1	1.35
9.	Workers of different factories belonging to press unit.	70	97.22	2	2.78	0	0.00
10.	Salaried workers.	219	92.41	16	6.75	2	0.84

(Contd.)

11. Contractual workers	234	97.91	5	2.09	0	0.00
12. Male workers	436	94.99	21	4.58	2	0.44
13. Female workers	13	92.86	1	7.14	0	0.00
14. Literate workers	218	98.20	3	1.35	1	0.45
15. Illiterate workers	232	92.06	19	7.54	1	0.40
16. Joint family workers	334	96.25	13	3.75	0	0.00
17. Nuclear family workers	116	91.34	9	7.09	2	1.57
18. Rural workers	114	89.76	13	10.24	0	0.00
19. Urban workers	310	96.57	9	2.80	2	0.62
20. Hindu workers	135	92.47	11	7.53	0	0.00
21. Muslim workers	315	96.04	11	3.53	2	0.61
22. Workers in income group 0–3000	339	94.69	18	5.03	1	0.28
23. Workers in income group of 3000 and above	111	95.69	4	3.45	1	0.86
24. Workers belonging to Labour Class	364	93.81	22	5.67	2	0.52
25. Workers belonging to Management Class	83	100.0	0	0	0	0

workers receiving salary up to Rs. 3000/- and 95.69% workers receiving salary of more than 3000/-per month; 93.81% workers hailing from Labour class and 100.00% workers hailing from management group expressed their agreement with the statement.

It can, thus, be concluded that the respondents representing different units of the factory as well as majority of the total subjects (94.94%) have expressed their agreement with the statement that "community members lacking the required political awareness in selecting right type of person or party do not caste their votes."

Table 4.70 reveals that majority of workers (95.36%) representing different units of 55 factories agreed that political parties and independent candidates mostly make false promises at the time of elections but never attend to them. While 4.43% exhibited their indifference, only 0.21% have expressed their disagreement with the statement.

Unit-wise analysis reveals that 96.23% workers hailing from assembly units; 96.55% from die-making units; 97.67% from furnace and dispatch units; 94.64% from key-making units; 91.23% from nickle polish units; 100.00% from Office; 90.54% from packing units; 97.22% from press units; 92.83% salaried workers and 97.91% contractual workers; 95.42% male workers and 92.86% female workers; 98.20% literate workers and 92.86% illiterate workers; 96.54% workers from joint family system and 92.13% representing nuclear family system; 92.16% rural and 96.88% urban workers; 92.47% Hindu workers and 96.65% Muslim workers; 94.97% workers receiving salary up to Rs. 3000/- and 96.55% workers receiving salary of more than 3000/- per month; 94.33% workers hailing from Labour class and 100.00% workers hailing from management group expressed their agreement with the statement.

It can, thus, be concluded that the respondents representing different units of the factory as well as majority of the total subjects (95.36%) expressed their agreement with the statement that "political parties and independent candidates mostly make false promises at the time of elections but never attend to them".

TABLE 4.70 POLITICAL PERCEPTION: (10) POLITICAL PARTIES AND INDEPENDENT CANDIDATES MOSTLY MAKE FALSE PROMISES AT THE TIME OF ELECTIONS BUT NEVER ATTEND TO THEM

	RESPONDENTS CATEGORY	*YES*	*%*	*INDIFF.*	*%*	*NO*	*%*
1.	Workers of different industrial units belonging to same factory.	452	95.36	21	4.43	1	0.21
2.	Workers of different factories belonging to assembly unit.	51	96.23	2	3.77	0	0.00
3.	Workers of different factories belonging to die making unit.	56	96.55	2	3.45	0	0.00
4.	Workers of different factories belonging to furnace & dispatch unit.	42	97.67	1	2.33	0	0.00
5.	Workers of different factories belonging to key making unit.	53	94.64	3	5.36	0	0.00
6.	Workers of different factories belonging to nickle polish unit	52	91.23	5	8.77	0	0.00
7.	Workers of different factories belonging to Office.	61	100.00	0	0.00	0	0.00
8.	Workers of different factories belonging to packing unit.	67	90.54	6	8.11	1	1.35
9.	Workers of different factories belonging to press unit.	70	97.22	2	2.78	0	0.00
10.	Salaried workers.	220	92.83	16	6.75	1	0.42

(Contd.)

11.	Contractual workers	234	97.91	5	2.09	0	0.00
12.	Male workers	438	95.42	20	4.36	1	0.22
13.	Female workers	13	92.86	1	7.14	0	0.00
14.	Literate workers	218	98.20	3	1.35	0	0.45
15.	Illiterate workers	234	92.86	18	7.14	1	0.00
16.	Joint family workers	335	96.54	12	3.46	0	0.00
17.	Nuclear family workers	117	92.13	9	7.09	1	0.79
18.	Rural workers	141	92.16	12	7.84	0	0.00
19.	Urban workers	311	96.88	99	2.80	1	0.31
20	Hindu workers	135	92.47	11	753	0	0.00
21.	Muslim workers	317	96.65	10	3.05	1	0.30
22.	Workers in income group 0–3000	340	94.97	17	4.75	1	0.28
23.	Workers in income group of 3000 and above	112	96.55	4	3.45	0	0.00
24.	Workers belonging to Labour Class	366	94.33	21	5.41	1	0.26
25.	Workers belonging to Management Class	83	100.0	0	0	0	0

Table 4.71 reveals that majority of the workers (95.36%) representing different units of 55 factories agreed that generating judicious and ethical political awareness among the masses of the community, if and when they get an opportunity not to adopt unethical parties in the political affairs of the society. While 2.53% have exhibited their in difference, only 2.11% have expressed their disagreement with the statement.

Unit-wise analysis reveals that 98.11% workers hailing from assembly units; 94.83% from die-making units; 100.00% from furnace and dispatch units; 98.21% from key-making units; 92.98% from nickle polish units; 98.36% from Office; 90.54% from packing units; and 93.06% from press units; 94.94% salaried workers; 96.23% contractual workers; 95.42% male workers and 92.86% female workers; 98.65% literate workers and 92.46% illiterate workers; 96.25% workers from joint family system and 92.91% representing nuclear family system; 92.16% rural workers and 96.88% urban workers; 92.47% Hindu workers and 96.65% Muslim workers; 94.41% workers receiving salary up to Rs. 3000/- and 98.28% workers receiving salary more than 3000/- per month; 94.33% workers hailing from Labour class and 100.00% workers hailing from management group expressed their agreement with the statement.

It can, thus, be concluded that the respondents representing different units of the factory as well as majority of the total subjects (95.36%) expressed their agreement with the statement that "generating judicious and ethical political awareness among the masses of the community, if and when they get an opportunity not to adopt unethical practices in the political affairs of the society".

Table 4.72 reveals that majority of the workers (93.04%) representing different units of 55 factories agreed that to propagate among the members of the society to support political parties on the basis of their election manifesto and not on any other consideration, while 4.64% exhibited their indifference towards the statement and only 2.32% have expressed their disagreement with the statement.

Unit-wise analysis reveals that 92.45% workers hailing from assembly units; 91.38% from die-making units; 100.00% from furnace

TABLE 4.71 GENERATING JUDICIOUS AND ETHICAL POLITICAL AWARENESS AMONG MASSES OF THE COMMUNITY IF AND WHEN THEY GET AN OPPORTUNITY NOT TO ADOPT UNETHICAL PRACTICES IN POLITICAL AFFAIRS OF THE SOCIETY

	RESPONDENTS CATEGORY	*YES*	*%*	*INDIFF.*	*%*	*NO*	*%*
1.	Workers of different industrial units belonging to same factory.	452	95.36	12	2.53	10	2.11
2.	Workers of different factories belonging to assembly unit.	52	98.11	1	1.89	0	0.00
3.	Workers of different factories belonging to die making unit.	55	94.83	1	1.72	2	3.45
4.	Workers of different factories belonging to furnace & dispatch unit.	43	100.00	0	0.00	0	0.00
5.	Workers of different factories belonging to key making unit.	55	98.21	0	0.00	1	1.79
6.	Workers of different factories belonging to nickle polish unit.	60	98.36	1	1.64	0	0.00
7.	Workers of different factories belonging to Office.	60	98.36	1	1.64	0	0.00
8.	Workers of different factories belonging to packing unit.	67	90.54	4	5.41	3	4.05
9.	Workers of different factories belonging to press unit.	67	93.06	3	4.17	2	2.78
10.	Salaried workers.	225	94.94	9	3.80	3	1.27

(Contd.)

11.	Contractual workers	230	96.23	3	1.26	6	2.51
12.	Male workers	438	95.42	12	2.61	9	1.96
13.	Female workers	13	92.86	0	0.00	1	7.14
14.	Literate workers	219	98.65	2	0.90	1	0.45
15.	Illiterate workers	233	92.46	10	3.97	9	3.57
16.	Joint family workers	334	96.25	4	1.15	9	2.59
17.	Nuclear family workers	118	92.91	8	6.30	1	0.79
18.	Rural workers	141	92.16	4	2.61	8	5.23
19.	Urban workers	311	96.88	8	2.49	2	0.62
20.	Hindu workers	135	92.47	6	4.11	5	3.42
21.	Muslim workers	317	96.65	6	1.83	5	1.52
22.	Workers in income group 0-3000	338	94.41	10	2.79	10	2.79
23.	Workers in income group 3000 and above	114	98.28	2	1.72	0	0.00
24.	Workers belonging to Labour Class	366	94.33	12	3.09	10	2.58
25.	Workers belonging to Management Class	83	100		0	0	0

TABLE 4.72 POLITICAL ASPIRATION: (2) TO PROPAGATE AMONG MEMBERS OF THE SOCIETY TO SUPPORT POLITICAL PARTIES ON THE BASIS OF THEIR ELECTION MANIFESTO AND NOT ON ANY OTHER CONSIDERATION

	RESPONDENTS CATEGORY	*YES*	*%*	*INDIFF.*	*%*	*NO*	*%*
1.	Workers of different industrial units belonging to same factory.	441	93.04	22	4.64	11	2.32
2.	Workers of different factories belonging to assembly unit.	49	92.45	4	7.55	0	0.00
3.	Workers of different factories belonging to die making unit.	53	91.38	2	3.45	3	5.17
4.	Workers of different factories belonging to furnace & dispatch unit.	43	100.00	0	0.00	0	0.00
5.	Workers of different factories belonging to key making unit.	53	94.64	2	3.57	1	1.79
6.	Workers of different factories belonging to nickle polish unit.	51	89.47	5	8.77	1	1.75
7.	Workers of different factories belonging to Office.	59	96.72	2	3.28	0	0.00
8.	Workers of different factories belonging to packing unit.	65	87.84	5	6.76	4	5.41
9.	Workers of different factories belonging to press unit.	68	94.44	2	2.78	2	2.78
10.	Salaried workers.	215	90.72	15	6.33	7	2.95

(*Contd*)

11. Contractual workers	229	95.82	7	2.93	3	1.26
12. Male workers	427	93.03	21	4.58	11	2.40
13. Female workers	13	92.86	1	7.14	0	0.00
14. Literate workers	215	96.85	4	1.80	3	1.35
15. Illiterate workers	226	89.68	18	7.14	8	3.17
16. Joint family workers	327	94.24	12	3.46	8	2.31
17. Nuclear family workers	114	89.76	10	7.87	3	2.36
18. Rural workers	135	88.24	11	7.19	7	4.58
19. Urban workers	306	95.33	11	3.43	4	1.25
20. Hindu workers	130	89.04	12	8.22	4	2.74
21. Muslim workers	311	94.82	10	3.05	7	2.13
22. Workers in income group 0–3000	332	92.74	16	4.47	10	2.79
23. Workers in income group of 3000 and above	109	93.97	6	5.17	1	0.86
24. Workers belonging to Labour Class	357	92.01	20	5.15	11	2.84
25. Workers belonging to Management Class	81	97.59	2	2.41	0	0

and dispatch units; 94.64% from key-making units; 89.47% from nickle polish units; 96.72% from Office; 87.84% from packing units; 94.44% from press units; 90.72% salaried workers and 95.82% contractual workers; 93.03% male workers and 92.86% female workers; 96.85% literate workers and 89.68% illiterate workers; 94.24% workers from joint family system and 89.76% representing nuclear family system; 88.24% rural workers and 95.33% urban workers; 89.04% Hindu workers and 94.82% Muslim workers; 92.74% workers receiving salary up to Rs. 3000/- and 93.97% workers receiving salary of more than 3000/- per month; 92.01% workers hailing from Labour class; and 97.59% workers hailing from management group have also expressed their agreement with the statement.

It can, thus, be concluded that the respondents representing different units of the factory as well as majority of the total subjects (93.04%) expressed their agreement with the statement that "to propagate among the members of the society to support political parties on the basis of their election manifesto and not on any other consideration."

Table 4.73 reveals that majority of workers (90.51%) representing different units of 55 factories agreed that becoming members of some such organization which may fight against mal-practices operative during elections. While 6.54% exhibited their indifference, only 2.95% have expressed their disagreement with the statement.

Unit-wise analysis reveals that 90.57% workers hailing from assembly units; 89.66% from die-making units; 93.02% from furnace and dispatch units; 92.86% from key-making units; 89.47% from nickle polish units; 93.44% from Office; 87.84% from packing units; 88.89% from press units; 89.45% salaried workers and 92.05% contractual workers; 90.41% male workers and 92.86% female workers; 93.24% literate workers and 88.10% illiterate workers; 90.78% workers from joint family system and 89.76% representing nuclear family system; 87.58% rural workers and 91.90% urban workers also exhibit their support to the statement. 85.62% Hindu

TABLE 4.73 POLITICAL ASPIRATION: (3) BECOMING MEMBER OF SOME SUCH ORGANISATION WHICH MAY FIGHT AGAINST MAL-PRACTICES OPERATIVE DURING ELECTIONS

	RESPONDENTS CATEGORY	*YES*	*%*	*INDIFF.*	*%*	*NO*	*%*
1.	Workers of different industrial units belonging to same factory.	429	90.51	31	6.54	14	2.95
2.	Workers of different factories belonging to assembly unit.	48	90.57	5	9.43	0	0.00
3.	Workers of different factories belonging to die-making unit.	52	89.66	2	3.45	4	6.90
4.	Workers of different factories belonging to furnace & dispatch unit.	40	93.02	2	4.65	1	2.33
5.	Workers of different factories belonging to key making unit.	52	92.86	4	7.14	0	0.00
6.	Workers of different factories belonging to nickle polish unit.	51	89.47	5	8.77	1	1.75
7.	Workers of different factories belonging to Office.	57	93.44	1	1.64	3	4.92
8.	Workers of different factories belonging to packing unit.	65	87.84	8	10.81	1	1.35
9.	Workers of different factories belonging to press unit.	64	88.89	4	5.56	4	5.56
10.	Salaried workers.	212	89.45	16	6.75	9	3.80

(Contd.)

11.	Contractual workers	220	92.05	15	6.28	4	1.67
12.	Male workers	415	90.41	30	6.54	14	3.05
13.	Female workers	13	92.86	1	7.14	0	0.00
14.	Literate workers	207	93.24	8	3.60	7	3.15
15.	Illiterate workers	222	88.10	23	9.13	7	2.78
16.	Joint family workers	315	90.78	21	6.05	11	3.17
17.	Nuclear family workers	114	89.76	10	7.87	3	2.36
18.	Rural workers	134	87.58	13	8.50	6	3.92
19.	Urban workers	295	91.90	18	5.61	8	2.49
20.	Hindu workers	125	85.62	18	12.33	3	2.05
21.	Muslim workers	304	92.68	13	3.96	11	3.35
22.	Workers in income group 0–3000	319	89.11	27	7.54	12	3.35
23.	Workers in income group of 3000 and above	110	94.83	4	3.45	2	1.72
24.	Workers belonging to Labour Class	347	89.43	30	7.73	11	2.84
25.	Workers belonging to Management Class	79	95.18	1	1.20	3	3.61

workers and 92.68% Muslim workers; 89.11% workers receiving salary up to Rs. 3000/- and 94.83% workers receiving salary of more than 3000/- per month; 89.43% workers hailing form Labour class; and 95.18% workers Hailing from management group expressed their agreement with the statement.

It can, thus, be concluded that the respondents representing different units of the factory as well as majority of the total subjects (90.51%) expressed their agreement with the statement that "becoming member of some such organisation, which may fight against the mal-practices, operative during elections."

Table 4.74 reveals that majority of workers (82.49%) representing different units of 55 factories agreed that to expose such political person who misuse their positions and power for their selfish ends. While 15.61% exhibited their indifference, only 1.90% expressed their disagreement with the statement.

Unit-wise analysis reveals that 80.33% workers hailing from assembly units; 84.48% from die-making units; 81.40% from furnace and dispatch units; 87.50% from key-making units; 78.95% from nickle polish units; 87.30% from Office; 87.78% from packing units; 76.39% from press unit;81.86% salaried workers and 83.68% contractual workers; 82.35% male workers and 85.71% female workers; 79.28% literate workers and 85.32% illiterate workers; 80.98% workers from joint family system and 86.61% representing nuclear family system; 79.08% rural workers and 84.11% urban workers; 76.03% Hindu workers and 85.37% Muslim workers; 83.80% workers receiving salary up to Rs. 3000/- and 78.45% workers receiving salary of more than 3000/- per month; 81.19% workers hailing from Labour class and 87.95% workers hailing from management group have also expressed their agreement with the statement.

It can, thus, be concluded that respondents representing different units of the factory as well as majority of the total subjects (82.49%) expressed their agreement "to expose such political persons who misuse their positions and power for their selfish ends."

TABLE 4.74 POLITICAL ASPIRATION: (4) TO EXPOSE SUCH POLITICAL PERSONS WHO MISUSE THEIR POSITION AND POWER FOR SELFISH ENDS

RESPONDENTS CATEGORY	*YES*	*%*	*INDIFF.*	*%*	*NO*	*%*
1. Workers of different industrial units belonging to same factory.	391	82.49	74	15.61	9	1.90
2. Workers of different factories belonging to assembly unit.	49	80.33	11	18.03	1	1.64
3. Workers of different factories belonging to die making unit.	49	84.48	5	8.62	4	6.90
4. Workers of different factories belonging to furnace & dispatch unit.	35	81.40	8	18.60	0	0.00
5. Workers of different factories belonging to key making unit.	49	87.50	7	12.50	0	0.00
6. Workers of different factories belonging to nickle polish unit	45	78.95	10	17.54	2	3.51
7. Workers of different factories belonging to Office.	45	78.95	10	17.54	2	3.51
8. Workers of different factories belonging to packing unit.	55	87.30	6	9.52	2	3.17
9. Workers of different factories belonging to press unit.	55	76.39	15	20.83	2	2.78
10. Salaried workers	194	81.86	38	16.03	5	2.11

11. Contractual workers	200	83.68	35	14.64	4	1.67
12. Male workers	378	82.35	72	15.69	9	1.96
13. Female workers	12	85.71	2	14.29	0	0.00
14. Literate workers	176	79.28	41	18.47	5	2.25
15. Illiterate workers	215	85.32	33	13.10	4	1.59
16. Joint family workers	281	80.98	58	16.71	8	2.31
17. Nuclear family workers	110	86.61	16	12.60	1	0.79
18. Rural workers	121	79.08	31	20.26	1	0.65
19. Urban workers	270	84.11	43	13.40	8	2.49
20. Hindu workers	111	76.03	33	22.60	2	1.37
21. Muslim workers	280	85.37	41	12.50	7	2.13
22. Workers in income group 0–3000	300	83.80	53	14.80	5	1.40
23. Workers in income group of 3000 and above	91	78.45	21	18.10	4	3.45
24. Workers belonging to Labour Class	315	81.19	64	16.49	9	2.32
25. Workers belonging to Management Class	73	87.95	10	12.05	0	0

Table 4.75 reveals that majority of workers (78.27%) representing different units of 55 factories agreed to work and raise voice against such parties and persons who use money and muscle power during elections. While 19.41% exhibited their indifference, only 2.32% expressed their disagreement with the statement.

Unit-wise analysis reveals that 75.47% workers hailing from assembly units; 84.48% from die-making units; 86.05% from furnace and dispatch units; 78.57% from key-making units; 77.19% from nickle polish units; 73.77% from Office; 75.68% from packing units; 77.78% from press units; 77.22% salaried workers and 79.92% contractual workers; 77.78% male workers and 92.86% female workers; 78.38% literate workers and 78.17% illiterate workers; 76.08% workers from joint family system and 84.25% representing nuclear family system; 77.12% rural workers and 78.82% urban workers; 77.40% Hindu workers and 78.66% Muslim workers; 77.65% workers receiving salary up to Rs. 3000/- and 80.17% workers receiving salary of more than 3000/- per month; 78.35% workers hailing from Labour class and 77.11% workers hailing from management group expressed their agreement with the statement.

It can, thus, be concluded that the respondents representing different units of the factory as well as majority of the total subjects (78.27%) expressed their agreement "to work and raise voice against such parties and persons who use money and muscle power during elections".

Table 4.76 reveals that majority of the workers (81.22%) representing different units of 55 factories agreed to demand strongly that government should impose some financial limits. In election expenditure which should be subject to accountability. While 13.08% exhibited their indifference only 5.70% expressed their disagreement with the statement.

Unit-wise analysis reveals that 84.91% workers hailing from assembly units; 79.31% from die-making units; 86.05% from furnace and dispatch units; 80.36% from key-making units; 78.95% from

TABLE 4.75 POLITICAL ASPIRATION: (5) TO WORK AND RAISE VOICE AGAINST SUCH PARTIES AND PERSONS WHO USE MONEY AND MUSCLE POWER DURING ELECTIONS

	RESPONDENTS CATEGORY	*YES*	*%*	*INDIFF.*	*%*	*NO*	*%*
1.	Workers of different industrial units belonging to same factory.	371	78.27	92	19.41	11	2.32
2.	Workers of different factories belonging to assembly unit.	40	85.47	11	20.75	2	3.77
3.	Workers of different factories belonging to die making unit.	49	84.48	8	13.79	1	1.72
4.	Workers of different factories belonging to furnace & dispatch unit.	37	86.05	6	13.95	0	0.00
5.	Workers of different factories belonging to key making unit.	44	78.57	11	19.64	1	1.79
6.	Workers of different factories belonging to nickle polish unit.	44	77.19	9	15.79	4	7.02
7.	Workers of different factories belonging to Office.	45	73.77	15	24.59	1	1.64
8.	Workers of different factories belonging to packing unit.	45	73.77	15	24.59	1	1.64
9.	Workers of different factories belonging to press unit.	56	77.78	15	20.83	1	1.39
10.	Salaried workers.	138	77.22	49	20.68	5	2.11

(*Contd.*)

11. Contractual workers	191	79.92	42	17.57	6	2.51
12. Male workers	357	77.78	91	19.83	11	0.00
13. Female workers	13	92.86	1	7.14	0	2.25
14. Literate workers	174	78.17	43	19.37	5	2.25
15. Illiterate workers	197	76.08	49	19.44	6	2.38
16. Joint family workers	264	84.25	75	21.61	8	2.31
17. Nuclear family workers	107	77.12	17	13.39	3	2.36
18. Rural workers	118	78.82	33	21.57	2	1.31
19. Urban workers	253	77.40	59	18.38	9	2.80
20. Hindu workers	113	78.66	29	19.86	4	2.74
21. Muslim workers	258	77.65	63	19.21	7	2.13
22. Workers in income group 0–3000	278	77.65	71	19.83	9	2.51
23. Workers in income group of 3000 and above	93	80.17	21	18.10	2	1.72
24. Workers belonging to Labour Class	304	78.35	74	19.07	10	2.58
25. Workers belonging to Management Class	64	77.11	18	21.69	1	1.20

TABLE 4.76 POLITICAL ASPIRATION: (6) TO DEMAND STRONGLY THAT GOVERNMENT SHOULD IMPOSE SOME FINANCIAL LIMIT ON ELECTION EXPENDITURE WHICH SHOULD BE SUBJECT TO STRICT ACCOUNTABILITY

	RESPONDENTS CATEGORY	*YES*	*%*	*INDIFF.*	*%*	*NO*	*%*
1.	Workers of different industrial units belonging to same factory.	385	81.22	62	13.08	27	5.70
2.	Workers of different factories belonging to assembly unit	45	84.91	4	7.55	4	7.55
3.	Workers of different factories belonging to die making unit	46	79.31	8	13.79	4	6.90
4.	Workers of different factories belonging to furnace & dispatch unit.	37	86.05	4	9.30	2	4.65
5.	Workers of different factories belonging to key making unit.	45	80.36	9	16.07	2	3.57
6.	Workers of different factories belonging to nickle polish unit.	45	78.95	10	17.54	2	3.51
7.	Workers of different factories belonging to Office.	54	88.52	4	6.56	3	4.92
8.	Workers of different factories belonging to packing unit.	58	78.38	11	14.86	5	6.76
9.	Workers of different factories belonging to press unit.	55	76.39	12	16.67	5	9.94
10.	Salaried workers.	188	79.32	29	12.24	20	8.44

(Contd.)

11.	Contractual workers	200	83.68	32	13.39	7	2.93
12.	Male workers	376	81.92	56	12.20	27	5.88
13.	Female workers	8	57.14	6	42.86	0	0.00
14.	Literate workers	192	86.49	20	9.01	10	4.50
15.	Illiterate workers	193	76.59	42	16.67	17	6.50
16.	Joint family workers	294	84.73	37	10.66	16	6.75
17.	Nuclear family workers	91	71.65	25	19.69	11	4.61
18.	Rural workers	121	79.08	24	15.69	8	5.23
19.	Urban workers	264	82.24	38	11.84	19	5.92
20.	Hindu workers	112	76.71	23	15.75	11	7.53
21.	Muslim workers	273	83.23	39	11.89	16	4.88
22.	Workers in income group 0–3000	294	82.12	48	13.41	16	4.47
23.	Workers in income group of 3000 and above	91	78.45	14	12.07	11	9.48
24.	Workers belonging to Labour Class	309	79.64	56	14.43	23	5.93
25.	Workers belonging to Management Class	73	87.95	6	7.23	4	4.82

nickle polish units; 88.52% from Office; 78.38% from packing units; and 76.39% from press units; 79.32% salaried workers and 83.68% contractual workers; 81.92% male workers and 57.14% female workers; 86.49% literate workers and 76.59% illiterate workers; 84.73% workers from joint family system and 71.65% representing nuclear family system; 79.08% rural workers and 82.24% urban workers; 76.71% Hindu workers and 83.23% Muslim workers; 82.12% workers receiving salary up to Rs. 3000/-and 78.45% workers receiving salary of more than 3000/- per month; 79.64% workers hailing from Labour class; 87.95% workers hailing from management group expressed their agreement with the statement.

It can, thus, be concluded that respondents representing different units of the factory as well as majority of the total subjects (81.22%) expressed their agreement "to demand strongly that government should impose some financial limit on election expenditure, which should be subject to strict accountability."

Table 4.77 reveals that majority of the workers (91.77%) representing different units of 55 factories agreed that to pursue the enlightened and judicious members of the community to pressurize government to impose ban on contestants having criminal background seeking election. While 7.81% exhibited their indifference, only 0.42% have expressed their disagreement with the statement.

Unit-wise analysis reveals that 94.34% workers hailing from assembly units; 87.93% from die-making units; 97.67% from furnace and dispatch units; 91.07% from key-making units; 91.23% from nickle polish units; 96.72% from Office; 85.14% from packing units; 93.06% from press units; 88.24% salaried workers and 95.40% contractual workers; 91.94% male workers and 85.71% female workers; 95.05% literate workers and 88.889% illiterate workers; 91.93% workers from joint family system and 99.15% representing nuclear family system; 87.58% rural and 93.77% urban worker also exhibit their support of the statement. 91.10% Hindu workers and 92.07% Muslim workers; 91.62% workers receiving salary up to Rs.

TABLE 4.77 POLITICAL ASPIRATION: (7) TO PURSUE THE ENLIGHTENED AND JUDICIOUS MEMBERS OF THE COMMUNITY TO PRESSURISE GOVERNMENT TO IMPOSE BAN ON CONTESTANTS HAVING CRIMINAL BACKGROUND SEEKING ELECTION

	RESPONDENTS CATEGORY	*YES*	*%*	*INDIFF.*	*%*	*NO*	*%*
1.	Workers of different industrial units belonging to same factory.	436	91.77	37	7.81	02	0.42
2.	Workers of different factories belonging to assembly unit.	50	94.34	3	5.66	0	0.00
3.	Workers of different factories belonging to die making unit.	51	87.93	6	10.34	1	1.72
4.	Workers of different factories belonging to furnace & dispatch unit.	42	97.67	1	2.33	0	0.00
5.	Workers of different factories belonging to key making unit.	51	91.07	5	8.93	0	0.00
6.	Workers of different factories belonging to nickle polish unit.	52	91.23	5	8.77	0	0.00
7.	Workers of different factories belonging to Office.	59	96.72	2	3.28	0	0.00
8.	Workers of different factories belonging to packing unit.	63	85.14	11	14.86	0	0.00
9.	Workers of different factories belonging to press unit.	67	93.06	4	5.56	0	1.39
10.	Salaried workers.	210	88.24	27	11.34	1	0.42

11. Contractual workers	228	95.40	10	4.18	1	0.42
12. Male workers	422	91.94	35	7.63	2	0.44
13. Female workers	12	85.71	2	14.29	0	0.00
14. Literate workers	211	95.05	11	4.95	0	0.00
15. Illiterate workers	224	88.89	26	10.32	2	0.79
16. Joint family workers	319	91.93	26	7.49	2	0.58
17. Nuclear family workers	116	99.15	1	0.85	0	0.00
18. Rural workers	134	87.58	18	11.76	1	0.65
19 Urban workers	301	93.77	19	5.92	1	0.31
20. Hindu workers	133	91.10	12	8.22	1	0.68
21. Muslim workers	302	92.07	25	7.62	1	0.30
22. Workers in income group 0–3000	328	91.62	28	7.82	2	0.56
23. Workers in income group of 3000 and above	107	92.24	9	7.76	0	0.00
24. Workers belonging to Labour Class	351	90.48	35	9.02	2	0.52
25. Workers belonging to Management Class	82	98.80	1	1.20	0	0

3000/- and 92.24% workers receiving salary of more than 3000/- per month; 90.48% workers hailing from Labour class and 98.80% workers hailing from management group expressed their agreement with the statement.

It can, thus, be concluded that the respondents representing different units of the factory as well as majority of the total subject (91.77%) expressed their agreement "to pursue the enlightened and judicious members of the community to pressurize government to impose ban on constants having criminal background seeking election."

Table 4.78 reveals that majority of the workers (94.09%) representing different units of 55 factories agreed that to protest vigorously through some organization or independently against such political parties and independent candidates who, in order to win elections, spoil the election scene on the basis of religion/caste. While 5.06% have exhibited their indifference, only 0.84% have expressed their disagreement with the statement.

Unit-wise analysis reveals that 96.23% workers hailing from assembly units; 94.83% from die-making units; 97.67% from furnace and dispatch units; 92.86% from key-making units; 91.23% from nickle polish units; 100.00% from Office; 89.19% from packing units; and 93.06% from press units; 91.98% salaried workers and 96.65% contractual workers; 94.12% male workers and 92.86% female workers; 98.65% literate workers and 91.53% illiterate workers; 95.10% workers from joint family system and 91.34% representing nuclear family system; 86.71% rural workers and 97.20% urban workers; 90.41% Hindu workers and 95.73% Muslim workers; 93.58% workers receiving salary up to Rs.3000/- and 95.69% workers receiving salary of more than 3000/- per month; 92.78% workers hailing from Labour class and 100.00% workers hailing from management group expressed their agreement with the statement.

It can, thus, be concluded that the respondents representing different units of the factory as well as majority of the total subjects (94.09%) have expressed their agreement "to protest vigorously through some organization or independently, against such political

TABLE 4.78 POLITICAL ASPIRATION: (8) TO PROTEST VIGOROUSLY THROUGH SOME ORGANIZATION OR INDEPENDENTLY AGAINST SUCH POLITICAL PARTIES AND INDEPENDENT CANDIDATES WHO, IN ORDER TO WIN ELECTIONS, SPOIL THE ELECTION SCENE ON THE BASIS OF RELIGION/CASTE

	RESPONDENTS CATEGORY	*YES*	*%*	*INDIFF.*	*%*	*NO*	*%*
1.	Workers of different industrial units belonging to same factory.	446	94.09	24	5.06	4	0.84
2.	Workers of different factories belonging to assembly unit.	51	96.23	2	3.77	0	0.00
3.	Workers of different factories belonging to die making unit.	55	94.83	3	5.17	0	0.00
4.	Workers of different factories belonging to furnace & dispatch unit.	42	97.67	1	2.33	0	0.00
5.	Workers of different factories belonging to key making unit.	52	92.86	4	7.14	0	0.00
6.	Workers of different factories belonging to nickle polish unit.	52	91.23	5	8.77	0	0.00
7.	Workers of different factories belonging to Office.	61	100.00	0	0.00	0	0.00
8.	Workers of different factories belonging to packing unit.	66	89.19	6	8.11	2	2.70
9.	Workers of different factories belonging to press unit.	67	93.06	3	4.17	2	2.78
10.	Salaried workers.	218	91.98	18	7.59	1	0.42

11.	Contractual workers	231	96.65	5	2.09	3	1.26
12.	Male workers	432	94.12	24	5.23	3	0.65
13.	Female workers	13	92.86	0	0.00	1	7.14
14.	Literate workers	219	98.65	3	1.35	0	0.00
15.	Illiterate workers	227	91.53	21	8.47	0	0.00
16.	Joint family workers	330	95.10	15	4.32	2	0.58
17.	Nuclear family workers	116	91.34	9	7.09	2	1.57
18.	Rural workers	124	86.71	16	11.19	3	2.10
19.	Urban workers	312	97.20	8	2.49	1	0.31
20.	Hindu workers	132	90.41	10	6.85	4	2.74
21.	Muslim workers	314	95.73	14	4.27	0	0.00
22.	Workers in income group 0–3000	335	93.58	19	5.31	4	1.12
23.	Workers in income group of 3000 and above	111	95.69	5	4.31	0	0.00
24.	Workers belonging to Labour Class	360	92.78	24	6.19	4	1.03
25.	Workers belonging to Management Class	83	100.00	0	0	0	0

parties and independent candidates who, in order to win elections spoil the election scene on the basis of religion/ caste".

Table 4.79 reveals that majority of the workers (90.93%) representing different units of 55 factories agreed to educate independently or through some organisation to press the members of the community to caste their votes and support right type of person or party based on their election manifesto. While 8.23% have exhibited their indifference, only 0.84% have expressed their disagreement with the statement.

Unit-wise analysis reveals that 94.34% workers hailing from assembly units; 87.93% from die-making units; 97.67% from furnace and dispatch units; 91.07% from key-making units; 87.72% from nickle polish units; 93.44% from Office; 86.49% from packing units; and 91.67% from press units; 86.50% salaried workers and 95.82% contractual workers; 90.85% male workers and 92.86% female workers; 95.05% literate workers and 87.30% illiterate workers 92.80% workers from joint family system and 85.83% representing nuclear family system; 87.58% rural workers and 92.52% urban workers; 89.04% Hindu workers and 91.77% Muslim workers; 91.62% workers receiving salary up to Rs.3000/- and 88.79% workers receiving salary of more than 3000/- per month; 89.95% workers hailing from Labour class and 95.18% workers hailing from management group expressed their agreement with the statement.

It can, thus, be concluded that the respondents representing different units of the factory as well as majority of the total subjects (90.93%) expressed their agreement "to educate independently or through some organisation to press the members of the community to caste their votes and support right type of person or party based on their election manifesto".

Table 4.80 reveals that majority of the workers 94.09 representing different units of 55 factories agreed join some such non-political organization through which voice may be raised to highlight nonfulfilment of promises made to the communities by the political parties and independent candidates who failed to fulfil them after

TABLE 4.79 POLITICAL ASPIRATION: (9) TO EDUCATE INDEPENDENTLY OR THROUGH SOME ORGANIZATION TO PRESS THE MEMBERS OF THE COMMUNITY TO CASTE THEIR VOTES AND SUPPORT RIGHT TYPE OF PERSON OR PARTY BASED ON THEIR ELECTION MANIFESTO

	RESPONDENTS CATEGORY	*YES*	*%*	*INDIFF.*	*%*	*NO*	*%*
1.	Workers of different industrial units belonging to same factory.	431	90.93	39	8.23	4	0.84
2.	Workers of different factories belonging to assembly unit.	50	94.34	3	5.66	0	0.00
3.	Workers of different factories belonging to die making unit.	51	87.93	7	12.07	0	0.00
4.	Workers of different factories belonging to furnace & dispatch unit.	42	97.67	1	2.33	0	0.00
5.	Workers of different factories belonging to key making unit.	51	91.07	5	8.93	0	0.00
6.	Workers of different factories belonging to nickle polish unit.	50	87.72	7	12.28	0	0.00
7.	Workers of different factories belonging to Office.	57	93.44	4	6.56	0	0.00
8.	Workers of different factories belonging to packing unit.	64	86.49	8	10.81	2	2.70
9.	Workers of different factories belonging to press unit.	66	91.67	4	5.56	2	2.78
10.	Salaried workers.	205	86.50	31	13.08	1	0.42

(Contd)

11. Contractual workers	229	95.82	7	2.93	3	1.26
12. Male workers	417	90.85	39	8.50	3	0.65
13. Female workers	13	92.86	0	0.00	1	7.14
14. Literate workers	211	95.05	11	4.95	0	0.00
15. Illiterate workers	220	87.30	28	11.11	4	1.59
16. Joint family workers	322	92.80	21	6.05	4	1.15
17. Nuclear family workers	109	85.83	18	14.17	0	0.00
18. Rural workers	134	87.58	17	11.11	2	1.31
19. Urban workers	297	92.52	22	6.85	2	0.62
20. Hindu workers	130	89.04	14	9.59	2	1.37
21. Muslim workers	301	91.77	25	7.62	2	0.61
22. Workers in income group 0–3000	328	91.62	26	7.26	4	1.12
23. Workers in income group of 3000 and above	103	88.79	13	11.21	0	0.00
24. Workers belonging to Labour Class	349	89.95	35	9.02	4	1.03
25. Workers belonging to Management Class	79	95.18	4	4.82	0	0

TABLE 4.80 POLITICAL ASPIRATION: (10) TO JOIN SOME SUCH NON-POLITICAL ORGANISATION THROUGH WHICH CHOICE MAY BE RAISED TO HIGHLIGHT NONFULFILMENT OF PROMISES MADE TO THE COMMUNITIES MADE BY THE POLITICAL PARTIES AND INDEPENDENT CANDIDATES WHO FAILED TO FULFIL THEM AFTER WINNING

	RESPONDENTS CATEGORY	*YES*	*%*	*INDIFF.*	*%*	*NO*	*%*
1.	Workers of different industrial units belonging to same factory.	446	94.09	26	5.49	2	0.42
2.	Workers of different factories belonging to assembly unit.	50	94.34	3	5.66	0	0.00
3.	Workers of different factories belonging to die making unit.	53	91.38	3	5.17	2	3.45
4.	Workers of different factories belonging to furnace & dispatch unit.	42	97.67	1	2.33	0	0.00
5.	Workers of different factories belonging to key making unit.	52	92.86	4	7.14	0	0.00
6.	Workers of different factories belonging to nickle polish unit	52	91.23	5	8.77	0	0.00
7.	Workers of different factories belonging to Office.	61	100.00	0	0.88	0	0.00
8.	Workers of different factories belonging to packing unit.	68	91.89	6	8.11	0	0.00
9.	Workers of different factories belonging to press unit.	68	94.44	4	5.56	0	0.00
10.	Salaried workers.	216	91.14	19	8.02	2	0.84

(Contd.)

11. Contractual workers	233	97.49	6	2.51	0	0.00
12. Male workers	431	93.90	26	5.66	2	0.44
13. Female workers	14	100.00	0	0.00	0	0.00
14. Literate workers	216	97.30	4	1.80	2	0.90
15. Illiterate workers	230	91.27	22	8.73	0	0.00
16. Joint family workers	331	95.39	16	4.61	0	0.00
17. Nuclear family workers	115	90.55	10	7.87	2	1.57
18. Rural workers	137	89.54	16	10.46	0	0.00
19. Urban workers	309	96.26	10	3.12	2	0.62
20. Hindu workers	136	93.15	10	6.85	0	0.00
21. Muslim workers	310	94.51	16	4.88	2	0.61
22. Workers in income group 0–3000	336	93.85	21	5.87	1	0.28
23. Workers in income group of 3000 and above	110	94.83	5	4.31	1	0.86
24. Workers belonging to Labour Class	360	92.78	26	6.70	2	0.52
25. Workers belonging to Management Class	83	100.00	0	0	0	0

winning elections. While 5.49% exhibited their indifference, only 0.42% expressed their disagreement with the statement.

Unit-wise analysis reveals that 94.34% workers hailing from assembly units; 91.38% from die-making units; 97.67% from furnace and dispatch units; 92.86% from key-making units; 91.23% from press units; 91.14% salaried workers and 97.49% contractual workers; 93.90% male workers and 100.00% female workers; 97.30% literate workers and 91.27% illiterate workers; 95.39% workers from joint family system and 90.55% representing nuclear family system; 89.54% rural workers and 96.26% urban workers; 93.15% Hindu workers and 94.51% Muslim workers; 93.85% workers receiving salary up to Rs. 3000/- and 94.83% workers receiving salary of more than 3000/-per month; 92.78% workers hailing from Labour class and 100.00% workers hailing from management group expressed their agreement with the statement.

It can, thus, be concluded that respondents representing different units of the factory as well as majority of the total subjects (94.09%) expressed their agreement "to join some such non-political organization through which voice may be raised to highlight nonfulfilment of promises made communities by the political parties and independent candidates who failed to fulfil them after winning elections."

Table 4.81 reveals that a very low percentage of workers (14.14%) representing different units of 55 factories agreed that in the present era of advancement the community members are satisfied with the prevailing education system. While 1.69% exhibited their indifference, 84.18% expressed their disagreement with the statement.

Unit-wise analysis reveals that 7.55% workers hailing from assembly units; 18.97% from die-making units; 2.33% from furnace and dispatch units; 10.71% from key-making units; 12.28% from nickle polish units; 9.84% from Office; 24.32% from packing units; 19.44% from press units; 16.88% salaried workers and 10.88% contractual workers; 13.73% male workers and 28.57% female workers; 8.11% literate workers and 42.33% illiterate workers; 11.53% workers from joint family system and 21.26% representing nuclear family system; 23.53% rural workers and 9.66% urban workers;

TABLE 4.81 EDUCATIONAL PERCEPTION: (1) IN THE PRESENT ERA OF ADVANCEMENT, THE COMMUNITY MEMBERS ARE SATISFIED WITH THE PREVAILING EDUCATION SYSTEM

RESPONDENTS CATEGORY	*YES*	*%*	*INDIFF.*	*%*	*NO*	*%*
1. Workers of different industrial units belonging to same factory.	67	14.14	8	1.69	399	84.18
2. Workers of different factories belonging to assembly unit.	4	7.55	1	1.89	48	90.57
3. Workers of different factories belonging to die making unit.	11	18.97	1	1.72	46	79.31
4. Workers of different factories belonging to furnace & dispatch unit.	1	2.33	0	0.00	42	97.67
5. Workers of different factories belonging to key making unit.	6	10.71	0	0.00	50	89.29
6. Workers of different factories belonging to nickle polish unit.	7	12.28	2	3.51	48	84.21
7. Workers of different factories belonging to Office.	6	9.84	0	0.00	55	90.16
8. Workers of different factories belonging to packing unit.	18	24.32	2	2.70	54	72.97
9. Workers of different factories belonging to press unit.	14	19.44	2	2.78	56	77.78
10. Salaried workers.	40	16.88	6	2.53	6	80.59

(Contd.)

11.	Contractual workers	26	10.88	2	0.84	2	88.28
12.	Male workers	63	13.73	8	1.74	8	84.53
13.	Female workers	4	28.57	0	0.00	0	71.43
14.	Literate workers	18	8.11	4	1.80	4	90.09
15.	Illiterate workers	149	42.33	4	1.14	4	56.53
16.	Joint family workers	40	11.53	4	1.15	4	87.32
17.	Nuclear family workers	27	21.26	4	3.15	4	75.59
18.	Rural workers	36	23.53	1	0.65	1	75.82
19.	Urban workers	31	9.66	7	2.18	7	88.16
20.	Hindu workers	31	21.23	5	3.42	5	75.34
21.	Muslim workers	36	10.98	3	0.91	3	88.11
22.	Workers in income group 0–3000	58	16.20	6	1.68	6	82.12
23.	Workers in income group of 3000 and above	9	7.76	2	1.72	2	90.52
24.	Workers belonging to Labour Class	63	16.24	8	2.06	8	81.70
25.	Workers belonging to Management Class	4	4.82	0	0.00	0	95.18

21.23% Hindu workers and 10.98% Muslim workers; 16.20% workers receiving salary up to Rs. 3000/- and 7.76% workers receiving salary of more then 3000/- per month; 81.70% workers hailing from Labour class; 16.24% workers from Labour class only 4.82% expressed their agreement with the statement.

It can, thus, be concluded that the respondents representing different units of the factory as well as majority of the total subjects (84.18%) have expressed their disagreement with the statement that "in the present era of advancement the community members are satisfied with the prevailing education system". Only a small percentage of respondents either exhibited their indifference the statement.

Table 4.82 reveals that majority of the workers (93.67%) representing different units of 55 factories agreed that on account of higher cost of education majority of people hailing from economically weaker sections do not encourage their children to receive full education. While 5.06% exhibited their indifference, only 1.27% have expressed their disagreement with the statement.

Unit-wise analysis reveals that 96.23% workers hailing from assembly units; 96.55% from die-making units; 97.67% from furnace and dispatch units; 96.43% from key-making untis; 91.23% from nickle polish units; 91.80% from Office; 89.19% from packing units; 93.06% from press units; 93.67% salaried workers and 93.72% contractual workers; 93.46% male workers and 100.00% female workers; 93.69% literate workers and 93.65% illiterate workers; 95.10% workers from joint family system and 89.76% representing nuclear family system; 94.77% rural workers and 93.15% urban workers; 90.41% Hindu workers and 95.12% Muslim workers; 93.30% workers receiving salary up to Rs. 3000/- and 94.83% workers receiving salary of more than 3000/- per month; 93.30% workers hailing from Labour class; 95.18% workers hailing from management group expressed their agreement with the statement.

It can, thus, be concluded that respondents representing different units of the factory as well as majority of the total subjects (93.67%) expressed their agreement with the statement that "on account of

TABLE 4.82 EDUCATIONAL PERCEPTION: (2) ON ACCOUNT OF HIGHER COST OF EDUCATION MAJORITY OF PEOPLE HAILING FROM ECONOMICALLY WEAKER SECTIONS DO NOT ENCOURAGE THEIR CHILDREN TO RECEIVE FULL EDUCATION

	RESPONDENTS CATEGORY	*YES*	*%*	*INDIFF.*	*%*	*NO*	*%*
1.	Workers of different industrial units belonging to same factory.	444	93.67	24	5.06	06	1.27
2.	Workers of different factories belonging to assembly unit.	51	96.23	2	3.77	0	0.00
3.	Workers of different factories belonging to die making unit.	56	96.55	2	3.45	0	0.00
4.	Workers of different factories belonging to furnace & dispatch unit.	42	97.67	1	2.33	0	0.00
5.	Workers of different factories belonging to key making unit.	54	96.43	2	3.57	0	0.00
6.	Workers of different factories belonging to nickle polish unit.	52	91.23	4	7.02	1	1.75
7.	Workers of different factories belonging to Office.	56	91.80	5	8.20	0	0.00
8.	Workers of different factories belonging to packing unit.	66	89.19	4	5.41	4	5.41
9.	Workers of different factories belonging to press unit.	67	93.06	4	5.56	1	1.39
10.	Salaried workers.	222	93.67	14	5.91	1	0.42

(Contd.)

11. Contractual workers	224	93.72	10	4.18	5	2.09
12. Male workers	429	93.46	24	5.23	6	1.31
13. Female workers	14	100.00	0	0.00	0	0.00
14. Literate workers	208	93.69	12	5.41	2	0.90
15. Illiterate workers	236	93.65	12	4.76	4	1.59
16. Joint family workers	330	95.10	13	3.75	4	1.15
17. Nuclear family workers	114	89.76	11	8.66	2	1.57
18. Rural workers	145	94.77	4	2.61	4	0.61
19. Urban workers	299	93.15	20	6.23	2	0.62
20. Hindu workers	132	90.41	9	6.16	5	3.42
21. Muslim workers	312	95.12	15	4.57	1	0.30
22. Workers in income group 0–3000	334	93.30	19	5.31	5	1.40
23. Workers in income group of 3000 and above	110	94.83	5	4.31	1	0.86
24. Workers belonging to Labour Class	362	93.30	20	5.15	6	1.55
25. Workers belonging to Management Class	79	95.18	4	4.82	0	0.00

higher cost of education majority of people hailing from economically weaker sections do not encourage their children to receive full education."

Table 4.83 reveals that majority of workers (91.14%) representing different units of 55 factories agreed that education mainly responsible for socio-economic development. While 5.49% exhibited their indifference, only 3.38% have expressed their disagreement with the statement.

Unit-wise analysis reveals that 92.45% workers hailing from assembly units; 84.48% from die-making units; 97.67% from furnace and dispatch units; 94.64% from key-making units; 87.72% from nickle polish units; 93.44% from Office; 90.54% from packing units; and 90.28% from press units; 89.45% salaried workers and 93.31% contractual workers; 91.29% male workers and 85.71% female workers; 92.79% literate workers and 89.68% illiterate workers; 93.95% workers from joint family system and 83.46% representing nuclear family system; 89.54% rural workers and 91.90% urban workers; 87.67% Hindu workers and 92.68% Muslim workers; 96.73% workers receiving salary up to Rs. 3000/- and 92.24% workers receiving salary of more than 3000/- per month; 90.21% workers hailing from Labour class and 95.18% workers hailing from management group expressed their agreement with the statement.

It can, thus, be concluded that respondents representing different units of the factory as well as majority of the total subjects (91.14%) expressed their agreement with the statement that, "education is mainly responsible for socio-economic development."

Table 4.84 reveals that only 26.16% workers (26.16%) representing different units of 55 factories agreed that educated persons of the community as compared to others are more successful in business and trade. While 6.96% have exhibited their indifference, only 66.88% have expressed their disagreement with the statement.

TABLE 4.83 EDUCATIONAL PERCEPTION: (3) EDUCATION IS MAINLY RESPONSIBLE FOR SOCIO-ECONOMIC DEVELOPMENT

RESPONDENTS CATEGORY	*YES*	*%*	*INDIFF.*	*%*	*NO*	*%*
1. Workers of different industrial units belonging to same factory.	432	91.14	26	5.49	16	3.38
2. Workers of different factories belonging to assembly unit.	49	92.45	4	7.55	0	0.00
3. Workers of different factories belonging to die making unit.	49	84.48	3	5.17	6	10.34
4. Workers of different factories belonging to furnace & dispatch unit.	42	97.67	1	2.33	0	0.00
5. Workers of different factories belonging to key making unit.	53	87.72	1	1.79	2	3.57
6. Workers of different factories belonging to nickle polish unit.	50	87.44	4	7.02	3	5.26
7. Workers of different factories belonging to Office.	57	93.44	4	6.56	0	0.00
8. Workers of different factories belonging to packing unit.	67	90.54	3	4.05	4	5.41
9. Workers of different factories belonging to press unit.	65	90.28	6	8.33	1	1.39
10. Salaried workers.	212	89.45	15	6.33	10	4.22

(Contd.)

11. Contractual workers	223	93.31	11	4.60	5	2.09
12. Male workers	419	91.29	25	5.45	15	3.27
13. Female workers	12	85.71	1	7.14	1	7.14
14. Literate workers	206	89.79	9	4.05	7	3.15
15. Illiterate workers	226	89.68	17	6.75	9	3.57
16. Joint family workers	326	93.95	13	3.75	8	2.31
17. Nuclear family workers	106	83.46	13	10.24	8	6.30
18. Rural workers	137	89.54	10	6.54	6	3.92
19. Urban workers	295	91.90	16	4.98	10	3.12
20. Hindu workers	128	87.67	11	7.53	7	4.79
21. Muslim workers	304	92.68	15	4.57	9	2.74
22. Workers in income group 0–3000	325	96.73	10	2.98	1	0.30
23. Workers in income group of 3000 and above	107	92.24	4	3.45	5	4.31
24. Workers belonging to Labour Class	350	90.21	22	5.67	16	4.12
25. Workers belonging to Management Class	79	95.18	4	4.82	0	0.00

TABLE 4.84 EDUCATIONAL PERCEPTION: (4) EDUCATED PERSONS OF THE COMMUNITY, AS COMPARED TO OTHERS, ARE MORE SUCCESSFUL IN BUSINESS AND TRADE

	RESPONDENTS CATEGORY	*YES*	*%*	*INDIFF.*	*%*	*NO*	*%*
1.	Workers of different industrial units belonging to same factory.	124	26.16	33	6.96	317	66.88
2.	Workers of different factories belonging to assembly unit.	13	24.53	2	3.77	38	71.70
3.	Workers of different factories belonging to die making unit.	16	27.59	3	5.17	39	67.24
4.	Workers of different factories belonging to furnace & dispatch unit.	9	20.93	2	4.65	32	74.42
5.	Workers of different factories belonging to key making unit.	11	20.37	3	5.56	40	74.07
6.	Workers of different factories belonging to nickle polish unit.	13	22.81	5	8.77	39	68.42
7.	Workers of different factories belonging to Office.	18	29.51	1	1.64	42	68.85
8.	Workers of different factories belonging to packing unit.	21	28.38	10	13.51	43	58.11
9.	Workers of different factories belonging to press unit.	21	29.17	7	9.72	44	61.11
10.	Salaried workers.	58	24.47	17	7.17	162	68.35

(Contd.)

11. Contractual workers	66	27.62	16	6.69	157	65.69
12. Male workers	118	25.71	31	6.75	310	67.54
13. Female workers	6	42.86	2	14.29	6	42.86
14. Literate workers	54	24.32	8	3.60	160	72.07
15. Illiterate workers	70	27.78	25	9.92	157	62.30
16. Joint family workers	86	24.78	23	6.63	238	68.59
17. Nuclear family workers	38	29.92	10	7.87	79	62.20
18. Rural workers	44	28.76	15	9.80	94	61.44
19. Urban workers	80	24.92	18	5.61	223	69.47
20. Hindu workers	36	24.66	16	10.69	94	64.38
21. Muslim workers	88	26.83	17	5.18	223	67.99
22. Workers in income group 0–3000	97	27.09	29	8.10	232	64.80
23. Workers in income group of 3000 and above	27	23.28	4	3.45	85	73.28
24. Workers belonging to Labour Class	99	25.52	32	8.25	257	66.24
25. Workers belonging to Management Class	25	30.12	1	1.20	57	68.67

Unit-wise analysis reveals that 24.53% workers hailing from assembly units; 27.59% from die-making units; 20.93% from furnace and dispatch units; 20.37% from key-making units; 22.81% from nickle polish units; 2951% from Office; 28.38% from packing units; and 29.17% from press units; 24.47% salaried workers and 27.62% contractual workers; 25.71% male workers and 42.86% female workers; 24.32% literate workers and 27.78% illiterate workers; 24.78% workers from joint family system and 29.92% representing nuclear family system; 28.76% rural workers and 24.92% urban workers; 24.66% Hindu workers and 26.83% Muslim workers; 27.09% workers receiving salary up to Rs. 3000/- and 23.28% workers receiving salary of more than 3000/-per month; 66.24% workers hailing from labour class exhibited their disagreement with the statement, while only 25.52% have expressed their agreement. Similarly, against 68.67% workers hailing from management group expressing their agreement only 30.12% expressed their agreement with the statement.

It can, thus, be concluded that the respondents representing different units of the factory as well as majority of the total subjects (66.88%) expressed their disagreement with the statement that "educated persons of the community as compared to others were more successful in business and trade". On the other hand while only 6.96% of the respondents exhibited their indifference towards the statement, only 26.16% of the respondents exhibited their agreement towards the statement. Similar trend was also noticeable among respondents representing different units of the factory.

Table 4.85 reveals that only 14.14% workers representing different units of 55 factories agreed that advice of educated persons of the community was always sought by the uneducated or less educated ones to settle their disputes. While 4.43% have exhibited their indifference, only 81.43% have expressed their disagreement with the statement.

Unit-wise analysis reveals that 7.55% workers hailing from assembly units; 15.52% from die-making units; 6.98% from furnace and dispatch units; 8.93% from key making units; 8.77% from nickle polish units; 13.11% from Office; 27.03% from packing units; and

TABLE 4.85 EDUCATIONAL PERCEPTION: (5) ADVICE OF EDUCATED PERSONS OF THE COMMUNITY WAS ALWAYS SOUGHT BY UNEDUCATED OR LESS EDUCATED ONES TO SETTLE THEIR DISPUTES

	RESPONDENTS CATEGORY	*YES*	*%*	*INDIFF.*	*%*	*NO*	*%*
1.	Workers of different industrial units belonging to same factory.	67	14.14	21	4.43	386	81.43
2.	Workers of different factories belonging to assembly unit.	4	7.55	0	0.00	49	92.45
3.	Workers of different factories belonging to die making unit.	9	15.52	3	5.17	46	79.31
4.	Workers of different factories belonging to furnace & dispatch unit.	3	6.98	0	0.00	40	93.02
5.	Workers of different factories belonging to key making unit.	5	8.93	1	1.79	50	89.29
6.	Workers of different factories belonging to nickle polish unit.	5	8.77	4	7.02	48	84.21
7.	Workers of different factories belonging to Office.	8	13.11	2	3.28	51	83.61
8.	Workers of different factories belonging to packing unit.	20	27.03	4	5.41	50	67.57
9.	Workers of different factories belonging to press unit.	13	18.06	7	9.72	52	72.22
10.	Salaried workers.	40	16.88	14	5.91	183	77.22

(Contd.)

11. Contractual workers	27	11.30	7	2.93	205	85.77
12. Male workers	62	13.51	21	4.58	376	81.92
13. Female workers	5	35.71	0	0.00	9	64.29
14. Literate workers	26	11.71	6	2.70	190	85.59
15. Illiterate workers	41	16.27	15	5.95	196	77.78
16. Joint family workers	3	11.24	11	3.17	297	85.59
17. Nuclear family workers	28	22.05	10	7.87	89	70.08
18. Rural workers	28	18.30	11	7.19	114	74.58
19. Urban workers	39	12.15	10	3.12	272	4.741
20. Hindu workers	28	19.18	10	6.85	108	73.97
21. Muslim workers	39	11.89	11	3.35	278	84.76
22. Workers in income group 0–3000	54	15.08	17	4.75	287	80.17
23. Workers in income group of 3000 and above	13	11.21	4	3.45	99	85.34
24. Workers belonging to Labour Class	59	15.21	19	4.90	310	79.90
25. Workers belonging to Management Class	8	9.64	2	2.41	73	87.95

18.06% from press units; 16.88% salaried workers and 11.30% contractual workers; 13.51% male workers and 35.71% female workers; 11.71% workers from joint family system and 22.05% representing nuclear family system; 18.30% rural workers and 12.15% urban workers; 19.18% Hindu workers and 11.89% Muslim workers; 15.08% workers receiving salary up to Rs. 3000/- and 11.21% workers receiving salary of more than 3000/- per month 15.21% workers from Labour class; and 9.64% workers from management class 79.90% workers hailing from Labour class against thing as among as while and 87.95% workers hailing from management group expressed their disagreement with the statement.

It can, thus, be concluded that respondents representing different units of the factory as well as majority of the total subjects (81.43%) expressed their disagreement with the statement that, advice of educated persons of community was always sought by uneducated or less educated ones to settle their disputes. As against this, only 4.43% of the respondents have exhibited their indifference, only 14.14% of the respondents exhibited their agreement towards the statement. A similar trend is also noticeable among respondents representing different units of the factory.

Table 4.86 reveal that majority of the workers (64.98%) representing different units of 55 factories agreed that parents of the community were more in favour of imparting religious education to their children, instead of scientific education. While 4.85% exhibited their indifference, only 30.17% expressed their disagreement with the statement.

Unit-wise analysis reveals that 64.15% workers hailing from assembly units; 63.79% from die-making units; 67.44% from furnace and dispatch units; 60.71% from key-making units; 64.91% from nickle polish units; 62.30% from Office; 72.60% from packing units; 63.89% from press units; 62.87% salaried workers and 67.65% contractual workers; 64.85% male workers and 71.43% female workers; 68.78% literate workers and 61.90% illiterate workers 65.90% workers from joint family system and 62.99% representing nuclear family system; 61.44% rural workers and 66.88% urban

TABLE 4.86 EDUCATIONAL PERCEPTION: (6) PARENTS OF THE COMMUNITY ARE MORE IN FAVOUR OF IMPARTING RELIGIOUS EDUCATION TO THEIR CHILDREN INSTEAD OF SCIENTIFIC EDUCATION

	RESPONDENTS CATEGORY	*YES*	*%*	*INDIFF.*	*%*	*NO*	*%*
1.	Workers of different industrial units belonging to same factory.	308	64.98	23	4.85	143	30.17
2.	Workers of different factories belonging to assembly unit.	34	64.15	1	1.89	18	33.96
3.	Workers of different factories belonging to die making unit.	37	63.79	2	3.45	19	32.76
4.	Workers of different factories belonging to furnace & dispatch unit.	29	67.44	0	0.00	14	32.56
5.	Workers of different factories belonging to key making unit.	34	60.71	3	3.35	19	33.93
6.	Workers of different factories belonging to nickle polish unit	37	6491	2	3.51	18	31.58
7.	Workers of different factories belonging to Office.	38	62.30	3	4.92	20	32.79
8.	Workers of different factories belonging to packing unit.	53	72.60	5	6.85	15	20.55
9.	Workers of different factories belonging to press unit.	46	63.89	6	8.33	20	27.78
10.	Salaried workers	149	62.87	13	5.49	75	31.65

(Contd.)

11. Contractual workers	161	67.65	9	3.78	68	28.57
12. Male workers	297	64.85	22	4.80	139	30.35
13. Female workers	10	71.43	0	0.00	4	28.57
14. Literate workers	152	68.78	6	2.71	63	28.51
15. Illiterate workers	156	61.90	16	6.35	80	31.75
16. Joint family workers	228	65.90	11	3.18	107	30.92
17. Nuclear family workers	80	62.99	11	8.66	36	28.35
18. Rural workers	94	61.44	13	8.50	46	30.07
19. Urban workers	214	66.88	9	2.81	97	30.31
20. Hindu workers	90	62.07	7	4.83	48	33.10
21. Muslim workers	218	66.46	15	4.57	95	28.96
22. Workers in income group 0–3000	229	64.15	21	5.88	107	29.97
23. Workers in income group of 3000 and above	79	68.10	1	0.86	36	31.03
24. Workers belonging to Labour Class	257	66.41	20	5.17	110	28.42
25. Workers belonging to Management Class	48	57.83	2	2.41	33	39.76

workers; 62.07% Hindu workers and 66.46% Muslim workers; 64.15% workers receiving salary up to Rs. 3000/- and 68.10% workers receiving salary of more than 3000/- per month; 66.41% workers hailing from Labour class and 57.83% workers hailing from management group expressed their agreement with the statement.

It can, thus, be concluded that the respondents representing different units of the factory as well as majority of the total subjects (64.98%) expressed their agreement with the statement that "parents of the community are more in favour of imparting religious education to their children, instead of scientific education".

Table 4.87 reveals that majority of workers (92.62%) representing different units of 55 factories agreed that majority of the parents of the community are ignoring about importance of their children's education. While 61.12% exhibited their indifference, only 1.27% have expressed their disagreement with the statement.

Unit-wise analysis reveals that 98.11% workers hailing from assembly units; 93.10% from die-making units; 93.02% from furnace and dispatch units; 37.50% from key-making units; 91.23% from nickle polish units; 98.36% from Office; 87.84% from packing units; 93.06% from press units; 89.87% salaried workers and 95.82% contractual; 92.59% male workers and 92.86% female workers; 95.05% literate workers and 90.48% illiterate workers; 93.95% workers from joint family system and 88.98% representing nuclear family system; 89.04% Hindu workers and 94.21% Muslim workers; 91.90% workers receiving salary up to Rs. 3000/- and 94.83% workers receiving salary of more than 3000/- per month; 91.48% workers hailing from Labour class; 97.59% workers hailing from management group have also expressed their agreement with the statement.

It can, thus, be concluded that the respondents representing different units of the factory as well as majority of the total subjects (92.62%) have expressed their agreement with the statement that, "majority of the parents of the community are ignorant about importance of their children's education".

TABLE 4.87 EDUCATIONAL PERCEPTION: (7) MAJORITY OF PARENTS OF THE COMMUNITY ARE IGNORANT ABOUT IMPORTANCE OF THEIR CHILDREN'S EDUCATIONS

	RESPONDENTS CATEGORY	YES	%	INDIFF.	%	NO	%
1.	Workers of different industrial units belonging to same factory.	439	92.62	29	6.12	6	1.27
2.	Workers of different factories belonging to assembly unit.	52	98.11	1	1.89	0	0.00
3.	Workers of different factories belonging to die making unit.	54	93.10	3	5.17	1	1.72
4.	Workers of different factories belonging to furnace & dispatch unit.	40	93.02	2	4.65	1	2.33
5.	Workers of different factories belonging to key making unit.	49	87.50	6	10.71	1	1.79
6.	Workers of different factories belonging to nickle polish unit.	52	91.23	5	8.77	0	0.00
7.	Workers of different factories belonging to Office.	60	98.36	0	0.00	1	1.64
8.	Workers of different factories belonging to packing unit.	65	87.84	7	9.46	2	2.70
9.	Workers of different factories belonging to press unit.	67	93.06	5	6.94	0	0.00
10.	Salaried workers.	213	89.87	20	8.44	4	1.69

(Contd.)

11. Contractual workers	229	95.82	8	3.35	2	0.84
12. Male workers	425	92.59	28	6.10	6	1.31
13. Female workers	13	92.86	1	7.14	0	0.00
14. Literate workers	211	95.05	8	3.60	3	1.35
15. Illiterate workers	228	90.48	21	8.33	3	1.19
16. Joint family workers	326	93.95	18	5.19	3	0.86
17. Nuclear family workers	113	88.98	11	8.66	3	2.36
18. Rural workers	132	86.27	19	12.42	2	1.31
19. Urban workers	307	95.64	10	3.12	4	1.25
20. Hindu workers	130	89.04	14	9.59	2	1.37
21. Muslim workers	309	94.21	15	4.57	4	1.22
22. Workers in income group 0–3000	329	91.90	25	6.98	4	1.12
23. Workers in income group of 3000 and above	110	94.83	4	3.45	2	1.72
24. Workers belonging to Labour Class	355	91.49	29	7.47	4	1.02
25. Workers belonging to Management Class	81	97.59	0	0.00	2	2.41

Table 4.88 reveals that majority of the workers (94.51%) representing different units of 55 factories agreed that women of their community were more educationally backward as compared to the women of other communities. While 5.49% exhibited their indifference, only expressed their disagreement with the statement.

Unit wise analysis reveals that 98.11% workers hailing from assembly units; 94.83% from die-making units; 97.67% from furnace and dispatch units; 91.07% from key-making units; 91.23% from nickle polish units; 100.00% from Office; 91.89% from packing units; and 93.06% from press units; 92.41% salaried workers and 97.07% contractual workers; 94.34% male workers and 100.00% female workers; 97.75% literate workers and 91.67% illiterate workers; 95.68% workers from joint family system and 91.34% representing nuclear family system; 88.89% rural workers and 97.20% urban workers; 91.78% Hindu workers and 95.86% Muslim workers; 99.41% workers receiving salary up to Rs. 3000/- and 96.55% workers receiving salary of more than 3000/- per month; 93.30% workers hailing from Labour class and 100.00% workers hailing from management group expressed their agreement with the statement.

It can, thus, be concluded that respondents representing different units of the factory as well as majority of the total subjects (94.51%) expressed their agreement with the statement that, "women of their community are more educationally backward as compared to women of other communities".

Table 4.89 reveals that majority of workers (94.51%) representing different units of 55 factories agreed that leaders of community were indifferent towards upliftment of the community and do not seek help from the government. While 5.49% exhibited their indifference, only 0.00% expressed their disagreement with the statement.

Unit-wise analysis reveals that 98.11% workers hailing from assembly units; 94.83% from die-making units; 97.67% from furnace and dispatch units; 91.07% from key-making units; 91.23% from nickle polish units; 100.00% from Office; 91.89% from packing units;

TABLE 4.88 EDUCATIONAL PERCEPTION: (8) WOMEN OF THEIR COMMUNITY ARE MORE EDUCATIONALLY BACKWARD AS COMPARED TO THE WOMEN OF OTHER COMMUNITIES

	RESPONDENTS CATEGORY	*YES*	%	*INDIFF.*	%	*NO*	%
1.	Workers of different industrial units belonging to same factory.	448	94.51	26	5.49	0	0.00
2.	Workers of different factories belonging to assembly unit	52	98.11	1	1.89	0	0.00
3.	Workers of different factories belonging to die making unit	55	94.83	3	5.17	0	0.00
4.	Workers of different factories belonging to furnace & dispatch unit.	42	97.67	1	2.33	0	0.00
5.	Workers of different factories belong to key making unit.	51	91.07	5	8.93	0	0.00
6.	Workers of different factories belonging to nickle polish unit.	52	91.23	5	8.77	0	0.00
7.	Workers of different factories belonging to Office.	61	100.00	0	0.00	0	0.00
8.	Workers of different factories belonging to packing unit.	68	91.89	6	8.11	0	0.00
9.	Workers of different factories belonging to press unit.	67	93.06	5	6.94	0	0.00
10.	Salaried workers.	219	92.41	18	7.59	0	0.00

(Contd.)

11.	Contractual workers	232	97.07	7	2.93	0	0.00
12.	Male workers	433	93.34	26	5.66	0	0.00
13.	Female workers	14	100.00	0	0.00	0	0.00
14.	Literate workers	217	97.75	5	2.25	0	0.00
15.	Illiterate workers	231	91.67	21	8.33	0	0.00
16.	Joint family workers	332	95.68	15	4.32	0	0.00
17.	Nuclear family workers	116	91.34	11	8.66	0	0.00
18.	Rural workers	136	88.89	17	11.11	0	0.00
19.	Urban workers	312	97.20	9	2.80	0	0.00
20.	Hindu workers	134	91.78	12	8.22	0	0.00
21.	Muslim workers	324	95.86	14	4.14	0	0.00
22.	Workers in income group 0–3000	336	99.41	2	0.59	0	0.00
23.	Workers in income group of 3000 and above	112	96.55	4	3.45	0	0.00
24.	Workers belonging to Labour Class	362	93.30	26	6.70	0	0.00
25.	Workers belonging to Management Class	83	100.00	9	0.00	0	0.00

TABLE 4.89 EDUCATIONAL PERCEPTION: (9) LEADERS OF THE COMMUNITY ARE INDIFFERENT TOWARDS UPLIFTMENT OF THE COMMUNITY AND DO NOT SEEK HELP FROM THE GOVERNMENT

	RESPONDENTS CATEGORY	*YES*	*%*	*INDIFF.*	*%*	*NO*	*%*
1.	Workers of different industrial units belonging to same factory.	448	94.51	26	5.49	0	0.00
2.	Workers of different factories belonging to assembly unit	52	98.11	1	1.89	0	0.00
3.	Workers of different factories belonging to die making unit	55	94.83	3	5.17	0	0.00
4.	Workers of different factories belonging to furnace & dispatch unit.	42	97.67	1	2.33	0	0.00
5.	Workers of different factories belonging to key making unit.	51	91.07	5	8.93	0	0.00
6.	Workers of different factories belonging to nickle polish unit	52	91.23	5	8.77	0	0.00
7.	Workers of different factories belonging to Office.	61	100.00	0	0.00	0	0.00
8.	Workers of different factories belonging to packing unit.	68	91.89	6	8.11	0	0.00
9.	Workers of different factories belonging to Press unit.	67	93.06	5	6.94	0	0.00
10.	Salaried workers.	219	92.41	18	7.59	0	0.00

(Contd.)

11.	Contractual workers	232	97.07	7	2.93	0	0.00
12.	Male workers	433	94.34	26	5.66	0	0.00
13.	Female workers	14	100.00	0	0.00	0	0.00
14.	Literate workers	217	97.75	5	2.25	0	0.00
15.	Illiterate workers	231	91.67	21	8.33	0	0.00
16.	Joint family workers	332	95.68	15	4.32	0	0.00
17.	Nuclear family workers	116	91.34	11	8.66	0	0.00
18.	Rural workers	136	88.89	17	11.11	0	0.00
19.	Urban workers	312	97.20	9	2.80	0	0.00
20.	Hindu workers	134	91.78	12	8.22	0	0.00
21.	Muslim workers	314	95.73	14	4.27	0	0.00
22.	Workers in income group 0–3000	336	93.85	22	6.15	0	0.00
23.	Workers in income group of 3000 and above	112	96.55	4	3.45	0	0.00
24.	Workers belonging to Labour Class	362	93.30	26	6.70	0	0.00
25.	Workers belonging to Management Class	83	100.00	0	0.00	0	0.00

93.06% from press units; 92.41% salaried workers and 97.07% contractual workers; 94.34% male workers and 100.00% female workers; 97.75% literate workers and 91.67% illiterate workers; 95.68% workers from joint family system and 91.34% representing nuclear family system; 88.89% rural workers and 97.20% urban workers; 91.78% Hindu workers and 95.86% Muslim workers; 93.85% workers receiving salary up to Rs.3000/- and 96.55% workers receiving salary of more than 3000/ per month; 93.30% workers hailing from Labour class and 100.00% workers hailing from management group expressed their agreement with the statement.

It can, thus, be concluded that the respondents representing different units of the factory as well as majority workers (94.51%) expressed their agreement with the statement that leaders of the community were indifferent towards the upliftment of the community and did not seek help from the government."

Table 4.90 reveals that majority of workers (94.30%) representing different units of 55 factories agreed that in the present era, education has become highly commercialized because teachers do not judiciously perform their teaching duties in school and colleges as either they have opened their coaching centers or were teaching in other coaching centers on payment. While 5.49% exhibited their indifference, only 0.21% expressed their disagreement with the statement.

Unit wise analysis reveals that 98.11% workers hailing from assembly units; 94.83% from die-making units; 97.67% from furnace and dispatch units; 91.07% from key-making units; 91.23% from nickle polish units; 100.00% from Office; 91.78% from packing units; and 93.06% from press units; 91.98% salaried workers and 97.07% contractual workers; 94.34% male workers and 92.86% female workers; 97.75% literate workers and 91.27% illiterate workers; 95.39% workersfrom joint family system and 91.34% representing nuclear family system; 88.24% rural workers and 97.20% urban workers; 91.10% Hindu workers and 95.73% Muslim workers; 93.85% workers receiving salary up to Rs. 3000/- and 96.55% workers receiving salary of more than 3000/- per month; 93.04% workers

TABLE 4.90 EDUCATIONAL PERCEPTION: (10) IN THE PRESENT ERA EDUCATION HAS BECOME HIGHLY COMMERCIALIZED BECAUSE TEACHERS DO NOT JUDICIOUSLY PERFORM THEIR TEACHING DUTIES IN SCHOOL AND COLLEGES AS EITHER THEY HAVE OPENED THEIR COACHING CENTERS OR WHERE TEACHING IN OTHER COACHING CENTERS ON PAYMENT

	RESPONDENTS CATEGORY	*YES*	*%*	*INDIFF.*	*%*	*NO*	*%*
1.	Workers of different industrial units belonging to same factory.	447	94.30	26	5.49	0	0.00
2.	Workers of different factories belonging to assembly unit.	52	98.11	1	1.89	0	0.00
3.	Workers of different factories belonging to die making unit.	55	94.83	3	5.17	0	0.00
4.	Workers of different factories belonging to furnace & dispatch unit.	42	97.67	1	2.33	0	0.00
5.	Workers of different factories belonging to key making unit.	51	91.07	5	8.93	0	0.00
6.	Workers of different factories belonging to nickle polish unit.	52	91.23	5	8.77	0	0.00
7.	Workers of different factors belonging to Office.	61	100.00	0	0.00	0	0.00
8.	Workers of different factories belonging to packing unit.	67	91.78	6	8.22	0	0.00
9.	Workers of different factories belonging to press unit.	67	93.06	5	6.94	0	0.00
10.	Salaried workers.	218	91.98	18	7.59	1	0.42

(Contd.)

11. Contractual workers	232	97.07	7	2.93	0	0.00
12. Male workers	433	94.34	26	5.66	0	0.00
13. Female workers	13	92.86	0	0.00	1	7.14
14. Literate workers	217	97.75	5	2.25	0	0.00
15. Illiterate workers	230	91.27	21	8.33	1	0.40
16. Joint family workers	331	95.39	15	4.32	1	0.29
17. Nuclear family workers	116	91.34	11	8.66	0	0.00
18. Rural workers	135	88.24	17	11.11	1	0.65
19. Urban workers	312	97.20	9	2.80	0	0.00
20. Hindu workers	133	91.10	12	8.22	1	0.68
21. Muslim workers	314	95.73	14	4.27	0	0.00
22. Workers in income group 0–3000	335	93.58	22	6.15	1	0.28
23. Workers in income group of 3000 and above	112	96.55	4	3.45	0	0.00
24. Workers belonging to Labour Class	351	93.04	26	6.70	1	0.26
25. Workers belonging to Management Class	83	100.00	0	0.00	0	0.00

hailing from Labour class and 100.00% workers hailing from management group expressed their agreement with the statement.

It can, thus, be concluded that respondents representing different units of the factory as well as majority of the total subjects (94.30%) expressed their agreement with the statement that, "in the present era, education has become highly commercialized because teachers do not judiciously perform their teaching duties in schools and colleges as either they have opened their coaching centers or were teaching in other coaching centers on payment."

Table 4.91 reveals that majority of the workers (58.23%) representing different units of 55 factories have agreed to establish contact with the members of the community connected with the education system to suggest ways and means to the government so that some better system of education may be evolved. While 1.27% exhibited their indifference, only 40.51% have expressed their disagreement with the statement.

Unit-wise analysis reveals that 56.60% workers hailing from assembly units; 58.62% from die-making units; 5581% from furnace and dispatch units; 53.57% from key-making units; 61.40% from nickle polish units; 55.74% from Office; 63.51% from packing units; and 58.33% from press units; 56.96% salaried workers and 41.89% contractual workers; 57.73% male workers and 71.43% female workers; 55.41% literate workers and 60.71% illiterate workers; 60.23% workers from joint family system and 52.76% representing nuclear family system; 64.05% rural workers and 55.45% urban workers; 67.81% Hindu workers and 53.96% Muslim workers; 60.61% workers receiving salary up to Rs. 3000/- and 50.86% workers receiving salary of more than 3000/- per month; 60.57% workers hailing salary up to Rs. 3000/- and 50.86% workers receiving salary more than 3000/- per month; 60.57% workers hailing from Labour class and 45.78% workers hailing from management group expressed their agreement with the statement.

It can, thus, be concluded that majority of the respondents (58.23%) representing different units of the factory expressed their agreement to establish contact with the members of the community connected

TABLE 4.91 EDUCATIONAL PERCEPTION: (1) TO ESTABLISH CONTACT WITH MEMBERS OF THE COMMUNITY CONNECTED WITH EDUCATION SYSTEM TO SUGGEST WAYS AND MEANS TO THE GOVERNMENT SO THAT SOME BETTER SYSTEM OF EDUCATION MAY BE EVOLVED

	RESPONDENTS CATEGORY	*YES*	*%*	*INDIFF.*	*%*	*NO*	*%*
1.	Workers of different industrial units belonging to same factory.	276	58.23	6	1.27	192	40.51
2.	Workers of different factories belonging to assembly unit.	30	56.60	1	1.89	22	41.51
3.	Workers of different factories belonging to die making unit.	34	58.62	0	0.00	24	41.38
4.	Workers of different factories belonging to furnace & dispatch unit.	24	55.81	0	0.00	19	44.19
5.	Workers of different factories belonging to key making unit.	30	53.57	1	1.79	25	44.64
6.	Workers of different factories belonging to nickle polish unit.	35	61.40	0	0.00	22	38.60
7.	Workers of different factories belonging to Office.	34	55.74	0	0.00	27	44.26
8.	Workers of different factories belonging to packing unit.	47	63.51	1	1.35	26	35.14
9.	Workers of different factories belonging to press unit.	42	58.33	3	4.17	27	37.50
10.	Salaried workers.	135	56.96	2	0.84	100	42.19

(Contd.)

11. Contractual workers	142	41.89	4	1.18	193	56.93
12. Male workers	265	57.73	6	1.31	188	40.96
13. Female workers	10	71.43	0	0.00	4	28.57
14. Literate workers	217	97.75	5	2.25	0	0.00
15. Illiterate workers	153	60.71	5	1.98	94	37.30
16. Joint family workers	209	60.23	4	1.15	134	38.62
17. Nuclear family workers	67	52.76	2	1.57	58	45.67
18. Rural workers	98	64.05	4	2.61	51	33.33
19. Urban workers	178	55.45	2	0.62	141	43.93
20. Hindu workers	99	67.81	3	2.05	44	30.14
21. Muslim workers	177	53.96	3	0.91	148	45.12
22. Workers in income group 0–3000	217	60.61	6	1.68	135	37.71
23. Workers in income group of 3000 and above	59	50.86	0	0.00	57	49.14
24. Workers belonging to Labour Class	235	60.57	6	1.55	147	37.89
25. Workers belonging to Management Class	38	45.78	0	0.00	45	54.22

with the education system to suggest ways and means to the government so that some better system of education may be evolved. The trend indicates that the respondents wanted to work and pursue with the government for evolving better system of education. While only 1.27% of the respondents exhibited their indifference, 40.51% of the respondents exhibited their disagreement towards the statement. Similar trend was also noticeable among the respondents representing different units of the factory. It can, thus, be inferred that majority of the respondents were in favour of the statement.

Table 4.92 reveals the majority of the workers (92.83%) representing different units of 55 factories agreed to work and fight independently or through some social organisation to press the government for free and full education to the children hailing from economically backward strata of the community. While 6.12% exhibited their indifference, only 1.05% have expressed their disagreement with the statement.

Unit-wise analysis reveals that 90.57% workers hailing from assembly units; 94.83% from die-making units; 93.02% from furnace and dispatch units; 94.64% from key-making units; 94.74% from nickle polish units; 86.89% from Office; 91.89% from packing units; and 95.83% from press units; 91.14% salaried workers and 94.56% contractual workers; 92.81% male workers and 92.86% female workers; 92.79% literate workers and 92.86% illiterate workers; 94.81% workers from joint family system and 87.40% representing nuclear family system; 92.81% rural workers and 92.83% urban workers; 93.84% Hindu workers and 92.38% Muslim workers; 92.74% workers receiving salary up to Rs. 3000/-and 93.10% workers receiving salary of more than 3000/- per month; 93.04% workers hailing from Labour class and 91.57% workers hailing from management group expressed their agreement with the statement.

It can, thus, be concluded that respondents representing different units of the factory as well as majority of the total subjects (92.83%) expressed their agreement "to work and fight independently or through some social organisation to press the government for free and full education to the children hailing from economically backward strata of the community."

TABLE 4.92 EDUCATIONAL ASPIRATION: (2) TO WORK AND FIGHT INDEPENDENTLY OR THROUGH SOME SOCIAL ORGANIZATION TO PRESS THE GOVERNMENT FOR FREE AND FULL EDUCATION TO CHILDREN HAILING FROM ECONOMICALLY BACKWARD STRATA OF THE COMMUNITY

	RESPONDENTS CATEGORY	*YES*	*%*	*INDIFF.*	*%*	*NO*	*%*
1.	Workers of different industrial units belonging to same factory.	440	92.83	29	6.12	5	1.05
2.	Workers of different factories belonging to assembly unit.	48	90.57	5	9.43	0	0.00
3.	Workers of different factories belonging to die making unit.	55	94.83	3	5.17	0	0.00
4.	Workers of different factories belonging to furnace & dispatch unit.	40	93.02	2	4.65	1	2.33
5.	Workers of different factories belonging to key making unit.	53	94.64	1	1.79	2	3.57
6.	Workers of different factories belonging to nickle polish unit.	54	94.74	2	3.51	1	1.75
7.	Workers of different factories belonging to Office.	53	86.89	7	11.48	1	1.64
8.	Workers of different factories belonging to packing unit.	68	91.89	6	8.11	0	0.00
9.	Workers of different factories belonging to press unit.	69	95.83	3	4.17	0	0.00
10.	Salaried workers.	216	91.14	18	7.59	3	1.27

(*Contd.*)

11. Contractual workers	226	94.65	11	4.60	2	0.84
12. Male workers	426	92.81	28	6.10	5	1.09
13. Female workers	13	92.86	1	7.14	0	0.00
14. Literate workers	206	92.79	14	6.31	2	0.90
15. Illiterate workers	234	92.86	15	5.95	3	1.19
16. Joint family workers	329	94.81	13	3.75	5	1.44
17. Nuclear family workers	111	87.40	16	12.60	0	0.00
18. Rural workers	142	92.81	9	5.988	2	1.31
19. Urban workers	298	92.83	20	6.23	3	0.93
20. Hindu workers	137	93.84	7	4.79	2	1.37
21. Muslim workers	303	92.38	22	6.71	3	0.91
22. Workers in income group 0–3000	332	92.74	21	5.87	5	1.40
23. Workers in income group of 3000 and above	108	93.10	8	6.90	0	0.00
24. Workers belonging to Labour Class	361	93.04	23	5.93	4	1.03
25. Workers belonging to Management Class	76	91.57	6	7.23	1	1.20

Table 4.93 reveals that majority of the workers (54.64%) representing different units of 55 factories agreed to work with some social organisation of the community, which claim to look after the interest of the poor' children hailing from lower economic strata. While 5.72% exhibited their indifference, only 39.66% expressed their disagreement with the statement.

Unit-wise analysis reveals that 54.72% workers hailing from assembly units; 58.62% from die-making units; 62.79% from furnace and dispatch units; 46.43% from key-making units; 47.37% from nickle polish units; 50.82% from Office; 60.81% from packing units; 55.56% from press units; 56.96% salaried workers and 52.72% contractual workers; 54.90% male workers and 42.86% female workers; 55.86% literate workers and 53.57% illiterate workers; 56.20% workers from joint family system and 50.39% representing nuclear family; 58.82% rural workers and 52.65% urban workers; 63.01% Hindu workers and 50.91% Muslim workers; 56.15% workers receiving salary up to Rs. 3000/- and 50.00% workers receiving salary of more than 3000/- per month; 56.70% workers hailing from Labour class; 46.99% workers hailing from management group expressed their agreement with the statement.

It can, thus, be concluded that majority of the respondents (54.64%) representing different units of the factory expressed their agreement to work with some social organisation of the community which claim to look after the interest of the poor's children hailing from the lower economic strata. The trend indicates that the respondents wanted to work with some social organisation of the community for looking after the interests of the poor children of their community. While 5.72% of the respondents exhibited their indifference, 39.66% of the respondents exhibited their disagreement towards the statement. Similar trend was also noticeable among respondents representing different units of the factory. It can, thus, be concluded that majority of the respondents were in favour the statement.

TABLE 4.93 EDUCATIONAL ASPIRATION: (3) TO WORK WITH SOME SOCIAL ORGANIZATIONS OF THE COMMUNITY, WHICH CLAIM TO LOOK AFTER THE INTEREST OF POORS' CHILDREN HAILING FROM THE LOWER ECONOMIC STRATA

	RESPONDENTS CATEGORY	*YES*	*%*	*INDIFF.*	*%*	*NO*	*%*
1.	Workers of different industrial units belonging to same factory.	259	54.64	27	5.72	188	39.66
2.	Workers of different factories belonging to assembly unit.	29	54.72	4	7.55	20	37.74
3.	Workers of different factories belonging to die making unit.	34	58.62	2	3.45	22	37.93
4.	Workers of different factories belonging to furnace & dispatch unit.	27	62.79	0	0.00	16	37.21
5.	Workers of different factories belonging to key making unit.	26	46.43	5	8.93	25	44.64
6.	Workers of different factories belonging to nickle polish unit.	27	47.37	4	7.02	26	45.61
7.	Workers of different factories belonging to Office.	31	40.82	3	4.92	27	44.26
8.	Workers of different factories belonging to packing unit.	45	60.81	5	6.76	24	32.43
9.	Workers of different factories belonging to press unit.	40	55.56	4	5.56	28	32.43
10.	Salaried workers.	135	56.96	12	5.06	90	37.97

(Contd.)

11. Contractual workers	126	52.72	14	5.86	99	41.42
12. Male workers	252	54.90	26	5.66	181	39.43
13. Female workers	6	42.86	1	7.14	7	50.00
14. Literate workers	124	55.86	7	3.15	91	40.99
15. Illiterate workers	135	53.57	20	7.94	97	38.49
16. Joint family workers	195	56.20	17	4.90	135	38.90
17. Nuclear family workers	64	50.39	10	7.87	53	41.73
18. Rural workers	90	58.82	48	31.37	15	9.80
19. Urban workers	169	52.65	12	3.74	140	43.61
20. Hindu workers	92	63.01	9	6.16	45	30.82
21. Muslim workers	167	50.91	18	5.49	143	43.60
22. Workers in income group	201	56.15	24	6.70	133	37.15
23. Workers in income group	58	50.00	3	2.59	55	47.41
24. Workers belonging to Labour Class	220	56.70	24	6.19	144	37.77
25. Workers belonging to Management Class	39	46.99	3	3.61	41	49.40

Table 4.94 reveals that majority of workers (77.85%) representing different units of 55 factories agreed to propagate that children must not be engaged in any economic activity till they receive proper education so that they may be more successful in business and trade. While 7.17% have exhibited their indifference, only 14.98% have expressed their disagreement with the statement.

Unit-wise analysis reveals that 75.47% workers hailing from assembly units; 81.03% from die-making units; 74.42% from furnace and dispatch units; 78.57% from key-making units; 77.19% from nickle polish units; 81.97% from Office; 75.68% from packing units; 78.38% from press units; 78.06% salaried workers and 78.24% contractual workers; 78.43% male workers and 64.29% female workers; 80.18% literate workers and 75.79% illiterate workers; 76.95% workers from joint family system and 80.31% representing nuclear family system; 79.74% rural workers and 76.95% urban workers; 78.08% Hindu workers and 77.74% Muslim workers; 75.70% workers receiving salary up to Rs. 3000/- and 84.48% workers receiving salary of more than 3000/- per month; 76.80% workers hailing from Labour class and 81.93% workers hailing from management group expressed their agreement with the statement.

It can, thus, be concluded that respondents representing different units of the factory as well as majority of the total subjects (77.85%) expressed their agreement "to propagate that children must not be engaged in any economic activity till they receive proper education so that they may be more successful in business and trade".

Table 4.95 reveals that majority of workers (85.44%) representing different units of 55 factories agreed that to educate the uneducated or less educated masses of the community to settle their disputes amicably with the help of educated person and not to use physical force or adopt unethical practices or to go to court of law as it was very expensive and time consuming. While 6.33% exhibited their indifference, only 8.23% expressed their disagreement with the statement.

Unit-wise analysis reveal that 88.68% workers hailing from assembly units; 84.48% from die-making units; 88.37% from furnace

TABLE 4.94 EDUCATIONAL ASPIRATION: (4) TO PROPAGATE THAT CHILDREN MUST NOT BE ENGAGED IN ANY ECONOMIC ACTIVITY TILL THEY RECEIVE PROPER EDUCATION SO THAT THEY MAY BE MORE SUCCESSFUL IN BUSINESS AND TRADE

	RESPONDENTS CATEGORY	*YES*	*%*	*INDIFF.*	*%*	*NO*	*%*
1.	Workers of different industrial units belonging to same factory.	369	77.85	34	7.17	71	14.98
2.	Workers of different factories belonging to assembly unit.	40	75.47	4	7.55	9	16.98
3.	Workers of different factories belonging to die making unit.	47	81.03	3	5.17	8	13.79
4.	Workers of different factories belonging to furnace & dispatch unit	32	74.42	2	4.65	9	20.93
5.	Workers of different factories belonging to key making unit.	44	78.57	5	8.93	7	12.50
6.	Workers of different factories belonging to nickle polish unit	44	77.19	4	7.02	9	15.79
7.	Workers of different factories belonging to Office.	50	81.97	2	3.28	9	14.75
8.	Workers of different factories belonging to packing unit.	56	75.68	6	8.11	12	16.22
9.	Workers of different factories belonging to press unit.	58	78.38	8	10.81	8	10.81
10.	Salaried workers	185	78.06	19	8.02	33	13.92

(Contd.)

11. Contractual workers	187	78.24	14	5.86	38	15.90
12. Male workers	360	78.43	32	6.97	67	14.60
13. Female workers	9	64.29	2	14.29	3	21.43
14. Literate workers	178	80.18	10	4.50	34	15.32
15. Illiterate workers	191	75.79	24	9.52	37	14.68
16. Joint family workers	267	76.95	26	7.49	54	15.56
17. Nuclear family workers	102	80.31	8	6.30	17	13.39
18. Rural workers	122	79.74	17	11.11	14	9.15
19. Urban workers	247	76.95	17	5.30	57	17.76
20. Hindu workers	114	78.08	17	11.64	15	10.27
21. Muslim workers	255	77.74	17	5.18	56	17.07
22. Workers in income group .	271	75.70	29	8.10	58	16.20
23. Workers in income group	98	84.48	5	4.31	13	11.21
24. Workers belonging to Labour Class	298	76.80	31	7.99	59	15.21
25. Workers belonging to Management Class	68	81.93	3	3.61	12	14.46

TABLE 4.95 EDUCATIONAL ASPIRATION: (5) TO EDUCATE THE UNEDUCATED OR LESS EDUCATED MASSES OF THE COMMUNITY TO SETTLE THEIR DISPUTES AMICABLY WITH THE HELP OF EDUCATED PERSONS AND NOT TO USE PHYSICAL FORCE OR ADOPT UNETHICAL PRACTICES OR TO GO TO COURT OF LAW AS IT WAS VERY EXPENSIVE AND TIME CONSUMING

	RESPONDENTS CATEGORY	*YES*	*%*	*INDIFF.*	*%*	*NO*	*%*
1.	Workers of different industrial units belonging to same factory.	405	85.44	30	6.33	39	8.23
2.	Workers of different factories belonging to assembly unit.	47	88.68	1	1.89	5	9.43
3.	Workers of different factories belonging to die making unit.	49	84.48	5	8.62	4	6.90
4.	Workers of different factories belonging to furnace & dispatch unit.	38	88.37	1	2.33	4	9.30
5.	Workers of different factories belonging to key making unit.	50	89.29	3	5.36	3	5.36
6.	Workers of different factories belonging to nickle polish unit.	48	84.21	3	5.26	6	10.53
7.	Workers of different factories belonging to Office.	55	90.16	1	1.64	5	8.20
8.	Workers of different factories belonging to packing unit.	59	79.73	8	10.81	7	9.46
9.	Workers of different factories belonging to press unit.	59	81.94	8	11.11	5	6.94
10.	Salaried workers.	192	81.01	17	7.17	28	11.81

(Contd.)

11. Contractual workers	216	90.38	12	5.02	11	4.60
12. Male workers	391	85.19	29	6.32	39	8.50
13. Female workers	13	92.86	1	7.14	0	0.00
14. Literate workers	187	84.23	5	2.25	30	13.51
15. Illiterate workers	218	86.51	25	9.92	9	3.57
16. Joint family workers	298	85.88	16	4.61	33	9.51
17. Nuclear family workers	107	84.25	14	11.02	6	4.72
18. Rural workers	116	75.82	20	13.07	17	11.11
19. Urban workers	289	90.03	10	3.12	22	6.85
20. Hindu workers	118	80.82	12	8.22	16	10.96
21. Muslim workers	287	87.50	18	5.49	23	7.01
22. Workers in income group 0–3000	308	86.03	27	7.54	23	6.42
23. Workers in income group of 3000 and above	97	83.62	3	2.59	16	13.79
24. Workers belonging to Labour Class	325	83.76	29	7.47	34	8.76
25. Workers belonging to Management Class	77	92.77	1	1.20	5	6.02

and dispatch units; 89.29% from key-making units; 8421% from nickle polish units; 90.16% from Office; 79.73% from packing units; 81.94% from press units; 81.01% salaried workers and 90.38% contractual workers; 85.19% male workers and 92.86% female workers; 84.23% literate workers and 86.51% illiterate workers; 85.88% workers from joint family system and 84.25% representing nuclear family system; 75.82% rural workers and 90.03% urban workers; 8082% Hindu workers and 87.50% Muslim workers; 86.03% workers receiving salary up to Rs. 3000/- and 83.62% workers receiving salary of more than 3000/- per month; 83.76% workers hailing from Labour class and 92.77% workers hailing from management group expressed their agreement with the statement.

It can, thus, be concluded that the respondents representing different units of the factory as well as majority of the total subjects (85.44%) expressed their agreement "to educated the uneducated or less educated masses of the community to settle their disputes amicably with the help of educated persons and not to use physical force or adopt unethical practices or to go tocourt of law as it is very expensive and time consuming".

Table 4.96 reveals that only 45.57% workers representing different units of 55 factories agreed that to propagate among the masses of the community about the usefulness of scientific education based on analytical and rational principles instead of religious education alone. While 7.51% exhibited their indifference, only 46.84% expressed their disagreement with the statement.

Unit-wise analysis reveals that 45.28% workers hailing from assembly units; 44.83% from die-making units; 51.16% form furnace and dispatch units; 42.86% from key-making units; 45.61% from nickle polish units; 44.26% from Office; 47.30% from packing units; and 44.44% from press units; 43.04% salaried workers and 48.12% contractual workers; 44.88% male workers and 64.29% female workers; 47.30% literate workers and 44.05% illiterate workers; 48.41% workers from joint family system and 37.80% representing nuclear family system; 44.44% rural workers 46.11% urban workers; 47.95% Hindu workers and 44.51% Muslim workers; 39.26% workers

TABLE 4.96 EDUCATIONAL ASPIRATION: (6) TO PROPAGATE AMONG THE MASSES OF THE COMMUNITY ABOUT THE USEFULNESS OF SCIENTIFIC EDUCATION BASED ON ANALYTICAL AND RATIONAL PRINCIPLES INSTEAD OF RELIGIOUS EDUCATION ALONE

	RESPONDENTS CATEGORY	*YES*	%	*INDIFF.*	%	*NO*	%
1.	Workers of different industrial units belonging to same factory.	216	45.57	36	7.51	222	46.84
2.	Workers of different factories belonging to assembly unit.	24	45.28	3	5.66	26	49.06
3.	Workers of different factories belonging to die making unit.	26	44.83	6	10.34	26	44.83
4.	Workers of different factories belonging to furnace & dispatch unit.	22	51.16	1	2.33	20	46.51
5.	Workers of different factories belonging to key making unit.	24	42.86	3	5.35	29	51.79
6.	Workers of different factories belonging to nickle polish unit	26	45.61	3	5.26	28	49.12
7.	Workers of different factories belonging to Office.	27	44.26	3	8.20	29	47.54
8.	Workers of different factories belonging to packing unit.	35	47.30	8	10.81	31	41.89
9.	Workers of different factories belonging to press unit.	32	44.44	7	9.72	33	45.83
10.	Salaried workers	102	43.04	24	10.13	111	46.84

(Contd.)

11. Contractual workers	115	48.12	11	4.60	113	47.28
12. Male workers	206	44.88	35	7.63	218	47.49
13. Female workers	9	64.29	1	7.14	4	28.57
14. Literate workers	105	47.30	13	5.86	104	86.85
15. Illiterate workers	111	44.05	23	9.13	118	46.83
16. Joint family workers	168	48.41	22	6.34	157	45.24
17. Nuclear family workers	48	37.80	14	11.02	65	51.18
18. Rural workers	68	44.44	17	11.11	68	44.44
19. Urban workers	148	46.11	19	5.92	154	47.98
20. Hindu workers	70	47.95	13	8.90	63	43.15
21. Muslim workers	146	44.51	23	7.01	159	48.48
22. Workers in income group 0–3000	117	39.26	25	8.39	156	52.35
23. Workers in income group of 3000 and above	39	33.62	11	9.48	66	56.90
24. Workers belonging to Labour Class	184	47.42	32	8.25	172	44.33
25. Workers belonging to Management Class	29	34.94	4	4.82	50	60.24

receiving salary up to Rs. 3000/- and 33.62% workers receiving salary of more than 3000/- per month; 47.42% workers hailing from Labour class; 43.94% workers hailing from management group expressed their agreement with the statement. It may be noted that 44.33% of workers from Labour class and a high figure of 60.24% expressed their disagreement with the statement.

It can, thus, be concluded that a minority of respondents (45.57%) representing different units of the factory expressed their agreement to propagate among the masses of the community about the usefulness of scientific education based on analytical and rational principles instead of religious education alone. The trend indicates that the respondents wanted to work and propagate among the community members for the scope and necessity of scientific education instead of religious education alone. While only 7.51% of the respondents exhibited their indifference, a majority of workers (46.84%) exhibited their disagreement with the statement. Similar trend was also noticeable among the respondents representing different units of the factory. It can, thus, be inferred that majority of the respondents were not in favour of the statement.

Table 4.97 reveals that majority of workers (91.77%) representing different units of 55 factories agreed to seek help from educated members of the community to enlighten the ignorant persons about the importance of children's education. While 4.85% exhibited their indifference, only 3.38% have expressed their disagreement with the statement.

Unit-wise analysis reveals that 45.28% workers hailing from assembly units; 44.83% from die-making units; 51.16% from furnace and dispatch units; 42.86% from key-making units; 45.61% from nickle polish units; 44.26% from Office; 47.30% from packing units; 44.44% from press units; 43.04% salaried workers and 48.12% contractual workers; 44.88% male workers and 64.29% female workers; 47.30% literate workers and 44.05% illiterate workers; 48.41% workers from joint family system and 37.08% representing nuclear family system; 44.44% rural workers and 46.11% urban

TABLE 4.97 EDUCATIONAL ASPIRATION: (7) TO SEEK HELP FROM THE EDUCATED MEMBERS OF THE COMMUNITY TO ENLIGHTEN THE IGNORANT PERSONS ABOUT THE IMPORTANCE OF CHILDREN'S EDUCATION

	RESPONDENTS CATEGORY	*YES*	*%*	*INDIFF.*	*%*	*NO*	*%*
1.	Workers of different industrial units belonging to same factory.	435	91.77	23	4.85	16	3.38
2.	Workers of different factories belonging to assembly unit.	50	45.28	1	5.66	2	49.06
3.	Workers of different factories belonging to die making unit.	53	44.83	3	10.34	2	44.83
4.	Workers of different factories belonging to furnace & dispatch unit.	41	51.16	1	2.33	1	46.51
5.	Workers of different factories belonging to key-making unit.	50	42.86	4	5.36	2	51.79
6.	Workers of different factories belonging to nickle polish unit	49	45.61	4	5.26	4	49.12
7.	Workers of different factories belonging to Office.	60	44.26	0	8.20	1	47.54
8.	Workers of different factories belonging to packing unit.	66	47.30	6	10.81	2	41.89
9.	Workers of different factories belonging to press unit.	66	44.44	4	9.72	2	45.83
10.	Salaried workers.	217	43.04	17	10.13	3	46.84

(Contd.)

11. Contractual workers	220	48.12	5	4.60	14	27.28
12. Male workers	420	44.88	23	7.63	16	47.49
13. Female workers	14	64.29	0	7.14	0	28.57
14. Literate workers	213	47.30	5	5.86	4	46.85
15. Illiterate workers	222	44.05	18	9.13	12	46.83
16. Joint family workers	327	48.41	13	6.34	7	45.24
17. Nuclear family workers	108	37.80	10	11.02	9	51.18
18. Rural workers	132	44.44	15	11.11	6	44.44
19. Urban workers	303	46.11	8	5.92	10	47.98
20. Hindu workers	127	47.95	11	8.90	8	43.15
21. Muslim workers	308	44.51	12	7.01	8	48.43
22. Workers in income group 0--3000	324	39.26	20	8.39	14	52.35
23. Workers in income group of 3000 and above	111	33.62	3	9.48	2	56.90
24. Workers belonging to Labour Class	350	90.21	23	5.93	15	3.87
25. Workers belonging to Management Class	82	98.80	0	0.00	1	1.20

workers; 47.95% Hindu workers and 44.51% Muslim workers; 39.26% workers receiving salary up to Rs. 3000/- and 33.62% workers receiving salary of more than 3000/- per month; and 90.21% workers hailing from Labour class and 98.80% workers hailing from management group have also expressed their agreement with the statement.

It can, thus, be concluded that the respondents representing different units of the factory as well as majority of the total subjects (91.77%) expressed their agreement "to seek help from the educated members of the community to enlighten the ignorant persons about the importance of children's education."

Table 4.98 reveals that majority of the workers (92.41%) representing different units of 55 factories agreed to establish some women social organisation in the community to enlighten and encourage women of the community to receive education so that they may not remain educationally backward. While 5.27% exhibited their indifference, only 2.32% expressed their disagreement with the statement.

Unit-wise analysis reveals that 96.23% workers hailing from assembly units; 89.66% from die-making units; 97.67% from furnace and dispatch units; 91.07% from key-making units; 89.47% from nickle polish units; 95.08% from Office; 89.19% from packing units; 93.06% from press units; 88.61% salaried workers and 96.65% contractual workers; 92.16% male workers; 92.16% male workers and 100.00% female workers; 94.59% literate workers and 90.48% illiterate workers; 94.24% workers from joint family system and 87.40% representing nuclear family system; 89.54% rural workers and 93.77% urban workers; 90.41% Hindu workers and 93.29% Muslim workers; 92.74% workers receiving salary up to Rs. 3000/ - and 91.38% workers receiving salary of more than 3000/- per month; 91.49% workers hailing from Labour class and 96.39% workers hailing from management group expressed their agreement with the statement.

TABLE 4.98 EDUCATIONAL ASPIRATION: (8) TO ESTABLISH SOME WOMEN SOCIAL ORGANIZATION IN THE COMMUNITY TO ENLIGHTEN AND ENCOURAGE WOMEN OF THE COMMUNITY TO RECEIVE EDUCATION SO THAT THEY THEN MAY NOT REMAIN EDUCATIONALLY BACKWARD

	RESPONDENTS CATEGORY	*YES*	*%*	*INDIFF.*	*%*	*NO*	*%*
1.	Workers of different industrial units belonging to same factory.	438	92.41	25	5.27	11	2.32
2.	Workers of different factories belonging to assembly unit	51	96.23	1	1.89	1	1.89
3.	Workers of different factories belonging to die making unit	52	89.66	4	6.90	2	3.45
4.	Workers of different factories belonging to furnace & dispatch unit.	42	97.67	1	2.33	0	0.00
5.	Workers of different factories belonging to key making unit.	51	91.07	4	7.14	1	1.79
6.	Workers of different factories belonging to nickle polish unit	51	89.47	5	8.77	1	1.75
7.	Workers of different factors belonging to Office.	58	95.08	0	0.00	3	4.92
8.	Workers of different factories belonging to packing unit.	66	89.19	6	8.11	2	2.70
9.	Workers of different factories belonging to press unit.	67	93.06	4	5.56	1	1.39
10.	Salaried workers	210	88.61	18	7.59	9	3.80

11. Contractual workers	231	96.65	6	2.51	2	0.84
12. Male workers	423	92.16	25	5.45	11	2.40
13. Female workers	14	100.00	0	0.00	0	0.00
14. Literate workers	210	94.59	6	2.70	6	2.70
15. Illiterate workers	228	90.48	19	7.54	5	1.98
16. Joint family workers	327	94.24	14	4.03	6	1.73
17. Nuclear family workers	111	87.40	11	8.66	5	3.94
18. Rural workers	137	89.54	15	9.80	1	0.65
19. Urban workers	301	93.77	10	3.12	10	3.12
20. Hindu workers	132	90.41	12	8.22	2	1.37
21. Muslim workers	306	93.29	13	3.96	9	2.74
22. Workers in income group 0–3000	332	92.74	20	5.59	6	1.68
23. Workers in income group of 3000 and above	106	91.38	5	4.31	5	4.31
24. Workers belonging to Labour Class	355	91.49	25	6.44	8	2.06
25. Workers belonging to Management Class	80	96.39	0	0.00	3	3.61

It can, thus, be concluded that the respondents representing different units of the factory as well as majority of the total subjects (92.41%) expressed their agreement "to establish some women social organisation in the community to enlighten and encourage women of the community to receive education so that they may not remain educationally backward".

Table 4.99 reveals that majority of workers (94.51%) representing different units of 55 factories agreed that educated and respectable members of the community should keep regular contacts with the leaders of the community and press them to work and seek government's help in getting adequate educational facilities for the sake of community. While 5.27% exhibited their indifference, 0.21% expressed their disagreement with the statement.

Unit-wise analysis reveals that 98.11% workers hailing from assembly units; 94.83% from die-making units; 97.67% from furnace and dispatch units; 92.86% from key-making units; 89.47% from nickle polish units; 100.00% from Office; 91.89% from packing units; and 93.06% from press units; 92.41% salaried workers and 97.07% contractual workers; 94.34% male workers; 94.34% male workers and 100.00% female workers; 97.75% literate workers and 91.67% illiterate workers; 95.97% workers from joint family system and 90.55% representing nuclear family system; 88.89% rural workers and 97.20% urban workers; 90.41% Hindu workers and 96.34% Muslim workers; 93.85% workers receiving salary up to Rs. 3000/ - and 96.55% workers receiving salary of more than 3000/- per month; 93.30% workers hailing from Labour class and 100.00% workers hailing from management group expressed their agreement with the statement.

It can, thus, be concluded that respondents representing different units of the factory as well as majority of the total subjects (94.51%) have expressed their agreement that "educated and respectable members of the community should keep regular contacts with the leaders of the community and press them to work and seek government's help in getting adequate educational facilities for the sake of the community".

TABLE 4.99 EDUCATIONAL ASPIRATION: (9) EDUCATED AND RESPECTABLE MEMBERS OF THE COMMUNITY SHOULD KEEP REGULAR CONTACTS WITH THE LEADERS OF THE COMMUNITY AND PRESS THEM TO WORK AND SEEK GOVERNMENT'S HELP IN GETTING ADEQUATE EDUCATIONAL FACILITIES FOR THE SAKE OF THE COMMUNITY

	RESPONDENTS CATEGORY	*YES*	*%*	*INDIFF.*	*%*	*NO*	*%*
1.	Workers of different industrial units belonging to same factory.	448	94.51	25	5.27	1	0.21
2.	Workers of different factories belonging to assembly unit.	52	98.11	1	1.89	0	0.00
3	Workers of different factories belonging to die making unit.	55	94.83	3	5.17	0	0.00
4.	Workers of different factories belonging to furnace & dispatch unit.	42	97.67	1	2.33	0	0.00
5.	Workers of different factories belonging to key making unit.	52	92.86	4	7.14	0	0.00
6.	Workers of different factories belonging to nickle polish unit.	51	89.47	5	8.77	1	1.75
7.	Workers of different factories belonging to Office.	61	100.00	0	0.00	0	0.00
8.	Workers of different factories belonging to packing unit.	68	91.89	6	8.11	0	0.00
9.	Workers of different factories belonging to press unit.	67	93.06	5	6.94	0	0.00
10.	Salaried workers	219	92.41	18	7.59	0	0.00

(Contd.)

11. Contractual workers	232	97.07	6	2.51	1	0.42
12. Male workers	433	93.34	25	5.45	1	0.22
13. Female workers	14	100.00	0	0.00	0	0.00
14. Literate workers	217	97.75	5	2.25	0	0.00
15. Illiterate workers	231	91.67	20	7.94	1	0.40
16. Joint family workers	333	95.97	13	3.75	1	0.29
17. Nuclear family workers	115	90.55	12	9.45	0	0.00
18. Rural workers	136	88.89	16	10.46	1	0.65
19. Urban workers	312	97.20	9	2.80	0	0.00
20. Hindu workers	132	90.41	13	8.90	1	0.68
21. Muslim workers	316	96.34	12	3.66	0	0.00
22. Workers in income group 0–3000	336	93.85	21	5.87	1	0.28
23. Workers in income group of 3000 and above	112	96.55	4	3.45	0	0.00
24. Workers belonging to Labour Class	362	93.30	25	6.44	1	0.26
25. Workers belonging to Management Class	83	100.00	0	0.00	0	0.00

Table 4.100 reveals that majority of workers (94.51%) representing different units of 55 factories agreed that the services of teachers who are not performing their educational duties in their institutions and are engaged in coaching centers should be terminated and the coaching centers be banned. While 5.06% have exhibited their indifference, only 0.42% have expressed their disagreement with the statement.

Unit-wise analysis reveals that 96.23% workers hailing from assembly units; 94.83% from die-making units; 97.67% from furnace and dispatch units; 92.86% from key-making units; 91.23% from nickle polish units; 100.00% from Office; 90.54% from packing units; and 94.44% from press units; 92.41% salaried workers and 97.07% contractual workers; 94.34% male workers and 100.00% female workers; 97.75% literate workers and 91.67% illiterate workers; 95.68% worker from joint family system and 91.34% representing nuclear family system; 90.20% rural workers and 96.57% urban workers; 91.78% Hindu workers and 95.73% Muslim workers; 93.85% workers receiving salary up to Rs. 3000/- and 96.55% workers receiving salary of more than 3000/- per month; 93.56% workers hailing from Labour class and 98.80% workers hailing from management group expressed their agreement with the statement.

It can, thus, be concluded that the respondents representing different units of the factory as well as majority of the total subjects (94.51%) expressed their agreement with the statement that, "services of the teachers who are not performing their educational duties in their institutions and are engaged in coaching centers should be terminated and such coaching centers be banned."

TABLE 4.100 EDUCATIONAL ASPIRATIONS: (10) SERVICES OF TEACHERS WHO ARE NOT PERFORMING THEIR EDUCATIONAL DUTIES IN THEIR INSTITUTIONS AND ARE ENGAGED IN COACHING CENTERS SHOULD BE TERMINATED AND SUCH COACHING CENTERS BE BANNED

	RESPONDENTS CATEGORY	*YES*	%	*INDIFF.*	%	*NO*	%
1.	Workers of different industrial units belonging to same factory.	448	94.51	24	5.06	2	0.42
2.	Workers of different factories belonging to assembly unit.	51	96.23	1	1.89	1	1.89
3.	Workers of different factories belonging to die making unit.	55	94.83	3	5.17	0	0.00
4.	Workers of different factories belonging to furnace & dispatch unit.	42	97.67	1	2.33	0	0.00
5.	Workers of different factories belonging to key making unit.	52	92.86	4	7.14	0	0.00
6.	Workers of different factories belonging to nickle polish unit.	52	91.23	5	8.77	0	0.00
7.	Workers of different factories belonging to Office.	61	100.00	C	0.00	0	0.00
8.	Workers of different factories belonging to packing unit.	67	90.54	5	8.11	1	1.35
9.	Workers of different factories belonging to press unit.	68	94.44	4	5.56	0	0.00
10.	Salaried workers.	219	92.41	17	7.17	1	0.42

(*Contd.*)

11.	Contractual workers	232	97.07	6	2.51	1	0.42
12.	Male workers	433	94.34	24	2.23	2	0.44
13.	Female workers	14	100.00	0	0.00	0	0.00
14.	Literate workers	217	97.75	5	2.25	0	0.00
15.	Illiterate workers	231	91.67	19	7.54	2	0.79
16.	Joint family workers	332	95.68	13	3.75	2	0.58
17.	Nuclear family workers	116	91.34	11	8.66	0	0.00
18.	Rural workers	138	90.20	15	9.80	0	0.00
19.	Urban workers	310	96.57	9	2.80	2	0.62
20.	Hindu workers	134	91.78	12	8.22	0	0.00
21.	Muslim workers	314	95.73	12	3.66	2	0.61
22.	Workers in income group 0–3000	336	93.85	20	5.59	2	0.56
23.	Workers in income group of 3000 and above	112	96.55	4	3.45	0	0.00
24.	Workers belonging to Labour Class	362	93.56	24	6.19	1	0.26
25.	Workers belonging to Management Class	82	98.80	0	0.00	1	1.20

Table 4.101 reveals that only a thin percentage of workers (18.78%) representing different units of 55 factories agreed that majority of the members of the community offer prayers regularly as prescribed. While 0.63% exhibited their indifference, only 80.59% have expressed their disagreement with the statement.

Unit-wise analysis reveals that 11.32% workers hailing from assembly units; 18.97% from die-making units; 4.65% from furnace and dispatch units; 10.71% from key-making units; 19.30% from press units; 21.61% salaried workers and 15.48% contractual workers; 17.86% male workers and 28.57% female workers; 12.61% literate workers and 24.30% illiterate workers; 15.32% workers from joint family system and 28.35% representing nuclear family system; 25.66% rural workers and 14.84% urban workers; 11.76% Hindu workers and 14.77% Muslim workers; 20.17% workers receiving salary up to Rs. 3000/- and 14.66% workers receiving salary of more than 3000/- per month have also exhibited their agreement with the statement. While a big majority of 79.07% workers hailing from Labour class exhibited their disagreement with the statement, only 20.41% expressed their agreement. Similarly, while 87.95% workers hailing from management class disagreed with the statement, only 12.05% have expressed their agreement with the statement.

It can, thus, be concluded that only a weak percentage (18.78%) of respondents representing different units of the factory as well as of the total subjects expressed their agreement with the statement While only 0.63% of the respondents exhibited their indifference an overwheling majority of 80.59% of the respondents exhibited their disagreement towards the statement. Similar trend was also noticeable among the respondents representing different units of the factory.

Table 4.102 reveals that a weak minority of the worker (13.08%) representing different units of 55 factories agreed that members of the community strictly follow and practice the laws as prescribed in holy scriptures. While 5.49% have exhibited their indifference, 81.43% expressed their disagreement with the statement.

TABLE 4.101 RELIGIOUS PERCEPTIONS: (1) MAJORITY OF MEMBERS OF THE COMMUNITY OFFER PRAYERS REGULARLY AS PRESCRIBED

	RESPONDENTS CATEGORY	*YES*	*%*	*INDIFF.*	*%*	*NO*	*%*
1.	Workers of different industrial units belonging to same factory.	89	18.78	2	0.62	382	80.59
2.	Workers of different factories belonging to assembly unit.	6	11.32	0	0.00	47	88.68
3.	Workers of different factories belonging to die making unit.	11	18.97	0	0.00	47	81.03
4.	Workers of different factories belonging to furnace & dispatch unit.	2	4.65	0	0.00	41	95.35
5.	Workers of different factories belonging to key making unit.	6	10.71	1	1.79	49	87.50
6.	Workers of different factories belonging to nickle polish unit.	11	19.30	1	1.75	45	78.95
7.	Workers of different factories belonging to Office.	12	19.67	0	0.00	49	80.33
8.	Workers of different factories belonging to packing unit.	23	31.08	0	0.00	51	68.92
9.	Workers of different factories belonging to press unit.	18	25.35	0	0.00	53	74.65
10.	Salaried workers	51	21.61	2	0.85	183	77.54

(Contd.)

11. Contractual workers	37	15.48	0	0.00	202	84.52
12. Male workers	85	17.86	4	0.84	387	81.30
13. Female workers	4	28.57	0	0.00	10	71.43
14. Literate workers	28	12.61	0	0.00	194	87.39
15. Illiterate workers	61	24.30	2	0.80	188	74.90
16. Joint family workers	53	15.32	2	0.58	291	84.10
17. Nuclear family workers	36	28.35	0	0.00	91	71.65
18. Rural workers	39	25.66	2	1.32	111	73.03
19. Urban workers	50	14.84	16	4.75	271	80.42
20. Hindu workers	14	11.76	0	0.00	105	88.24
21. Muslim workers	48	14.77	2	0.62	275	84.62
22. Workers in income group 0–3000	72	20.17	2	0.56	283	79.27
23. Workers in income group of 3000 and above	17	14.66	0	0.00	99	85.34
24. Workers belonging to Labour Class	79	20.41	2	0.52	306	79.07
25. Workers belonging to Management Class	10	12.05	0	0.00	73	87.95

TABLE 4.102 RELIGIOUS PERCEPTIONS: (2) MEMBERS OF THE COMMUNITY STRICTLY FOLLOW AND PRACTICE THE LAWS AS PRESCRIBED IN HOLY SCRIPTURES

	RESPONDENTS CATEGORY	YES	%	INDIFF.	%	NO	%
1.	Workers of different industrial units belonging to same factory.	62	13.08	26	5.49	386	81.43
2.	Workers of different factories belonging to assembly unit	4	7.55	1	1.89	48	90.57
3.	Workers of different factories belonging to die making unit	4	7.14	3	5.36	49	87.50
4.	Workers of different factories belonging to furnace & dispatch unit.	2	4.65	1	2.33	40	93.02
5.	Workers of different factories belonging to key making unit.	4	7.14	3	5.36	49	87.50
6.	Workers of different factories belonging to nickle polish unit	9	15.79	3	5.26	45	78.95
7.	Workers of different factories belonging to Office.	6	9.84	5	8.20	50	81.97
8.	Workers of different factories belonging to packing unit.	18	24.32	5	6.76	51	68.92
9.	Workers of different factories belonging to press unit.	13	18.06	5	6.94	54	75.00
10.	Salaried workers	34	14.35	20	8.44	183	77.22

(Contd.)

11. Contractual workers	28	47.46	5	8.47	26	44.07
12. Male workers	85	17.49	26	5.35	375	77.16
13. Female workers	4	28.57	0	0.00	10	71.43
14. Literate workers	15	6.76	11	4.95	196	88.29
15. Illiterate workers	47	18.65	15	5.95	190	75.40
16. Joint family workers	41	11.82	16	4.61	290	83.57
17. Nuclear family workers	21	16.54	10	7.87	96	75.59
18. Rural workers	35	22.80	10	6.54	108	70.59
19. Urban workers	27	7.40	60	16.44	278	76.16
20. Hindu workers	35	23.97	9	6.16	102	69.86
21. Muslim workers	27	8.23	17	5.18	284	86.59
22. Workers in income group 0–3000	55	15.36	18	5.03	285	79.61
23. Workers' income group of 3000 and above	7	6.03	8	6.90	101	87.07
24. Workers belonging to Labour Class	28	14.95	21	5.41	309	79.64
25. Workers belonging to Management Class	4	4.62	5	6.02	74	89.16

Unit-wise analysis reveals that 7.55% workers hailing from assembly units; 7.14% from die-making units; 4.65% from furnace and dispatch units; 7.14% from key-making units; 15.79% from nickle polish units; 9.84% from Office; 24.32% from packing unit and 18.06% from press units; 14.35% salaried workers and 47.46% contractual workers; 17.59% male workers and 28.57% female workers; 6.76% literate workers and 18.65% illiterate workers; 11.82% workers from joint family system and 16.54% representing nuclear family system; 22.88% rural workers and 7.40% urban workers; 23.97% Hindu workers and 8.23% Muslim workers; 15.36% workers receiving salary up to Rs. 3000/- and 6.03% workers receiving salary of more than 3000/- per month; 14.95% workers from Labour class; and only 4.62% workers from management class expressed their agreement with the statement. As against this, 79.64% workers hailing from Labour class 89.16% workers hailing from management group have also expressed their disagreement with the statement.

It can, thus, be concluded that only a thin minority (13.08%) of the respondents representing different units of the factory as well as of the total subjects expressed their agreement with the statement that "members of the community strictly followed and practiced the laws as prescribed in Holy Scriptures. While only 5.49% of the respondents exhibited their indifferent, whooping majority of 81.43% of the respondents exhibited their disagreement towards the statement. Similar trend was also noticeable among the respondents representing different units of the factories.

Table 4.103 reveals that a minority of the workers (27.00%) representing different units of 55 factories agreed that members of the community extend equal respect to other religions. While 5.70% exhibited their indifference, only 67.30% have expressed their disagreement with the statement.

Unit-wise analysis reveals that 22.64% workers hailing from assembly units; 25.86% form die-making units; 13.95% from furnace and dispatch units; 25.00% from key-making units; 28.07% from nickle polish units; 22.95% from Office; 36.49% from packing units; 33.33% from press units; 27.43% salaried workers and 76.78%

TABLE 4.103 RELIGIOUS PERCEPTIONS: (3) MEMBERS OF THE COMMUNITY EXTEND EQUAL RESPECT TO OTHER RELIGIONS

	RESPONDENTS CATEGORY	*YES*	*%*	*INDIFF.*	*%*	*NO*	*%*
1.	Workers of different industrial units belonging to same factory.	128	27.00	27	5.70	319	67.30
2.	Workers of different factories belonging to assembly unit.	12	22.64	1	1.89	40	75.47
3.	Workers of different factories belonging to die making unit.	15	25.86	3	5.17	40	68.97
4.	Workers of different factories belonging to furnace & dispatch unit.	6	13.95	3	6.98	34	79.07
5.	Workers of different factories belonging to key making unit.	14	25.00	4	7.14	38	67.86
6.	Workers of different factories belonging to nickle polish unit.	16	28.07	3	5.26	38	66.67
7.	Workers of different factories belonging to Office.	14	22.95	3	4.92	44	72.13
8.	Workers of different factories belonging to packing unit.	27	36.49	5	6.76	42	56.76
9.	Workers of different factories belonging to press unit.	24	33.33	5	6.94	43	59.72
10.	Salaried workers	65	27.43	14	5.91	158	66.67

(*Contd.*)

11.	Contractual workers	64	26.78	13	5.44	162	67.78
12.	Male workers	124	27.02	27	5.88	308	67.10
13.	Female workers	4	28.57	0	0.00	10	71.43
14.	Literate workers	40	18.02	12	5.41	170	76.58
15.	Illiterate workers	88	34.92	15	5.95	149	59.13
16.	Joint family workers	48	15.14	17	5.36	252	79.50
17.	Nuclear family workers	50	39.37	10	7.87	67	52.76
18.	Rural workers	55	35.95	9	5.88	89	58.17
19.	Urban workers	73	22.74	18	5.61	230	71.65
20.	Hindu workers	51	34.93	7	4.79	88	60.27
21.	Muslim workers	77	23.48	20	6.10	231	70.43
22.	Workers in income group 0–3000	103	28.77	25	6.98	230	64.25
23.	Workers in income group of 3000 and above	25	21.55	2	1.72	89	76.72
24.	Workers belonging to Labour Class	110	28.35	24	6.19	254	65.46
25.	Workers belonging to Management Class	18	21.69	3	3.61	62	74.70

contractual workers; 27.02% male worker and 28.57% female workers; 18.02% literate workers and 34.92% illiterate workers; 15.14% workers have joint family system and 39.37% representing nuclear family system; 35.95% rural workers and 22.74% urban workers; 34.93% Hindu workers and 23.48% Muslim workers; 28.77% workers receiving salary up to Rs. 3000/- and 21.55% workers receiving salary of more than 3000/- per month; 28.35% workers from Labours class and 21% 29% from management class expressed this agreement with the statement. As against this, a strong majority of 65.46% workers hailing from Labour class and 74.70% workers hailing from management group expressed their disagreement with the statement.

It can, thus, be concluded that a weak majority of respondents representing different units of the factory as well as the total subjects (27.00%) expressed their agreement with the statement that "members of the community extend equal respect to other religions". While 5.70% of the respondents exhibited their indifference, 67.30% exhibited their disagreement towards the statement. Similar trend was also noticeable among the respondents who exhibited their disagreement towards the statement.

Table 4.104 reveals that majority of workers (93.25%) representing different units of 55 factories agreed that certain members of the community deviate from the prescribed religious codes of conduct on account of their vested interests. While 4.01% have exhibited their indifference, only 2.74% expressed their disagreement with the statement.

Unit-wise analysis reveals that 96.23% workers from assembly units; 89.66% from die-making units; 96.23% from furnace and dispatch units; 82.54% from key-making units; 91.23% form Nickle polish units; 95.08% from Office; 90.54% from packing units; 95.83% from press units; 90.30% salaried workers and 96.65% contractual workers; 93.25% male workers and 92.86% female workers; 95.05% literate workers and 91.67% illiterate workers; 93.66% workers from joint family system and 92.13% representing nuclear family system;

TABLE 4.104 RELIGIOUS PERCEPTION: (4) CERTAIN MEMBERS OF THE COMMUNITY DEVIATE FROM THE PRESCRIBED RELIGIOUS CODES OF CONDUCT ON ACCOUNT OF THEIR VESTED INTERESTS

	RESPONDENTS CATEGORY	*YES*	*%*	*INDIFF.*	*%*	*NO*	*%*
1.	Workers of different industrial units belonging to same factory.	442	93.25	19	4.01	13	2.74
2.	Workers of different factories belonging to assembly unit.	51	96.23	2	3.77	0	0.00
3.	Workers of different factories belonging to die making unit.	52	89.66	4	6.90	2	3.45
4.	Workers of different factories belonging to furnace & dispatch unit.	51	96.23	0	0.00	2	3.77
5.	Workers of different factories belonging to key making unit.	52	82.54	3	4.76	8	12.70
6.	Workers of different factories belonging to nickle polish unit.	52	91.23	3	5.26	2	3.51
7.	Workers of different factories belonging to Office.	58	95.08	1	1.64	2	3.28
8.	Workers of different factories belonging to packing unit.	56	90.54	4	5.41	3	4.05
9.	Workers of different factories belonging to press unit.	69	95.83	2	2.78	1	1.39
10.	Salaried workers.	214	90.30	12	5.06	11	4.64

(*Contd.*)

11. Contractual workers	231	96.65	6	2.51	2	0.84
12. Male workers	428	93.25	18	3.92	13	2.83
13. Female workers	13	92.86	1	7.14	0	0.00
14. Literate workers	211	95.05	5	2.25	6	2.70
15. Illiterate workers	231	91.67	14	5.56	7	2.78
16. Joint family workers	325	93.66	11	3.17	11	3.17
17. Nuclear family workers	117	92.13	8	6.30	2	1.57
18. Rural workers	138	90.20	10	6.54	5	3.27
19. Urban workers	304	94.70	9	2.80	8	2.49
20. Hindu workers	132	90.41	10	6.85	4	2.73
21. Muslim workers	310	94.51	9	2.74	9	2.74
22. Workers in income group 0–3000	322	92.53	15	4.31	11	3.16
23. Workers in income group 3000 and above	110	94.83	4	3.45	2	1.72
24. Workers belonging to Labour Class	258	92.27	19	4.90	11	2.84
25. Workers belonging to Management Class	81	97.59	0	0.00	2	2.41

90.20% rural workers and 94.70% urban workers; 90.41% Hindu workers and 94.51% Muslim workers; 92.53% workers receiving salary up to Rs. 3000/- and 94.83% workers receiving salary of more than 3000/- per month; 92.27% workers hailing from Labour class and 97.59% workers hailing from management group expressed their agreement with the statement.

It can, thus, be concluded that the respondents representing different units of the factory as well as majority of the total subjects (93.2%) expressed their agreement with the statement that "certain members of the community deviate from the prescribed religious codes of conduct on account of their vested interests".

Table 4.105 reveals that majority of workers (94.94%) representing different units of 55 factories agreed that certain sections of the community, on account of their ignorance about teachings of religion, maintain social distance with members hailing from other religions. While 4.01% exhibited their indifference, only 1.05% have expressed their disagreement with the statement.

Unit-wise analysis reveals that 98.11% workers from assembly units; 96.55% form die-making units; 95.3% from furnace and dispatch units; 94.64% from key-making units; 94.74% from nickle polish units; 100.00% from Office; 87.84% from packing units; 94.44% from press units; 94.33% salaried workers and 95.82% contractual workers; 94.77% male workers and 100.00% female workers; 96.85% literate workers and 93.25% illiterate workers; 95.68% workers from joint family system and 92.91% representing nuclear family system; 89.54% rural workers and 97.51% urban workers; 91.10% Hindu workers and 96.65% Muslim workers; 94.13% workers receiving salary up to Rs. 3000/- and 97.41% workers receiving salary of more than 3000/- per month; and 100.00% workers hailing from management group have also expressed their agreement with the statement.

It can, thus, be concluded that respondents representing different units of the factory as well as majority of the total subjects (94.94%) expressed their agreement with the statement that "certain section

TABLE 4.105 RELIGIOUS PERCEPTIONS: CERTAIN (5) SECTIONS OF THE COMMUNITY, ON ACCOUNT OF THEIR IGNORANCE ABOUT TEACHINGS OF RELIGION, MAINTAIN SOCIAL DISTANCE WITH MEMBERS HAILING FROM OTHER RELIGIONS

	RESPONDENTS CATEGORY	*YES*	*%*	*INDIFF.*	*%*	*NO*	*%*
1.	Workers of different industrial units belonging to same factory.	450	94.94	19	4.01	5	1.05
2.	Workers of different factories belonging to assembly unit.	52	98.11	1	1.89	0	0.00
3.	Workers of different factories belonging to die making unit.	56	96.55	2	3.45	0	0.00
4.	Workers of different factories belonging to furnace & dispatch unit.	41	95.35	1	2.33	1	2.33
5.	Workers of different factories belonging to key making unit.	53	94.64	1	1.79	2	3.57
6.	Workers of different factories belonging to nickle polish unit	54	94.74	3	5.26	0	0.00
7.	Workers of different factories belonging to Office.	61	100.00	0	0.00	0	0.00
8.	Workers of different factories belonging to packing unit.	65	87.84	8	10.81	1	1.35
9.	Workers of different factories belonging to press unit.	68	94.44	3	4.17	1	1.39
10.	Salaried workers.	233	94.33	11	4.45	3	1.21

(*Contd.*)

11. Contractual workers	229	95.82	8	3.35	2	0.84
12. Male workers	435	94.77	19	4.14	5	1.09
13. Female workers	14	100.00	0	0.00	0	0.00
14. Literate workers	215	96.85	4	1.80	3	1.35
15. Illiterate workers	235	93.25	15	5.95	2	0.79
16. Joint family workers	332	95.68	12	3.46	3	0.86
17. Nuclear family workers	118	92.91	7	5.51	2	1.57
18. Rural workers	137	89.54	13	8.50	3	1.96
19. Urban workers	313	97.51	6	1.87	2	0.62
20. Hindu workers	133	91.10	11	7.53	2	1.37
21. Muslim workers	317	96.65	8	2.44	3	0.91
22. Workers in income group 0–3000	337	94.13	16	4.47	5	1.40
23. Workers in income group of 3000 and above	113	97.41	3	2.59	0	0.00
24. Workers belonging to Labour Class	364	93.81	19	4.90	5	1.29
25. Workers belonging to Management Class	83	100.00	0	0.00	0	0.00

of the community, on account of their ignorance about teachings of religion, maintain social distance with members hailing from other religions".

Table 4.106 reveals that majority of workers (85.44%) representing different units of 55 factories agreed that preachers of religion of your community have not adequately succeeded in transmitting proper understanding and knowledge about religion to the masses. While 5.70% exhibited their indifference, only 8.86% expressed their disagreement with the statement.

Unit-wise analysis reveals that 90.57% workers from assembly units; 82.76% from die-making units; 90.70% from furnace and dispatch units; 87.50% from key-making units; 85.96% from nickle polish units; 88.52% from Office; 85.14% from packing units; 76.93% from press units; 83.54% salaried workers and 87.45% contractual workers; 85.19% male workers and 92.86% female workers; 88.29% literate workers and 82.94% illiterate workers; 88.47% workers from joint family system and 77.17% representing nuclear family system; 80.39% rural workers and 87.85% urban workers 82.88% Hindu workers and 89.59% Muslim workers; 85.20% workers receiving salary up to Rs. 3000/- and 86.21% workers receiving salary of more than 3000/- per month; 85.05% workers hailing from Labour class and 88.75% workers hailing from management group their agreement with the statement.

It can, thus, be concluded that respondents representing different units of the factory as well as majority of the total subjects (85.44%) expressed their agreement with the statement that "preachers of religion of your community have not adequately succeeded in transmitting proper understanding and knowledge about religion to the masses".

TABLE 4.106 RELIGIOUS PERCEPTIONS: (6) PREACHERS OF RELIGION OF YOUR COMMUNITY HAVE NOT ADEQUATELY SUCCEEDED IN TRANSMITTING PROPER UNDERSTANDING AND KNOWLEDGE ABOUT RELIGION TO THE MASSES

	RESPONDENTS CATEGORY	YES	%	INDIFF.	%	NO	%
1.	Workers of different industrial units belonging to same factory.	405	85.44	27	5.70	42	8.86
2.	Workers of different factories belonging to assembly unit.	48	90.57	1	1.89	4	7.55
3.	Workers of different factories belonging to die making units	48	82.76	3	5.17	7	12.07
4.	Workers of different factories belonging to furnace & dispatch unit.	39	90.70	1	2.33	3	6.98
5.	Workers of different factories belonging to key making unit.	49	87.50	1	1.79	6	10.71
6.	Workers of different factories belonging to nickle polish unit.	49	85.96	4	7.02	4	7.02
7.	Workers of different factories belonging to Office	54	88.52	2	3.28	5	8.20
8.	Workers of different factories belonging to packing unit.	63	85.14	6	8.11	5	6.76
9.	Workers of different factories belonging to press unit.	55	76.39	9	12.50	8	11.11
10.	Salaried workers.	198	83.54	15	6.33	24	10.13

(Contd.)

11. Contractual workers	209	87.45	12	5.02	18	7.53
12. Male workers	391	85.19	26	5.66	42	9.15
13. Female workers	13	92.86	1	7.14	0	0.00
14. Literate workers	196	88.29	8	3.60	18	8.11
15. Illiterate workers	209	82.94	19	7.54	24	9.52
16. Joint family workers	307	88.47	17	4.90	23	6.63
17. Nuclear family workers	98	77.17	10	7.87	19	14.96
18. Rural workers	123	80.39	15	9.80	15	9.80
19. Urban workers	282	87.85	12	3.74	27	8.41
20. Hindu workers	121	82.88	15	10.27	10	6.85
21. Muslim workers	284	86.59	12	3.66	32	9.76
22. Workers in income group 0–3000	305	85.20	24	6.70	29	8.10
23. Workers in income group of 3000 and above	100	86.21	3	2.59	13	11.21
24. Workers belonging to Labour Class	330	85.05	25	6.44	33	8.51
25. Workers belonging to Management Class	72	86.75	2	2.41	9	10.84

Tabel 4.107 reveals that majority of workers (91.77%) representing different units of 55 factories agreed that religious heads of the community have imposed certain such restrictions which are not prescribed in the holy scriptures. While 4.64% have exhibited their indifference, only 3.59% have expressed their disagreement with the statement.

Unit-wise analysis reveals that 94.34% workers hailing from assembly units; 94.83% from die-making units; 100.00% from furnace and dispatch units; 98.21% from key-making units; 89.47% from nickle polish units; 90.00% from Office; 87.84% from packing units; and 84.72% from press units; 90.30% salaried workers and 93.31% contractual workers; 91.94% male workers and 85.71% female workers; 94.14% literate workers and 89.68% illiterate workers; 93.95% workers from joint family system and 85.83% representing nuclear family system; 89.54% rural workers and 92.83% urban workers; 89.99% Hindu workers and 93.33% Muslim workers; 91.62% workers receiving salary up to Rs. 3000/- and 92.24% workers receiving salary of more than 3000/- per month; 91.49% workers hailing from Labour class and 95.06% workers hailing from management group expressed their agreement with the statement.

It can, thus, be concluded that respondents representing different units of the factory as well as majority of the total subjects (91.77%) expressed their agreement with the statement that "religious heads of the community have imposed certain such restrictions, which are not prescribed in the Holy Scriptures."

Table 4.108 reveals that majority of workers (94.51%) representing different units of 55 factories agreed that religious heads of the community, on account of their vested material gains and popularity, offer their services to political parties during elections, which is against their religious ethics. While 5.27% exhibited their indifference, only 0.21% expressed their disagreement with the statement.

Unit-wise analysis reveals that 94.34% workers hailing from assembly units; 94.83% from die-making units; 100.00% from furnace

TABLE 4.107 RELIGIOUS PERCEPTIONS: (7) RELIGIOUS HEADS OF THE COMMUNITY HAVE IMPOSED CERTAIN SUCH RESTRICTIONS WHICH ARE NOT PRESCRIBED IN THE HOLY SCRIPTURES

	RESPONDENTS CATEGORY	*YES*	*%*	*INDIFF.*	*%*	*NO*	*%*
1.	Workers of different industrial units belonging to same factory.	435	91.77	22	4.64	17	3.59
2.	Workers of different factories belonging to assembly unit	50	94.34	2	3.77	1	1.89
3.	Workers of different factories belonging to die making unit.	55	94.83	1	1.72	2	3.45
4.	Workers of different factories belonging to furnace & dispatch unit.	43	100.00	0	0.00	0	0.00
5.	Workers of different factories belonging to key making unit.	55	98.21	0	0.00	1	1.79
6.	Workers of different factories belonging to nickle polish unit.	51	89.47	3	5.26	3	5.26
7.	Workers of different factors belonging to Office	54	90.00	2	3.33	4	5.26
8.	Workers of different factories belonging to packing unit.	65	87.84	6	8.11	3	6.67
9.	Workers of different factories belonging to press unit.	61	84.72	8	11.11	3	4.05
10.	Salaried workers	214	90.30	12	5.06	11	4.64

(Contd.)

11. Contractual workers	223	93.31	10	4.18	6	2.51
12. Male workers	422	91.94	20	4.36	17	3.70
13. Female workers	12	85.71	2	14.29	0	0.00
14. Literate workers	209	94.14	5	2.25	8	3.60
15. Illiterate workers	226	86.68	17	6.75	9	3.57
16. Joint family workers	326	93.95	11	3.17	10	2.88
17. Nuclear family workers	109	85.83	11	8.66	7	5.51
18. Rural workers	137	89.54	13	8.50	3	1.96
19. Urban workers	298	92.83	9	2.80	14	4.36
20. Hindu workers	127	86.99	16	10.96	3	2.05
21. Muslim workers	308	93.33	8	2.42	14	4.25
22. Workers in income group 0–3000	328	91.62	19	5.31	11	3.07
23. Workers in income group of 3000 and above	107	92.24	3	2.59	6	5.17
24. Workers belonging to Labour Class	355	91.49	20	5.15	13	3.35
25. Workers belonging to Management Class	77	95.06	0	0.00	4	4.94

TABLE 4.108 RELIGIOUS PERCEPTIONS: (8) RELIGIOUS HEADS OF THE COMMUNITY ON ACCOUNT OF THEIR VESTED MATERIAL GAINS & POPULARITY OFFER THEIR SERVICES TO THE POLITICAL PARTIES DURING ELECTIONS WHICH IS AGAINST THEIR RELIGIOUS ETHICS

	RESPONDENTS CATEGORY	*YES*	*%*	*INDIFF.*	*%*	*NO*	*%*
1.	Workers of different industrial units belonging to same factory.	448	94.51	25	5.27	1	0.21
2.	Workers of different factories belonging to assembly unit.	51	94.34	2	3.77	0	1.89
3.	Workers of different factories belonging to die making unit.	54	94.83	4	1.72	0	3.45
4.	Workers of different factories belonging to furnace & dispatch unit.	52	100.00	1	0.00	0	0.00
5.	Workers of different factories belonging to key making unit.	53	98.21	2	0.00	1	1.79
6.	Workers of different factories belonging to nickle polish unit.	50	89.47	7	5.26	0	5.26
7.	Workers of different factors belonging to Office.	61	90.00	0	3.33	0	6.67
8.	Workers of different factories belonging to packing unit.	68	87.84	6	8.11	0	4.05
9.	Workers of different factories belonging to press unit.	69	84.72	3	11.11	0	4.17
10.	Salaried workers.	220	90.30	17	5.06	0	4.64

(Contd.)

11. Contractual workers	231	93.31	7	4.18	1	2.51
12. Male workers	433	91.94	1	4.36	25	3.70
13. Female workers	14	85.71	0	14.29	0	0.00
14. Literate workers	216	94.14	6	2.25	0	3.60
15. Illiterate workers	232	89.68	19	6.75	1	3.57
16. Joint family workers	332	93.95	14	3.17	1	2.88
17. Nuclear family workers	116	85.83	11	8.66	0	5.51
18. Rural workers	138	89.54	14	8.50	1	1.96
19. Urban workers	310	92.83	11	2.80	0	4.36
20. Hindu workers	134	86.99	12	10.96	0	2.05
21. Muslim workers	314	93.33	13	2.42	1	4.24
22. Workers in income group 0–3000	336	91.62	21	5.31	1	3.07
23. Workers income group of 3000 and above	112	92.24	4	2.59	0	5.17
24. Workers belonging to Labour Class	362	93.30	25	6.44	1	0.26
25. Workers belonging to Management Class	83	100.00	0	0.00	0	0.00

and dispatch units; 98.21% from key-making units; 89.47% from nickle polish units; 90.00% from Office; 87.84% from packing units; 84.72% from press units; 90.30% salaried workers and 93.31% contractual workers; 91.94% male workers and 85.71% female workers; 94.14% literate workers and 89.68% illiterate workers; 93.95% workers from joint family system and 85.83% representing nuclear family system; 89.54% rural workers and 92.83% urban workers; 86.99% Hindu workers and 93.33% Muslim workers; 91.62% workers receiving salary up to Rs. 3000/- and 92.24% workers receiving salary of more than 3000/- per month; 93.30% workers hailing from Labour class and 100.00% workers hailing from management group expressed their agreement with the statement.

It can, thus, be concluded that respondents representing different units of the factory as well as majority of the total subjects (94.51%) expressed their agreement with the statement that "religious heads of the community, on account of their vested material gains and popularity, offer their services to the political parties during elections, which is against their religious ethics."

Table 4.109 reveals that the majority of workers (94.51%) representing different units of 55 factories agreed that members in the society are distinctly discriminated on the basis of religion and caste in all matters of life. While 5.49% exhibited their indifference only 0.00% expressed their disagreement with the statement.

Unit-wise analysis reveals that 96.23% workers hailing from assembly units; 93.10% from die-making units; 97.67% from furnace and dispatch units; 92.86% from key-making units; 89.47% from nickle polish units; 98.36% from Office; 93.24% from packing units; 95.83% from press units; 91.98% salaried workers and 97.49% contractual workers; 94.34% male workers and 100.00% female workers; 97.30% literate workers and 92.06% illiterate workers; 95.68% workers from joint family system and 91.384% representing nuclear family system; 88.89% rural workers and 97.20% urban workers; 91.10% Hindu workers and 96.04% Muslim workers; 93.85%

TABLE 4.109 RELIGIOUS PERCEPTIONS: (9) MEMBERS IN THE SOCIETY ARE DISTINCTLY DISCRIMINATED ON THE BASIS OF RELIGION AND CASTE IN ALL MATTERS OF LIFE

	RESPONDENTS CATEGORY	*YES*	*%*	*INDIFF.*	*%*	*NO*	*%*
1.	Workers of different industrial units belonging to same factory.	448	94.51	26	5.49	0	0.00
2.	Workers of different factories belonging to assembly unit.	51	96.23	2	3.77	0	0.00
3.	Workers of different factories belonging to die making unit.	54	93.10	4	6.90	0	0.00
4.	Workers of different factories belonging to furnace & dispatch unit.	42	97.67	1	2.33	0	0.00
5.	Workers of different factories belonging to key making unit.	52	92.86	4	7.10	0	0.00
6.	Workers of different factories belonging to nickle polish unit.	51	89.47	6	10.53	0	0.00
7.	Workers of different factories belonging to Office.	60	98.36	1	1.64	0	0.00
8.	Workers of different factories belonging to packing unit.	69	93.24	5	6.76	0	0.00
9.	Workers of different factories belonging to press unit.	69	95.83	3	4.17	0	0.00
10.	Salaried workers.	218	91.98	19	8.02	0	0.00

(Contd.)

11. Contractual workers	233	97.49	6	2.51	0	0.00
12. Male workers	433	94.34	26	5.66	0	0.00
13. Female workers	14	100.00	0	0.00	0	0.00
14. Literate workers	216	97.30	6	2.70	0	0.00
15. Illiterate workers	232	92.06	20	7.94	0	0.00
16. Joint family workers	332	95.68	15	4.32	0	0.00
17. Nuclear family workers	116	91.34	11	8.66	0	0.00
18. Rural workers	136	88.89	17	11.11	0	0.00
19. Urban workers	312	97.20	9	2.80	0	0.00
20. Hindu workers	133	91.10	13	8.90	0	0.00
21. Muslim workers	315	96.04	13	3.96	0	0.00
22. Workers in income group 0–3000	336	93.85	22	6.15	0	0.00
23. Workers in income group of 3000 and above	112	96.55	4	3.45	0	0.00
24. Workers belonging to Labour Class	365	93.56	25	6.44	0	0.00
25. Workers belonging to Management Class	82	96.80	1	1.20	0	0.00

workers receiving salary up to Rs. 3000/-and 96.55% workers receiving salary of more than 3000/- per month; 93.56% workers hailing from Labour class and 98.80% workers hailing from management group expressed their agreement with the statement.

It can, thus, be concluded that the respondents representing different units of the factory as well as majority of the total subjects (94.51%) expressed their agreement with the statement that "members in the society are distinctly discriminated on the basis of religion and caste in all matters of life".

Table 4.110 reveals that majority of workers (94.51%) representing different units of 55 factories agreed that funds collected in the name of religion by the religious leaders of the community were not utilized religiously by them. While 5.27% exhibited their indifference, only 0.21% expressed their disagreement with the statement.

Unit-wise analysis reveals that 96.23% workers hailing from assembly units; 90.00% from die-making units; 97.67% from furnace and dispatch units; 92.86% from key-making units; 89.47% from nickle polish units; 100.00% from Offices; 91.89% from packing units; and 95.83% from press units; 91.98% salaried workers and 97.49% contractual workers; 94.55% male workers and 92.86% female workers; 97.75% literate workers and 91.67% illiterate workers; 95.68% workers from joint family system and 91.34% representing nuclear family system; 91.89% rural workers and 97.20% urban workers; 91.10% Hindu workers and 96.04% Muslim workers; 93.85% workers receiving salary up to Rs. 3000/- and 96.55% workers receiving salary of more than 3000/- per month; 93.30% workers hailing from Labour class and 100.00% workers hailing from management group expressed their agreement with the statement.

It can, thus, be concluded that the respondents representing different units of the factory as well as majority of the total subjects (94.51%) expressed their agreement with the statement that, "funds collected in the name of religion by the religious leaders of the community are not utilized religiously by them".

TABLE 4.110 RELIGIOUS PERCEPTIONS: (10) FUNDS COLLECTED IN THE NAME OF RELIGION BY THE RELIGIOUS LEADERS OF THE COMMUNITY ARE NOT UTILIZED RELIGIOUSLY BY THEM

	RESPONDENTS CATEGORY	*YES*	%	*INDIFF.*	%	*NO*	%
1.	Workers of different industrial units belonging to same factory.	448	94.51	25	5.27	1	0.21
2.	Workers of different factories belonging to assembly unit.	51	96.23	2	3.77	0	0.00
3.	Workers of different factories belonging to die making unit.	54	90.00	4	6.67	2	3.33
4.	Workers of different factories belonging to furnace & dispatch unit.	42	97.67	1	2.33	0	0.00
5.	Workers of different factories belonging to key making unit.	52	92.86	4	7.14	0	0.00
6.	Workers of different factories belonging to nickle polish unit.	51	89.47	6	10.53	0	0.00
7.	Workers of different factories belonging to Office.	61	100.00	0	0.00	0	0.00
8.	Workers of different factories belonging to packing unit.	68	91.89	5	6.67	1	1.35
9.	Workers of different factories belonging to press unit.	69	95.83	3	4.17	0	0.00
10.	Salaried workers.	218	91.98	18	7.59	1	0.42

(Contd.)

11. Contractual workers	233	97.49	6	2.51	0	0.00
12. Male workers	434	94.55	25	5.45	0	0.00
13. Female workers	13	92.86	0	0.00	1	7.14
14. Literate workers	217	97.75	5	2.25	0	0.00
15. Illiterate workers	231	91.67	20	7.94	1	0.40
16. Joint family workers	332	95.67	14	4.03	1	0.29
17. Nuclear family workers	116	91.34	11	8.66	0	0.00
18. Rural workers	136	91.89	11	7.43	1	0.68
19. Urban workers	312	97.20	9	2.80	0	0.00
20. Hindu workers	133	91.10	12	8.22	1	0.68
21. Muslim workers	315	96.04	13	3.96	0	0.00
22. Workers in income group 0–3000	336	93.85	21	5.87	1	0.28
23. Workers in income group of 3000 and above	112	96.55	4	3.45	0	0.00
24. Workers belonging to Labour Class	362	93.30	25	6.44	1	0.26
25. Workers belonging to Management Class	83	100.00	0	0.00	0	0.00

Table 4.111 reveal that majority of workers 95.57% representing different units of 55 factories agreed to educate importance of offering prayers to such members of the community who do not offer prayers regularly as prescribed. While 3.59% have exhibited their indifference, only 0.84% have expressed their disagreement with the statement.

Unit-wise analysis reveal that 100.00% workers hailing from assembly units; 94.83% from die-making units; 100.00% from furnace and dispatch units; 94.64% from key-making units; 91.23% from nickle polish units; 96.72% from Office; 94.39% from packing units; 94.44 from press units; 94.09% salaried workers and 97.07% contractual workers; 95.42% male workers and 100.00% female workers; have also expressed their 94.44% from press units; 94.09% salaried workers and 97.07% contractual workers; 95.42% male workers and 100.00% female workers; 97.75% literate workers and 93.65% illiterate workers; 95.10% ;workers from joint family system and 96.85% representing nuclear family system; 92.81% rural workers and 96.88% urban workers; 93.84% Hindu workers and 96.34% Muslim workers; 94.69% workers receiving salary up to Rs. 3000/ and 98.28% workers receiving salary of more than 3000/- per month; 94.85% workers hailing from Labour class; 98.80% workers hailing from management group expressed their agreement with the statement.

It can, thus, be concluded that respondents representing different units of the factory as well as majority of the total subjects (95.57%) "to educate the importance of offering prayers to such members of community who do not offer prayers regularly as prescribed".

Table 4.112 reveals that majority of workers (94.51%) representing different units of 55 factories agreed that to follow and educate other members of the community to follow and practice laws as laid down in the holy scriptures. While 4.64% exhibited their indifference, only 0.84% expressed their disagreement with the statement.

Unit-wise analysis reveal that 96.23% workers from assembly units; 98.28% from die-making units; 97.67% from furnace and dispatch units; 92.86% from key-making units; 94.74% from nickle

TABLE 4.111 RELIGIOUS ASPIRATIONS: (1) TO EDUCATE IMPORTANCE OF OFFERING PRAYERS TO SUCH MEMBERS OF THE COMMUNITY WHO DO NOT OFFER PRAYERS REGULARLY AS PRESCRIBED

	RESPONDENTS CATEGORY	*YES*	*%*	*INDIFF.*	*%*	*NO*	*%*
1.	Workers of different industrial units belonging to same factory.	453	95.57	17	3.59	4	0.84
2.	Workers of different factories belonging to assembly unit.	53	100.00	0	0.00	0	0.00
3.	Workers of different factories belonging to die making unit.	55	94.83	3	5.17	0	0.00
4.	Workers of different factories belonging to furnace & dispatch unit.	43	100.00	0	0.00	0	0.00
5.	Workers of different factories belonging to key making unit.	53	94.64	3	5.36	0	0.00
6.	Workers of different factories belonging to nickle polish unit.	52	91.23	4	7.02	1	1.75
7.	Workers of different factories belonging to Office.	59	96.72	2	3.28	0	0.00
8.	Workers of different factories belonging to packing unit.	70	94.59	1	1.35	3	4.05
9.	Workers of different factories belonging to press unit.	68	94.44	4	5.56	0	0.00
10.	Salaried workers.	223	94.09	11	4.64	3	1.27

(*Contd.*)

11. Contractual workers	232	97.07	6	2.51	1	0.42
12. Male workers	438	95.42	17	3.70	4	0.87
13. Female workers	14	100.00	0	0.00	0	0.00
14. Literate workers	217	97.75	5	4.25	0	0.00
15. Illiterate workers	236	93.65	12	4.76	4	1.59
16. Joint family workers	330	95.10	14	4.03	3	0.86
17. Nuclear family workers	123	96.85	3	2.36	1	0.79
18. Rural workers	142	92.81	9	5.88	2	1.31
19. Urban workers	311	96.88	8	2.49	2	0.62
20. Hindu workers	137	93.84	8	5.48	1	0.68
21. Muslim workers	316	96.34	9	2.74	3	0.91
22 Workers in income group 0–3000	339	94.69	15	4.19	4	1.12
23. Workers in income group of 3000 and above	114	98.28	2	1.72	0	0.00
24. Workers belonging to Labour Class	368	94.85	16	4.12	4	1.03
25. Workers belonging to Management Class	82	98.80	1	1.20	0	0.00

TABLE 4.112 RELIGIOUS ASPIRATIONS: (2) TO FOLLOW AND EDUCATE OTHER MEMBERS OF COMMUNITY TO FOLLOW AND PRACTICE AND LAWS AS LAID DOWN IN THE HOLY SCRIPTURES

	RESPONDENTS CATEGORY	*YES*	*%*	*INDIFF.*	*%*	*NO*	*%*
1.	Workers of different industrial units belonging to same factory.	448	94.51	22	4.64	4	0.84
2.	Workers of different factories belonging to assembly unit.	51	96.23	2	3.77	0	0.00
3.	Workers of different factories belonging to die making unit.	57	98.28	1	1.72	0	0.00
4.	Workers of different factories belonging to furnace & dispatch unit.	42	97.67	1	2.33	0	0.00
5.	Workers of different factories belonging to key making unit.	52	92.86	3	5.36	1	1.79
6.	Workers of different factories belonging to nickle polish unit.	54	94.74	2	3.51	1	1.75
7.	Workers of different factories belonging to Office.	58	95.08	3	4.92	0	0.00
8.	Workers of different factories belonging to packing unit.	69	93.24	4	5.41	1	1.35
9.	Workers of different factories belonging to press unit.	66	91.67	5	6.94	1	1.39
10.	Salaried workers	223	94.09	11	4.64	3	1.27

11. Contractual workers	228	95.40	10	4.18	1	0.42
12. Male workers	434	94.55	21	4.58	4	0.87
13. Female workers	14	100.00	0	0.00	0	0.00
14. Literate workers	216	97.30	5	2.25	1	0.45
15. Illiterate workers	233	92.46	3	1.19	16	6.35
16. Joint family workers	232	95.68	11	3.17	4	1.15
17. Nuclear family workers	117	91.41	10	7.81	1	0.78
18. Rural workers	144	94.12	7	4.58	2	1.31
19. Urban workers	305	95.02	14	4.36	2	0.62
20. Hindu workers	134	91.78	11	7.53	1	0.68
21. Muslim workers	315	96.04	10	3.05	3	0.91
22. Workers in income group 0–3000	336	93.85	18	5.03	4	1.12
23. Workers in income group of 3000 and above	113	97.41	3	2.59	0	0.00
24. Workers belonging to Labour Class	365	94.07	19	4.90	4	1.03
25. Workers belonging to Management Class	81	97.59	2	2.41	0	0.00

polish units; 95.08% from Office; 93.24% from packing units; 91.67% from press units; 94.09% salaried workers and 95.40% contractual workers; 94.55% male workers and 100.00% female workers; 97.30% literate workers and 92.46% illiterate workers; 95.68% workers from joint family system and 91.41% representing nuclear family system; 94.12% rural workers and 95.02% urban workers; 91.78% Hindu workers and 96.04% Muslim workers; 93.85% workers receiving salary up to Rs. 3000/- and 97.41% workers receiving salary of more than 3000/ per month; 94.07% workers hailing from Labour class and 97.59% workers hailing from management group expressed their agreement with the statement.

It can, thus, be concluded that respondents representing different units of the factory as well as majority of the total subjects (94.51%) "to follow and educate other members of the community to follow practice and laws as laid down in the holy scriptures".

Table 4.113 reveals that majority of workers (90.30%) representing different units of 55 factories agreed that to educate such members of the community to extend equal respect to other religions who out of their ignorance, were failing to offer equal respect to other religions. While 8.65% exhibited their indifference, only 1.05% have expressed their disagreement with the statement.

Unit-wise analysis reveals that 88.68% workers hailing from assembly units; 87.93% from die-making units; 95.35% from furnace and dispatch units; 94.64% from key-making units; 85.96% from nickle polish units; 90.16% from Office; 91.89% from packing units; 88.89% from press units; 88.61% salaried workers and 92.47% contractual workers; 89.98% male workers and 100.00% female workers; 92.79% literate workers and 88.10% illiterate workers; 92.51% workers from joint family system and 84.25% representing nuclear family system; 90.20% rural workers and 90.34% urban worker; 89.73% Hindu workers and 90.55% Muslim workers; 90.78% workers receiving salary up to Rs. 3000/- and 88.79% workers receiving salary of more than 3000/- per month; 90.21% workers

TABLE 4.113 RELIGIOUS ASPIRATIONS: (3) TO EDUCATE SUCH MEMBERS OF THE COMMUNITY TO EXTEND EQUAL RESPECT TO OTHER RELIGIONS WHO OUT OF THEIR IGNORANCE, ARE FAILING TO OFFER EQUAL RESPECT TO OTHER RELIGIONS

	RESPONDENTS CATEGORY	*YES*	*%*	*INDIFF.*	*%*	*NO*	*%*
1.	Workers of different industrial units belonging to same factory.	428	90.30	41	8.65	5	1.05
2.	Workers of different factories belonging to assembly unit.	47	88.68	6	11.32	0	0.00
3.	Workers of different factories belonging to die making unit.	51	87.93	7	12.07	0	0.00
4.	Workers of different factories belonging to furnace & dispatch unit.	41	95.35	2	4.65	0	0.00
5.	Workers of different factories belonging to key making unit.	53	94.64	3	5.36	0	0.00
6.	Workers of different factories belonging to nickle polish unit.	49	85.96	7	12.28	1	1.75
7.	Workers of different factories belonging to Office	55	90.16	6	9.84	0	0.00
8.	Workers of different factories belonging to packing unit.	68	91.89	5	6.76	1	1.35
9.	Workers of different factories belonging to press unit.	64	88.89	5	6.94	3	4.17
10.	Salaried workers.	210	88.61	27	11.39	0	0.00

(Contd.)

11. Contractual workers	221	92.47	13	5.44	5	2.09
12. Male workers	413	89.98	41	8.93	5	1.09
13. Female workers	14	100.00	0	0.00	0	0.00
14. Literate workers	206	92.79	15	6.76	1	0.45
15. Illiterate workers	222	88.10	26	10.32	4	1.59
16. Joint family workers	321	92.51	23	6.63	3	0.86
17. Nuclear family workers	107	84.25	18	14.17	2	1.57
18. Rural workers	138	90.20	13	8.50	2	1.31
19. Urban workers	290	90.34	28	8.72	3	0.93
20. Hindu workers	131	89.73	11	7.53	4	2.74
21. Muslim workers	297	90.55	30	9.15	1	0.30
22. Workers in income group 0–3000	325	90.78	28	7.82	5	1.40
23. Workers in income group of 3000 and above	103	88.79	13	11.21	0	0.00
24. Workers belonging to Labour Class	350	90.21	33	8.51	5	1.29
25. Workers belonging to Management Class	75	90.36	8	9.64	0	0.00

hailing from Labour class and 90.36% workers hailing from management group expressed their agreement with the statement.

It can thus be concluded that respondents representing different units of the factory as well as majority of the total subjects (90.30%) "to educate such members of the community to extend equal respect to other religions who, out of hier ignorance, are failing to offer equal respect to other religions".

Table 4.114 reveals that majority of workers 89.03% representing different units of 55 factories agreed that to enlighten members of the community not to violate the prescribed religious prescriptions for the sake of their personal gains. While 8.44% exhibited their indifference, only 2.53% expressed their disagreement with the statement.

Unit wise analysis reveals that 92.45% workers hailing from assembly units; 87.93% from die-making units; 100.00% from furnace and dispatch units; 89.29% from key-making units; 92.98% from nickle polish units; 88.52% from Office; 85.14% from packing units; and 84.51% from press units; 91.56% salaried workers and 87.82% contractual workers; 89.52% male workers and 85.71% female workers; 90.99% literate workers and 88.05% illiterate workers; 88.18% workers from joint family system and 92.86% representing nuclear family system; 86.18% rural workers and 90.97% urban workers; 88.36% Hindu workers and 90.00% Muslim workers; 88.80% workers receiving salary up to Rs. 3000/- and 91.38% workers receiving salary of more than 3000/- per month; 88.63% workers hailing from Labour class and have 92.77% workers hailing from management group expressed their agreement with the statement.

It can, thus, be concluded that respondents representing different units of the factory as well as majority of the total subjects (89.03%) "to enlighten members of the community not to violate and prescribed religious prescriptions for the sake of their personal gains."

TABLE 4.114 RELIGIOUS ASPIRATIONS: (4) TO ENLIGHTEN MEMBERS OF THE COMMUNITY NOT TO VIOLATE THE PRESCRIBED RELIGIOUS PRESCRIPTIONS FOR THE SAKE OF THEIR PERSONAL GAINS

	RESPONDENTS CATEGORY	YES	%	INDIFF.	%	NO	%
1.	Workers of different industrial units belonging to same factory.	442	89.03	40	8.44	12	2.53
2.	Workers of different factories belonging to assembly unit.	49	92.45	3	5.66	1	1.89
3.	Workers of different factories belonging to die making unit.	51	87.93	4	6.90	3	5.17
4.	Workers of different factories belonging to furnace & dispatch unit.	43	100.00	0	0.00	0	0.00
5.	Workers of different factories belonging to key making unit.	50	89.29	6	10.71	0	0.00
6.	Workers of different factories belonging to nickle polish unit.	53	92.98	3	5.26	1	1.75
7.	Workers of different factories belonging to Office.	54	88.52	7	11.48	0	0.00
8.	Workers of different factories belonging to packing unit.	63	85.14	7	9.46	4	5.41
9.	Workers of different factories belonging to press unit.	60	84.51	9	12.68	2	2.82
10.	Salaried workers.	217	91.56	15	6.33	5	2.11

(Contd.)

11. Contractual workers	209	87.82	23	9.66	6	2.52
12. Male workers	410	89.52	38	8.30	10	2.18
13. Female workers	12	85.71	1	7.14	1	7.14
14. Literate workers	202	90.99	15	6.76	5	2.25
15. Illiterate workers	221	88.05	24	9.56	6	2.39
16. Joint family workers	306	88.18	33	9.51	8	2.31
17. Nuclear family workers	117	92.86	6	4.76	3	2.38
18. Rural workers	131	86.18	15	9.87	6	3.95
19. Urban workers	292	90.97	24	7.48	5	1.56
20. Hindu workers	129	88.36	13	8.90	4	2.74
21. Muslim workers	297	90.00	26	7.88	7	2.12
22. Workers in income group 0–3000	317	88.80	31	8.68	9	2.52
23. Workers in income group of 3000 and above	106	91.38	8	6.90	2	1.72
24. Workers belonging to Labour Class	343	88.63	33	8.53	11	2.84
25. Workers belonging to Management Class	77	92.77	6	7.23	0	0.00

Table 4.115 reveals that majority of workers 72.57% representing different units of 55 factories agreed to enlighten certain prevailing misconceptions about teachings of religion so that community members do not maintain social distance from followers of other religions. While 18.99% have exhibited their indifference, only 8.44% expressed their disagreement with the statement.

Unit-wise analysis reveals that 77.36% workers hailing from assembly units; 74.14% from die-making units; 67.44% from furnace and dispatch units; 71.43% from key-making units; 71.93% from nickle polish units; 72.13% from Office; 70.27% from packing units; 75.00% from press units; 67.09% salaried workers and 78.24% contractual workers; 72.11% male workers and 85.71% female workers; 69.37% literate workers and 75.40% illiterate workers; 74.15% workers from joint family system and 75.59% representing nuclear family system; 69.28% rural workers and 74.14% urban workers; 6849% Hindu workers and 74.39% Muslim workers; 72.07% workers receiving salary up to Rs. 3000/- and 74.14% workers receiving salary of more than 3000/- per month; 72.16% workers hailing from Labour class and 74.70% from management class exhibited their agreement with the statement.

It can, thus, be concluded that the respondents representing different units of factory as well as majority of the total subjects (72.57%) agreed "to enlighten certain prevailing misconceptions about teachings of religions so that community members do not maintain social distance from followers of other religions."

Table 4.116 reveals that majority of workers (86.71%) representing different units of 55 factories agreed that to gain full and real religious knowledge from scholars for transmitting it judiciously to masses of the community during spare time. While 10.34% exhibited their indifference only 2.95% have expressed their disagreement with the statement.

Unit-wise analysis reveals that 90.57% workers hailing from assembly units; 89.66% from die-making units; 88.37% from furnace

TABLE 4.115 RELIGIOUS ASPIRATIONS: (5) TO ENLIGHTEN CERTAIN PREVAILING MISCONCEPTIONS ABOUT TEACHINGS OF RELIGION SO THAT COMMUNITY MEMBERS DO NOT MAINTAIN SOCIAL DISTANCE FROM FOLLOWERS OF OTHER RELIGIONS

	RESPONDENTS CATEGORY	*YES*	*%*	*INDIFF.*	*%*	*NO*	*%*
1.	Workers of different industrial units belonging to same factory.	344	72.57	90	18.99	40	8.44
2.	Workers of different factories belonging to assembly unit.	41	77.36	9	16.98	3	5.66
3.	Workers of different factories belonging to die making unit.	43	74.14	9	15.52	6	10.34
4.	Workers of different factories belonging to furnace & dispatch unit.	29	67.44	11	25.58	3	6.98
5.	Workers of different factories belonging to key making unit.	40	71.43	12	21.43	4	7.14
6.	Workers of different factories belonging to nickle polish unit.	41	71.93	11	19.30	5	8.77
7.	Workers of different factories belonging to Office.	44	72.13	11	18.03	6	9.84
8.	Workers of different factories belonging to packing unit.	52	70.27	16	21.62	6	8.11
9.	Workers of different factories belonging to press unit.	54	75.00	11	15.28	7	9.72
10.	Salaried workers.	159	67.09	53	22.36	25	10.55

(Contd.)

11. Contractual workers	187	78.24	37	15.48	15	6.28
12. Male workers	331	72.11	88	19.17	40	8.71
13. Female workers	12	85.71	2	14.29	0	0.00
14. Literate workers	154	69.37	54	24.32	14	6.31
15. Illiterate workers	190	75.40	36	14.29	26	10.32
16. Joint family workers	284	74.15	66	17.23	53	8.62
17. Nuclear family workers	96	75.59	24	18.90	7	5.51
18. Rural workers	106	69.28	32	20.92	15	9.80
19. Urban workers	238	74.14	58	18.07	25	7.79
20. Hindu workers	100	68.49	34	23.29	12	8.22
21. Muslim workers	244	74.39	56	17.07	28	8.54
22. Workers in income group 0–3000	258	72.07	70	19.55	30	8.38
23. Workers in income group of 3000 and above	86	74.14	20	17.24	10	8.62
24. Workers belonging to Labour Class	280	72.16	77	19.85	31	7.99
25. Workers belonging to Management Class	62	74.70	12	14.46	9	10.84

TABLE 4.116 RELIGIOUS ASPIRATIONS: (6) TO GAIN FULL AND REAL RELIGIOUS KNOWLEDGE FROM SCHOLARS FOR TRANSMITTING IT JUDICIOUSLY TO THE MASSES OF THE COMMUNITY DURING SPARE TIME

	RESPONDENTS CATEGORY	*YES*	*%*	*INDIFF.*	*%*	*NO*	*%*
1.	Workers of different industrial units belonging to same factory.	411	86.7	49	10.34	14	2.95
2.	Workers of different factories belonging to assembly unit.	48	90.57	3	5.66	2	3.77
3.	Workers of different factories belonging to die making unit.	52	89.66	5	8.62	1	1.72
4.	Workers of different factories belonging to furnace & dispatch unit.	38	88.37	5	11.63	0	0.00
5.	Workers of different factories belonging to key making unit.	48	85.71	6	10.71	2	3.57
6.	Workers of different factories belonging to nickle polish unit.	52	91.23	2	3.51	3	5.26
7.	Workers of different factories belonging to Office.	84	88.52	6	9.84	1	1.64
8.	Workers of different factories belonging to packing unit.	60	81.08	12	16.22	2	2.70
9.	Workers of different factories belonging to press unit.	60	83.33	9	12.50	3	4.17
10.	Salaried workers.	201	84.81	31	13.08	5	2.11

11.	Contractual workers	214	89.54	16	6.69	9	3.77
12.	Male workers	402	87.58	43	9.37	14	3.05
13.	Female workers	9	64.29	5	35.71	0	0.00
14.	Literate workers	196	88.29	22	9.91	4	1.80
15.	Illiterate workers	216	85.71	26	10.32	10	3.97
16.	Joint family workers	305	87.90	31	8.93	11	3.17
17.	Nuclear family workers	107	84.25	17	13.39	3	2.36
18.	Rural workers	123	80.39	23	15.03	7	4.58
19.	Urban workers	289	90.03	25	7.79	7	2.18
20.	Hindu workers	120	82.19	22	15.07	4	2.74
21.	Muslim workers	292	89.02	26	7.93	10	3.05
22.	Workers in income group 0–3000	307	85.75	39	10.89	12	3.35
23.	Workers income group of 3000 and above	105	90.52	9	7.76	2	1.72
24.	Workers belonging to Labour Class	336	86.60	39	10.05	13	3.35
25.	Workers belonging to Management Class	73	87.95	9	10.84	1	1.20

and dispatch units; 85.71% from key-making units; 91.23% from nickle polish units; 88.52% from Office; 81.08% from packing units; 83.33% from press units; 84.81% salaried workers and 89.54% contractual workers; 87.58% male workers and 64.29% female workers; 88.29% literate workers and 85.71% illiterate workers; 87.90% workers from joint family system and 84.25% representing nuclear family system; 80.39% rural workers and 90.03% urban workers; 82.19% Hindu workers and 89.02% Muslim workers; 85.75% workers receiving salary up to Rs. 3000/- and 90.32% workers receiving salary of more than 3000/- per month; 86.60% workers hailing from Labour class 87.95% workers hailing from management group expressed their agreement with the statement.

It can, thus, be concluded that respondents representing different units of the factory as well as majority of the total subjects (86.57%) agreed "to gain full and real religious knowledge from the scholars for transmitting it judiciously to the masses of community during spare time."

Table 4.17 reveals that majority of workers 90.72% representing different units of 55 factories agreed take guidance from religious scholars and fight against such restrictions which were not prescribed in the religious scriptures but have been imposed by the preachers. While 8.02% exhibited their indifference, only 1.27% expressed their disagreement with the statement.

Unit-wise analysis reveals that 90.57% workers hailing from assembly units; 89.66% from die-making units; 95.35% from furnace and dispatch units; 94.64% from key-making units; 87.72% from nickle polish units; 93.44% from Office; 87.84% from packing units; 87.50% from press units; 84.45% salaried workers and 91.63% contractual workers; 90.85% male workers and 78.57% female workers; 94.14% literate workers and 87.30% illiterate workers; 91.93% workers from joint family system and 67.90% representing nuclear family systems 86.27% rural workers and 92.52% urban workers; 85.62% Hindu workers and 92.68% Muslim 90.50% workers

TABLE 4.117 RELIGIOUS ASPIRATIONS: (7) TAKING GUIDANCE FROM RELIGIOUS SCHOLARS AND FIGHTING AGAINST SUCH RESTRICTIONS WHICH ARE NOT PRESCRIBED IN RELIGIOUS SCRIPTURES BUT HAVE BEEN IMPOSED BY PREACHERS

	RESPONDENTS CATEGORY	*YES*	%	*INDIFF.*	%	*NO*	%
1.	Workers of different industrial unit belonging to same factory.	430	90.72	38	8.02	6	1.27
2.	Workers of different factories belonging to assembly unit.	48	90.57	4	7.55	1	1.89
3.	Workers of different factories belonging to die making unit.	52	89.66	5	8.62	1	1.72
4.	Workers of different factories belonging to furnace & dispatch unit.	41	95.35	1	2.33	1	2.33
5.	Workers of different factories belonging to key making unit.	53	94.64	3	5.36	0	0.00
6.	Workers of different factories belonging to nickle polish unit.	50	87.72	6	10.53	1	1.75
7.	Workers of different factories belonging to Office.	57	93.44	4	6.56	0	0.00
8.	Workers of different factories belonging to packing unit.	65	87.84	8	10.81	1	1.35
9.	Workers of different factories belonging to press unit.	63	87.50	8	11.11	1	1.39
10.	Salaried workers	212	89.45	22	9.28	3	1.27

(Contd.)

11. Contractual workers	219	91.63	17	7.11	3	1.26
12. Male workers	417	90.85	36	7.84	6	1.31
13. Female workers	11	78.57	3	21.43	0	0.00
14. Literate workers	209	94.14	12	5.41	1	0.45
15. Illiterate workers	220	87.30	27	10.71	5	1.98
16. Joint family workers	219	91.93	24	6.92	4	1.15
17. Nuclear family workers	110	67.90	50	30.86	2	1.23
18. Rural workers	132	86.27	18	11.76	3	1.96
19. Urban workers	297	92.52	21	6.54	3	0.93
20. Hindu workers	125	85.68	19	13.01	2	1.37
21. Muslim workers	304	92.68	20	6.10	4	1.22
22. Workers in income group 0–3000	324	90.50	29	8.10	5	1.40
23. Workers in income group of 3000 and above	105	90.52	10	8.62	1	0.86
24. Workers belonging to Labour Class	348	89.69	35	9.02	5	1.29
25. Workers belonging to Management Class	78	93.98	4	4.82	1	1.20

receiving salary up to Rs. 3000/- and 90.52% workers receiving salary of more than 3000/- per month; 89.69% workers hailing from Labour class and 93.98% workers hailing from management group expressed their agreement with the statement.

It can, thus, be concluded that respondents representing different units of the factory as well as majority of the total subjects (90.72%) agreed to "take guidance from religious scholars and fight against such striations which are not prescribed in the religious scriptures but have been imposed by the preachers."

Table 4.118 reveals that majority of workers (89.03%) representing different units of 55 factories agreed to raise voice to condemn such religious heads of the community who were offering services to political parties for their vested interests. While 6.12% have exhibited their indifference, only 4.85% have expressed their disagreement with the statement.

Unit-wise analysis reveals that 90.57% workers hailing from assembly units; 89.66% from die-making units; 93.02% from furnace and dispatch units; 87.50% from key-making units; 85.96% from nickle polish units; 90.16% from Offices; 87.84% from packing units; 90.28% from press units; 87.76% salaried workers and 90.38% contractual workers; 88.89% male workers and 100.00% female workers; 92.34 literate workers and 86.51% illiterate workers; 91.07% workers from joint family system and 84.25% representing nuclear family system; 84.97% rural workers and 91.28% urban workers; 84.25% Hindu workers and 91.46% Muslim workers; 88.55% workers receiving salary up to Rs. 3000/- and 91.38% workers receiving salary of more than 3000/- per month; 88.66% workers hailing from Labour class and 91.57% workers hailing from management group expressed their agreement with the statement.

It can, thus, be concluded that respondents representing different units of the factory as well as majority of the total subjects (89.03%) "raising of voice to condemn such religious heads of the community which offer services to political parties for their vested interests".

TABLE 4.118 RELIGIOUS ASPIRATIONS: (8) RAISING VOICE TO CONDEMN SUCH RELIGIOUS HEADS OF THE COMMUNITY OFFERING SERVICES TO POLITICAL PARTIES FOR THEIR VESTED INTERESTS

	RESPONDENTS CATEGORY	*YES*	%	*INDIFF.*	%	*NO*	%
1.	Workers of different industrial unit belonging to same factory.	422	89.03	29	6.12	23	4.85
2.	Workers of different factories belonging to assembly unit.	48	90.57	2	3.77	3	3.66
3.	Workers of different factories belonging to die making unit.	52	89.66	3	5.17	3	5.17
4.	Workers of different factories belonging to furnace & dispatch unit.	40	93.02	2	4.65	1	2.33
5.	Workers of different factories belonging to key making unit.	49	87.50	4	7.14	3	5.36
6.	Workers of different factories belonging to nickle polish unit	49	85.96	5	8.77	3	5.26
7.	Workers of different factories belonging to Office.	55	90.16	3	4.92	3	4.92
8.	Workers of different factories belonging to packing unit.	65	87.84	5	6.76	4	5.41
9.	Workers of different factories belonging to press unit.	65	90.28	4	5.56	3	4.17
10.	Salaried workers.	208	87.76	21	8.86	8	3.38

(*Contd.*)

11. Contractual workers	216	90.38	6	2.51	17	7.11
12. Male workers	408	88.89	28	6.10	23	5.01
13. Female workers	14	100.00	0	0.00	0	0.00
14. Literate workers	205	92.34	8	3.60	9	4.05
15. Illiterate workers	218	86.51	20	7.94	14	5.56
16. Joint family workers	316	91.07	19	5.48	12	3.46
17. Nuclear family workers	107	84.25	9	7.09	11	8.66
18. Rural workers	130	84.97	15	9.80	8	5.23
19. Urban workers	293	91.28	13	4.05	15	4.67
20. Hindu workers	123	84.25	14	9.59	9	6.16
21. Muslim workers	300	91.46	14	4.27	14	4.27
22. Workers in income group 0–3000	317	88.55	21	5.87	20	5.59
23. Workers in income group of 3000 and above	106	91.38	7	6.03	3	2.59
24. Workers belonging to Labour Class	344	88.66	24	6.19	20	5.15
25. Workers belonging to Management Class	76	91.57	4	4.82	3	3.61

Table 4.119 reveals that majority of workers (83.33%) representing different units of 55 factories agreed to work and fight against the operative practices of discrimination in society by seeking support from enlightened members hailing from other communities. While 13.92% exhibited their indifference, only 2.74% have expressed their disagreement with the statement.

Unit wise analysis reveals that 90.57% workers hailing from assembly units; 82.76% from die-making units; 88.37% from furnace and dispatch units; 82.14% from key-making units; 80.70% from nickle polish units; 81.97% from Office; 79.73% from packing units; 84.72% from press units; 79.75% salaried workers and 87.45% contractual workers; 83.22% male workers and 92.86% female workers; 85.59% literate workers and 81.75% illiterate workers; 87.90% workers from joint family system and 84.14% representing nuclear family system; 79.74% rural workers and 85.36% urban workers; 84.93% Hindu workers and 82.93% Muslim workers; 83.80% workers receiving salary up to Rs. 3000/- and 92.76% workers receiving salary of more than 3000/- per month; 83.51% workers hailing from Labour class and 83.13% workers hailing from management group expressed their agreement with the statement.

It can, thus, be concluded that respondents representing different units of the factory as well as majority of the total subjects (83.33%) "to work and fight against the operative practices of discrimination in the society by seeking support from enlightened members hailing from other communities."

TABLE 4.119 RELIGIOUS ASPIRATIONS: (9) TO WORK AND FIGHT AGAINST THE OPERATIVE PRACTICES OF DISCRIMINATION IN THE SOCIETY BY SEEKING SUPPORT FROM ENLIGHTENED MEMBERS HAILING FROM OTHER COMMUNITIES

	RESPONDENTS CATEGORY	*YES*	*%*	*INDIFF.*	*%*	*NO*	*%*
1.	Workers of different industrial units belonging to same factory.	395	83.33	66	13.92	13	2.74
2.	Workers of different factories belonging to assembly unit.	48	90.57	3	5.66	2	3.77
3.	Workers of different factories belonging to die making unit.	48	82.76	8	13.79	2	3.45
4.	Workers of different factories belonging to furnace & dispatch unit.	38	88.37	4	9.30	1	2.33
5.	Workers of different factories belonging to key making unit.	46	82.14	9	16.07	1	1.79
6.	Workers of different factories belonging to nickle polish unit	46	80.70	10	17.54	1	1.75
7.	Workers of different factories belonging to Office.	50	81.97	9	14.75	2	3.28
8.	Workers of different factories belonging to packing unit.	59	79.73	13	17.57	2	2.70
9.	Workers of different factories belonging to press unit.	61	84.72	9	12.50	2	2.78
10.	Salaried workers.	189	79.75	42	17.72	6	2.53

(Contd.)

11. Contractual workers	209	87.45	23	9.62	7	2.93
12. Male workers	382	83.22	64	13.94	13	2.83
13. Female workers	13	92.86	1	7.14	0	0.00
14. Literate workers	190	85.59	24	10.81	8	3.60
15. Illiterate workers	206	81.75	41	16.27	5	1.98
16. Joint family workers	305	87.90	33	9.51	9	2.59
17. Nuclear family workers	191	84.14	32	14.10	4	1.76
18. Rural workers	122	79.74	26	16.99	5	3.27
19. Urban workers	274	85.36	39	12.15	8	2.49
20. Hindu workers	124	84.93	18	12.33	4	2.74
21. Muslim workers	272	82.93	47	14.33	9	2.74
22. Workers in income group 0–3000	300	83.80	46	12.85	12	3.35
23. Workers in income group of 3000 and above	96	82.76	19	16.38	1	0.86
24. Workers belonging to Labour Class	324	83.51	53	13.66	11	2.84
25. Workers belonging to Management Class	69	83.13	12	14.46	2	2.41

Table 4.120 reveals that majority of workers (94.94%) representing different units of 55 factories agreed to propagate in community that religious fund collectors must submit the programmes and regular accounts before the general body of the community so that misuse of funds may be checked. While 5.06% have exhibited their indifference, only 0.00% have expressed their disagreement with the statement.

Unit-wise analysis reveals that 98.11% workers hailing from assembly units; 94.83% from die-making units; 97.67% from furnace and dispatch units; 92.86% from key-making units; 91.23% from nickle polish units; 98.36% from Office; 93.24% from packing units; 95.83% from press units; 92.83% salaried workers and 97.91% contractual workers; 94.99% male workers and 100.00% female workers; 97.30% literate workers and 93.25% illiterate workers; 95.97% workers from joint family system and 92.91% representing nuclear family system; 90.85% rural workers and 97.20% urban workers; 91.78% Hindu workers and 96.65% Muslim workers; expressed their agreement with the statement. 94.69% workers receiving salary up to Rs. 3000/- and 96.55% workers receiving salary of more than 3000/- per month; 94.33% workers hailing from Labour class and 98.80% workers hailing from management group expressed their agreement with the statement.

It can, thus, be concluded that respondents different units of the factory as well as majority of the total subjects (94.94%) "to propagate in the community that religious fund collectors must submit details of programmes and regular accounts before the general body of the community so that misuse of funds may be checked".

TABLE 4.120 RELIGIOUS ASPIRATIONS: (10) TO PROPAGATE IN THE COMMUNITY THAT RELIGIOUS FUND COLLECTORS MUST SUBMIT DETAILS OF PROGRAMMES AND REGULAR ACCOUNTS BEFORE GENERAL BODY OF THE COMMUNITY SO THAT MISUSE OF FUNDS MAY BE CHECKED

	RESPONDENTS CATEGORY	*YES*	*%*	*INDIFF.*	*%*	*NO*	*%*
1.	Workers of different industrial units belonging to same factory.	450	94.94	24	5.06	0	0.00
2.	Workers of different factories belonging to assembly unit.	52	98.11	1	1.89	0	0.00
3.	Workers of different factories belonging to die making unit.	55	94.83	3	5.17	0	0.00
4.	Workers of different factories belonging to furnace & dispatch unit.	42	97.67	1	2.33	0	0.00
5.	Workers of different factories belonging to key making unit.	52	92.86	4	7.14	0	0.00
6.	Workers of different factories belonging to nickle polish unit.	52	91.23	5	8.77	0	0.00
7.	Workers of different factories belonging to Office.	60	98.36	1	1.64	0	0.00
8.	Workers of different factories belonging to packing unit.	69	93.24	5	6.76	0	0.00
9.	Workers of different factories belonging to press unit.	69	95.83	3	4.17	0	0.00
10.	Salaried workers	220	92.83	17	7.17	0	0.00

(Contd)

11. Contractual workers	234	97.91	5	2.09	0	0.00
12. Male workers	436	94.99	23	5.01	0	0.00
13. Female workers	14	100.00	0	0.00	0	0.00
14. Literate workers	216	97.30	6	2.70	0	0.00
15. Illiterate workers	235	93.25	17	6.75	0	0.00
16. Joint family workers	333	95.97	14	4.03	0	0.00
17. Nuclear family workers	118	92.91	9	7.09	0	0.00
18. Rural workers	139	90 85	14	9.15	0	0.00
19. Urban workers	312	97.20	9	2.80	0	0.00
20. Hindu workers	134	91.78	12	8.22	0	0.00
21. Muslim workers	317	96.65	11	3.35	0	0.00
22. Workers in income group 0–3000	339	94.69	19	5.31	0	0.00
23. Workers in income group of 3000 and above	112	96.55	4	3.45	0	0.00
24. Workers belonging to Labour Class	366	94.33	22	5.67	0	0.00
25. Workers belonging to Management Class	82	98.80	1	1.20	0	0.00

CHAPTER

5

CONCLUSION AND SUGGESTIONS

Following survey technique of sociological empirical research, are interview schedule was administered on all the respondents all hailing from different working groups of Aligarh lock industries. The interview schedule contained 100 questions covering various parameters of the study related to the problem. The sample of respondents was drawn by random sampling method, selecting 474 workers from 55 lock industries out of 7795 workers from 1612 registered lock industries situated in the vicinity of Industrial Estate and other parts of Aligarh City. The conclusions and suggestions discussed in the chapter are based on scientific analysis of their responses.

Initially, the data was analysed with the help of Item analysis. Later, T-test and MicroSoft Excel tests were also applied to find out significant difference if any, and to work out comparative analysis among the respondents. The data was compared and analysed on the basis of differentials of perceptions and aspirations among the respondents hailing from different industrial units of Aligarh Lock Industry; workers representing different religions, workers hailing from different backgrounds like urban and rural areas, joint and nuclear families, literate and illiterate workers, male and female salaried and contractual workers, management and labour class and on the basis of different income groups of Lock Industry workers. On account of paucity of space, presentation of analysis in this chapter has been restricted only to those items, which have obtained maximum and minimum preferences from the respondents representing different areas under study.

On the basis of interpretation and data analysis, the following conclusions have been drawn:

1. To the best of knowledge of this researcher little work has been done so far on perceptions and aspirations among the Aligarh Lock Industry workers.
2. Percentage wise and t-value analysis of perceptions and aspirations of the respondents hailing from various groups of Aligarh Lock Industries reveals that:
   - Majority of respondents expressed their agreement with the statement that, "earnings are not sufficient to meet their familial responsibilities and other obligations".
   - Majority of respondents perceived that because of economic reasons people of their community, despite mental and physical exploitation permit their children to seek employment.
   - Majority of respondents expressed their agreement with the statement that, "because of economic constraints majority of the people of their community fail to fulfil their socio-cultural commitments".
   - Majority of respondents perceived that on account of economic considerations people of their community give preference to sons in place of daughters.
   - Majority of respondents expressed their agreement with the statement that, "some families within the community, where women are also working along with men, are economically much better off as compared to others".
   - Majority of respondents perceived that constant hike in the cost of living and limited income has compelled the economically weaker sections of their community to accept all kinds of exploitations.
   - Majority of respondents expressed their disagreement with the statement that, "on account of limited opportunities of employment, educated youths of the community have adopted unethical and illegal means to earn money".

- Majority of respondents expressed their agreement with the statement that "continuous disturbed conditions like strikes and riots in the society certainly affect economic activities and per capita income of the people of the society".
- Majority of respondents expressed their agreement with the statement that, "educated and capable youths of the community are not making adequate use of governmental programmes or schemes meant for economic welfare of the people".
- Majority of respondents expressed their agreement with the statement that "on account of financial reasons, children of the community are unable to receive adequate education as mostly parents in general, and economically weaker sections in particular, are unable to meet the prevailing high educational expenses".
- Majority of respondents aspired to supplement their earnings by taking up some part-time jobs or economic activities.
- Majority of respondents wished to raise their voice and fight the implementation of labour laws pertaining to children so that they may be saved from exploitations.
- Majority of respondents aspired to take up some extra economic activity, which may yield monetary returns to fulfill their socio-cultural commitments.
- Majority of the respondents desired to educate and enlighten the ignorant members of the community to encourage women for taking part in economic activities along with their male counterparts to achieve greater economic stability and prosperity.
- Majority of respondents agreed to educate the economically weaker sections of the community to fight against any kind of exploitation and start some extra economic activities, initially on a small scale, for countering exploitation.
- Majority of respondents intended to educate unemployed educated youths of their community that instead of using

unethical and illegal means of earning money, they should avail loan facilities as offered by the government, to start independent economic activity.

- Majority of respondents wished to join some judicious and nonpolitical organisations which may prove useful instrument in settling strikes and in maintaining communal harmony at the time of riot and to educate the deserving youths of the community to avail the provisions and benefits of government sponsored employment programmes and schemes for economic upliftment.
- Majority of respondents wished to raise voice through some social organisation or agency for pressuring the government and welfare bodies of the community for providing reading material on subsidised rates, in general, and scholarships, in particular, for economically weaker sections.
- Majority of respondents expressed their agreement with the statement that "boys' parents, at the time of marriage, directly or indirectly demand gift in cash and kind from the parents of the girls which is not permissible in their religion and law."
- Majority of respondents expressed their agreement with the statement that girls were subjected to humiliation if they fail to bring with them the committed gifts and cash at the time of their marriage.
- Majority of respondents expressed their agreement with the statement that "earnings are not sufficient to meet the familial responsibilities and other obligations".
- Majority of respondents expressed their agreement with the statement that "men and women are enjoying equal authority in family matters."
- Majority of respondents expressed their agreement with the statement that "educated couples are more happily settled in their lives as compared to less or uneducated couples."

- Majority of respondents expressed their agreement with the statement that "people are going for early marriage of their daughters even to elderly settled persons because of economic reasons".
- Majority of respondents expressed their agreement with the statement that "divorce has become fairly common among the members of the society amounting to family disorganisation".
- Majority of respondents expressed their agreement with the statement that "widows' remarriage, though legally permissible, yet is being discouraged by certain sections of the communities."
- Majority of respondents expressed their agreement with the statement that "it is difficult to find suitable matches for educated boys and girls."
- Majority of respondents expressed their agreement with the statement that "on account of growing nuclear family patterns the traditional familial bonds and feelings of belonging among members of the community have weakened".
- Majority of respondents wished to work against the system of demanding cash or gifts in kind by the boys' parents at the time of the marriage which is not permissible in their religion and by law, and intended to organize or join some such organisation which is working for rehabilitation of the girls who become victims of humiliation after marriage.
- Majority of respondents desired to appeal to the enlightened, educated and expert members of their community to come forward and educate the masses about socio-economic and physiological advantages of family planning.
- Majority of respondents intended to raise voice in support of women's rights of equality in family matters of their community.

- Majority of the respondents wished to educate members of their community for not marrying off their children till they receive proper education and also to apprise the members of the community for not marrying their daughters to elderly settled persons due to economic reasons and instead start some extra economic activity to improve their financial conditions.
- Majority of respondents wished to propagate against the evils of divorce for saving families from disorganisation and also to encourage widow remarriage to rehabilitate and rescue them from expected future exploitation.
- Majority of respondents wanted to be associated with some such voluntary social organisations which may help in selecting matches for educated boys and girls of their community.
- Majority of respondents agreed to enlighten the community members to interact among themselves quite frequently so that he traditional bonds of family proximity were maintained.
- Majority of respondents expressed their agreement with the statement that their community members take keen interest in the political affairs and also adopt unethical practices to achieve their goals.
- Majority of respondents expressed their agreement with the statement that "members of the society do not support political parties on the basis of their election manifesto".
- Majority of respondents disagreed with the statement that "fair elections are held in our society".
- Majority of respondents expressed their agreement with the statement that "political bosses misuse their position and power for selfish ends by exploiting their authority."
- Majority of respondents expressed their agreement with the statement that "candidates and political parties freely use money and muscle power during elections".

- Majority of respondents expressed their agreement with the statement that, "economically well off people extend financial support to important parties and candidates because they cash them after their victories."
- Majority of respondents expressed their agreement with the statement that "in elections political parties issue tickets and extend full support to the persons having established criminal background".
- Majority of respondents expressed their agreement with the statement that "political parties or even independent candidates, for winning the election, do not hesitate in giving communal or caste turn to any event during election period if its suits them".
- Majority of respondents expressed their agreement with the statement that "community members lacking the required political awareness in selecting right type of person or party do not caste their votes".
- Majority of respondents expressed their agreement with the statement that "political parties and independent candidates mostly make false promises at the time elections but never attend to them".
- Majority of respondents wished to generate judicious and ethical political awareness among masses of the community, if and when they get an opportunity, not to adopt unethical practices in the political affairs of the society.
- Majority of respondents wished to propagate among members of the society to support political parties on the basis of their election manifesto and not on any other consideration.
- Majority of respondents desired to become member of some such organisation which may fight against the mal-practices, which are operative during elections.
- Majority of respondents intended to expose such political persons who misuse their position and power for their selfish ends and wished to work and raise voice against

such practices and persons who use money and muscle power during elections.

- Majority of respondents wished to raise their voice that government should impose some financial limits in election expenditure, which should be also subjected to accountability.
- Majority of respondents desired to persuade the enlightened and judicious members of the community to pressurize the government impose to ban on permitting any contestant who has criminal background to seek election and wished to protest vigorously through some organisation or independently against such political parties and independent candidates who, in order to win elections spoil the election, science on the basis of religion/caste.
- Majority of respondents intended to educate independently or through some organisation to press the members of their community to caste their votes and support right type of person or party based on their election manifesto.
- Majority of respondents wished to join some such non-political organisation through which voice may be raised in highlighting the nonfulfilment of promises to the communities made by the political parties and independent candidates after winning elections.
- Majority of respondents expressed their agreement with the statement that "in the present era of advancement, the community members are not satisfied with the prevailing education system."
- Majority of respondents expressed their agreement with the statement that, "on account of higher cost of education majority of the people hailing from economically weaker section do not encourage their children to receive full education".
- Majority of respondents expressed their agreement with the statement that "education is mainly responsible for the socio-economic development".

- Majority of the respondents expressed their agreement with the statement that "educated persons of the community, as compared to others, are more successful in business and trade".
- Majority of respondents expressed their agreement with the statement that "advice of educated persons of the community is always sought by the uneducated or less educated ones to settle their disputes".
- Majority of respondents expressed their agreement with the statement that "parents of the community are more in favour of imparting religious education to their children instead of scientific education".
- Majority of respondents expressed their agreement with the statement that "woman of their community is more educationally backward as compared to women of other communities".
- Majority of respondents expressed their agreement with the statement that "leaders of their community are indifferent towards upliftment of the community and do not seek help from government".
- Majority of respondents expressed their agreement with the statement that "in the present era, education has become highly commercialised because teachers do not judiciously perform their teaching duties in schools and colleges as either they had opened their own coaching centers or were teaching in other coaching centers on payment.
- Majority of respondents desired to establish contact with members of their community connected with the education system to suggest ways and means to the government so that some better system of education may be evolved.
- Majority of respondents wished to work and fight independently or through some social organisations to press the government for free and full education to the children hailing from the economically backward strata of their community.

- Majority of respondents were eager to work with some social organisations of their community who claim to look after the interest of the poor children hailing from the lower economic strata.
- Majority of respondents were keen to propagate that children should be not engaged in any economic activity till they receive proper education so that they may be more successful in business and trade.
- Majority of respondents desired to teach the uneducated or less educated masses of their community to settle their disputes amicably with the help of educated persons and not to use physical force or adopt unethical practices or to go court of law as it was very expensive and time consuming.
- Majority of respondents wished to propagate among the masses of their community the usefulness of scientific education based on analytical and rational principles instead of religious education alone.
- Majority of respondents agreed to seek help from educated members of their community to enlighten the ignorant persons about the importance of children's education.
- Majority of respondents wished to establish some women social organisations in their community to enlighten and encourage women of the community to receive education and not remain educationally backward.
- Majority of respondents expressed their agreement with the statement that "educated and respectable members of their community should keep regular contact with leaders of their community and press them to work and seek government's help in getting adequate educational facilities for the sake of their community".
- Majority of respondents expressed their agreement with the statement that "services of the teachers who are not performing their educational duties in their institutions and

were engaged in coaching centers should be terminated and the coaching centers be banned".

- Majority of respondents expressed their agreement with the statement that "majority of members of their community offer prayers regularly as prescribed".
- Majority of respondents expressed their agreement with the statement that "members of their community strictly follow and practice the laws as prescribed in holy scriptures."
- Majority of respondents expressed their agreement with the statement that "members of their community extend equal respect to other religions."
- Majority of respondents expressed their agreement with the statement that certain members of their community deviate from the prescribed religious codes of conduct on account of their vested interests."
- Majority of respondents expressed their agreement with the statement that "sections of their community on account of their ignorance about teachings of religion, maintain social distance with the members hailing from other religions."
- Majority of respondents expressed their agreement with the statement that "the preachers of religion of your community have not adequately succeeded in transmitting the proper understanding and knowledge about religion to the masses."
- Majority of respondents expressed their agreement with the statement that "religious heads of their community have imposed certain such restrictions which are not prescribed in the holy scriptures."
- Majority of respondents expressed their agreement with the statement that, "religious heads of their community, on account of their vested material gains and popularity, offer their services to political parties during elections which is against their religious ethics."

- Majority of respondents expressed their agreement with the statement that "members in the society are distinctly discriminated on the basis of religion and caste in all matters of life".
- Majority of respondents expressed their agreement with the statement that "funds collected in the name of religion by the religious leaders of their community are not utilized religiously by them."
- Majority of respondents wished to educate the importance of offering payers to such members of the community who did not offer prayers regularly as prescribed.
- Majority of respondents desired to follow and educate other members of the community to follow and practice laws as laid down in the holy scriptures.
- Majority of respondents desired to educate such members of their community to extend equal respect to other religions who out of their ignorance, were failing to offer equal respect to other religions.
- Majority of respondents intended to enlighten members of their community not to violate the prescribed religious prescriptions for the sake of their personal gains and wished to tell them about certain prevailing misconceptions about teachings of religion so that the community members do not maintain social distance with the follower of other religions.
- Majority of respondents desired to gain full and real knowledge of religion from the scholars for transmitting it judiciously to the masses of their community during spare time.
- Majority of respondents wished to take guidance from religious scholars to fight against such restrictions which are not prescribed in the religious scriptures but have been imposed by the preachers.

- Majority of respondents desired to raise their voice to condemn such religious heads of the community who offer service to political parties for their vested interests.
- Majority of respondents intended to work and fight against the operative practices of discrimination in the society by seeking support from the enlightened members hailing from other communities.
- Majority of respondents wished to propagate in their community that religious fund collectors must submit details of programmes and regular accounts before the general body of their community so that misuse of funds may be checked.

3. Percentage-wise analysis and *chi*-square value pertaining to perceptions among the Hindu and Muslim workers of Aligarh Lock Industry revealed that no significant variation was noticeable.
4. Percentage-wise analysis and *chi*-square value pertaining to aspirations among the Hindu and Muslim workers revealed that, in general a little variation was noticeable.
5. Percentage-wise analysis and *chi*-square value pertaining to perceptions and aspirations among the workers hailing from Assembly Unit, Die Making Unit, Furnace and Dispatch Unit Key making Unit, Nickle Polish Unit, Packing Unit and Press Unit revealed that in general significant variations were noticeable.
6. Percentage-wise analysis and *chi*-square value pertaining to perceptions and aspirations among workers hailing from the families with two or less children (hence adopting small family norms) and from the families with more than two children (hence not adopting small family norms) of Aligarh Lock Industry revealed that little variations were noticeable.
7. Percentage-wise analysis and *chi*-square value pertaining to perceptions and aspirations among the salaried and contractual workers revealed that, in general, little variations were noticeable.

8. Percentage-wise analysis *chi*-square value pertaining to perceptions and aspirations among male and female workers revealed that, in general, little variations were noticeable.
9. Percentage-wise analysis and *chi*-square value pertaining to perceptions and aspirations among literate and illiterate workers revealed that in general little variations were noticeable.
10. Percentage wise analysis and *chi*-square value pertaining to perceptions and aspirations among workers hailing from joint family system and the workers coming from nuclear family system of Aligarh Lock Industry revealed that no significant variations were noticeable.
11. Percentage-wise analysis and *chi*-square value pertaining to perceptions and aspirations among workers hailing from rural areas and the workers coming from urban areas of the Aligarh Lock Industry revealed that no significant variations were noticeable.
12. Percentage-wise analysis and *chi*-square value pertaining to perceptions and aspirations among the labour and management groups revealed that in general, little variations were noticeable.
13. Percentage-wise analysis and *chi*-square value pertaining to perceptions and aspirations among the workers hailing from income groups of below Rs. 3000/- per month and of Rs. 3000/- and above revealed that, in general, little variations noticeable.

On the basis of variations in perceptions and aspirations a comparative analysis among the respondents hailing from different working groups and total respondents towards statements related to different areas under study was attempted as under:

1. ECONOMIC PERCEPTIONS AND ASPIRATIONS

Percentage-wise comparison exhibited that there were significant differences in the economic perceptions among respondents hailing from different working groups.

Percentage-wise comparison exhibited that there were significant differences in the economic aspirations of respondents hailing from different working groups. But insignificant variations were noticeable pertaining to Item No. 4.

Percentage-wise comparision exhibited that there seemed to be insignificant variations in the economic perceptions among the Hindu and Muslim workers hailing from different working groups of Aligarh Lock Industries but significant variations were noticeable pertaining to Item No. 5, 7 and 8.

Percentage-wise comparision exhibited that there seemed to be insignificant variations in the economic aspirations among Hindu and Muslim workers hailing from different working groups of Aligarh Lock Industries, but significant variations were noticeable pertaining to Item No.6.

Percentage wise comparison showed that there seemed to be significant variations in the economic perceptions of the salaried workers and contractual workers in Aligarh Lock Factories.

Percentage-wise comparison exhibited that there seemed to be significant variations in the economic aspirations of the salaried workers and contractual workers in Aligarh Lock Factories but insignificant variations were noticeable pertaining to Item Nos. 1, 2 and 8.

Percentage-wise comparision showed that there seemed to be insignificant variations in the economic perceptions of the Male and Female workers in Aligarh Lock Factories but significant variations were noticeable pertaining to Item Nos. 5, 6 and 9.

Percentage-wise comparison exhibited that there seemed to be significant variations in the economic aspirations of the Male and Female workers in Aligarh Lock Factories but insignificant variations were noticeable pertaining to Item Nos. 2, 3, 8, 9 and 10.

Percentage-wise comparison showed that there seemed to be insignificant variations in economic perceptions of the literate and illiterate workers in Aligarh Lock Factories but significant variations were noticeable pertaining to Item No. 7.

Percentage-wise comparison exhibited that there seemed to be significant variations in the economic aspirations of the literate and illiterate workers in Aligarh Lock Factories but insignificant variations were noticeable pertaining to Item Nos. 1, 2, 3, and 8.

Percentage-wise comparison exhibited that there seems to be insignificant variations in the economic perceptions of the workers hailing from joint families and nuclear families in Aligarh Lock Factories but significant variations were noticeable pertaining to Item No. 5.

Percentage-wise comparison exhibited that there seemed to be insignificant variations in the economic aspirations of the workers hailing from joint families and nuclear families in Aligarh Lock Factories but significant variations were noticeable pertaining to Item Nos. 4, 9 and 10.

Percentage-wise comparison showed that there seemed to be insignificant variations in the economic perceptions of the workers hailing from rural and urban areas in Aligarh Lock Factories but significant variations were noticeable pertaining to Item Nos. 7, 8 and 9.

Percentage-wise comparison exhibited that there seemed to be insignificant variations in the economic aspirations of the workers hailing from rural and urban areas in Aligarh Lock Factories but significant variations were noticeable pertaining to Item Nos. 5 and 6.

Percentage-wise comparison showed that there seemed to be significant variations in the economic perceptions of the workers belonging to management group and labour Class in Aligarh Lock Factories but insignificant variations were noticeable pertaining to Item Nos. 1, 2, 3, 4, and 5.

Percentage-wise comparison exhibited that there seemed to be significant variations in the economic aspirations of the workers belonging to management group and labour class in Aligarh Lock Factories but insignificant variations were noticeable pertaining to Item Nos. 1, 2, 5, 7, 8 and 10.

Percentage-wise comparison exhibited that there seemed to be insignificant variations in the economic perceptions of the workers belonging to different income groups: (1). Below Rs. 3000/- and (2). Above Rs. 3000 in Aligarh Lock Factories but significant variations were noticeable pertaining to Item Nos. 5 and 7.

Percentage-wise comparison exhibited that there seemed to be insignificant variations in the economic aspirations of the workers belonging to different income groups: (1) below Rs. 3000/- and (2) Above Rs. 3000) in Aligarh Lock Factories.

Percentage-wise comparison exhibited that there seemed to be significant variations in the economic perceptions of the workers hailing from families adopting small family norms and those not adopting small family norms in Aligarh Lock Factories, but insignificant variations were noticeable pertaining to Item Nos. 4 and 8.

Percentage-wise comparison exhibited that there seemed to be significant variations in the economic aspirations of the workers hailing from the families adopting small family norms and those not adopting small family norms in Aligarh Lock Factories, but insignificant variations were noticeable pertaining to Item Nos. 1, 5 and 7.

2. SOCIAL PERCEPTIONS AND ASPIRATIONS

The percentage-wise comparison showed that there were insignificant differences in the social perceptions of the respondents hailing from different working groups. But significant variations were noticeable pertaining to Item Nos. 4 and 8.

The percentage-wise comparison exhibited that there were insignificant differences in the social aspirations of respondents hailing from different working groups. But significant variations were noticeable pertaining to Item Nos. 3 and 4.

Percentage-wise comparison showed that there seemed to be insignificant variations in the social perceptions among the Hindu and Muslim workers hailing from different working groups of Aligarh Lock Industries but significant variations were noticeable pertaining to Item Nos. 1, 5, & 7.

Percentage-wise comparison exhibited that there seemed to be insignificant variations in the social aspirations among the Hindu and Muslim workers hailing from different working groups of Aligarh Lock Industries but significant variations were noticeable pertaining to Item Nos. 1, 4, 6, 7, & 8.

Percentage-wise comparison showed that there seemed to be insignificant variations in the social perceptions of the salaried workers and contractual workers in Aligarh Lock Factories but significant variations were noticeable pertaining to Item No. 4 & 8.

Percentage-wise comparison exhibited that there seemed to be insignificant variations in the social aspirations of the salaried workers and contractual workers in Aligarh Lock Factories but significant variations were noticeable pertaining to Item Nos. 3 & 4.

Percentage-wise comparison showed that there seemed to be significant variations in the social perceptions of the male and female workers in Aligarh lock factories, but insignificant variations were noticeable pertaining to Item No. 1, 2, 4, & 7.

Percentage-wise comparison showed that there seemed to be significant variations in the social aspirations of the male and female workers in Aligarh lock factories, but insignificant variations were noticeable pertaining to item No. 7.

Percentage-wise comparison exhibited that there seemed to be insignificant variations in the social perceptions of the literate and illiterate workers in Aligarh lock factories, but significant variations were noticeable pertaining to Item Nc. 6, 7, 8, & 9.

Percentage-wise comparison exhibited that there seemed to be significant variations in the social aspirations of the literate and illiterate workers in Aligarh lock factories, but insignificant variations were noticeable pertaining to Item Nos. 1, 4, & 6.

Percentage-wise comparison exhibited that there seemed to be insignificant variations in the social perceptions of the workers hailing from joint families and nuclear families in Aligarh lock factories but significant variations were noticeable pertaining to Item Nos. 4, 5, 6, 7 and 9.

Percentage-wise comparison exhibited that there seemed to be insignificant variations in the social aspirations of the workers hailing from joint families and nuclear families in Aligarh lock factories, but significant variations were noticeable pertaining to Item Nos. 1, 6, 7 and 8.

Percentage-wise comparison exhibited that there seemed to be significant variations in the social perceptions of the workers hailing from rural and urban areas in Aligarh Lock Factories, but insignificant variations were noticeable pertaining to Item No. 2, 9 & 10.

Percentage-wise comparison exhibited insignificant variations in the social aspirations of the workers hailing from rural and urban areas in Aligarh lock factories but significant variations were noticeable pertaining to Item Nos. 2, 4, 7 & 8.

Percentage-wise comparison exhibited that there seemed to be significant variations in the social perceptions of the workers belonging to management group and labour class in Aligarh Lock Factories but insignificant variations were noticeable pertaining to Item No. 2, 3, 7 and 10.

Percentage-wise comparison showed that there seemed to be insignificant variations in the social aspirations of the workers belonging to management group and labour class in Aligarh Lock Factories but significant variations were noticeable pertaining to Item Nos. 2, 7, 8 & 9.

Percentage-wise comparison exhibited that there seemed to be significant variations in the social perceptions of the workers belonging to different income groups: (1) below Rs. 3000/ and (2) above Rs. 3000 in Aligarh lock factories but insignificant variations were noticeable pertaining to Item Nos. 2, 3, 7, 9 and 10.

Percentage-wise comparison showed insignificant variations in the social aspirations of the workers belonging to different income groups: (1) below Rs. 3000 and (2) above Rs. 3000 in Aligarh lock factories, but significant variations were noticeable pertaining to Item Nos. 2, 3, and 8.

Percentage-wise comparison exhibited significant variations in the social perceptions of the workers hailing from the families adopting small family norms and those not adopting small family norms in Aligarh lock factories, but insignificant variations were noticeable pertaining to Item Nos. 2, 3, 8, 9, & 10.

Percentage-wise comparison showed significant variations in the social aspirations of the workers hailing from the families adopting small family norms and those not adopting small family norms in

Aligarh lock factories, but insignificant variations were noticeable pertaining to Item Nos. 2, 3, 5, 7 & 8.

3. POLITICAL PERCEPTIONS AND ASPIRATIONS:

Percentage-wise comparison exhibited significant differences in political perceptions of respondents hailing from different working groups.

Percentage-wise comparison exhibited that there were significant differences in the political aspirations of respondents hailing from different working groups.

Percentage-wise comparison exhibited insignificant variations in the political perceptions among the Hindu and Muslim workers hailing from different working groups of Aligarh Lock Industries, but significant variations were noticeable pertaining to Item Nos. 1, 3, and 8.

Percentage-wise comparison showed insignificant variations in political aspirations among the Hindu and Muslim workers hailing from different working groups of Aligarh Lock Industries but significant variations were noticeable pertaining to Item Nos. 1, 5, 7, 9 and 10.

Percentage-wise comparison exhibited insignificant variations in the political perceptions of salaried workers and contractual workers in Aligarh Lock Factories, but significant variation was noticeable pertaining to Item No. 1.

Percentage-wise comparison showed insignificant variations in political aspirations of salaried workers and contractual workers in Aligarh Lock Factories but significant variations were noticeable pertaining to Item Nos. 3, 4, 5 and 6.

Percentage-wise comparison exhibited insignificant variations in political perceptions of the male and female workers in Aligarh Lock Factories but significant variations were noticeable pertaining to Item Nos. 1, 3, 4, 5, 7 and 8.

Percentage-wise comparison exhibited insignificant variations in the political aspirations of the male and female workers in Aligarh Lock Factories but significant variations were noticeable pertaining to Item Nos. 5, 6, 7 and 10.

Percentage-wise comparison showed significant variation in the political perceptions of the literate and illiterate workers in Aligarh lock factories, but insignificant variations were noticeable pertaining to Item Nos. 2 and 6.

Percentage-wise comparison showed significant variations in political aspirations of the literate and illiterate workers in Aligarh Lock Factories, but insignificant variations were noticeable pertaining to Item No. 5.

Percentage wise comparison exhibited insignificant variations in the political perceptions of the workers hailing from joint families and nuclear families in Aligarh Lock Factories but significant variations were noticeable pertaining to Item Nos. 1 and 10.

Percentage-wise comparison exhibited significant variations in political aspirations of the workers hailing from joint families and nuclear families in Aligarh Lock Factories but significant variations were noticeable pertaining to Item Nos. 1, 8, and 9.

Percentage-wise comparison exhibited significant variations in political perceptions of the workers hailing from rural and urban areas in Aligarh Lock Factories, but insignificant variations were noticeable pertaining to Item Nos. 2, 6, 9 and 10.

Percentage-wise comparison exhibited significant variations in political aspirations of the workers hailing from rural and urban areas in Aligarh Lock Factories, but insignificant variations were noticeable pertaining to Item Nos. 1, 3, 5, and 6.

Percentage-wise comparison exhibited significant variations in political perceptions of the workers belonging to management group and labour class in Aligarh Lock Factories, but insignificant variations were noticeable pertaining to Item No. 5.

Percentage-wise comparison exhibited significant variations in political aspirations of the workers belonging to management group and labour class in Aligarh Lock Factories, but insignificant variations were noticeable pertaining to Item No. 5.

Percentage-wise comparison exhibited significant variations in political perceptions of the workers belonging to different income groups (1). Below Rs. 3000/ and (2). Above Rs. 3000 in Aligarh Lock Factories, but insignificant variations were noticeable pertaining to Item Nos. 2, 7, 8, 9, and 10.

Percentage-wise comparison exhibited insignificant variations in political aspirations of the workers belonging to different income groups : (1). Below Rs. 3000/ and (2). above Rs. 3000) in Aligarh Lock Factories, but significant variations were noticeable pertaining to Item Nos. 3 and 4.

Percentage wise comparison exhibited that there seemed to be significant variations in political perceptions of the workers hailing from the families adopting small family norms and those not adopting small family norms in Aligarh Lock Factories but insignificant variations were noticeable pertaining to Item No. 6.

Percentage wise comparison exhibited that there seemed to be significant variations in political aspirations of the workers hailing from the families adopting small family norms and those not adopting small family norms in Aligarh Lock Factories but insignificant variations were noticeable pertaining to Item No. 4 and 5.

iv. Educational Perceptions and Aspirations:

The percentage wise comparison exhibited that there were significant difference in the educational perceptions of the respondents hailing from different working groups.

The Percentage wise comparison exhibited that there were significant differences in the educational aspirations of the respondents hailing from different working groups, but insignificant variations were noticeable pertaining to Item No. 1 and 6.

Percentage wise comparison exhibited that there seemed to be significant variations in the educational perceptions among the Hindus and Muslims workers hailing from different working groups of Aligarh Lock Industries but insignificant variations were noticeable pertaining to Item No. 4, 6, 8, 9 and 10.

Percentage wise comparison exhibited that there seemed to be significant variations in the educational aspirations among the Hindus and Muslims workers hailing from different working groups of Aligarh

Lock Industries but insignificant variations were noticeable pertaining to Item No. 2, 4, 6, 7 and 8.

Percentage wise comparison exhibited that there seemed to be insignificant variations in the educational perceptions of the salaried workers and contractual workers in Aligarh Lock Factories but significant variations were noticeable pertaining to Item No. 1, 7 and 10.

Percentage wise comparison exhibited that there seemed to be insignificant variations in the educational aspirations of the salaried workers and contractual workers in Aligarh Lock Factories but significant variations were noticeable pertaining to Item No. 1, 5, and 8.

Percentage wise comparison exhibited that there seemed to be significant variations in the educational perceptions of the male and female workers in Aligarh Lock Factories but insignificant variations were noticeable pertaining to Item No. 7 and 10.

Percentage wise comparison exhibited that there seemed to be significant variations in the educational aspirations of the male and female workers in Aligarh Lock Factories but insignificant variations were noticeable pertaining to Item No. 2.

Percentage wise comparison exhibited that there seems to be significant variations in the educational perceptions of the literate and illiterate workers in Aligarh Lock Factories but insignificant variations were noticeable pertaining to Item No. 2, 3, and 4.

Percentage wise comparison exhibited that there seems to be significant variations in the educational aspirations of the literate and illiterate workers in Aligarh Lock Factories but insignificant variations were noticeable pertaining to Item No. 2 and 3.

Percentage wise comparison exhibited that there seemed to be significant variations in the educational perceptions of the workers hailing from joint families and nuclear families in Aligarh Lock Factories but insignificant variations were noticeable pertaining to Item No. 4. 5 and 10.

Percentage wise comparison exhibited that there seemed to be significant variations in the educational aspirations of the workers hailing from joint families and nuclear families in Aligarh Lock Factories but insignificant variations were noticeable pertaining to Item No. 4, 5, 9, 10.

Percentage wise comparison exhibited that there seemed to be significant variations in the educational perceptions of the workers hailing from rural and urban areas in Aligarh Lock Factories but insignificant variations were noticeable pertaining to Item No. 2, 3 and 4.

Percentage wise comparison exhibited that there seemed to be significant variations in the educational aspirations of the workers hailing from rural and urban areas in Aligarh Lock Factories but insignificant variations were noticeable pertaining to Item No. 2, 4, 6, 7 and 8.

Percentage wise comparison exhibited that there seemed to be significant variations in the educational perceptions of the workers belonging to management group and labour class in Aligarh Lock Factories but insignificant variations were noticeable pertaining to Item No. 2.

Percentage wise comparison exhibited that there seemed to be significant variations in the educational aspirations of the workers belonging to management group and labour class in Aligarh Lock Factories but insignificant variations were noticeable pertaining to Item No. 2.

Percentage wise comparison exhibited that there seemed to be insignificant variations in the educational perceptions of the workers belonging to different income groups (1). Below Rs. 3000/-(2). above Rs. 3000) in Aligarh Lock Factories but significant variations were noticeable pertaining to Item No. 1.

Percentage wise comparison exhibited that there seemed to be significant variations in the educational aspirations of the workers belonging to different income groups (1). below Rs. 3000/-(2). above Rs. 3000) in Aligarh Lock Factories but insignificant variations were noticeable pertaining to Item No. 2, 5, 8, 9 and 10.

Percentage wise comparison exhibited that there seemed to be significant variations in the educational perceptions of the workers hailing from the families adopting small family norms and those not adopting small family norms in Aligarh Lock Factories but insignificant variations were noticeable pertaining to Item No. 6.

Percentage wise comparison exhibited that there seemed to be significant variations in the educational aspirations of the workers hailing from the families adopting small family norms and those not adopting small family norms in Aligarh Lock Factories but insignificant variations were noticeable pertaining to Item No. 4 and 5.

5. RELIGIOUS PERCEPTIONS AND ASPIRATIONS:

Percentage wise comparison exhibited that there were significant differences in the religious perceptions of the respondents hailing from different working groups.

Percentage wise comparison exhibited that there seemed to be significant variations in the religious perceptions among the Hindu and Muslim workers hailing from different working groups of Aligarh Lock Industries but insignificant variations were noticeable pertaining to Item No. 1, 4, and 6.

Percentage wise comparison exhibited that there seemed to be significant variations in the religious aspirations among the Hindu and Muslim workers hailing from different working groups of Aligarh Lock Industries but insignificant variations were noticeable pertaining to Item No. 1, 3, 4 and 9.

Percentage wise comparison exhibited that there seemed to be insignificant variations in the religious perceptions of the Salaried workers and contractual workers in Aligarh Lock Factories but significant variations were noticeable pertaining to Item No. 3, 5, 6, 7 & 8.

Percentage wise comparison exhibited that there seemed to be significant variations in the religious aspirations of the salaried workers and contractual workers in Aligarh Lock Factories but insignificant variations were noticeable pertaining to Item No. 5, 6, 9 and 10.

Percentage wise comparison exhibited there seemed to be significant variations in the religious perceptions of the male and female workers in Aligarh Lock Factories but insignificant variations were noticeable pertaining to Item No. 3, 4 and 10.

Percentage wise comparison exhibited that there seemed to be significant variations in the religious aspirations of the male and female workers in Aligarh Lock Factories but Insignificant variations are noticeable pertaining to Item No. 8.

Percentage wise comparison exhibited that there seemed to be significant variations in the religious perceptions of the literate and illiterate workers in Aligarh Lock Factories but insignificant variations were noticeable pertaining to Item No. 5.

Percentage wise comparison exhibited that there seemed to be significant variations in the religious aspirations of the literate and illiterate workers in Aligarh Lock Factories but insignificant variations were noticeable pertaing to Item No. 1, 4, 6, 9 and 10.

Percentage wise comparison exhibited that there seemed to be insignificant variations in the reloigious perceptions of the workers hailing from joint families and nuclear families in Aligarh Lock Factories but significant variations were noticeable pertaining to Item No. 4, 5, 9 and 10.

Percentage wise comparison exhibited that there seemed to be insignificant variations in the religious aspirations of the workers hailing from joint families and nuclear families in Aligarh Lock Factories but significant variations were noticeable pertaining to Item No. 3, 7 and 8.

Percentage wise comparison exhibited that there seemed to be significant variations in the social perceptions of the workers hailing from rural and urban areas in Aligarh Lock Factories but insignificant variations were noticeable pertaining to Item No. 4 and 8.

Percentage wise comparison exhibited that there seemed to be significant variations in the religious aspirations of the workers hailing from rural and urban areas in Aligarh Lock Factories but insignificant variations were noticeable pertaining to Item No. 1, 12, 3, and 4.

Percentage wise comparison exhibited that there seemed to be significant variations in the religious perceptions of the workers belonging to management group and labour class in Aligarh Lock Factories but insignificant variations were noticeable pertaining to Item No 6 and 7.

Percentage wise comparison exhibited that there seemed to be significant variations in the religious aspirations of the workers belonging to management groups and labour class in Aligarh Lock Factories.

Percentage wise comparison exhibited that there seemed to be insignificant variations in the religious perceptions of the workers belonging to different income group (1). below Rs. 3000/-(2). above Rs. 3000) in Aligarh Lock Factories but significant variations were noticeable pertaining to Item No. 1, 2, and 3.

Percentage wise comparison exhibited that there seemed to be insignificant variations in the religious aspirations of the workers belonging to different income groups (1). below Rs. 3000/-(2). above Rs. 3000) in Aligarh Lock Factories

Percentage wise comparison exhibited that there seemed to be significant variations in the religious perceptions of the workers hailing from the families adopting small family norms and those not adopting small family norms in Aligarh Lock Factories but insignificant variations were noticeable pertaining to Item No. 2 and 5.

Percentage wise comparison exhibited that there seemed to be significant variations in the religious aspirations of the workers hailing from the families adopting small family norms and those not adopting small family norms in Aligarh Lock Factories but insignificant variations were noticeable pertaining to Item No. 1, 2, 4, 7 and 10.

SUGGESTIONS

The analysis of the data pertaining to Social, Educational, Political, religious and economic perceptions and aspirations of the respondents reveals that majority of the respondents out of the total sample of 474 have expressed their agreement with the statements. Keeping in view the responses of the subjects following suggestions according to the areas of the investigation are tentatively proposed.

ECONOMIC AREA:

The Majority of the community have expressed their earnings are not sufficient to meet their family responsibilities and other obligations. In order to achieve the objective is suggested that they should supplement their earnings by taking up some part time jobs or economic activities.

It has been said by the respondents that because of economic reasons people of their community despite mental and physical exploitation permit their children to seek employment. In order to protect children from exploitation it is suggested that people should raise their voice and fight for the implementation of labour laws pertaining to children so that they may be saved from exploitation.

It has been accepted by the respondents that because of economic constraints majority of the people of their community fail to fulfil their socio-cultural commitments. In order to arrest economic constraints it is suggested that the members of the community should take up some extra economic activities which may yield monetary returns in order to fulfil their socio-cultural commitments.

It has been observed that on account of economic considerations people of their community give preference to their sons in place of daughters. It is suggested that people should work and educate the community members to treat their sons and daughters on equal terms keeping in view the trends and changing laws of the land.

It has been said by the respondents that some families within their community where women are also working along with men are economically much better off as compared to others. It is proposed that the people of their community educate and enlighten the ignorant members of the community to encourage women for taking part in economic activities along with their male counterparts in order to achieve greater economic stability and prosperity.

It has been accepted by the respondents that constant hikes in the cost of lives and limited income has compelled the economically weaker sections of their community to accept all kinds of exploitation. It is proposed that the economically weaker section of their community be educated to fight against any kind of exploitation and start some extra economic activities, initially on a small scale, for controlling the exploitation.

It has been stated by the respondents that on account of limited opportunities of employment, the educated youths of the community have adopted unethical and illegal means to earn money. It is suggested that the unemployed educated youths of their community are educated that instead of using unethical & illegal means of earning money they should avail loan facilities as offered by the government to start their own independent economic activity.

It has been observed that continual disturbed conditions like strikes and riots in the society certainly affect economic activities and per capita income of the people of the society. It is proposed that the people of their community should form some judicious and nonpolitical organisation which may prove useful instrument in settling strikes and in maintaining communal harmony so that economic activities and per capita income of the members of the society are not affected negatively.

It has been observed that educated and capable youths of the community are not making adequate use of governmental programmes or schemes meant for economic welfare to the people. The objective to some extent can be achieved if the people come forward and educate the deserving youths of the community to avail the provisions and benefits of government sponsored employment programmes and schemes for achieving economic upliftment.

It has been observed that on account of financial reasons children of the community are unable to receive adequate education as mostly parents in general and the economically weaker ones in particular are unable to meet the prevailing high educational expenses. The objective to some extent can be achieved if voice is raised through some social organisation or agency for pressurizing the government and welfare bodies of their communities for providing reading materials on subsidized rates in general and scholarships for the economically weaker sections in particular.

SOCIAL AREA:

It has been observed that boys' parents of the community demand kind and cash directly or indirectly as gifts from the parents of the girls which is not permissible in religion as well as in the law of the land. In order to check the prevailing system it is suggested that firstly the boy be educated and encouraged by the enlightened members of their community to raise their voice against their parents if they demand kind and cash at the time of marriage. Furthermore, the honest an judicious members of the community jointly condemn and oppose such members of their community. Moreover, anti dowry act be made practically operative among the members of the society hailing from any caste of religion.

It has been observed that the girls of the community are subjected to humiliation if they fail to bring with them the committed gifts and cash at the time of their marriage. In order to check the operative system it is suggested that people of the community should organize or join such organizations, which are working for the rehabilitation and welfare of such girls becoming victims of humiliation after marriage.

It has been observed that the members of their community on account of religious consideration and ignorance do not follow family planning programmes and practices. In order to achieve this objective it is suggested that the enlightened, educated and expert members of the community be approached to come forward and educate the masses about the socio-economic and physiological advantages of family planning.

It has been observed that men and women are not enjoying equal authority in family matters. In order to achieve this objective it is suggested that educated and enlightened people of their community should raise voice in support of women's rights of equality in family matters of their community.

It has been observed that educated couples are more happily settled in their lives as compared to less or uneducated couples. In order to achieve the objective it is suggested that the people of their community should come forward to educate the members of the community not to marry their children till they receive proper and maximum education.

It has been observed that members of the community go for early marriage of their daughters even to elderly settled persons because of economic reasons. The above situations can be checked if the members of their community are apprised not to marry their daughters to elderly settled persons due to economic reasons rather to start some extra economic activity to improve their financial conditions.

It has been observed that divorce has become fairly common among the members of the society amounting to family disorganization. In order to save the families from disorganization it is suggested that people should propagate against the evils of divorce. Further more the elderly and enlightened members of the community should take initiative for amicable compromise among such couple who are going for divorce. Even law courts instead of deciding divorce cases on the basis of any group shall first make use of their good offices for a compromise.

It has been observed that widow remarriage though legally permissible yet is being discouraged by certain section of the communities. In order to achieve the objective it is suggested that the enlightened and educated members of the community should educate the members of their community not to discrouge/oppose widow remarriage in order to rehabilitate and rescue them from expected future exploitation.

It has been observed that it is somewhat difficult to find suitable matches for educated boys and girls. In order to achieve the objective it is suggested that the members of the community should associate themselves with some such voluntary social organisations which may help in selecting matches for educated boys and girls of their community.

Moreover, community wise marriage bureau be established by the members of the community.

It has been observed that on account of growing nuclear family patterns, the traditional familial bonds among the members of the community have weakened. In order to retain the familial bonds it is suggested that members of the community should enlighten the community members to interact among themselves quite frequently so that the traditional bond of family proximity are maintained.

POLITICAL AREA:

It has been observed that community members take keen interest in the political affairs and also do not adopt unethical practices to achieve their goals. It is suggested that the members of the their community should never deviate from this fair approach. Moreover, they should also keep an eye on the illiterate members of the community as well as on the children that they also do not deviate.

It has been observed that the members of the society do not support political parties on the basis of their elections manifestos. In order to achieve the objective it is suggested that people should propagate and work sincerely among the members of the society to educate the masses to support political parties on the basis of their election manifestos and not on any other consideration.

The respondents have disagreement that fair elections are held in our society. It is suggested that people should form or become members of some such organization, which may raise their voice and fight through court of law against the malpractices, which are operative during elections.

It has been observed that political bosses misuse their position and power for selfish ends by exploiting the authorities. In order to avoid such situations it is suggested that people should expose such political persons with evidence who misuse their positions and power for their selfish ends.

It has been observed that candidates and political parties freely use money and muscle power during elections. In order to avoid such situations it is suggested that people should work earnestly and raise voice against such parties and persons using money and muscle power during elections. It is further suggested that the government should take strict action against such parties or persons as per laws of the election.

It has been observed that economically well off people extend financial support to the important parties and candidates because they cash them after their victories. In order to discourage such mal practices it is suggested that people should raise voice that the government should impose some financial limits in election expenditure which should be subject to public accountability.

It has been observed that in the elections political parties issue tickets and extend full support to persons having established criminal background. It order to discourage this operative practice it is suggested that people should pursue the enlightened and judicious members of the community to pressurize the government to put a ban on permitting any contestant having criminal background to seek election. Moreover, the members of the society should also make a principle not to vote such persons having criminal background.

It has been observed that political parties or even independent candidates for winning the election do not hesitate in giving communal or caste turn to any event during election period if it suits them. In order to avoid such situations it is suggested that people should protest vigorously through some organisation or independently against such political parties and independent candidates who in order to win election spoil the election scene on the basis of religion or caste. It is further suggested that strict penal action be taken against such persons or parties.

It has been observed that community members lacking the required political awareness in selecting right type of person or party do not caste their votes. It is thus suggested that the enlightened members of the community should educate the masses of their community to caste their votes and support right type of person or party based on their elections manifesto.

It has been observed that political parties and independent

candidates mostly make false promises at the time of elections but never attend to them. It is suggested that people of the society should form some such non political organizations which may raise their voice against such political parties or independent candidates who fail to fulfil their promises so that an awareness of accountability may emerge among the political aspirants and the masses.

Educational Area:

It has been observed that in the present era of advancement community members are not satisfied with the prevailing education system. In order to achieve the objective it is suggested that people should establish contact with the members of their community connected with the education system to suggest ways and means to the government so that some better system of education may be evolved.

It has been observed that on account of higher cost of education majority of the people hailing from economically weaker section do not encourage their children to receive full education. In order to achieve the objective it is suggested that people should work and fight independently or through some social organisation to press the government for free and full education of the children hailing from the economically backward strata of the community.

It has been observed that education is mainly responsible for the socio-economic development of the members of the community. In order to achieve this objective it is tentatively suggested that economically well off and educated people of the community should establish some such organization which may look after the educational interest of the children hailing from lower strata of their community.

It has been observed that educated persons of the community as compared to others are more successful in business and trade. It is suggested that people should propagate and practice that children are not engaged in any economic activity till they receive proper education so that they may be more successful in business and trade in times to come.

It has been observed that the advice of educated persons of the community is not always sought by the uneducated or less educated ones to settle their disputes. It is suggested that people should teach the uneducated or less educated masses of their community to settle their disputes amicably with the help of educated judicious persons of the community and not to use physical force or adopt unethical practices or to go court of law as it is very expensive and time consuming.

It has been observed that parents of the community are more in favour of imparting religious education to their children instead of scientific education. It is suggested that people besides religious education should propagate among the masses of their community about the usefulness of scientific education based on analytical and rational principles instead of religious education alone.

It has been observed that majority of the parents of the community are ignorant about the importance of their children's education. In order to achieve this objective it is suggested that people should seek help from the educated members of the society to enlighten the ignorant persons of their community about the importance of children's education.

It has been observed that the members of the community feel that the women of their community are educationally more backward as compared to women hailing from other communities. In order to remove educational backwardness among the members of their community it is tentatively suggested that enlightened and educated members of their community should come forwarded and establish some social organization to look after the problem of education which women of the community are facing. Furthermore, such organizations should encourage and enlighten the women of their community about the importance of ecucation for the womanhood in the changing society of today.

It has been observed that the leader of the community are indifferent towards the educational upliftment of the community and do not seek help from the government. In order to achieve this objective it is suggested that people should request and pursue the respectable members of their community to maintain regular contacts with the leaders of the community and press them to work and seek government's help in getting adequate assistance and educational facilities for the sake of the community.

It has been observed that in the present era education has become highly commercialized because teachers do not judiciously perform their teaching duties in school and colleges as either they have opened their own coaching centers or teaching in other coaching centers on payment. It is suggested that the services of the teachers who are not performing their educational duties in their institutions properly and are engaged in coaching centers should be terminated and the coaching centers banned by the government.

RELIGIOUS AREAS

It has been observed that majority members of the community offer prayers regularly as prescribed. It is suggested that people should educate the importance of offering prayers to such members of their community who do not offer prayers regularly as prescribed.

It has been observed that members of the community strictly follow and practice the laws as prescribed in Holy Scriptures. It is suggested that people should educate other members of their community who do not follow and practice to follow and practice the laws as laid down in the Holy Scriptures.

It has been observed that members of the community extend equal respect to the religions. It is suggested that people should educate such members of their community to extend equal respect to other religions who out of their ignorance and other reasons are failing to offer equal respect to other religions.

It has been observed that certain members of the community deviate from the prescribed religious codes of conduct on account of their vested interests. It is suggested that people should enlighten members of their community not to violate the prescribed religious prescriptions for the sake of their personal gains as it would be against the teachings of reiigion.

It has been observed that some sections of the community on account of their ignorance about the teachings of religion maintain social distance with the members hailing from other religions. It is suggested that persons having full or better understanding about their religion should come forward and work judiciously in removing the prevailing misconceptions about the teaching of their religion so that the members of other community may not retain social distance with the members following other religions.

It has been observed that the preachers of religion of their community have not adequately succeeded in transmitting the proper understanding and knowledge about religion to the masses. It is suggested that people should come forward to gain full and real religious knowledge from the religion scholars in transmitting it judiciously to the masses of community during spare time.

It has been observed that religious heads of the community have imposed certain such restrictions which are not prescribed in the Holy Scriptures. It is suggested that people should take guidance from religion scholars and fight against such restrictions which are not prescribed in the scriptures but have been imposed by the preachers.

It has been observed that religious heads of the community on account of their vested material gains & popularity offer their services to the political parties during elections which is against their religious ethics. It is suggested that people should raise their voice and condemn such religious heads of the community who offer services to political parties for their vested interests as such services are not sanctioned in religious prescription.

It has been observed that members in the society are distinctly discriminated on the basis of religion and caste in all the matters of life. It is suggested that people should work and fight against the operative practices of discrimination in the society by seeking legal help and support from the enlightened members hailing from other communities.

It has been observed that funds collected in the name of religion by the religious leaders of the community are not utilized religiously by them. It is suggested that people should propagate in their community that the religious fund collectors must submit the programmes and regular accounts before the general body fo the community so that misuse of funds may be checked and the feeling of accountability may emerge among the members of the community.

COMMENTS:

On the basis of reports of lock industries the following has been observed and suggestions are given as under:

The early momentum of growth which the industry had received from the state has worn off due to indifferent attitude of the state towards its problems. On the contrary, the new lock enterprises are receiving full benefits and support from the State assistance in Haryana, Punjab, Gujarat, Tamil Nadu and other States. It has adversely affected Aligarh Lock Industry. If the industry continues to be a victim of the State apathy, thousands of workers may face retrenchment. The industry contributes to the economic growth as a net foreign exchange earner. The State must expedite measures to ameliorate the problems of the Aligarh lock industry in the larger interest of the State which need to be transformed into an industrial economy. To enhance productivity, it is necessary to have facilities for proper training of workers. It is a tragic commentary that the state training center in Aligarh has not been functioning since long, which should be revived to motivate youngsters towards the same. However, as a step forward the central government has recently provided funds for research and training for the development of lock production in Aligarh with latest and modern techniques for manufacturing the magnetic and electronic locks.

In brief, Aligarh Lock Industry can still play a leading role in the state economy if remedial measures are initiated by the industry with the state assistance.

Easy credit, training of the workers, steady supply of power and some agencies to undertake marketing of the products produced by artisans and entrepreneur, would indeed, enhance productivity and contribute to economic viability of the Aligarh lock industry.

Therefore concerted and coordinated efforts are required to be made by all the agencies in order to eradicate the handicaps which have been crept into the organizational set up of Aligarh lock Industry. All these measures would go a long way in accelerating the development of the industry and making of it a vital segment of Utter Pradesh Economy.

BIBLIOGRAPHY

Ahmed, K. (1968), *Social Background of women undergraduates of Delhi University*, quoted from *Survey in Research Education* by M.B. Buch, 1974.

Akers, Marilyn, O.S. (1981), *Perceptions of Selected Eighth Grade Students Concerning Academic Achievement and Influence of Family Encouragement and Expectation; Dissertation Abstracts International Series* 4, Vol. 21 (4).

Akers, Marilyn, O.S. (1981), Perceptions of Selected Eighth Grade Students Concerning Academic Achievement and Influence of Family Encouragement and Expectation, Dissertation Abstracts International Series 4, Vol. 42(4) Sept.–Oct. 1981.

Adler, A (1925), *Individual Psychology*, Harcourt Brace, New York, 1925.

Ahmad, Ishtiyaque (1988), H. *St. J. Phiby's Perceptions of Islam and the Arabs.*

Ali, S. Nisar (1975), *Effects of Stress on the Level of Aspiration as Related to EGO-Strength and Rigidity.*

Braccia, M.C. (1981), *A Comparison of Changes in Perceptions of Leader Behaviour in Interpersonal Communication, and Work Motivation Attitudes of Students in an Enducational Administration Programme Who Have and Have Not Completed; International, Series,* 4 Vol. 42 (4).

Boyed F. G. (1952), The Level of Aspiration of White and Negro Children in a Non-segreated Elementary School, Journal of Social Psychology, Vol. 36, 1952.

Bon Haller Glammer (1967), *Industrial Psychology*, McGraw Hill Book Company, New York, 1967.

Clyton Kirkpatric (1945), "Labor's Goodwill Goal of Management", Reprinted from *Chicago Tribune*, Sep. 1945, Quoted by Willard Praker.

Dass, M.N. (1959 *Economic and Social Development of Modern India,* Calcutta.

Decoleav, R. (1981), *Perceptions of Selected Group Toward the Current and Ideal Role of Special Education Directors as Administrative Leaders in North Dakota Schools Which Have High Concentration of Indian Students, Dissertation Abstracts International,* Series 4, Vol. 42(4).

Davis, K. (1980)*Human Behaviour at Work*, Tata McGraw Hill Book Company. New Delhi.

Dussing Andre (1983), Work Situation and Job Satisfaction, (Kolner Zeitschift Fur Sociologic and Sozinal Psychologic), 1983, 35, 4 (Dec.)

Faridi, F.R. and Siddiqi, M.M. (1992), *The Social Structure of Indian Muslims*. Ist Edition, Delhi.

Forgus, Ronald H. L.E. and Melamed (1976), *Perception – A Cognitive Stage Approach*, Mc.Graw Hill Book Company, New York.

Fair Child, H.P. (1967), *Dictionary of Sociology,* Little Field, Adams and Company, Totawa, New Jersey, 1967.

Frutcher Benjamin (1967), *Introduction to Factor Analysis*, Affiliated East West Press, New Delhi, 1967.

Flanagan Robert, J. George Strauss and Liyod Ulman (1974), "Worker Discontent and Work Place Behaviour", *Industrial Relations*, 1974, 13, 2 May.

Guilford, J.P. (1973), *Fundamental Statistics in Psychology and Education*. McGraw Hill Book Co., New York.

Gupta, Giri Raj (1974), *Marriage, Religion and Society pattern of change in an Indian Village*, Vikas Publishing House, Delhi.

Gupta, Jagdish Prasad (1971), *Phonetic Analysis and Perception of Vowel Sounds.*

Giri, V. V. (1959), *Labour Problems in India Industry*, Asia Publishing House, Bombay.

Gisbert, P. (1982), *Fundamentals of Industrial Sociology*, Tata McGraw Hill Bombay.

Glass Udyog (1983), *Journal of the All India Class Manufactures Federation*, Vol. XII, No. 3, Sept., 1983.

Gains Lary K. (1984), Van Tubergen H., and Paiva Michael A., "*Police Officer's Perceptions of Promotions As a Source of Motivation*", Journal of Criminal Justice, 1984, Vol. 12 (3).

Haq, Jalalul (1978), *Bertrand Russell's Philosophy of Perception.*

Hurlock, Elizabeth B. (1974), *Personality and Development*, Mc. Graw Hill, New York.

Jackson, S.J. (1988), *The Muslims of India: Beliefs and Practices*, Bangalore.

Jain, Shashi (1988), *Status and Role Perceptions of Middle Class Women*, Puja Publications, New Delhi, 1988.

Julian, E. Hochberg, "Introduction" in David L. Sill (Ed.) *International Encycl opedia off Social Sciences*, Vol. II, McMillan and Free Press, NY.

Kuanr, J.P. and Patel, S. (1984), *Changes in Socio-Economic Life of Tribals in Phulbani District of Orissa.*

Kumar, Sanjay (1993), *Talon Mein Taley Aligarh Key Taley,* Asmita Prakashan, Gandinagar, Delhi, 1993.

Khan, Naushad (1995), *Security Perceptions in the Gulf.*

Kuk, Linda, S. (1981), "Perceptions of the Work Climate and Their Relationship to the Career Aspiration of Women Students Affairs Administrators", *Dissertation Abstracts International, Series* 4, Vol. 42(4).

Lal, Shoe Kumar (1976), *Occupational Aspirations of Schedule Caste's Students, Social Change*, Vol. 6 (1 and 2).

Lewin,Kurt (1944), Level of Aspirations; in J. Mc. V. Hunt (Ed.), *Personality And Behaviour Disorders*, The Ronald Press Company, New York, 1944.

Lawler, E.E. (1971), *Pay and Organizational Effectiveness, A Psychological View*, McGraw Hill Book Company Inc., New York.

Lathan, Garry, P. (1985), Establishment of Goals, Feedback and Motivation of the Industrial Employees, *Revista Interamericana De Psicologia Occupational*, 1985, Vol. 4(3).

Lee, Raymonds and Wibur, Elizabeth, R. (1929), "*Age, Education Job Tenure, Salary, Job – characteristics and Job Satisfaction.* A Mltivariate Analysis, *Human Relations*, 1985 (Aug.), 38 (8).

Moreland, W.H. (1929), *Agrarian System of Muslim India – A Historical Essay with Appendices*. Central Book Depot, Allahabad.

Muthayya, B.C. (1971), *Farmers and Their Aspirations*, Hyderabad, N.I.C.D.

Mukerjee Radha Kamal (1951), *The Indian Working Class*, Hind Kitabs Ltd. Bombay.

M.C., Cornic, E.J. and Tiffin, J. (1969), *Industrial Psychology*, Prentice Hall of India New Delhi.

Muthayya, B.C. (1971), *Level of Aspiration and Frustration Reality, Researches in Personality and Social Problems*, Deptt. of Psychology, University of Madras.

Miller Jon and Sanford Labovitiz (1973), "Individual Relations to Organizational Conflict and Change", *Socialogical Quarterly*, 1973, 11, 4 Autumn.

Mallort Jose (1975), "Work Condition", *Revista de Psicologian General Y. Applicada*, 1975, (Jan – Feb), Vol. 30 (132).

Mamoria, C.B. (1975), *Industrial Labour and Industrial Relations in India*, Vol. 1, Kitab Mahal, Allahabad.

Mohanty G. (1976), "Sex Differences in Shifts and Rigidity in level of Aspiration Experiment", *Journal of Psychological Researches,* Vol. 22(1).

Mongia, J. N. (1980), *Reading in India Labour and Social Welfare*, Atma Ram and Sons, Delhi.

Mustafa, S. M. (1980), *A Study of Labour Problems in Sugar Industry of Eastern* U.P., Department of Commerece, A.M.U., Aligarh.

Mirza Masood Ali (1984), *Worker's Participation in Public Sector Enterprises with Special References Insecticides Ltd.*(Thesis presented to AMU) Commerce Department, A.M.U., Aligarh.

Mc Guir, J.B. and Liro, J.R. (1986), "Flexible Work Schedule, Work Attitude and Perceptions of Productivity", *Public Personnel Management*. 1986, (spring), Vol. 15(1).

Nizam-ud-Din (1920), *Tabaqat-I-Akbari* (3 vols), Locknow.

Neviol, H.R. (1945), *District Gazetteer of the United Provinces*, VI, Aligarh.

Norsworthy, J.R. and Zebala Craig, A. (1985), "Worker Attitudes, Worker Behaviour and Productivity in the U. S. Automobile Industry", *Industrial and Labour Relations Review*, 1985, 38, 4 July.

Neider Peter (1975), "Relationship Between Leadership, Level of Productivity and Satisfaction", *Gruppendynamilk (Forachung and Praxis)*, 1975 (Apr.) Vol. 2 (6).

Norton Steven D. (1976), "Employee Central Management Participation in Descision–Making and Satisfaction With Work Itself", *Psychological Reports*, 1976, (Aprs.), Vol. 38 (2).

Oldham, Grag, R. (1976), "Conditions under which Employees Respond Positively to Enriched Work," *Journal of Applied Psychology*, 1976, Vol. 61 (4) Aug.

Sharma, R. Rani (1981), "Self-concept, Level of Aspiration and Mental Health as Factors in Academic Achievement", *Indian Educational Review*, Vol. XVI(2).

Shamsi, Amir Mohammad (1989), *Trikh-I-Rajouri*, Islamic Book Centre, Rajouri, Kashmir.

Siddiqi, Jamal Muhammad (1981), *Aligarh District: A Historical Survey.* Munshiram Manoharlal, New Delhi.

S. Robert, W. Kleomeir (1951), *Human Relations in Supervision*, McGraw Hill Book New York.

Saxena, R.C. (1968), *Labour Problems and Social Welfare*, Jai Prakash Nath & Co., Meerut.

Schneider, E.V. (1969), *Industrial Sociology*, McGraw Hill Book. London.

Spaulding Charles, B. (1970), *An Introduction to Industrial Sociology*, D.B. Taraporevala Sons Bombay.

Schneider, B. and Synder, R. A. (1975), "*Some Relationship Between Job Satisfaction and organization Climate*", *Journal of Applied Psychology*, 1975, Vol. 60(3), June.

Singhal Sushila (1976), "Need Gratification under which Employees Respond Positively to Enriched Work", *Journal of Applied Psychology*, 1976, Vol. 61(4) Aug.

Swaleha, B. (1979), "A Study of Age, Socio-economic Differences in Level of Aspiration, Manavdarshan, Vol. 14, 15 – 17.

Thompson, D.B. and Richard, P.B. (1973), A case study of Employee's attitude and Labour Unrest, *Industrial and Relations Review*, 1973, 27 Oct.

Uniyal, M.P. (1981), "The Level of Aspiration of Teacher Trainees of Rural and Urban Areas in Relation to Their Achievement, *Indian Educational Review*, Vol XVI, No. (2).

Uplaonkar, Ambarao, t. (1983), "Occupational Aspirations of College students, *Social change*, Vol. 3(2).

Vaid, K.N. (1968), "*The New Workers (A Study at Kota)*, Asia Publishing House, Bombay.

Veale David John. (1982), *Thesis on Organizational Status and Employee Attitude*, Universtiy California, Santacruz.

Zirbel, Dirk Drawin (1985), "*Job Satisfaction Between Part time and Full time Grocery Employees*, Ph.D Thesis submitted to United States International University.

Research Work:

Alka, Kulshreshtha (1982), "A Study of Principles's Own Perception How He Should Behave with the Staff", perception and Behaviour.

Deocoleav, R. (1981), "Perceptions of Selected Group Toward the Current and Ideal Role of Special Education Directors as Administrative Leaders in North Dakota Schools which have High Concentration of Indian Students", *Dissertation Abstracts International,* Series 4, vol. 42(4).

Hamid, Rukhsana (1983), Study of Self Awareness in Relation to Interpersonal and Interpersonal Perception of Adolescents.

Hamid Karbassi Abdol (1980), "Social Adjustment and Occupational aspirations of Iranian Students in Berlin and Honnover".

Jabeen, Jahan Ara (1993), "A comparative Study of perceptions and Aspirations of Women Students Studying in the Colleges and Kashmir University, unpublished thesis *Abstract*, Department of Sociology, AMU, Aligarh.

Khan, Mahmood Subuktageen 1993), "Aspiration Levels in Disadvantaged and Advantaged Students Groups".

Khan, Sajid Ali (1989), "Study of Adjustment Anxiety and Level of Aspiration Among Criminals and Psychosomatic Patients".

Khan, Mohd Ilyas (1980), "Aspiration Levels in Repressors and Senitizers Under Stress.

Khan, Mahmood Subuktageen (1984), Realism in the Level of Aspiration of Disadvantaged and Advantaged Children.

Kamat, P.A. (1969), A Comparative Study of Achievements of Girls with their Intelligence and Socio-economic Status of the Parents, Unpublished M. Ed. Dissertation, M.S. University of Baroda.

Khan, Rahat, Ali (1980), "Fear of Failure in Relation to Anxiety and Level of Aspiration Among University Students".

Khan, Sajid Ali Kr. (1986), "Study of Anxiety and Level of Aspiration of Criminals Convicted for Crimes Against Person and Property".

Mutayya B.C. (1971), "Level of Aspiration and Frustration Reality", *Researches in Personality and Social Problems*, Department of Psychology, University of Madras, 1971.

Madihur, Suhaib Rehman (1992), "Themes of Development of the Child's Perception in the Novels of Mark Twain.

Nootan, Kaushik (1986), Sex Differences in Perception of Psysique-Attractiveness Stereotyping.

Prakash, N. and Srivastava, A.L. (1991), "Perception of Schedule Castes Towards Education", *Journal of Indian Education*, Vol. XVI(5).

Rashid Tabassum (1986), "Study of Trait Evaluation in Self & Other Perception of Populatrs, Neglected and Isolates: a Pilot Study".

Rashid, Tabassum (1989), Study of Biased Components and Evaluation of Traits in Self and Others Perception of Populars, Neglecteds and Isolateds".

Sahoo, Basudev and Ajay Kumar (1984), "Industrialisation and Changing Pattern of Socio-economic Life of Tribals – A Case Study in the Lathikata Region of Sundergarh.

Shah, A.M. (1993), "Lineage, Structure and Change in a Gujarat Village". Quoted from *Family Kinship and Marriage in India* (Patricia Uberoi), Delhi

Singer H. (1916), A Note on Education in the State of Jammu and Kashmir, Calcutta.

Singer Milton (1975), *Traditional India: Structure and Change*, Rawat Publications Jaipur.

Singh, C.P. (1976), "Educational Aspirations of Schedule Caste Students in Eastern Uttar Pradesh", *Social Change*, Vol. 6.

Swaleha, B. (1979), "A Study of Age, Socio-economic Difference in Level of Aspiration, Manaudasshan, Sundergarh. Vol. 14, 15–17.

Sultana, Jafri Bilquis (1992), "Values and Aspirations of Undergraduate Women Students in Aligarh: A Comparative Study of Tika Ram Girls College and Aligarh Muslim University".

Sunita, Sachdeva (1983), "Times Perception of Intervals filled with Identional and Non-identional Activities in Introverts and xtroverts".

Shivanarain (1992), *Gandhian Perception of the Harijan Problems*.

Sunita, Tandon (1989), "Need Pattern and Perception of Deprivation Among Scheduled Caste and Non-scheduled Caste Men and Women.

Singh, Karuna (1996), Perception of stress and Psychological well-being in doctors exposed to condition of threat.

Uplaonkar, Ambaraso, T. (1983), Occupational Aspirations of College Students, Social Change, Vol. 3(2).

Zeeshan, Mohammad (1996), Job Satisfaction and Perception ofQuality of Working Life of Middle Level Manger.

Journals:

Anand, A.L. (1982), Souvenier, Seminar on Locks, March 21, 1982.

Boyd, F.G. (1952), Journal of Social Psychology, Vol. 36. The Level of Aspiration of white and Negro Children in a Non-segregated Elementary School.

Gould, R. (1941), Journal of Social Psychology. Some Scociological Determinants of Goal Settings.

Mohanty, G. (1976), Journal of Psychological Research Vol. 22(1). Sex Differences in shifts and Rigidity in level of Aspiration Experiments.

Shah, V.P. (1971), Sociological Bulletin. Social Class and Educational Aspirations in an Indian Metropolitan.

The Lock Times **(Aug. 1996),** Published by All India Lock Manufactures Associations, Parker Lock Builing, Parao Dubey, Aligarh.

The Lock Times **(May 1997),** Published by All India Lock Manufactures Associations, Parker Lock Builing, Parao Dubey, Aligarh.

The Lock Times **(June 1997),** Published by All India Lock Manufactures Associations, Parker Lock Builing, Parao Dubey, Aligarh.

The Lock Times **(January 1998),** Published by All India Lock Manufactures Associations, Parker Lock Building, Parao Dubey, Aligarh.

The Lock Times **(April 1998),** Published by All India Lock Manufactures Associations, Parker Lock Building, Parao Dubey, Aligarh.

The Lock Times **(March 1999),** Published by All India Lock Manufactures Associations, Parker Lock Building, Parao Dubey, Aligarh.

The Lock Times **(Apri9l 1999),** Published by All India Lock Manufactures Associations, Parker Lock Building, Parao Dubey, Aligarh.

The Lock Times **(May 1999)**,Published by All India Lock Manufactures Associations, Parker Lock Building Parao Dubey, Aligarh.

The Lock Times **(June 1999)**, Published by All India Lock Manufacturers Associations, Parker Lock Builing, Parao Dubey, Aligarh.

The Lock Times **(July 1999)**, Published by All India Lock Manufactures Associations, Parker Lock Bui9lding, Parao Dubey, Aligarh.

International Encyclopedia of Social Science **(1968)**, Vol. 12, The Macmillan Company and the Press Press.

Report of the National Commission on Labour **(1975)**, Quoted by Mamoria, C.B., Industrial Labour and Industrial Relatins I India, Vol. 1 Kitab Mahal, Allahabad.

INDEX

C

D

E

9788176580342